M̶a̶...

To Jim

with all good wishes

from Joan

THE NOVEL POETICS OF GOETHE'S
WILHELM MEISTERS WANDERJAHRE

THE NOVEL POETICS OF GOETHE'S
WILHELM MEISTERS WANDERJAHRE
Eine zarte Empirie

Joan Wright

Studies in German Language and Literature
Volume 33

The Edwin Mellen Press
Lewiston•Queenston•Lampeter

Library of Congress Cataloging-in-Publication Data

Wright, Joan, 1946-
   The novel poetics of Goethe's Wilhelm Meisters Wanderjahre : eine zarte Empirie /
Joan Wright.
      p. cm. -- (Studies in German language and literature ; v. 33)
   Includes bibliographical references and index.
   ISBN 0-7734-7014-X
   1. Goethe, Johann Wolfgang von, 1749-1832. Wilhelm Meisters Wanderjahre. 2.
Modernism (Literature) I. Title. II. Series.

PT1982 .W75 2002
833'.6--dc21

                                                                    2002067770

This is volume 33 in the continuing series
Studies in German Language and Literature
Volume 33 ISBN 0-7734-7014-X
SGLL Series ISBN 0-88946-578-0

A CIP catalog record for this book is available from the British Library

The Edwin Mellen Press   The Edwin Mellen Press
Box 450   Box 67
Lewiston, New York   Queenston, Ontario
USA 14092-0450   CANADA L0S 1L0

The Edwin Mellen Press, Ltd.
Lampeter, Ceredigion, Wales
UNITED KINGDOM SA48 8LT

Printed in the United States of America

To my beloved parents

Wilfred Horace Wright (1912-1976)
and
Helen McCaig Wright (1916-2001)

durch wundersame Pfade zum stillen Ort
along wondrous pathways to the still place

Contents

Acknowledgements   ix

Abbreviations   xi

Foreword   xiii

Chapter 1   The tradition of the self-reflexive text.   1

     Daphnis and Chloe: 'a complete world'   11
     Laurence Sterne: 'in everything a guide and inspiration'   18
     Jean Paul: 'a very gifted spirit'   37
     A reception history of the *Wanderjahre*   50

Chapter 2   Reader, writer and text in Goethe's work   69

     Metafictional elements in the earlier novels   89

     Die Leiden des jungen Werther   92
     Wilhelm Meisters Lehrjahre   97
     Die Wahlverwandtschaften   110

Chapter 3   Reader and writer in the *Wanderjahre*   123

     The text-internal narrator   132
     Wilhelm: 'as representative of all'   145
     Lenardo: 'really no story'   156
     Makarie: 'a blessed spirit'   161
     Excursus: *Die neue Melusine*, a paradigm of mis-reading   181

Chapter 4   'A very intricate work of art'   191

     The *Wanderjahre* as a paradigm of 'world literature'   191
     The interaction of text and image   200
     Weaving the labyrinth of the text   222
     Excursus: *Wer ist der Verräter?*   254

Epilogue   The aesthetic of the open work   259

Bibliography   271

Index   281

ix

Acknowledgements

This book is the fruit of research undertaken for a PhD thesis in the Department of German at University College Dublin while I was a Faculty of Arts Research and Teaching Fellow. During that time I received the unstinting support and encouragement of the Head of Department, Professor Hugh Ridley and of my supervisor Dr Daniel Farrelly. To both of them my thanks and gratitude are due.

Translations are by the author unless otherwise stated.

Abbreviations

CollG	*Colloquia Germanica.*
DVjs	*Deutsche Vierteljahresschrift für Literaturwissenschaft und Geistesgeschichte.*
Gräf	Gräf, Hans Gerhard, *Goethe über seine Dichtungen*, 3 volumes, Frankfurt am Main, 1902, (rep. Darmstadt), 1968
GJb	*Goethe-Jahrbuch.*
Goethe	*Goethe. Neue Folge des Jahrbuchs der Goethe-Gesellschaft.*
GQ	*The German Quarterly.*
GRM	*Germanisch-Romanisch Monatschrift.*
GYb	*Goethe Yearbook.*
H.A.	Goethe, J.W., *Werke*, Hamburger Ausgabe, edited by Erich Trunz, 14 volumes, Hamburg, 1949-67 & revised edition, München, 1981
JbDSG	*Jahrbuch der Deutschen Schillergesellschaft.*
JbGG	*Jahrbuch der Goethe-Gesellschaft.*
JbJPG	*Jahrbuch der Jean-Paul-Gesellschaft.*
Lj.	Goethe, J.W., *Wilhelm Meisters Lehrjahre*, (Volume 5, H.A.).
MLN	*Modern Language Notes.*
Monatshefte	*Monatshefte für deutschen Unterricht, deutsche Sprache und deutsche Literatur.*
OL	*Orbis litterarum.*
PEGS	*Publications of the English Goethe Society.*
PMLA	*Proceedings of the Modern Language Association of America.*
RechG	*Recherches germaniques.*
SuF	*Sinn und Form.*
W.A.	Goethe, J.W., *Werke*, Weimarer Ausgabe, 143 volumes in 4 parts, edited under commission by Grand Duchess Sophie von Sachsen, Weimar, 1887-1919.
Wvw.	Goethe, J.W., *Die Wahlverwandtschaften* (Volume 6, H.A.).
WW	*Wirkendes Wort.*
ZfdPh	*Zeitschrift für deutsche Philologie.*

Foreword

Joan Wright's account of Goethe's last novel will surprise many a reader. Even the Goethe sceptics could feel challenged by her compelling arguments about Goethe's modernity: not only in his technique as a novel writer but also in his corresponding attitude towards the new age. Where his deliberate use of fragmentation in the novel – with its cluster of disparate literary forms and frequently changing perspectives – clearly anticipates the modern 20th century novel, his attitude towards solving problems equally reflects his modernity. He recognised – no doubt with deep regret, given the fundamentally organic nature of his thought – that his contemporary world was undergoing a process of fragmentation and specialisation.

Goethe is modern in not presuming to offer a solution to the problems arising from this process. In his novel, Joan Wright shows, he presents his material in such a way that his readers are left to find their own way through the complex maze. Each reading is an individual one, not one that can be presented as definitive. Furthermore, his attitude to problem-solving has a modern openness. When he says that the solution to a problem gives rise to new problems, this is not a counsel of despair but a realization that human life and human thought are caught up in a deep process of dynamic evolution.

A particularly refreshing aspect of Joan Wright's book is the excellent combination of deep learning and the skill and dexterity with which she handles her knowledge. The book reveals an impressive range of areas on which she is able to draw. In her direct discussion of Goethe she manifests the breadth and depth of knowledge we expect of a Goethe scholar, including a sound grasp of literary theory and a keen sensitivity to literary language. In addition, she brings to her writing an excellent knowledge of relevant aspects of the English and

Anglo-Irish literary traditions and exploits her solid education in Latin and Greek culture; she is even able to illuminate some aspects of her book through her knowledge of the history of painting. In more senses than one, this is a particularly Goethean book.

Finally: perhaps it is as a result of her extensive experience as a teacher of young people that the author achieves a high level of clarity which makes her book accessible to a relatively wide readership. As one of her distinguished mentors said: "She writes like an angel!"

DANIEL J. FARRELLY

CHAPTER 1

The tradition of the self-reflexive text

Das Buch ist selbst das, wovon es erzählt
The book is telling about itself

In 1829 at the age of eighty Goethe published the second version of his last novel *Wilhelm Meisters Wanderjahre*. The first version had already been published in 1821 without evoking any great response from the reading public. As the title indicates this novel was conceived as a continuation of *Wilhelm Meisters Lehrjahre*. The length of time it took to complete - rather more than twenty years - can perhaps in part be explained as the difficulty of attempting to write a social novel in a society that was becoming ever more complicated. The form is consciously fragmented. The work embraces a great variety of forms of writing: frame-narrative and novella, poem and song, diary and letter, factual and scientific report, collections of aphorisms and maxims. The ending remains open, with the last words being 'ist fortzusetzen' [to be continued]. Goethe was attempting, in the open form and the variety of perspectives, to reproduce in a literary work an analogy for the infinity and diversity of life itself. All aspects of life find their reflection in this novel: the life of the individual with its experience of the joys and pains of love; and also the concerns of the larger community which in the early nineteenth century included the beginnings of industrialisation and job-specialisation, emigration and the search for a new life and a new social order.

The eponymous hero, Wilhelm, and along with him the reader, makes his way, or rather is led, through a series of labyrinthine social models. In the diverse world-views he is offered a variety of confusing possibilities, which contradict and relativise each other. The author's intention is not to offer solutions to the social problems of the dawning modern age, but rather to challenge the reader to look for answers for himself. Through deliberate use of ambiguity Goethe aims at the education of the reader. He seeks to encourage the reader to become an active, reflective participant in the recreation of the meaning of the text or, perhaps more accurately, in the creation of an interpretation of the text.

In 1939 Thomas Mann gave an introductory lecture on the *Zauberberg* to students of Princeton University[1]. He emphasised that it was a highly self-conscious work, 'Das Buch ist selbst das, wovon es erzählt' [the book is telling about itself]. He claimed that his aim for this novel was to achieve complete consistency between form and content, essence and appearance so that it would always *be* what it dealt with and what it was about. In other words the *Zauberberg* should be understood as a work that thematises problems of novel-construction and novel-reading. These questions are also an important theme of the *Wanderjahre*. In the first collection of aphorisms, 'Betrachtungen im Sinne der Wanderer', one of the maxims alludes to exactly this close relationship between theory and practice, as well as to the demands that it makes of both writer and reader: 'Es gibt eine zarte Empirie, die sich mit dem Gegenstand innigst identisch macht und dadurch zur eigentlichen Theorie wird. Diese Steigerung des geistigen Vermögens aber gehört einer hochgebildeten Zeit an' (302) [there is a subtle kind of practice which makes itself most intimately identical with the subject and thereby actually becomes theory. This heightening of the intellectual capacities belongs, however, to a highly educated age] - a clear hint that we should see in the *Wanderjahre* a novel which simultaneously concerns itself with the poetics of the novel. This study considers to what extent the *Wanderjahre* can be described as metafiction: how far it can be seen as a work of art which takes itself as its subject and in the process of writing reflects on fiction and its relationship to

---

[1] Thomas Mann, 'Einführung in den Zauberberg für Studenten der Universität Princeton' Mai 1939 in: Gesammelte Werke, Volume 11, Frankfurt am Main 1990, page 612.

reality, on the role of art and the place of the artist in society[2]. It will examine the ways in which the work succeeds in being both a novel and a poetics of the novel.

Metafictional literature aims at a fusion of the creative with the critical, an amalgam of theory and praxis, so that it both thematises and incorporates within its structure its own critical system; at the same time literary work and literary criticism, its tendency is to blur the boundary, or rather to emphasise the uncertainty of the boundary, between art and life, truth and fiction, literary production and literary reception. It is interested in the literary work as both product and process, artefact and artifice - seeing it both as an object with an existence in its own right: a book manufactured from paper and ink, of more or less decorative appearance, with covers which can be opened and shut; and as a performance: as something that is called into existence by the kindred acts of writing and reading, whose existence is renewed and transformed by each new act of reading and which ceases to exist when it is no longer read.

It is essentially a didactic form, in that it aims at the education of the reader. Its didacticism, however, is not of that unsophisticated type whose objective is no more than the communication of a moral or ideological message. It sets itself the more complex task of giving the reader the means of developing an active, productive reading practice - a reading practice which will not only enable him to interpret the written text but also offers him a useful metaphor for his continuous struggle to interpret the 'text' of his lived experience[3]. In pursuance of

---

[2] Metafiction has been described as 'fiction that includes within itself a commentary on its own narrative and/or linguistic identity' - Linda Hutcheon, Narcissistic Narrative. The Metafictional Paradox, London & New York 1980, page 1. Cf. also Robert Alter, Partial Magic: The Novel as a Self-Conscious Genre, London & Berkeley 1975 and Patricia Waugh, Metafiction. The Theory and Practice of Self-Conscious Fiction, London & New York 1984. Patricia Waugh lists a range of characteristics which are commonly found in metafictional texts - including the obtrusive narrator, the dramatisation of the reader-role, Chinese box structures, self-reflexive images such as mirrors and mazes, and parody of literary conventions - and comments, 'In all of these what is foregrounded is the writing of the text as the most fundamentally problematic aspect of that text', pages 21-22.
[3] Cf. Waugh, page 18, 'Metafiction, then, does not abandon "the real world" for the narcissistic pleasures of the imagination. What it does is to re-examine the conventions of realism in order to discover - through its own self-reflection - a fictional form that is culturally relevant and comprehensible to contemporary readers. In showing us how literary fiction creates its imaginary

4

this educative aim the task of reading is made difficult and challenging. Reading becomes travail, a labour which it is anticipated may bring forth fruit. The reader is inspired, incited or impelled into ordering and interpreting the text, into making connections and leaps of the imagination[4]. But it also becomes pleasure, offering the possibility of choice and free play to the imagination[5]. The two aspects of play are incorporated in the text: its freedom from constraint and its organisation according to rules. The text is often seen as a puzzle to be solved, a game to be played, a knot to be unravelled or a maze to be negotiated. The reader must make as much effort to decode the script as the writer made to encode it. His role is envisaged as co-creator or co-producer, as travelling companion or accomplice of the writer[6]. Emphasis is laid on the creative processes of the reader as well as those of the writer[7]. At the same time the metafictional text, which by its very nature contains within itself its own poetics, is its own first critic and makes demands on the critical processes of reader as well as writer. Reader, writer and critic, therefore, become identified with each other in a coincidence of roles.

The reader is placed in the paradoxical situation of playing a role made up of apparently incompatible functions. He is invited to participate in the creation of the fictional world of the text, to become involved in the joys and sorrows of the

worlds, metafiction helps us to understand how the reality we live day by day is similarly constructed, similarly written'.

[4] Cf. Jean Ricardou, 'Pseudo-principes d'esthétique', in: *Nouveau Roman: hier, aujourd'hui 2* Paris 1972, 'The rules of the text are in the text. It's by reading that you learn to read: you can't do the work of reading for the reader', page 317.

[5] This twofold aspect of the text corresponds to the dual aims of literature - of offering both pleasure [delectare] and profit [prodesse] - expressed by Horace in the *Ars Poetica*, lines 333-4. In *Le plaisir du texte* Roland Barthes goes further and speaks of the possibilities of erotic pleasure in the relationship between reader, writer and text: 'the possibility of a dialectics of desire', Roland Barthes *le plaisir du texte*, Editions de Seuil, Paris, 1973, page 10. The metaphor of an erotic relationship between text, reader and writer is used very productively by Laurence Sterne in *Tristram Shandy*.

[6] The traditional topos of the journey or quest is a fruitful one for the metafictional writer. Reader, writer and fictional characters embark on a quest for a new Grail, a Grail embodied in the text itself: 'the traditional fictional quest has thus been transformed into a quest for fictionality', Waugh, page 10.

[7] Cf Roland Barthes, *S/Z*, Paris (Seuil) 1970, page 17. Barthes makes the distinction between texts which are 'lisible', which are designed to be consumed by their readers and the 'scriptible' text which inaugurates its reader as co-producer.

fictional characters and at the same time to remain aware of the status of the text as a fictional construct and alert to the possibilities of interpretation it offers. This paradoxical role dramatises the tension between subjectivity and objectivity in human experience, between the pull towards identification and involvement and the opposing pull towards self-awareness and detachment. The reader is called upon to participate in an act demanding the full use of his intellectual, affective and creative faculties. In return he is offered both freedom and responsibility. On the one hand he is given the freedom to complete a work which is 'open', although this freedom is naturally limited and symbolic of a potential, rather than unbounded and actual: the author ultimately retains a certain control over the text. On the other hand this freedom carries with it the responsibility of generating and activating the possibilities that lie dormant in the text.

The nexus of relationships between reader, writer, critic and text is often dramatised by the use of an intrusive narrator, who is a fictional character as much as an authorial voice and who thematises the problems and difficulties encountered in the creation of the literary work. This intrusive narrator also makes space for the reader within the text either by directly addressing him or by conjuring him up as an active presence. The fictional readers thus conjured up, as well as other characters within the text, can act as representatives of the 'real' reader, corroborating or contradicting his own attempts at interpretation and foregrounding the fictional nature of what he is reading. They are reader-surrogates who, by their very presence, accentuate the importance of the reader's role in constituting the text. The reader's desires and expectations are thematised, too, and the deliberate frustration of conventional expectations calls into question the validity of these stereotyped expectations and forces the reader to look beyond them.

The metafictional text tends to make the acts of writing and reading part of its theme. Story and fictional characters may function as an allegory for the narrative process. Fictional characters may refer explicitly to their own fictionality while the intrusive narrator constantly reminds us of their ontological

6

status, not as real beings but as words on the page[8]. Writing and reading often have a specific function on the diegetic level of the text. Characters produce their own texts of a factual or fictional nature: novels, letters, diaries, journals and poems, which may be commented on and criticised by themselves or other characters, so that the discussion of these fictional texts often plays a major role within the work itself. The fictional characters often, therefore, display an inordinately high degree of interest in the word, which results in a thematisation of the contradiction which lies at the heart of any consideration of language: the paradox of the tremendous power of the word, both as a means of manipulation and a means of expression and, at the same time, its total inadequacy, the whole realm of the inexpressible which lies beyond the boundaries of language.

This interest in the word is reflected on the meta-textual level by a high degree of intertextuality. Works contain, or are composed of, fragments of other texts; collage and montage techniques are employed, thus highlighting on the one hand the unfinished and provisional nature of the literary work, and, on the other hand, its collectivity. The metafictional work embraces parody, pastiche and 'plagiarism'. The parody of conventional literary forms opens the reader's eyes to his unconscious assumptions and opens up new literary possibilities. The imitation of a whole spectrum of traditional forms and the reference to, quotation of and 'borrowings' from other texts which the work incorporates within itself draw attention to its own 'situatedness' in the continuum of literary tradition while at the same time raising the question of the interaction of originality with that tradition in the creation of new literary works. As Edward Said says, 'The writer thinks less of writing originally, and more of rewriting. The image for writing changes from *original inscription* to parallel script, (...) from melody to fugue'[9].

---

[8] Cf. Waugh, page 26, 'Through continuous narrative intrusion, the reader is reminded that not only do characters verbally construct their own reality, they are themselves verbal constructions, *words* not *beings*'.
[9] Edward Said, in the essay 'On Originality' in: *The World, the Text and the Critic*, London 1981, pages 126-139. Said alludes to 'the way, for example, literature has made itself into a topos of

The image of the fugue indicates the inherently polyphonous nature of metafiction. Mikhail Bakhtin has characterised the novel form as essentially 'dialogic'. 'Dialogism' embraces not only the dialogue between conflicting and contradictory voices within the text but also the dialogue between different types (scientific, technical, poetic) of discourse, the dialogue between writer, reader and text and the dialogue between the fictional text, which of necessity implies limitation and finalisation and the chaotic limitlessness of lived experience[10]. Metafiction exploits and displays this inherent 'dialogism' of the novel form or of what Bakhtin calls 'novelness'. The text contains within itself a multiplicity of forms of discourse. The one dominant voice of the omniscient authorial narrator yields to a multitude of competing and conflicting voices offering a variety of perspectives, which supplement, relativise and comment on each other. This polyphony implies that meaning, too, is multifarious and denies the possibility of a resolution into one ultimate meaning.

Allied with this denial of the possibility of an ultimate meaning is a sense of the arbitrary nature of all beginnings, a consciousness that there was always something already there before the beginning and a concomitant sense of the impossibility of endings. The paradigmatic fictional happy ending may be parodied or called into question. The end may be left open or alternative endings may be offered for the reader to choose. The end may turn back upon itself and become identical with its beginning. There is a refusal of the closure implied both by ultimate meanings and by final endings.

writing', page 135. He is referring, in particular, to twentieth-century modernist writers, to Joyce, Eliot and Mann, but he is discussing a general metafictional feature.

[10] Cf. Michael Holquist, *Dialogism: Bakhtin and his world*, London and New York 1990. Holquist emphasises the way in which 'in dialogism, literature is seen as an activity that plays an important role in defining relations between individuals and society', page 86. He suggests that it provides a model for the individual to 'author' his own experience of the world, 'Literature has a particularly important role to play in the economy of dialogism, then, because it affords opportunities of a unique power to explore, to *teach* possibilities of authorship, where authorship is understood as consummating or 'finalizing' the unsigned world into an utterance in a manner that least restricts the world's possible meanings', pages 84-5.

8

Mirrors abound within the metafictional text just as they do in those self-conscious paintings such as van Eyck's 'Arnolfini Wedding' or Velázquez's 'Las Meninas' where the painted mirror reflects the scene being painted or the observers of that scene[11]. Stylistically the text is characterised by mirroring devices such as mise en abyme which tend to highlight its self-reflexivity. Mise en abyme is a term most specifically associated with the French 'nouveau roman' which has been defined as 'any internal mirror reflecting the narrative whole by simple, repeated or spacious reduplication'[12]. It is a technique, however, found throughout the whole tradition of the self-reflexive novel whereby the literary work contains within itself miniature analogues for the work itself, which reflect and accentuate its narrative structure and concerns.

The analogue may be overtly textual or it may be a textual description of a painting or other work of the visual arts and as such is closely connected with the technique of ekphrasis. The term ekphrasis has its origins in the technical language of Greek and Roman oratory and, in the rhetorical handbooks, referred to any descriptive passage used in a speech. In modern literary criticism it is used in a more specialised sense to refer to the description of a work of the visual arts, whether painting, sculpture or building, which is employed to particular purpose in a literary text: either as an analogy for the text itself and its own artistic concerns or as means of lending to the progressive temporality of the literary work something of the static spatiality of the visual arts, while at the same time indicating the 'inevitability of spatial language' in any attempt at concretisation of

---

[11] Velázquez's painting is a complex and ingenious exercise in mirroring: reflected in the mirror in the background of the painting is the large portrait of the king and queen on which Velázquez himself is working in the foreground, the back of which only can be seen. The king and queen themselves are to be imagined in the position of the observer, watching the scene of the painting as they 'sit' for the portrait which is being worked upon within the painting.

[12] Lucien Dällenbach, *Le Récit spéculaire. Essai sur la mise en abyme* Paris (Seuil) 1977, page 52. The term originated with André Gide who derived it from the heraldic emblem of a shield in whose centre is reproduced a miniature version of itself. Gide used the device in the *Faux-Monnayeurs* where the central character, Eduard, is a novelist working on a novel with the same title and a strong resemblance to the novel in which he is a character.

the text[13]. Together these devices help to call attention to the dual aspect of the literary work as both product and process, to the artefact which is created and to the artifice by which it is created.

Another technique borrowed from the visual arts is that of framing. The work may consist of a frame narrative with embedded novellas; it may contain stories within stories or fictional letters and diaries or purportedly factual reports and information, all of which focus attention on the composite nature of the novel genre[14]. There may be several levels or layers of fictionality with metaleptic moments, where characters move from one level of fictionality to another, as in Part Two of *Don Quixote* when the characters read about their own fictional adventures in Part One. This framing technique focuses attention on the perspectivity of all experience, on the structures through which we view what we think of as 'reality' and on the way in which 'one thinks that one is tracing the outline of the thing's nature over and over again and one is merely tracing round the frame through which we look at it'[15]. The breaking of the frame suggests the uncertainty of the boundary between reality and fiction, the impossibility of experience unmediated by the perspective, the structuring framework through which we experience it.

---

[13] Cf. Murray Krieger, *Ekphrasis: The Illusion of the Natural Sign*, Baltimore and London, 1992. Krieger discusses the use of spatial metaphors by writers, citing the example of Keats in 'Ode to a Grecian Urn', and the 'inevitability of spatial language used by the critic or by the poem itself as its own aesthetician'. He describes the way in which ekphrasis is 'introduced in order to use a plastic object as a symbol of the frozen, stilled world of plastic relationships which must be imposed upon literature's turning world to "still" it', and continues, 'I use, then, as the most obvious sort of poetic within the poem this anti-Lessing claim; the claim to form, to circular repetitiveness within the discretely linear, and this by the use of an object of spatial and plastic art to symbolise the spatiality and plasticity of literature's temporality', pages 265-6.

[14] Michael Holquist uses Mary Shelley's *Frankenstein* to illustrate this technique, suggesting that the monster's hybrid form is a metaphor for the hybrid form of the novel: 'that novel, like the monster, is made up of *disjecta membra*, story inside framed story, as Walton's letters surround Frankenstein's spoken tale that surrounds the monster's tale, that includes the story of Safie and the De Laceys, all encompassed at the end in Walton's diary. Not only is there a mix of narrators, there is a compound of genres - letters, diaries, and a variety of oral tales', Michael Holquist, *Dialogism,* page 97.

[15] Wittgenstein, quoted in Gabriel Josipovici, *The World and the Book: A Study of Modern Fiction*, London 1977.

The terms metafiction and self-reflexivity are relatively new, but there have been self-reflexive texts ever since the beginnings of storytelling[16]. Already in Homer's *Odyssey* there is a high degree of narrative self-consciousness. The *Odyssey*, too, is made up of 'story inside framed story' as the frame narrative surrounds Odysseus' own tales of his adventures, which leave us uncertain of where truth ends and fiction begins, and which themselves surround the tales told by Agamemnon, Menelaus and Achilles. The blind bard Demodocus is a poet figure within the text whose songs of the gods and of Odysseus' adventures at Troy reflect upon the rest of the text. There is an open-endedness in the text, too, as the blind prophet Teiresias foretells the travels of Odysseus still to come after the end of the *Odyssey*[17]. A further example from antiquity of a text displaying an awareness of its own status as a literary construct is the ancient Greek romance *Daphnis and Chloe* by Longus, a favourite book of Goethe[18]. The archetypal metafiction is Cervantes' *Don Quixote*, with its constant awareness of itself as a literary construct and its parodying of the outdated conventions of Romance narrative. The most striking examples of metafictional literature from the eighteenth century are the two novels of Laurence Sterne, *Tristram Shandy* and *A*

---

[16] John Banville recognises this when he describes his vision for a 'new fiction', a highly self-conscious form, thus, 'Modernism has run its course. So also, for that matter, has post-modernism. I believe, at least I hope, that we are on the threshold of a new *ism*, a new synthesis. What will it be? I do not know. But I hope it will be an art which is honest enough to despair and yet go on; rigorous and controlled, cool and yet passionate, without delusions, aware of its own possibilities and its own limits; an art which knows that truth is arbitrary, that reality is multifarious, that language is not a clear lens'; and then ends with the cry, 'Did I say *new*? What I have defined is as old as Homer', *Irish university review. A journal of Irish Studies. John Banville Special*, volume 11, no.1 (1981), page 17.

[17] Odysseus describes his wanderings after the sack of Troy to Alcinous and the Phaeacians in Books 9-12; later, on his return to Ithaca, before revealing his identity he entertains the swineherd Eumaeus with 'fictional' tales of his wanderings, which reflect upon the 'real' tales he had told earlier. Demodocus entertains Alcinous' court with his songs in Book 8. Menelaus tells his tale to Telemachus in Book 4 and the shades of Agamemnon and Achilles speak to Odysseus in Book 11. This 'Book of the Dead' also contains Teiresias' prophecies of Odysseus' further adventures after the end of the text.

[18] No detail survives of Longus' life but he is believed to have been a Sophist of the Second Sophistic movement between A.D.c.50-250, most probably writing during the late second and early third century A.D. Cf. R. L. Hunter *A Study of 'Daphnis & Chloe'*, Cambridge, 1983, pages 3-10 and Longus *Daphnis und Chloe* übersetzt und mit einem Nachwort von Arno Mauersberger, Insel, Frankfurt am Main 1976, pages 121-2.

Sentimental Journey, both of great influence on writers in eighteenth- and early nineteenth-century Germany. Goethe too enjoyed reading and rereading these novels and repeatedly referred to and invoked them in the *Wanderjahre*. They make constant play with their own form and are full of digressions, dead-ends and deviations. Goethe's contemporary and fellow fiction-writer, Jean Paul, was also influenced by Sterne, especially in his use of an intrusive narrator, who is constantly engaging the reader in his discourse and reflecting on his craft. Jean Paul, too, is a master of the curvilinear narrative. In the twentieth century - from Thomas Mann to Christa Wolf, from André Gide to Robbe-Grillet and the French 'nouveau roman', from John Barth to Angela Carter - this self-questioning, anti-illusionist tradition of metafiction has become the dominant form of narrative literature[19].

Daphnis and Chloe

eine vollständige Welt
a complete world

Daphnis and Chloe is mentioned on two occasions in Goethe's conversations with Eckermann. On the 9th March 1831 Eckermann tells Goethe that he is reading *Daphnis and Chloe* in the French translation by Courier. Goethe replies that it is a masterpiece which he has himself often read and admired. He goes on to compare the artistic merits of the work favourably with Virgil and praises its pictorial qualities whereby a landscape in the style of Poussin is realised in only a few brushstrokes[20].

---

[19] Martin Swales has emphasised the extent to which the genre of the German 'Bildungsroman' belongs to the tradition of the self-reflective novel (pages 147-8) and incorporates within itself 'the dialectical interaction of novel theory and novel practice' (page 161). Martin Swales, *The German Bildungsroman from Wieland to Hesse*, New Jersey and Guildford 1978.
[20]*Eckermanns Gespräche mit Goethe*, edited by Fritz Bergemann, Frankfurt am Main 1981, page 443. Goethe goes on to recount how the translator Courier had found a previously unknown manuscript of *Daphnis and Chloe* in the Laurentian library in Florence 'with the climax of the poem which the previous editions did not have'. Goethe confesses that he had often read and admired the work 'in its defective form' without sensing in any way that the climax was missing - a confession which, he suggests, must bear witness to the excellence of the work.

12

The second conversation takes place on the 20th March 1831. In the intervening ten days Goethe has been prompted to reread the novel and he now embarks on a more detailed analysis of its qualities. Again he emphasises its pictorial aspect, comparing it to the ancient Roman wall-paintings which he had seen in Herculaneum and Pompeii during his Italian journey. Another feature of the work praised by Goethe is the way in which it presents a restricted and enclosed world which is nevertheless complete and inhabited by human beings in all their diversity: 'and still, with all its modest self-containment (...) in it a complete world is developed. We see herdsmen of all kinds, cultivators of the land, gardeners, wine-growers, sailors, robbers, warriors und refined city-dwellers, great lords and serfs'. He emphasises, too, that through the particular and individual story of the lovers Daphnis and Chloe 'the deepest human concerns are given expression'.

In praising the beauty of the novel Goethe nevertheless points out that it does also deal with the most violent and distressing aspects of life, with rape, murder and warfare, but without an excessive preoccupation with them. They are assimilated into a world order which is essentially benevolent and harmonious: 'everything offensive that enters disruptively into the happy state of affairs in the work, such as assault, robbery and war, is always finished with as quickly as possible and leaves behind hardly a trace'. In contrast Goethe criticises Victor Hugo, whose talent he admired and whose *Notre Dame de Paris* he was reading in June 1831, for his obsession with the more repugnant elements of life and the way in which he torments and tortures his characters beyond endurance or belief, until all trace of plausibility, of natural event and circumstance disappears gradually into a chaos of atrocities[21]. In Hugo violence and cruelty become ends

---

[21] Goethe in a letter to Soret on 25th June 1831 as he returned to him the second part of *Notre Dame de Paris*, W.A. 4.48, page 254. Cf. also Goethe's diary entries for 14th, 15th and 20th June 1831; his letter to Soret on 19th June as he returned the first part of the work, W.A. 4.48, page 248; his conversation with Eckermann on 27th June 1831 and his letter to Zelter of 28th June 1831, H.A. Letters 4, page 435. In the conversation with Eckermann Goethe portrays Hugo as very much a product of his age and of the new direction Romanticism was taking in his obsession with the extremes of beauty and ugliness.

in themselves and are exploited for their shock effect, whereas in *Daphnis and Chloe* they are allotted a place within the whole cycle of human experience.

At the end of the conversation with Eckermann Goethe maintains that it would take a whole book to expatiate properly on the merits of *Daphnis and Chloe*. It is, he says, a book from which one can gain both profit and pleasure and whose benefits can only be harvested through regular rereading: 'one does well to reread it once a year, in order to learn from it again and again and to experience afresh the impression of its great beauty'.

In *Daphnis and Chloe* there is the same textual self-consciousness of its own status as artifice and artefact and the same interest in the relationship between the visual arts and literature which we will find in growing measure in all Goethe's narrative works and particularly in the *Wanderjahre*. The prologue begins with the description of a cult painting, which the narrator professes to have seen in the grove of the nymphs on the island of Lesbos. This painting is a simultaneous representation of all the many and varied stories which the narrator will go on to relate in the body of his text, and indeed it is his admiration of the painting which spurs him on to attempt to emulate it in his narrative. The whole of *Daphnis and Chloe* is therefore presented, in effect, as the verbal equivalent of a solid and concrete work of art. The painting stands as a metaphor for the literary work and is a self-conscious mirroring device, at once ekphrastic description and mise en abyme. The narrator calls attention to the correspondence between literary and visual work by describing the four books of his narrative as a 'lovely possession' and dedicating them as 'votive offerings to Eros, to the nymphs and to Pan'. Such votive offerings were usually artefacts of various kinds left in the shrines of gods by their followers, like the offerings of the shepherds described in the first book of the novel: 'and hung on the rock all around were milking pails, flutes and reed-pipes, votive offerings of shepherds long passed away'[22]. The identification of picture and narrative is reinforced at the end, as the novel comes

---

[22] Translations are taken from *The Pastoral Loves of Daphnis and Chloe*, done into English by George Moore, Heinemann, London 1924, pages 28 and 31.

14

full circle and describes the devotion of Daphnis and Chloe to the nymphs and to Pan and Eros and how they adorned the cave of the nymphs with images: votive offerings in which we can recognise the beautiful painting with which the prologue began.

Longus' use of the novel-as-painting analogy indicates the extent to which translation into text imposes limitation, closure and finalisation on the open-ended multifariousness of experience. The adventures of Daphnis and Chloe on the island of Lesbos occupy a space as defined as that of the painting within the framework of the prologue, with its description of the beautiful picture, and the ending in the cave of the nymphs, with its images and statues. The novel has 'a definite conclusion in the wedding night of Daphnis and Chloe which provides the climax towards which the whole work moves'[23]. At the same time it retains a certain open-endedness in that, already before the consummation of the marriage, it looks forward to the time after the wedding and the beginning of a whole new cycle of life in the birth of a boy and a girl to Daphnis and Chloe, children who are both similar and dissimilar to their parents.

In the prologue the narrator tells us that, before embarking on his task, he finds an expert who can interpret the painted scenes for him. In this complex device Longus suggests authentication for his story by creating an authority for the narrative, who is independent of the narrator, while at the same time avoiding himself vouching for its authenticity by representing it as something which was told to him. The need for an interpreter also suggests a mythical or legendary origin for the subject matter of the painted scenes and implies hidden layers of meaning, which tantalise the reader but continue to be ambiguous. The device also has the effect of gaining a sympathetic reading for the narrative by setting up an analogy between the narrator, listening to the interpretation of the paintings, and the reader of the text who will both accept what is told to him and seek to

---

[23] R.L. Hunter, page 42.

interpret it. The narrator here stands within his own text as the representative of the reader.

At the end of the prologue the narrator makes explicit his intentions for his text: that it should provide the reader with a mixture of the 'dulce' and the 'utile', with just that combination of profit and pleasure which Horace claimed as the true aim of literature[24]. The four books, he says, are not only votive offerings to Pan, Eros and the nymphs but also a gift to all men, 'that will help to cure the sick, to comfort the sorrowful, and recall memories of love to those whose time for love is over, and instruct those who have not yet loved' [25].

The fiction, which presents the novel as the story behind a 'narrative' painting of a cycle of separate but interconnected scenes, highlights the episodic structure of the narrative typical of romance. The episodes are linked not only by the setting on the island of Lesbos but also by the protagonists and the story of their progression towards an apparently pre-ordained union. This storyline, however, appears secondary to the portrayal of a profusion of incidents and scenes, which are all essentially autonomous although they reflect upon each other. In addition to this episodic structure the novel also contains digressions in the form of inserted narratives told by characters within the novel. In each of the first three books a short mythological story involving a metamorphosis is recounted. In the first book Daphnis tells Chloe the story of a girl who charms the cows she looks after with her beautiful singing voice. But when they are lured away by a boy in the neighbourhood who is also a cowherd and whose voice proves more attractive she begs the gods to turn her into a bird. Her wish is granted and she flies to and fro singing of the cows she has lost. In the second book Lamon, Daphnis' foster-father, tells Daphnis and Chloe the story of Syrinx, the nymph with the beautiful singing voice pursued by the god Pan and lost in the

---

[24] Cf. Horace *Ars Poetica*, lines 343-4, '...who mixed the useful with the pleasant/by diverting and instructing the reader in equal measure'. As we have seen, it was just this combination of profit and pleasure, which Goethe gave as the reason for reading and rereading the book, 'in order to learn from it again and again and experience afresh the impression of its great beauty'.
[25] Moore, page 29.

marshes when she hid from him in a bed of reeds. Pan immortalises her by making from the reeds, cut to different lengths, the first pan-pipes or syrinx, an instrument with which he can sing as beautifully as she did. In the third book Daphnis tells Chloe a variation on the story of Echo, daughter of a nymph and a mortal father. Echo sings beautifully and can play every kind of instrument. Pan, jealous of her musical talent and unable to win her love, drives the shepherds and goatherds mad so that they tear her apart like dogs or wolves. For the sake of the nymphs the earth buried her limbs where they were scattered and thereby preserved her song and music, the origin of the echo.

These three stories all mirror and reflect on the story of Daphnis and Chloe. The essentially erotic nature of each one underscores the main theme of the novel: 'the painted representation of a love story'. In each the idyllic world is overshadowed by an element of danger and violence, culminating in the tearing apart of Echo, a fate reminiscent of that of Orpheus at the hands of the Thracian maenads. In each, music plays a major part, as it does in the novel as a whole. The story of Echo, with its affinity to the myth of Orpheus, celebrates the potential of music, and by implication of all art, to survive and triumph over violence and devastation. Longus often explicitly indicates the links between the inserted stories and the story of Daphnis and Chloe: Daphnis introduces his story in the first book with the words, 'Once on a time, sweet maid, there was a maiden as beautiful as you and just of an age with you. She loved to sing and her cows delighted in her song'; the girl wears a garland of pine-needles just like Chloe and just as Daphnis and Chloe are shepherdess and goatherd, so the boy and girl in the story are cowherds[26]. After Lamon has told the story of Syrinx in the second book Daphnis and Chloe mime the action and, in so doing, suggest a similarity between themselves and the characters in the story. The fact that these three stories are myths also implies that the story of Daphnis and Chloe may be read on the level

---

[26] Moore, page 51.

of myth. In the lightest possible way Longus skilfully invests his simple story with the suggestion of multiple layers of meaning.

Instead of an inserted narrative in the fourth book there is a digression of a different kind: an ekphrastic description of Lamon's magnificent garden, with its echoes of the description of Alcinous' garden in the *Odyssey* - the archetypal rhetorical model for the description of a garden [27]. Lamon's garden has been seen as a 'microcosmic representation' of the world of the novel, again a mise en abyme or reflecting device, which enables the author to point up certain structural and thematic aspects of the novel[28]. Apart from its luxuriance, the most striking feature of the garden is the fusion of nature and art, which has gone to create it. In it, we are told, there are orchard trees of man's cultivation, but also forest trees which have planted themselves to form a natural wall. The branches of these trees are described as 'meeting and interweaving overhead so beautifully that nature seemed like art'[29]. There are cultivated flowers such as roses, hyacinths and lilies, but also wild flowers like violets, narcissi and daisies. A dominant theme of the novel - the relationship between nature and art - is here reflected in miniature in the garden. Longus' novel, too, represents a fusion of simple natural subject matter and complex, artificial literary technique.

This tension between the artificial and the natural and the preoccupation with the act of mimesis are also made manifest by the presentation of the novel as a complex and intricate 'work of art': the series of painted scenes described in the prologue. The prologue device highlights the status of the novel as an artistic construct. The novel, as a narrative 'description' of the painting, is an example of artifice doubly distanced from reality since it is the product of two distinct acts of

---

[27] *Odyssey*, Book 7, lines 112-32. The description of Lamon's garden also has striking topographical similarities with the various isolated landscape units, which are such a distinctive feature of the *Wanderjahre*: e.g. the uncle's estate, Makarie's realm, the 'pedagogical province'. In each the landscape description moves inwards from the margins and each contains in its centre a sanctuary: a building, like the temple to Dionysus in the centre of Lamon's garden, decorated with a frieze of pictures.

[28] Hunter, page 42.

[29] Moore, page 130.

18

imitation: that which produced the painting, and that which produced the 'story' of the painting. At the same time the mingling of genres seen in the prologue, the way in which it implies that the work represents an amalgam of the poetic and the historiographic traditions, points to the dialogic nature of the literary work and raises the question of the uncertainty of the boundaries between truth and fiction[30].

Laurence Sterne

in allem ein Andeuter und Erwecker
in everything a guide and inspiration

Goethe records in his diary that he was rereading Laurence Sterne's *Sentimental Journey* between the 10th and the 16th of September 1817. On the 16th he records further that he has begun *Tristram Shandy*, but his acquaintance with the works of Laurence Sterne stretches right back to the early 1770s, when Sterne was one of the foremost among the English writers who exercised such a strong influence on German 'Empfindsamkeit' [sentimentality][31]. Goethe's review of the second part of Schummel's *Empfindsame Reisen durch Deutschland* in the *Frankfurter gelehrte Anzeigen* in 1773 begins with the words, 'Alas poor Yorick!' and goes on to compare the work unfavourably with Sterne's *Sentimental Journey*. What he complains of is the apparent inauthenticity of the experiences of the present traveller in comparison with his exemplary predecessor, his lack of effectiveness in giving his readers a sense of directly experienced emotion and his inability to create credible characters who behave convincingly[32].

In the *Tages- und Jahreshefte* for 1789, when talking about his aims in his own travel writing, Goethe describes how he deliberately rejected the example of the 'unnachahmliche' [inimitable] sentimental journey of Sterne and, for his

---

[30] Cf. Hunter, page 52, 'The literary and rhetorical traditions are masterfully blended into an amusing and original form'.
[31] Cf. Goethe, 'Kampagne in Frankreich', H.A. Volume 10, pages 321-2. Further cf. Jean Paul *Vorschule der Ästhetik*, Meiner, Hamburg 1990, VII Programm, page 127. For Sterne's influence generally on the novel in eighteenth-century Germany cf. Peter Michelson, *Laurence Sterne und der deutsche Roman des 18 Jahrhunderts*, Göttingen, 1972.
[32] Goethe W.A. 1.37, page 214.

description of the Roman Carnival, sets up in opposition to the subjective-sentimental Sterne model which is devoted throughout to the emotions and opinions of the traveller, the model of a more objective form of travel writing whose aim is to bring out as clearly as possible the most typical features of the ethnic groups and their relationships[33].

There is little mention of Sterne again, before the diary references to the rereading of his works, apart from the use of the adjective 'altshändyscher' in a somewhat mocking poem on Klopstock[34]. In the 1820s, however, as Goethe looks back over his life and times, he repeatedly emphasises the impact of Laurence Sterne's works on general European culture, on German writers in particular and, most specifically, on his own development as a writer. In a conversation with Eckermann in 1828, for example, Sterne's name is one of the few which he chooses to highlight among the innumerable formative influences which he recognises have contributed to his cultural growth[35].

In 'Kampagne in Frankreich', written in 1820 and recalling his involvement in the Prussian campaign against the French revolutionary forces in 1792, Goethe focuses particularly on Sterne's influence on the 'Empfindsamkeit' of the 1770s. He describes a meeting with Professor Plessing in Duisburg after a gap of twenty years. This meeting prompts Goethe to reminisce over the circumstances of their first acquaintanceship in 1776 in Wernigerode and Weimar, when Goethe was already famous as the author of *Werther* and therefore, to some extent, the natural target for letters from gloomy, world-weary and introverted young men of artistic or intellectual bent. *Werther* became for its author a means of writing himself out of the melancholy, suicidal mood which had become fashionable among young people in the early 1770s - a period of peace and inactivity which so contrasted with the early 1790s. He suggests that much of the responsibility for stirring up this wave of sentimentality which was

[33] Goethe W.A. 1.35, pages 12-13.
[34] Goethe W.A. 1.5, page 37.
[35] Eckermann, 1987, page 281. Conversation of 16th December 1828.

sweeping through the young people of Germany lay with English writers of the mid-eighteenth century and particularly with the works of Laurence Sterne, but only because the essence of his work, when filtered through the German psyche, became translated into something utterly alien to its original spirit: the sentimentality, which in England was tempered by 'humorous irony' was transmogrified under German skies to 'a tiresome self-torment'[36]. The young Plessing, with whom Goethe tells us he conducted a 'sentimental novel-like relationship', personified for Goethe this particularly Germanic form of self-tormenting sentimentality, unmediated by the light touch of English self-mocking humour[37].

Goethe's most comprehensive discussion of Sterne's influence on European culture is the essay 'Lorenz Sterne' which was published in *Kunst und Altertum* for the year 1827. At the beginning he attributes to Sterne the function of a guide who can prevent us from wandering astray. He sees him as a great humanising force leavening the cultural atmosphere of the second half of the eighteenth century. What impresses him about Sterne is the sensitivity with which he is able to discover 'das Menschliche im Menschen' [what is most human in mankind], his willingness to interpret human eccentricities and idiosyncrasies - what Sterne describes as ruling passions or hobby-horses - in a positive light as signs of individuality rather than consigning them to one or other of the opposing categories of 'Irrthümer und Wahrheiten' [errors and truths]. Goethe here attributes to Sterne the characteristic of finding a third way between the extremes. It is a 'modus operandi' which accords with Goethe's own preferred way of looking at things. In the essay 'Über Wahrheit und Wahrscheinlichkeit der Kunstwerke' this way of looking at things is described by the lawyer as 'durch Gegensätze zu operieren, die Frage von zwei Seiten zu beantworten und so gleichsam die Sache in die Mitte zu fassen' [to operate through opposites, to

---

[36] H.A. Volume 10, page 321.
[37] Goethe, in fact, talks about 'the humorous irony of the Britons' but elsewhere refers to Sterne as the 'Irishman', just as he calls Carlyle the 'Scotsman' and makes clear his awareness of the different population groupings which go to make up the inhabitants of the British Isles.

answer the question from two sides and, as it were, to grasp the matter in the middle][38].

The means of grasping the matter in the middle is that form of benevolent irony which Goethe, in a letter to Zelter, ascribes to both Goldsmith and Sterne, and which he implicitly suggests is the legacy he hopes they have passed on to him[39]. In this letter, too, the writer's role is seen as that of a guide who helps us to develop the open-mindedness, which will enable us to find our way through the tortuous pathways of life. Finally Goethe distinguishes between Goldsmith, whose work he sees as 'ganz Form' [totally form], and Sterne, who he suggests 'inclines more towards the formless'; and claims that in this respect he has tended to follow Goldsmith. We will see presently, however, the extent to which he was influenced by Sterne's formless form in the construction of the *Wanderjahre*.

It is by no means fortuitous that Goethe's renewed interest in Sterne's influence on the late eighteenth century and upon his own writing coincided with his reworking of the *Wanderjahre* during the 1820s. In this second version of the *Wanderjahre* Goethe not only includes a kind of encoded blueprint of the extent of the work's indebtedness to Sterne, but also, in Makarie's archive, makes overt reference to Sterne and allows his voice to be heard directly through quotation from his work[40].

In Makarie's archive the spirit of Sterne is evoked in two series of aphorisms, 126 to 144 and 157 to 171, as well as in one or two other single aphorisms. The first series consists of a set of translated quotations from an English collection of aphorisms - *The Koran or Essays, Sentiments, Characters and Callimachies of Tria Juncta in Uno* - published in 1770 and believed by

---

[38] H.A. Volume 12, page 68. A similar idea is expressed by Montan in the *Wanderjahre* Book 2, Chapter 9 (H.A. Volume 8, page 262): "...indeed they say that the truth lies in the middle" – "By no means!" answered Montan: "in the middle the problem remains, perhaps impenetrable, but perhaps also accessible, if one embarks on the attempt". Cf. also the last aphorism in the 'Betrachtungen im Sinne der Wanderer' (309).
[39] Goethe to Zelter, 25th December 1829, W.A. 4.46, page 194.
[40] Cf. Jane K Brown, *Goethe's Cyclical Narratives. 'Die Unterhaltungen deutscher Ausgewanderten' and 'Wilhelm Meisters Wanderjahre'*, Chapel Hill (N.Carolina) 1975, pages 119-121.

Goethe and his contemporaries to be the work of Laurence Sterne[41]. This series of 'borrowings' follows directly upon references to two other writers, Shakespeare and Calderon, who were of especial significance to Goethe, and is framed by two direct references to Sterne. The introductory remark (No.126) characterises Sterne as 'der schönste Geist' [the finest spirit] and emphasises the beneficial effect of reading him, the liberating effect of his humour. The concluding remark (No.144) makes it clear that this beneficial influence is not confined to the eighteenth century, nor is it of just historical interest, but that the nineteenth century, too, could gain immeasurably from a reappraisal of his work.

The series of aphorisms thus framed, even if not collected and translated by Sterne himself, contains thoughts which accord with his way of thinking and reflects in particular some of the aspects of his thinking which appealed to Goethe[42]. It is apposite, given the doubt about their provenance, that one of their themes (Nos. 134 & 135) is the irrelevance of the name of the author to our engagement with a written work. The whole question of authorship and originality was of great interest to Goethe and was also thematised in the works of Sterne, which in themselves constitute an archive of quotations, references and 'borrowings' from his encyclopaedic reading. Tristram's mocking reference to his project as 'this cyclopaedia of arts and sciences' not only makes fun of the whole enterprise of encyclopaedia making, but also highlights the essentially 'dialogic' nature of the novel which can encompass a wide variety of genres[43]. Allied to this question is the scepticism about the possibility of, or indeed, necessity for, originality of thought which is the subject of aphorisms 174 and 175 and which

[41] The collection appeared in Sterne's collected works in 1775 and in 1795 but the author is now believed to be Richard Griffith (died 1788) or his son, also Richard Griffith (1752-1820).
[42] Such themes include Apollonian creativity (No.127); the proper use of time (Nos.131, 132 & 138); the value of tolerance and concern for one's fellow-men (Nos.129, 139 and also 181); the relationship between thought and action (No.130); the superior position of sight among the senses (No.128); and attempted definitions of art, science and poetry (Nos. 140-3).
[43] Volume 2, Chapter 17, page 98. Page references for *Tristram Shandy* are to the Penguin Classics edition of 1997.

indicates Goethe's (and Sterne's) appreciation of the writer's indebtedness to his predecessors, an awareness reflected in the intertextuality of their texts[44].

The second series of aphorisms concerned with Sterne (Nos. 157-171) comprise an attempt to characterise his qualities, embedded within which are quotations from his letters[45]. They are introduced by an assertion of the necessity to see him in the context of his time. The advantages and dangers of his particular type of humour are discussed. His ability to cut through all sham and distinguish the true from the false is praised along with his horror of all pedantry and his ability to highlight absurdity and triviality. His definition of 'Shandeism', as the inability to think about a serious subject for more than two minutes, is mentioned and his volatile nature with its mercurial shifts from gravity to levity is attributed to his Irish origins[46]. Goethe values in Sterne his appreciation of the contradictions of life and is impressed by the paradoxical delicacy of his lasciviousness. He stresses, however, that Sterne's qualities are inimitable and the concluding remark in this second series emphasises that he is to be regarded not as a model to be imitated but as a guide and a stimulator of the imagination: 'Er ist in nichts ein Muster und in allem ein Andeuter und Erwecker' [he is in nothing a model and in everything a guide and an inspiration] (No.171).

Occupying a central position in the second version of the *Wanderjahre*, towards the end of Book 2, is Wilhelm's explanatory letter to Natalie, which attempts to chart the agglomeration of experiences leading to his decision to train as a surgeon. Embedded within this letter is Wilhelm's own comment on its labyrinthine method of construction and the way in which it attempts to reach its goal by a very circuitous route, 'But if I now have to confess, after this

---

[44] In this sense they are examples of what Edward Said is describing in his essay 'On Originality' when he suggests, 'The image for writing changes from *original inscription* to parallel script, (...) from melody to fugue', page 135.

[45] Goethe records in his diary reading Sterne's letters on 3rd, 4th and 5th January 1826.

[46] An entry in Goethe's diary for 29th March 1828 records a conversation with his daughter-in-law Ottilie 'about the differences between the British nations and their characters, especially the character of the Irish' in conjunction with reading Sterne's *Sentimental Journey* on the evening of the same day.

24

convoluted explanation that I still haven't reached my intended goal and that I can only hope to get there by a roundabout way, what can I say! How can I excuse myself!' (279). The letter itself and Wilhelm's comment on the method of its construction have been taken by several critics as a model of the construction of the novel as a whole and as a comment on the way in which it is to be read[47]. It is also a homage to Laurence Sterne and an allusion to the ways in which the *Wanderjahre* has been shaped by his example.

In Wilhelm's comment Goethe thematises, along with the striking differences between himself and Sterne, his own marked indebtedness to Sterne's influence, especially with regard to the circuitous form of the *Wanderjahre* and its programme of drawing the reader into a productive involvement with the text. On the one hand he points out the obvious differences between his sensible, reasonable persona and Sterne's humorist, who allows himself the most extravagant flights of fancy. On the other hand he makes it clear that the intricate, digressive form of both letter and novel is inspired by the exuberant deviations characteristic of Sterne's work. At the same time he explains the purpose of this discursiveness, both in Sterne's work and in the *Wanderjahre*: the reader must be made to think, must be drawn actively into the construction of the meaning of the text. To this end 'he boldly leaves it to his reader to discover eventually at least something of what can be gathered from it'. Only when the writer constructs his text 'in an apparently peculiar way, by working roundabout towards many points', can he eventually bring his reader to the centre of the labyrinth where 'finally in a focal point one recognises them both in themselves and combined together and learns insight'. The vital importance of the reader's participation is further underscored by Wilhelm's injunction to Natalie, 'You must just possess your soul in patience, read and read further and at last it will suddenly leap out

---

[47] Cf. for example Heidi Gidion *Zur Darstellungsweise von 'Wilhelm Meisters Wanderjahre'*, Göttingen 1969 and Manfred Karnick *'Wilhelm Meisters Wanderjahre' oder die Kunst des Mittelbaren*, München 1968.

and appear quite natural to you even though it would have seemed very strange to you if it were stated explicitly' (280).

The first element alluded to in this passage as being inherited from Sterne is the device of the self-conscious narrator who makes his presence felt in his text as a person with a distinct cast of character and who comments both on his own skill as a writer and on the work itself as a literary product. The characterisation of the narrator is underscored by the careful distinction drawn between Sterne's whimsical narrators - Yorick and Tristram Shandy, the 'humorists' - and the sensible, reasonable persona assumed by the narrator of the *Wanderjahre*.

Sterne himself pays homage repeatedly in his work to his master Cervantes, to whom he was indebted not only for his 'cervantick tone', but also, to a large extent, for the device of the self-conscious narrator[48]. *Don Quixote* is the first major European novel to make extensive use of the intruding narrator. Indeed, Cervantes complicates the matter by introducing two narrators. The narrator of the preface, whom we first meet sitting at his desk struggling to compose his preface much in the manner of Tristram Shandy who only gets round to his preface in Volume 3, or Yorick in his 'desobligeant' at Calais, turns out to be the secondary narrator of this text, whose primary narrator appears at the end of Book One in the guise of the Arab chronicler Cid Hamet Benengeli and then intervenes at irregular intervals in a text which is seen principally through the eyes of the secondary narrator. Cervantes' narrator shows, on the one hand, an

---

[48] This homage is made explicit in The Invocation in Volume 9, Chapter 24, page 527, where the 'Gentle Spirit of sweetest humour, who erst didst sit upon the easy pen of my beloved CERVANTES' is invoked. Along with Lucian and 'my dear Rabelais', 'dearer Cervantes' is also invoked as Muse in Volume 3, Chapter 19 of *Tristram Shandy*, page 156. There are many scattered references in both *Tristram Shandy* and *A Sentimental Journey* to Sancho Panza and Don Quixote, Rosinante, Dulcinea and Cid Hamet. The constellation of Uncle Toby and his servant Trim might also be reminiscent of Don Quixote and Sancho Panza. Yorick, on his deathbed, is described as speaking with 'something of a cervantick tone'; Walter Shandy's 'cervantick gravity', page 139, persuades Dr. Slop to read aloud the curse of Ernulphus; and the amours of Uncle Toby are described as being of 'so Cervantick a cast'. In a letter Sterne defined 'Cervantick humour' as the art of 'describing silly and trifling events with the Circumstantial Pomp of great ones'.

awareness of his readers, and, on the other hand, must endure criticism from his own characters of his skill as an author.

It is this dialogic possibility of the self-conscious narrator which was perhaps of most interest to Sterne and which he developed to the highest degree. Not only does the eponymous hero of *Tristram Shandy* materialise before our eyes in his study to become the narrator of his own life-story but Sterne also conjures up along with him a collection of purported readers who will listen, argue, understand and misunderstand, be harassed and harangued and asked to move about and perform a variety of tasks as Tristram unrolls his narrative before them. These readers are individualised as 'Sir', the male reader, 'Madam', the female reader and 'your reverences and your worships', a group of influential figures: with each the narrator develops a distinctly differentiated relationship[49]. In Chapter 6 of Volume 1 Tristram imagines the relationship between reader and narrator developing from 'slight acquaintance' through 'familiarity' into 'friendship' as they 'jogg on' together in their journey through the text[50]. In Chapter 11 of Volume 2 this relationship is seen as a 'conversation' - a dialogue in which the reader participates along with the writer:

---

[49] Tristram sees the male reader as slow and unwilling and prone to misunderstanding and treats him in a rather off-hand manner; his influential and powerful readers command only good-natured disrespect; while a more animated and intimate relationship evolves between Tristram and the female reader.

[50] The key image of the hobby-horse is important in describing the relationship between reader and writer. Sometimes the reader is seen as the hobby-horse which is being ridden - e.g. page 184, 'like an unbacked filly'; sometimes the roles are reversed and sometimes it is the text itself which is the hobby-horse - page 488, ''Tis the sporting little filly-folly which carries you out for the present hour'. This confusion suggests the fruitful reciprocal interaction of reader and writer which is made explicit in Volume 1, Chapter 24: 'By long journies and much friction, it so happens that the body of the rider is at length fill'd as full of HOBBY-HORSICAL matter as it can hold; - so that if you are able to give but a clear description of the nature of the one, you may form a pretty exact notion of the genius and character of the other'. On this theme cf. Helen Ostovich, 'Reader as Hobby-Horse in *Tristram Shandy*' in the New Casebooks Series, *The life and opinions of Tristram Shandy, gentleman* edited by Melvin New, Macmillan, London 1992. She particularly brings out the way in which the sexual connotations of the hobby-horse are used to suggest the 'fertile creativity (...) inherent in the collaboration of writer and reader'; and points out that Tristram distinguishes three different aspects of this 'productive association: procreative (the book as child), recreative (the book as entertainment and as art), and generative (the book as proliferator of sensation and idea)', page 156. The relationship, which Ostovich goes on to describe (pages 157-8), between reader, writer and text has much in common with the erotic relationship posited by Roland Barthes in *Le Plaisir du Texte*.

> The truest respect which you can pay to the reader's understanding is to halve this matter amicably, and leave him something to imagine, in his turn, as well as yourself.
> For my own part, I am eternally paying him compliments of this kind, and do all that lies in my power to keep his imagination as busy as my own (88).

'The reader (...) shall decide', cries Tristram as he discusses the soundness of his father's judgement and later he even leaves a blank page for the reader to sketch his own subjective vision of the Widow Wadman's beauty. At the same time, however, Sterne makes us aware of the practical limitations on the reader's role as active participant. Even in the case of works such as *Tristram Shandy* or the *Wanderjahre*, which were composed over a number of years and exposed to public reaction while in the process of composition, the reader's scope for response was restricted. While ostensibly allowing his reader freedom of imagination Tristram often directs and manipulates the way that freedom is used. Yorick, at the end of *A Sentimental Journey*, leaves the reader to imagine the scene as he and the lady undress and get into bed, while at the same time telling him, 'There was but one way of doing it, and that I leave to the reader to devise; protesting as I do it, that if it is not the most delicate in nature, 'tis the fault of his own imagination - against which this is not my first complaint'[51]. The apparent liberties, which Tristram and Yorick allow their readers to take with their texts, are nevertheless emblematic of the openness and freedom of imagination, seen by both Sterne and Goethe as the necessary precondition for a productive reading practice.

Through his narrators Sterne reiterates the importance of reading and rereading. Wilhelm's injunction to Natalie to 'read and read further', is an echo in a different key of Tristram's exasperated exhortation to the male-reader, in Chapter 36 of Volume 3, to 'Read, read, read, read, my unlearned reader! read' (184). The importance of critical reading is brought vividly to life for the real reader when, at the beginning of Chapter 20 in the first volume, the fictional Madam is accused by Tristram of not paying close enough attention as she reads

---

[51] Laurence Sterne, *A Sentimental Journey and Other Writings*, edited by Tom Keymer, Everyman, London, 1994, page 104. Page references for *A Sentimental Journey* are to this edition.

and is forced to go back and reread the previous chapter, affording him the opportunity to give vent to the pious hope 'that all good people, both male and female, from her example, may be taught to think as well as read' (49)[52].

In his 'Author's Preface', inserted in the middle of Volume 3, Tristram/Sterne insists on the importance of the exercise of both wit and judgement for the effective writer as well as for the effective reader. Rather than seeing them as mutually exclusive faculties he sees them as complementary. Working together they provide 'that just balance betwixt wisdom and folly, without which a book would not hold together a single year' (515). In an extravagant flight of fancy he imagines the utopian, almost unbearably paradisical situation in which both writer and reader approach the text overflowing with wit and judgement. The combination of wit and judgement, encompassing as they do such things as 'memory, fancy, genius, eloquence, quick parts, and what not' (158), represent for Sterne the importance of the interaction of all aspects of the human personality, the intellectual, the emotional and the sensory in the production and reception of works of art[53].

Not only does Sterne emphasize the work's status as an artefact by keeping us constantly aware of the book's physical existence: it is handled and its pages are turned back and forth by his fictional readers, at one point a sermon falls out from between its pages, while at another Tristram threatens to tear out pages; but he also imports into his text the language of the visual artist to describe the techniques of the writer. He suggests, 'Writers of my stamp have one

---

[52] While Madam is thus occupied Tristram takes the opportunity to express another complaint which he has against his readership in general - 'a vicious taste which has crept into thousands besides herself, - of reading straight forward, more in quest of the adventures, than of the deep erudition and knowledge which a book of this cast, if read over as it should be, would infallibly impart with them' (48); that is, a reader fault of which both Goethe and Jean Paul complained with equal vehemence - the propensity to read just for the plot or the 'story'.

[53] This is summed up neatly at the end of Chapter 17 in Volume 6 when Tristram describes the kind of book he is writing and the effect it should have on the reader: 'I write a careless kind of a civil, nonsensical, good-humoured *Shandean* book, which will do all your hearts good - - And all your heads too, - provided you understand it'. As we shall see later this idea was also of great importance to Goethe, cf. 'Der Sammler und die Seinigen' where he says, 'But the human being (...) is a whole, a unity of manifold, intimately connected powers and the work of art must speak to this totality of the human being, it must accord with this rich unity, this united diversity in him'.

principle in common with painters - where an exact copy makes our pictures less striking, we choose the less evil; deeming it even more pardonable to trespass against truth than beauty' (74). When describing Corporal Trim, Tristram writes, 'I have but one more stroke to give to finish Corporal Trim's character' (77), and similarly he writes of giving the reader 'this stroke in my Uncle Toby's picture' (92). He refers repeatedly to Hogarth's *Analysis of Beauty* with its concept of the 'line of beauty', suggesting that a sentence, just as well as a statue or a figure in a painting may have a 'precise line of beauty' (81). Behind his description of Trim's stance or 'attitude' as he reads the sermon which has fallen out from between the pages of the book lies not only Hogarth's *Analysis of Beauty*, but also Leonardo da Vinci's *Treatise of Painting* and Tristram says of his father, 'Reynolds (...) might have painted him as he sat' (131)[54]. This sustained analogy of painting and literature serves to highlight the visual aspect of the literary work and the way in which the imagination of the reader works to convert the dynamic flow of words into a static image in his mind.

In his comment on his letter to Natalie Wilhelm points specifically to the link between the challenge to the reader offered by the text and its labyrinthine method of construction. Tristram, too, makes constant reference to the circuitous nature of his narrative[55]. Not only does he insist on the necessity of rereading, for example when he sends Madam back to reread the chapter where he feels she has missed something, but he also describes his own writing practice as one of constant movement backwards and forwards, 'For in good truth, when a man is telling a story in the strange way I do mine, he is obliged continually to be going backwards and forwards to keep all tight together in the reader's fancy', until he finds himself lost within the intricacies of his own text, 'And now you see I am

---

[54] Cf. *The Life and Opinions of Tristram Shandy*, page 572, note 1.
[55] Tristram characterises his writing practice as being governed by two apparently incompatible movements, 'By this contrivance the machinery of my work is of a species by itself, two contrary motions are introduced into it, and reconciled, which were thought to be at variance with each other. In a word, my work is digressive, and it is progressive too, - and at the same time'. (58). These two 'contrary motions' - digressive and progressive - are characteristic of the way one proceeds through a labyrinth - making progress by digression.

lost myself' (383). As he embarks upon his account of Toby's love entanglements his text and its theme of love become 'this mystick labyrinth' in which he envisages himself being 'entangled on all sides' (388). At the end of Volume 6 he abandons words altogether and resorts to several arabesque-like convoluted diagrams to describe the digressive course of his narrative. At the same time, in the figure of the single straight line, he satirises reader-expectations of a normal narrative that will progress through the standard 'Aristotelian' divisions directly to its goal[56].

The labyrinthine nature of Tristram's enterprise is echoed within his narrative by the preoccupations of his father Walter and of Uncle Toby. Toby has chosen his 'hobby-horse' - his obsessive interest in battles, sieges and fortifications - as a response to his wounding at the siege of Namur. He attempts to come to terms with this traumatic experience by endlessly replaying it, in the first instance by devoting himself to the study of all available maps and plans of contemporary siege-works and fortifications, and later by constructing miniature versions of the various fortifications on the bowling-green and acting out the sieges with his servant, Trim.

Not only are the original fortifications of Namur like a labyrinth in which Toby is trapped: '- the ground was cut and cross-cut with such a multitude of dykes, drains, rivulets, and sluices, on all sides'; but also any attempt to give an account of his experiences to friends and acquaintances develops into a verbal labyrinth in which he becomes hopelessly involved: 'and he would get so sadly bewilder'd and set fast amongst them, that frequently he could neither get backwards or forwards to save his life, and was oft times obliged to give up the attack upon that very account only' (68). Furthermore Tristram sees Toby's

---

[56] This satire of the straightforward narrative has already been fully verbalised in Volume 4 in Slawkenbergius' tale, where Slawkenbergius describes his own strict adherence to the 'Aristotelian' rule, 'In all my ten tales (...) have I, (...) tied down every tale of them as tightly to this rule'. We will see later how Goethe also addresses this dichotomy between progressive and digressive narrative practice in his introduction to 'The German *Gil Blas*'.

subsequent study of fortifications and siege plans as an equally labyrinthine enterprise and retrospectively warns him against it in his narrative:

> - stop! my dear uncle Toby, - stop! - go not one foot further into this thorny and bewilder'd track, - intricate are the mases of this labyrinth! intricate are the troubles which the pursuit of this bewitching phantom, KNOWLEDGE, will bring upon thee (73).

Toby, however, seems to be only secure when caught in one kind of labyrinth or another, as he moves from the complications of the siege-works to the complications of the heart and becomes exposed to the widow Wadman's amatory intrigues. In the widow Wadman the labyrinth image takes on human flesh as her devious nature is contrasted with Toby's simplicity, 'There was (...) in my uncle Toby (...) a plainness and simplicity of feeling, with such an unmistrusting ignorance of the plies and foldings of the heart of a woman' (378); and the landscape of his siege-works is replaced by the 'serpentine walks' of the garden which separates her house from his.

If Toby attempts to make sense of his experience by transcribing it into maps and plans and then giving it concrete form in the miniature fortifications that he builds, Walter attempts to impose order on the world through the abstract theories and hypotheses to which he tries to reduce its complexity. We are told, 'He was systematical, and, like all systematick reasoners, he would move both heaven and earth, and twist and torture every thing in nature to support his hypothesis' (45). Later his activity in defending his hypotheses is likened to Toby's siege-works: 'and in a word, would intrench and fortify them round with as many circumvallations and breast-works, as my uncle Toby would a citadel' (182). In his 'Tristrapaedia' he embarks upon the ill-fated attempt to compress a comprehensive system for the education of his son within the compass of one small volume. Sterne uses imagery of spinning and weaving, which we shall see is also closely allied to the imagery of the labyrinth in the *Wanderjahre*, to describe this enterprise, 'My father spun his, every thread of it, out of his own brain, - or reeled and cross-twisted what all other spinners and spinsters had spun before him, that 'twas pretty near the same torture to him' (307) [57]. The metaphor is continued to express the futility of his endeavours. On the one hand his dream of a small volume which 'might be rolled up in my mother's hussive' suggests that the thread which he spins will end up turned back upon itself in the sewing-case where it began, and on the other hand, the impossibility of such a dream makes clear the complexity of the world he is trying to encompass. This complexity becomes even clearer when Walter expounds his theory about auxiliary verbs and the system that was intended as simplification or short cut, as a 'North west passage to the intellectual world', reveals itself to be, not a simplification at all, but an intricate labyrinth producing a never-ending proliferation of new pathways: 'and by the versability of this great engine, round which they are twisted, to open new tracks of enquiry, and make every idea engender millions' (334).

Elsewhere Walter insists that the Gordian knot of intellectual argument must be untied and not severed, ' - That is cutting the knot, said my father, instead of untying it. - But give me leave to lead you brother Toby, a little deeper into the mystery' (228). And when Dr. Slop tries to sever the genuine 'hard knots' (138) with which Obadiah has secured his bag of obstetrical instruments his action leads to untold complications. Cutting the Gordian knot, like the 'Aristotelian' straight line of narrative, which affirms the feasibility of following a direct route to the heart of the maze, is revealed as an impossible simplification. When Tristram warns uncle Toby to fly from the intricate labyrinth into which the pursuit of knowledge will inevitably draw him, it is a warning to the reader, too, that there are no easy answers to the questions raised by the text; that he, too, is embarking on a journey which will have no end: '- Endless is the Search for Truth!' (73).

---

[57] Cf. Stephen Soud, '"Weavers, Gardeners, and Gladiators": Labyrinths in *Tristram Shandy*', in: *Eighteenth Century Studies* 28.4 (1995), pages 398-411, for an examination of the imagery of labyrinths, weaving and knots in *Tristram Shandy*. Soud links the imagery with the eighteenth-century love of garden mazes and their development out of the Elizabethan knot garden. It is striking how much of Goethe's labyrinth imagery, too, is linked to the landscape of garden and country estate, both in the *Wanderjahre* and in the *Wahlverwandtschaften*, as well as in short narratives such as 'Der neue Paris'.

This sense of the infinite complexity and unpredictability of life is, indeed, the serious import underlying the exuberant extravaganza of Sterne's text and it finds its most explicit expression in the labyrinthine image which describes Walter Shandy's reaction to the unforeseen accidents which accompany Tristram's birth:

> - But mark, madam, we live amongst riddles and mysteries - the most obvious things, which come in our way, have dark sides, which the quickest sight cannot penetrate into, and even the clearest and most exalted understandings amongst us find ourselves puzzled and at a loss in almost every cranny of nature's works, so that this, like a thousand other things, falls out for us in a way, which tho' we cannot reason upon it, - yet we find the good of it, may it please your reverences and your worships - and that's enough for us (241)[58].

The puzzling and challenging aspects of the literary work, which are highlighted by presenting it as a labyrinth, are also implied by the metaphor of the work as a collection of fragments. Early critics of *Tristram Shandy* were just as preoccupied as those of the *Wanderjahre* by the fragmentary nature of the work. One suggested that it had 'more the air of a collection of fragments, than of a regular work'[59]. Another, on the other hand, won Sterne's approval for his recognition that digression and fragmentation were the very essence of the work and for his ridiculing of those who sought to discover 'a close, connected Story' in it[60]. Both Sterne and Goethe go to great pains, in comments about the works and in the works themselves, to emphasise their deliberate and planned incompleteness and collectivity[61].

---

[58]This sensitivity, in the midst of all his gaiety, to the ineluctable human predicament, must have greatly contributed to the appeal which Sterne's work held for Goethe since it strikes a resonance with his own sense of the boundless enigma of human existence.

[59] John Ferrier, *Illustrations of Sterne*, 1797, reprinted New York 1971 page 4. Compare George Henry Lewes comment on the *Wanderjahre*: that he could not bring himself 'to regard the whole book as anything better than a collection of sketches and studies', George Henry Lewes *Life of Goethe* 2nd Ed, London 1864.

[60] Letter of the Reverend Robert Browne (Geneva 25th July 1760) to John Hall Stevenson, *Letters of Laurence Sterne*, edited by L. P. Curtis, Oxford 1935, pages 432-3. Cf. also Sterne's letter on page 122, 'They all look too high – 'tis ever the fate of low minds'. Goethe, too, criticised those of his readers, like Rochlitz, who had 'got hold of the foolish idea of wanting to construe and analyse the whole thing systematically' and insisted, 'That is completely impossible, the book only claims to be an aggregate'.

[61] The deliberate production of fragments - from the construction of 'follies' or artificial 'ancient' ruins in gardens to collections of literary fragments - was a phenomenon of the eighteenth century noted by Friedrich Schlegel, appropriately in a fragment, 'Many works of the ancients have become fragments. Many works of the moderns are already so from the beginning'. Athenäum-

Wilhelm's letter to Natalie, invoking Sterne as its model, is full of breaks and omissions, disjointed and incomplete. The novel contains other fragmentary texts, such as the novella 'Nicht zu weit' or the collections of aphorisms, by their very nature made up of discontinuous thoughts and quotations. Sterne includes in both *Tristram Shandy* and *A Sentimental Journey* sections explicitly labelled as fragments: the fragment about the Abderites in Volume 1 of *A Sentimental Journey* (itself incorporating a fragment of Euripides' lost *Andromeda*); the sheet of waste paper containing a part of the story of the old gentleman who had fallen on hard times in Volume 2; and in *Tristram Shandy* the fragment on whiskers in Chapter 1 of Volume 5. In addition both works are full of incomplete and unfinished elements from the snippet of dialogue with which *A Sentimental Journey* begins to its unfinished last sentence; from Slawkenbergius' tale in *Tristram Shandy*, mocking the 'Aristotelian' narrative conventions that its narrator purports to champion, to the cock and bull story with which the novel ends. These fragmentary elements, like the similar elements in the *Wanderjahre*, to be discussed later, contribute greatly to the self-reflective character of Sterne's works. They function as miniature reduplications of the work in which they occur, endlessly reflecting its fractured form in their own.

The fragmentary nature of the works also points to the importance accorded to the role of the reader by both writers. In Chapter 11 of Volume 2, when Tristram envisages the relationship between reader and writer as one of mutual involvement in a conversation or dialogue he connects the aesthetic of the unfinished with the aesthetic of reader-participation by saying that he has left certain things - the completion of Dr. Slop's tale, Obadiah's tale and the ensuing preparations for his own delivery - unfinished for the express purpose of giving

---

Fragment No.24, Friedrich Schlegel *Kritische und theoretische Schriften*, Stuttgart 1978, page 79. Schlegel's fragments were published in 1798 in the *Athenäum*, the literary journal he edited along with his brother August. Herder also produced a collection of fragments of literary criticism in the 1760s - *Über die neuere deutsche Literatur. Erste Sammlung von Fragmenten.*

the reader scope for the exercise of his imagination[62]. Sterne's comic muse then underscores this aesthetic of reader-participation by pushing its possibilities to the point of absurdity so that the reader's creative capacities are constantly being called upon to fill in the gaps behind dashes and asterisks, to invent and imagine, culminating in the blank page on which he is invited to sketch his own personal picture of widow Wadman.

The blank page is indicative of another element of this aesthetic of the unfinished. Both Sterne and Goethe were, paradoxically, passionate wordsmiths with a deep awareness of the limitations of language. In the *Wanderjahre* the voices of Hersilie and Montan expose the ambiguity and inadequacy of the word. Eventually the flow of words is brought to a complete standstill by the cryptic drawing of the key. Tristram exclaims of his Uncle Toby, '- by heaven! his life was put in jeopardy by words'. But he also suggests the paradoxical fruitfulness of language's ambiguity when he says, 'And a fertile source of obscurity it is, --- and ever will be,--- and that is the unsteady use of words which have perplexed the clearest and most exalted understandings' (71). In Sterne's work the power of the word is constantly being undercut by the blank page, by the dashes, dots and asterisks, or by the straight and arabesque lines which represent Tristram's journey through his text. The silence of man in the face of death is represented by the black page which is the only possible response to Yorick's death and near the end of Volume 3 the whole labyrinthine text is reduced to the one marbled page which is its 'motley emblem'.

Whereas, on the one hand, the fragment suggests the disintegration of language and the limits of what it can express, on the other hand, it is also used by both writers as an emblem of the boundless productivity of inspiration. They were both immersed in the language of the Bible and would have been very familiar with the story from Saint John's gospel of the miracle of the loaves and fishes and with Jesus' instruction to the disciples to 'gather up the fragments that remain,

---

[62] Cf. also Chapter 2 of Volume 2 where Tristram refers facetiously to the critics and says, 'I have left half a dozen places purposely open for them' (69).

that nothing be lost' (John 6:12-13)[63]. The essence of that story is the overflowing abundance contained within the apparent insufficiency of the five barley loaves and the two fishes. When put to productive use these fragmentary supplies increase and multiply far beyond their original proportions. In the same way the fragmentary thoughts which make up the aphorisms in Makarie's archive increase and multiply 'like seeds from a many-branched plant' (123), when they are put to productive use by being read aloud; and Walter's system of auxiliary verbs is designed to 'open new tracks of enquiry, and make every idea engender millions' (334).

For both Goethe and Sterne the fragment was, indeed, the emblem of profusion. In their fragmentary texts they were attempting to produce something of the polyphony, which is the hallmark of Mikhail Bakhtin's concept of dialogism, something that corresponds to the fragmentary and unfinished experience of life itself. When Sterne dedicated the second edition of the first two volumes of *Tristram Shandy* to William Pitt he referred expressly to 'this Fragment of Life'. When Goethe wrote to Rochlitz about the *Wanderjahre* he compared its heterogeneous form with that of life itself, 'But with such a book it is just like with life itself'[64].

Like *Tristram Shandy*, the *Wanderjahre* is a text vividly aware of its own status as an artistic construct. Both invoke the metaphor of weaving the textual labyrinth to describe their intricate and enigmatic form and the challenge they present to the reader. Both make us explicitly aware of the literary work as artefact by referring to the book's physical attributes and by likening it to works

---

[63] In Luther's translation, 'Sammelt die übrigen Brocken, daß nichts umkomme'. Herder quotes this passage when describing additions to his *Über die neuere deutsche Literatur. Erste Sammlung von Fragmenten* in 1768: 'so the fragments are gathered diligently enough, so that nothing is lost. But nevertheless everything remains just a fragment', in: *Sämtliche Werke*, Volume 2 edited by Suphan, Berlin 1879, page 4. Cf. Elizabeth W. Harries, 'Sterne's Novels: Gathering up the Fragments' in: *Contemporary critical essays on 'Tristram Shandy'* edited by Melvyn New, where she sketches in the eighteenth-century background of Sterne's aesthetic of the 'fragmentary' and relates it in particular to the Biblical and liturgical context of his life and thought.

[64] Hans Gerhard Gräf, *Goethe über seine Dichtungen*, Part 1, Volume 2, Frankfurt am Main 1902, page 1065. Letter to Johann Friedrich Rochlitz of 23rd November 1829.

of the visual arts. But both insist that the literary work is principally a process, which involves a constructive relationship between reader, writer and text and aims at inculcating in the reader a creative, productive reading practice.

Jean Paul

ein so begabter Geist
a very gifted spirit

Laurence Sterne also exercised a great influence on Goethe's younger contemporary, Jean Paul, who not only followed the 'Humorist' in his rapid changes from gravity to levity, but also took him as a model for his digressive style and use of an intrusive narrator. In a very early diary entry he explicitly points to Sterne's influence when describing his own tortuous, circuitous narrative style, which never follows one track, but in the pursuit of its prey, strays into every winding pathway[65]. Later, in a letter to Christian Otto, he makes clear that he is also following Sterne in his predilection for thematising in the text the relationship between narrator, reader and narrative: 'the absurd, discontinuous, attention-seeking style of narration is a habit I have unfortunately learned from Tristram'[66]. These aspects of his narrative technique led to Jean Paul, as well as Sterne, becoming both 'guide and inspiration' to Goethe during the period when he was writing the *Wanderjahre*.

At first glance Goethe and Jean Paul would seem to be strange bedfellows, not so much elective affinities as literary antipodes. From Jean Paul's first appearance in Weimar in the 1790s, shortly after the publication of *Hesperus*, to the end of his own life Goethe's verdicts on Jean Paul's literary work and on his personality exhibited a high degree of ambivalence. While recognising his talents as a writer and valuing what they saw as his desire for objectivity both Schiller

---

[65] 9th August 1782. Quoted by Peter Michelson in *Laurence Sterne und der deutsche Roman des 18.Jahrhunderts* Göttingen 1972, page 325.
[66] Letter of 28th June 1799. In Jean Paul, *Letters*, Volume 3, page 227.

and Goethe agreed upon his unworldliness[67]. According to Schiller he appeared as strange as someone who had fallen from the moon, and his eagerness to observe the objective world was accompanied by an inability to do so naturally with the organ with which one sees[68]. Ambivalence characterises, too, their reception of *Hesperus*, a work which they consider by no means without imagination and spirit, containing some strikingly original ideas, amusing reading matter for the long nights, but which they agree is very much a hybrid or composite creation, 'a tragelaph of the first order'[69].

That ambivalence often tipped over into aversion can only partly be explained by Jean Paul's deep admiration for and close attachment to Herder at the very time of his estrangement from Schiller and Goethe. The literary quarrel, combined with their stringently classical cultural programme, provides the explanation for the 'Xenien' directed against Jean Paul and for Goethe's lampoon 'Ein Chinese in Rom' which makes fun of the unappreciative philistine in the holy city of classical culture 'who compares his airy gossamer with the substantial weave/of an imperishable tapestry'. Even later in his life, however, Goethe was often very severe in his judgements on Jean Paul, describing him to Riemer as 'the personified nightmares of the age'; disclosing to Schopenhauer that he only had to read a few pages of Jean Paul to be overcome by a revulsion which made him lay the book aside; and in 1831 insisting to Eckermann in a fit of pique after Jean Paul had appropriated half of the title of *Dichtung und Wahrheit* for his own

---

[67] What Goethe referred to as his 'love of truth' and Schiller described as his eagerness to see 'the things outside of himself'.

[68] Letter from Schiller to Goethe 28th June 1896 and Goethe's reply on 29th June: *Der Briefwechsel zwischen Schiller und Goethe* edited by Emil Staiger, Frankfurt am Main, 1977, pages 216-7.

[69] Goethe/Schiller Briefwechsel, pages 110-15. 'Tragelaph' or 'goat-stag' was an epithet used by Euripides to describe Aeschylus' work (and he goes on to suggest that such hybrid figures were borrowed from Persian tapestries) in the *Frogs* by Aristophanes. That its use by Goethe and Schiller, even at this stage, is not entirely disparaging is suggested by the fact that, in his reply to Goethe, (12th June 1795) Schiller describes the *Horen* as a 'centaur'- another hybrid being, although perhaps a nobler one than the 'tragelaph'. It is this very metaphor 'tragelaph' which best characterises the heterogeneous nature of Goethe's own later work.

autobiographical writing, 'As if the truth about the life of such a man could be anything other than that the author was a philistine!'[70].

On the other hand, at much the same time as his comment to Schopenhauer, Goethe wrote very positively to Knebel about Jean Paul's essay on the 'Wichtigkeit der Erziehung', praising in particular its incredible maturity and the way in which his talent had managed to purify itself of dross[71]. Here there seems to be little more than the reappraisal of a writer who has begun to conform more to Goethe's own aesthetic principles. When we look, however, at what is perhaps Goethe's most positive appraisal of Jean Paul's literary work, the section entitled 'Vergleichung' in the 'Noten und Abhandlungen zu besserem Verständnis des *West-östlichen Divans*', which compares Jean Paul's work with the work of the Persian and Bedouin poets who are Goethe's own models for the 'Divan', we will notice the extent to which Goethe's later aesthetic - the aesthetic of *Faust II*, of *West-östlicher Divan* and of the *Wanderjahre* - entails a remarkable convergence with the aesthetic perspectives of Jean Paul[72].

After a section entitled 'Warnung', in which he expressly cautions against the dangers of literary comparisons, Goethe mischievously excuses himself for immediately embarking on such a comparison by attributing to a third party, to an expert on middle-eastern poetry, the idea that no German writer had come closer than Jean Paul to the poets and other writers of the orient[73]. As a starting point Goethe suggests the extent to which the personality of the writer can be deduced from his work and attributes to Jean Paul a combination of understanding, observation and insight, and benevolent concern. Indeed the characteristic which

---

[70] F.W. Riemer *Mitteilungen über Goethe*, edited by A.Pollmer, Leipzig 1921, page 286, (7th December 1807); F.von Biedermann *Goethe: Gespräche. Eine Sammlung zeitgenössischer Berichte aus seinem Umgang*, edited by W.Herwig, Volumes 1-4, Zürich, Stuttgart (Volume 4 München) 1965-84. Here Volume 2, page 938. No.4039: 1811-14 from J.Frauenstädt; Eckermann, 30th March 1831, page 461. Cf. Hendrik Birus *Vergleichung, Goethes Einführung in die Schreibweise Jean Pauls*, Stuttgart, 1986, for an account of the positive and negative elements in Goethe's attitude towards Jean Paul.
[71] Letter to Knebel 16th March 1814. H.A. Letters 3, page 265.
[72] Cf. Hendrik Birus, page 20.
[73] Joseph von Hammer-Purgstall (1774-1856) referred to Jean Paul in his book, *Geschichte der schönen Redekünste Persiens*, published in Vienna in 1818. Cf. H.A., Volume 2, page 681.

he stresses is just that found so lacking by Schiller in the Jean Paul of the 1790s, the ability to observe the world around him: 'Ein so begabter Geist blickt, nach eigentlichst orientalischer Weise, munter und kühn in seiner Welt umher' [a very gifted spirit looks around his world light-heartedly and fearlessly in the truest oriental manner].

What links him most closely to the Arabic poets is his delight in daring and often improbable similes and comparisons whereby he combines the most diverse and incompatible of items. In a previous section, 'Allgemeines' Goethe had used the image of an oriental bazaar or of a European trade-fair to describe the confusion to the imagination brought about by such heterogeneous and motley literary works where all the most disparate elements of life are mingled together in colourful disarray[74]. This variegated conglomerate is not, however, completely arbitrary, since 'the whole work is drawn to a certain unity by a secret, ethical thread that weaves itself through it'. In this image there is a return to the idea that the unifying element in such a work is the personality of the writer. Goethe uses the same image in the *Wahlverwandtschaften* in order to suggest how the miscellaneous series of perceptions, aphorisms and quotations which make up the contents of Ottilie's diary are linked together by the personality of the writer: 'in just such a way a thread of affection and devotion winds its way through Ottilie's diary, links everything and characterises the whole'[75].

Next a stark contrast is set up between the world of the Arabic poets who lived close to the natural source of inspiration and the fragmentary, over-differentiated, contemporary world in which Jean Paul and therefore, by

---

[74] H.A. Volume 2, page 163. In *Vorschule der Ästhetik* Jean Paul uses a similar image for the wide variety of Goethe's work when he writes, 'The first writers' school to which Goethe was sent, according to his autobiography, was assembled from craftsmen's workshops, painters' studios, coronation halls, state archives and from all of Frankfurt's trade fairs'. Jean Paul, *Vorschule der Ästhetik*, Hamburg, 1990, page 32.

[75] H.A. Volume 6, page 368. In a variation on this image, in one of his first references to the *Wanderjahre*, Goethe says that its disparate elements will be linked together by the 'romantic thread' of Wilhelm's travels. He also suggests later that it is the character of the writer which provides the unity of the work when he writes to Boisserée on 23rd July 1821, 'And if this work is not all of one piece, you will still certainly find it of one mind'. Gräf, 1.2, page 983.

implication, also Goethe himself must live and work. Living in 'a fresh, simple region' the Arab poets were still able to draw their similes 'from the first archetypal images' such as 'mountain and desert, cliff and plain, trees, herbs, river and sea and the starry firmament', whereas the contemporary European writer must reflect in his work a world compartmentalised 'through art, science, technology, politics, the transactions of war and peace, and devastation'. In order to illustrate the effect of this world on the literary work Goethe simply lists, without additional comment, some of the more specialised and unfamiliar terms, which the reader will encounter in the '10. Hundeposttag' of Jean Paul's *Hesperus*, and which he is expected to understand - at least with the help of the encyclopaedia. This idea of the encyclopaedic knowledge required of the contemporary reader of novels - or at least the necessity of having an encyclopaedia to hand - also occurs in the section 'Bedürfnis des gelehrten Witzes' in *Vorschule der Ästhetik* where Jean Paul conjures up a picture of a Germany dominated by 'ominscience and encyclopaedias' and asks disingenuously, 'And do I and other Germans – given that from time to time I make allusions to something foreign – not have Webel's encyclopaedic dictionary in 10 volumes (...), so that in order to read a heavy book, we need do nothing more than open a light one?'

In the next paragraph of his comparison Goethe draws a distinction between the poet and the prosaist. The former is allowed much more licence in his use of language because of the stringent demands of the form. The latter is held much more responsible for the liberties he takes with the language because of the freedom of the form. This observation leads to a consideration of the relationship between reader and writer. In the case of Jean Paul, the reader is attracted by the personality, which he detects behind the writing. Jean Paul is, in turn, concerned to engage the reader in dialogue: 'he stimulates our imaginative powers, he flatters our weaknesses and consolidates our strengths'. And finally Goethe suggests that the purpose of this engagement with the reader is to provoke him into using his wits and to confront him with the text as a puzzle for the solving, in whose 'colourfully woven world' he is presented with an analogy for the complexities of the world around him. The reader is, therefore, cast in the role of a collaborator, who works in co-operation with the writer in the production of the text. Important, too, for Goethe is the idea that Jean Paul's texts address all aspects of the human personality - the emotional, intellectual and the spiritual - and offer 'entertainment, excitement, emotion and, indeed, edification'. Like *Daphnis and Chloe* his novels offer the reader both profit and pleasure as well as themselves taking on a kind of endlessness since 'such a text can tempt one to boundless interpretation'.

At the height of his classical period, in a letter to Schiller in 1797, Goethe laments, 'that we moderns are so much inclined to mix the genres, indeed, that we are not capable of distinguishing them from each other'; and attempts to counter this tendency with a rigorous classical programme:

> The artist ought to withstand these really childish, barbaric, fatuous tendencies with all his powers; to separate work of art from work of art by impenetrable magic circles; to keep each one to its type and characteristics, just as the ancients did and thereby became and continued to be such good artists.

But he concludes with a rhetorical question which suggests a rueful awareness of how out of step this programme is with the spirit of the times, 'But who can separate his ship from the waves on which it sails? Against the current and the wind one only covers short distances'[76].

In his later work, however, the inevitable has been openly embraced to such an extent that diversity and heterogeneity of form and style have become a positive part of his aesthetic programme. With obvious satisfaction he tells Wilhelm von Humboldt that the Helena episode in *Faust II* covers a period of three thousand years 'from the fall of Troy to the capture of Missolunghi' and characterises it as a 'classical-romantic phantasmagoria'[77]. In a sequence of comments in the 'Maximen und Reflexionen' this delight in diversity is elevated into a principle of his poetics:

[76] Schiller/Goethe Briefwechsel, Letter to Schiller of 23rd December 1797, pages 518-19.
[77] Letter to Wilhelm von Humboldt of 22nd October 1826 in: H.A. Letters 4, page 205.

> But let us be many-sided. Carrots from the Mark-Brandenburg taste good, best mixed
> with chestnuts and these two noble fruits grow far apart. (966); Allow us in our mixed
> writings next to the western and northern forms also the eastern and southern ones! (967);
> One is only many-sided when one strives towards the highest, because one must (in all
> seriousness), and when one descends to the more trivial, when one wishes (for fun)[78].

In the light of these comments the description of Jean Paul's literary characteristics and techniques in 'Vergleichung' can be regarded as equally applicable to Goethe's own literary programme in the construction of the *Wanderjahre*[79]. It, too, is described as 'an aggregate', composed of the most diverse elements, through which it gains 'a kind of infinity'. It, too, is deliberately enigmatic with the intention of provoking the reader into active participation in the process of interpretation: 'it will make you think and that is, after all, what matters'[80].

The concept of the novel as a collection of fragments was an important element in Jean Paul's aesthetic. In the preface to the second edition he describes *Hesperus* as 'the aphroditographical fragments' and emphasises the digressive nature of the work, 'that circles around the sun in a by no means planetary ellipse with such obvious aberrations or deviations'[81]. The novel contains within itself a variety of genres: the 'Hundposttage'[dog-post days], which are supposed to concern themselves with the 'story'; the 'Schalttage' [leap-days] in which the narrator explicitly allows himself to digress; letters and idyllic descriptions; a chapter divided into five acts and characterised as a 'Lustspiel' [comedy]; another entitled 'Flüchtiges Extrablättchen' [brief extra page], which masquerades as a work of the visual arts and claims to be an elevation in perspective of the city of Little Vienna.

Jean Paul's work is fragmentary in another sense, too, in that it is characterised by a high degree of intertextuality. He was, like Sterne and Goethe,

---

[78] H.A. Volume 12, page 501.
[79] Cf. Birus, page 21, 'The description of Jean Paul's technique really reads like an anticipatory self-interpretation of the *Wanderjahre*'.
[80] Letter to Zelter, 30th October 1828. W.A. 4.45, page 37.
[81] Jean Paul, *Werke* Volume 1, Darmstadt 1970, page 485. The adjective 'aphroditographisch' presumably is an allusion to the fact that Hesperus, the evening star, was also the planet Venus.

a voracious reader. An acquaintance reported of him in 1799, 'And Jean Paul still reads daily, whatever comes into his hands, from Goethe, his idol, to the Leipzig directory'. He could, indeed, be said to be a prolific reader in that he had, from his earliest youth, made copious collections of excerpts from his reading[82]. The numerous notebooks, which housed these collections, became an inexhaustible quarry of material for his literary works[83].

The collective, digressive nature of Jean Paul's novels provoked much negative criticism from contemporary critics. He was described as writing just as his mood or his notebook of excerpts inspired him[84]. Some nineteenth-century commentators noted with disapproval the increasing correspondence between Goethe's later narrative style and the techniques of Jean Paul, particularly its digressive and fragmentary nature and the use of an intrusive narrator. Hermann Hettner saw signs of a loss of creativity in the *Wanderjahre* and complained that Goethe made use of the same stopgap measures as Jean Paul to gloss over his failing: the introduction of himself as reporter and editor of papers that had been entrusted to him[85]. Friedrich Hebbel felt that the inclusion of extracts from Ottilie's diary as supplementary material in the *Wahlverwandtschaften* was already evidence of Goethe's diminishing creative powers[86]. The concept of the

---

[82] *Jean Pauls Persönlichkeit in Berichten der Zeitgenossen. Jeans Pauls Sämtliche Werke Ergänzungsband*, edited by Eduard Berend, Berlin, 1956, page 53. Cf. also Ulrich Profitlich *Der Seelige Leser. Untersuchungen zur Dichtungstheorie Jean Pauls*, Bonn, 1968, pages 11-12.

[83] In 1798 Garlieb Merkel commented, 'He told me he read everything, everything that fell into his hands, and up to now no text has come to him in which he didn't find material for a comparison' in: *Jean Pauls Persönlichkeit in Berichten der Zeitgenossen*, page 36. For an account of the extent of his collections of words, excerpts and aphorisms cf. Eduard Berend, 'Jean Pauls handschriftlicher Nachlaß. Seine Eigenart und seine Geschichte' in: *JbJPG* 3 (1968), pages 13-22, esp. pages 14-16.

[84] By F. Nicolai in 'Zusatz eines andern Recensenten', quoted in Birus, page 51. Goethe, himself, on reading the first edition of Jean Paul's 'Levana' in 1806, commented to Riemer, 'One always hears the chain of quotations, excerpts, albums and so forth'.

[85] Hermann Hettner, *Geschichte der deutschen Literatur im achtzehnten Jahrhundert*, Volume 2, Berlin, 1961, 1st edtion, Braunschweig, 1879.

[86] Friedrich Hebbel, *Tagebücher - historisch-kritische Ausgabe*, edited by R.M.Werner, Volume 4 1854-63. Berlin Steglitz 1922, page 190, No.5896, 3rd May 1861. Even Jean Paul himself failed to recognise any structuring principle in the first edition of the *Wanderjahre* and was incensed by what he perceived to be its total lack of cohesion. He commented to Ludwig Rehstab on 28th August 1821,'How can he bring together in the book all the little novellas or fairytales which have

novel as a collective work and the inclusion of these 'borrowed' fragments, however, highlights the intertextuality and multi-perspectivity of the novel form and corresponds to Edward Said's image of the novel as 'fugue'.

The visual element in the reading process was also of considerable importance to Jean Paul. In the *Vorschule* he posits a division of novels as though they were paintings into three schools, the Italian, the German and the Dutch[87]. He suggests that Goethe's descriptions of landscape gain in vividness because of his experience as a painter since his painted landscapes are reflected in his literary landscapes[88]. Later he compares Goethe's prose work to a picture or statue gallery[89]. This metaphor of the picture gallery was often chosen by Jean Paul to describe the novel and it particularly emphasises the collective nature of the genre. In discussing the various 'schools' of novel writing he suggests that, like a picture gallery, most novels contain a mixture of elements from the three schools[90]. In the motto to *Hesperus* he describes the earth as 'the dark chamber full of pictures from a more beautiful world, which have been turned round and piled up together' and, in the preface to the third edition of the novel, the work itself becomes a picture gallery which the reader is imagined as struggling to reach through an ever-increasing suite of anterooms or prefaces until he dies on the way to the book[91]. We will see later how Goethe uses the metaphor of the picture gallery throughout the *Wanderjahre* to highlight its collective and reflective qualities.

---

already been published individually in Cotta's almanac, without any other motivation than that somebody needs to narrate something?' In: *Jean Pauls Persönlichkeit in Berichten der Zeitgenossen*, page 271.

[87] Jean Paul, *Vorschule* XII Programm, page 253. In this system he assigns Sterne and 'Goethe's *Meister* in part' to the German school.

[88] Jean Paul, *Vorschule*, I Programm, page 33.

[89] Jean Paul, *Vorschule*, XIV Programm, page 277.

[90] Jean Paul, *Vorschule*, XII Programm, page 255.

[91] Jean Paul, *Werke*, edited by Norbert Miller, München 1965, Volume 1, pages 474-5. Page references for *Hesperus* are to this edition. A little later Jean Paul uses another visual metaphor for his novel when he compares it to a house and suggests tongue-in-cheek that his own work lags far behind the fragmentary nature 'of the better modern novels' which 'resemble not, like my book, a single house, but a whole toy town from Nuremberg, whose loose, dismantled houses the child piles up in his toy cupboard, and whose mosaic of cottages the dear little one easily puts together alley by alley, just as he likes ', page 484.

The obverse side of the concept of the novel as a collection of fragments is the image of the novel as a 'poetic encyclopaedia'. In the *Vorschule der Ästhetik* Jean Paul discusses the problem of giving unity to such an expansive form as the novel, which exceeds all other art forms in the amount of paper it requires, and suggests that the majority of novel-writers begin well, then somehow manage to continue, but finally end wretchedly because of this very difficulty. He then goes on to suggest that the all-embracing form of the novel can be a positive advantage and lends itself to the creation of a work that is 'a poetic encyclopaedia, a poetic freedom of all freedoms'. The idea of the encyclopaedic, all-embracing novel, or the novel whose totality encompasses the complexities of a whole world, pervades the *Vorschule*. In the section 'Humoristische Totalität' he sees the 'universal humour' of Sterne and Rabelais as being generated through the great antitheses of life and describes the way in which Sterne's very sentence structure, and particularly his liberal use of dashes is an expression of the necessity he feels to adumbrate a totality within the confines of his pages[92].

In the *Vorschule* Jean Paul distinguishes between two types of novel, the epic and the dramatic: the extensiveness of the former offers a 'wide sweep of story' the restriction of the latter provides a 'racetrack for the characters'. It is the epic novel which corresponds to the poetic encyclopedia, embracing within itself a multiplicity of forms of discourse. Citing Goethe's *Lehrjahre* as an example of the epic novel, he suggests that it reflects or represents the world rather than one particular hero. In contrast to the dramatic form, the epic novel attempts to present a whole world ['die stehende Sichtbarkeit der Welt'] and therefore is allowed a slow breadth. Examples of this slow unfolding he finds in the work of Sterne and Cervantes where Yorick's whole journey in France lasts only three days and *one* evening in *one* tavern fills the whole fifth book of *Don Quixote*. In postulating the 'Gesetz der Langsamkeit' [law of slowness] for the epic novel,

---

[92] Jean Paul *Vorschule*, pages 127-8. The dash was a stylistic device enthusiastically adopted by Jean Paul from Sterne - a device, which not only allows disparate elements to be linked together, but also suggests the limitless possibilities that cannot be expressed in words.

Jean Paul sees it as being naturally composed of digressions and episodes, whereas drama hates the episodical. At the same time the epic novel, as a literary analogy for life itself, must be simultaneously short and long in order to imitate the varied pace of life. It must also allow space for a wide variety of characters, whereby the action is not so much slowed down as multiplied into a kaleidoscopic cycle of actions. This ever-changing sequence of episodes, which the reader is forced to traverse, helps to evoke a sense of the infinity of life itself.

The objective of the narrative complexity of this poetic encyclopedia is the education of the reader: 'literature teaches how to read'. Through his engagement with the text the reader will learn to read actively and productively. Jean Paul decries the overtly didactic text - the novel as 'unversifiertes Lehrgedicht' [unrhymed didactic poem] - which subordinates everything to a narrowly instructional goal, by comparing it to the educationalist Basedow who gave children biscuits in the shape of letters of the alphabet; and insists that the novel should be intrinsically educative like a flower which heralds the weather and the seasons by its opening and closing and even by its scent. The writer's role is then to provide guiding signs and the literary work becomes 'a dictionary and a grammar of signs' [93].

Within the novels themselves Jean Paul's concern for the reader is very apparent[94]. The proliferation of prefaces to the novels often contains reflections on the public for whom the texts are destined. In the *Vorschule* the word 'Publikum' is 'translated' into 'Vielkopf' [many-headed one] and in the preface to the second edition of *Hesperus* we are told that the reading public has at least 45 opinions

---

[93] *Vorschule* 'Über den Roman', page 250. A similar idea, that literature should be inherently educative, is expressed by Goethe in the essay 'Über das Lehrgedicht' where he says, 'All literature should be educational but imperceptibly; it should make a person aware of what is worth learning; he must draw the lesson from it himself, as from life'. And the writer's role as a guide is the theme of the first aphorism in Makarie's archive: 'but the poet points to the place'.

[94] It is apparent also in many of his comments about his working procedure, where he recommends the writer to invent a particular reader for his work in progress, 'The main rule: always invent for one person' and insists that the writer can only write for individuals, 'One must think of individuals when one writes'. Often Jean Paul chose real people such as Karl Philip Moritz, Nicolai or Böttinger as the imaginary addressees of his texts. Cf. Profitlich, page 119.

about *one* chapter. At the beginning of the preface to the first edition the narrator introduces 'several armies of readers whom I have nothing to offer in this book', and imagines himself as a doorman barring the way into the text to these unwelcome readers, including the members of 'the reading sisterhood of romances of chivalry'. In the preface to *Siebenkäs* the narrator posits a hierarchy of reading publics divided into three types to correspond to the division of man into 'body, soul and intellect': the body being those in the bookselling business; the soul being the frequenters of the lending libraries, girls, youths and the idle; and the intellect being artists themselves such as Herder, Goethe, Lessing, Wieland and several others. He suggests that the author need not concern himself too much with this latter group because they do not read his books.

Following the example of Sterne and Cervantes, Jean Paul makes extensive use of the intruding narrator, especially in the works written in the 1790s and most particularly in *Hesperus*. The narrator here is invested partly with the author's identity: he sometimes names himself as Jean Paul and even introduces one of his characters in the process of reading one of his, Jean Paul's, earlier novels, *Die unsichtbare Loge*. The narrator, however, is not identical with the author, but remains a fictitious figure within the work itself. At the same time he sets a mocking distance between himself and the story he is telling with the fiction that it is a 'Lebensbeschreibung' [biography] sent to him to turn into a novel by an unknown correspondent and delivered to him at intervals, as he sits on his island, by the dog, Spitz. Hence the story is divided, not into chapters but into 'Hundposttage'. Any deficiencies in the story can therefore be laid at the door of the unknown correspondent or else 'the dog must take responsibility for what he delivers' (519).

Like his mentors Jean Paul also exploits the dialogic possibility of the intruding narrator in order to draw the reader into the text and involve him actively in its construction. In *Hesperus* the narrator engages the reader in conversation while waiting for the dog to deliver the next chapter (564); he poses questions to the reader about his reactions to the story, only to complain about the inadequacy of the answer which he himself has put into his reader's mouth (650); and he plays with the idea of sending his whole readership off riding round the city to find out details of the story for themselves. Thus the fictitious reader enters the text and becomes both representative and foil for the real reader just as the fictitious narrator both is and is not Jean Paul.

The narrator is critical of the shortcomings of the reader whom he exhorts not to skip parts (489); and who, he constantly complains, is only interested in the story. In contrast the narrator claims to be only interested in digressions and deviations and regrets that he is wasting the colourful firework displays and magical tricks of his wit on his unappreciative readers (565). Reader and narrator are seen as two great opposing powers concluding a treaty to allow the narrator to include a witty and erudite digression, in which there is no narrative, after every fourth narrative chapter (566).

From the beginning, however, he also establishes his sympathy for the reader, evoking for him idyllic circumstances for his reading to compensate him for the hardships of his everyday life (511). The fiction of the 'Hundposttage' allows the narrator to play the role of the uninformed narrator who must wait along with his reader for the delivery of the next chapter. Thus he is allowed to identify with the reader and indeed he goes a step further and unites reader, writer and hero in their uncertainty, 'Viktor, the reader and I have only an indistinct, smudged chalk drawing of Matthieu in our heads' (540). The readers are allowed to join in the narration: 'the latest novelty that the readers have told me' (734); and Viktor, 'der Humorist' is identified with the writer whose mind contains 'a comic pocket-theatre of the Germans' (494-5). This identity of reader, writer and hero, as well as the polyphonous nature of the novel, is made explicit as Viktor sits in his study, 'in this concert hall of the finest voices gathered together from all times and places', and 'reading swept him into writing, writing into reading, reflection into perception and so on -' (588).

Elsewhere the reader and writer of the novel as poetic encyclopaedia are linked together by the demand made on them for all-knowingness, which is its

50

necessary concomitant. The image of the 'Allspieler' [one-man band] at the
beginning of the ninth chapter of *Siebenkäs*, who 'carried and played all
instruments with his one body alone', not only mocks the contemporary reader
who has achieved his omniscience 'through the English machinery of the
encyclopaedias', but is also a tongue-in-cheek description of the encyclopaedic
all-inclusive narrative style which Jean Paul himself advocates[95].

Another figure who is a representative within the text of the role of the
writer is the 'Luftschiffer [airship pilot] Gianozzo', hero of an appendix to *Titan*,
whose own narrative, couched in the form of a logbook or 'Seebuch', is a small-
scale reduplication of the novel to which it is appended and whose ever-changing
kaleidoscopic view of the world from the bird's eye perspective of his hot-air
balloon corresponds to the multi-perspectivity which is Jean Paul's narrative aim.
This narrative stance denies the possibility of the definitive statement and rejoices
in the uncertainty of the provisional. When Goethe says of Jean Paul's 'oriental'
use of metaphor, 'a very gifted intellect (...) creates the most curious connections
and links the incompatible', and Jean Paul, in his turn, compares Sterne's
metaphors to the vivid word-pictures contained in Homeric similes and oriental
metaphors, they are both also by implication describing their own narrative
programmes, which, through their manifold digressions and diversions, insist on
the boundlessness of the human experience of the world and attempt to represent
it in a way which imposes the least possible restriction on its diversity of
meanings[96].

A reception history of the *Wanderjahre*

nur Materialien zu einem Buch
just the materials for a book

The reception history of the *Wanderjahre* is a chronicle of polarised
critical positions. The form and structure of the novel in particular have exercised

[95] Cf. Wolfdietrich Rasch, *Die Erzählweise Jean Pauls*, München 1961, pages 9-10.
[96] Jean Paul, *Vorschule*, pages 142-3.

critics since its publication. On the one hand the fragmentary nature of the work, its apparent lack of unity and seemingly careless editing led to the view that what Goethe had produced was not a finished work but merely the material for a novel or 'just an unfinished fragment of a novel'[97]. Some critics attributed this to the diminishing creative powers of old age, but were willing to accept the lack of formal unity as the price for the wealth of ideas it contained[98]. George Henry Lewes, in his *Life of Goethe*, passed on to English readers this view of the unfinished and fragmentary nature of the work. He sees the whole book as nothing better than 'a collection of sketches and studies' and describes its composition as 'feeble and careless even to impertinence'. He also records, with some derision, how contemporary critics in the 1840s and 50s were beginning 'to see in it a social Bible – a Sybilline book'.[99]

On the other hand some of the earliest critics of the *Wanderjahre* insisted on the new and experimental nature of the work and suggested that the unusual form made heavy demands on the sensitivity and skill of the reader. This polarisation of critical positions is demonstrated in exemplary manner by two of the earliest reviews of the novel: the very positive articles by Gustav Heinrich Hotho from December 1829 and March 1830, and the rebuttal and counter-critic of Hotho's articles by the Young German writer and literary critic, Theodore Mundt. In these two reviews Goethe's novel becomes the arena for a confrontation between two opposing aesthetic directions. Hotho, professor of philosophy in Berlin, literary

---

[97] Theodor Mundt, Rezension von Goethes *Wanderjahre* 2 Fassung, Leipzig, 1830, republished in *Kritische Wälder, Blätter zur Beurteilung der Literatur, Kunst und Wissenschaft unserer Zeit*, Leipzig, 1933, here page 181. Wilhelm Scherer, *Geschichte der deutschen Literatur*, 1883, criticises the careless editing and describes the work as, 'nur Materialien zu einem Buch' [just the raw materials for a book].

[98] Cf., for example, G.G.Gervinus, who writes of the weariness of the elderly Goethe and maintains that Goethe himself was conscious that much in his later works exhibited signs of this diminishing creativity. G.G. Gervinus, *Neuere Geschichte der poetischen National-Literatur der Deutschen. Zweiter Teil*, Leipzig 1842. Hermann Hettner mentions among the signs of diminishing creative powers a 'lack of any unity of composition', the 'bundled together stockpiles of manuscript' and the fictional editor. Hermann Hettner, *Geschichte der deutschen Literatur in der 18 Jahrhundert*, Braunschweig, 1879. The wealth of ideas is stressed particularly by the 'socialist' interpreters of the *Wanderjahre* such as Ferdinand Gregorovius *Goethes 'Wilhelm Meister' in seinen sozialistischen Elementen entwickelt*, Königsberg, 1849.

[99] George Henry Lewes, *Life of Goethe*, 2nd Ed., London, 1864, pages 531-2.

historian and student of Hegel, gave lectures on Goethe's work and intended his review as the prelude to a more extensive treatise on the writer, which never came to fruition. He is an upholder of the still-dominant aesthetic norms of the 'Kunstperiode' [Weimar classicism]. Mundt, on the other hand, is a representative of that faction of the Young German writers who were hostile to Goethe. In denying artistic status to the *Wanderjahre* he uses his review to repudiate Weimar and all it stands for and to make a declaration of his own aesthetic position[100].

Hotho surveys all four of Goethe's novels, pointing continually to parallels between the *Wanderjahre* and the earlier novels. He posits a systematic and historical connection between all four novels, whose central concern he sees as the relationship between the individual and society. He suggests that a common feature of all four of Goethe's novels is the attempt to portray the 'poetry of feeling united with the so-called prose of the mundane world'. In this characterisation of the novels Hotho appears to have in mind Hegel's definition of the novel as presenting the 'conflict between the poetry of the heart and the opposing prose of circumstances'[101]. He regards the most striking achievement of the *Wanderjahre* to be the poeticising of that most prosaic of genres, the didactic novel. Where others saw only a lack of form, Hotho sees in the *Wanderjahre* originality of form resulting from the overstepping and shifting of the traditional boundaries of the novel. While acknowledging the difficult and experimental nature of the form that gives rise to a text which 'attracts and repels in equal measure', Hotho anticipates the direction of the most recent twentieth-century criticism of the novel by linking this originality of form to the challenge to the reader implicit in the text: 'only the sensitive reader with a broad education who is accustomed to reflect on and reproduce a work of art is in a position to enjoy this novel'. A century before Hermann Broch, Hotho was already claiming that Goethe had gained new territory for the modern novel[102].

---

[100] Cf. Klaus F.Gille, *'Wilhelm Meister' im Urteil der Zeitgenossen*, Assen, 1971, page 289.

[101] G.W.F. Hegel, *Ästhetik III. Die Poesie*, Reclam, Stuttgart 1971, page 177.

[102] Recent critics of the *Wanderjahre* have also developed fruitfully two other ideas raised by

Mundt, on the other hand, in pursuance of his aim of heralding the dawn of a new literary age, canonises Goethe as 'the most glorious hero of German literature', but at the same time suggests that his time is past. Far from seeing Goethe as writing something new and experimental in the *Wanderjahre* he evaluates Goethe's work as outdated and old-fashioned in comparison with the work of his own generation of writers, of whom he says, 'We belong to a new school of writing'[103]. He denies the novel the status of a finished work of art and, although he praises its aim of representing working life, he adds that the implementation of this aim 'has plunged the novel too deeply and irretrievably into prose'. Rejected, on the one hand, are those elements which, he feels, do not or could not exist in reality, such as the utopian 'League' or the mystical and mythical Makarie, and, on the other hand, those elements of nineteenth-century life which are all too much part of the everyday world of work: descriptions of technical, agricultural and economic processes. The source of this criticism seems to be his conviction that some material is not suitable for artistic treatment and has no place in a novel: that art belongs in its own special enclave from which all non-artistic elements are to be excluded. Paradoxically it is the radical Young German writer, Mundt, who insists that even the novel must have its boundaries, while the ostensibly more conservative Hotho rejoices in the overstepping of those very boundaries.

A third contemporary review of the novel was written by Varnhagen von Ense, who, with his wife Rahel Levin, was at the centre of a circle of admirers and supporters of Goethe. In his review of the first version of the novel in 1821

Hotho. Firstly, he emphasises the significance of the form of Wilhelm's labyrinthine letter to Natalie as a metaphor for the form of the whole novel. Secondly, he suggests that the intricacy and disturbing innovativeness of the text demands that the reader himself join the 'league of renunciation', in that he must be willing to renounce his normal expectations of a novel, in order to open himself to a new reading experience. This idea of the renunciation demanded of the reader has been developed effectively by Ehrhard Bahr in the section 'Poetik der Entsagung' of his essay on the *Wanderjahre* in: *Goethes Erzählwerk.Interpretationen*, edited by P.M. Lützeler and James E. McLeod, Stuttgart 1985. Cf. also Hans Vaget's article on the *Wanderjahre* in *Romane und Erzählungen zwischen Romantik und Realismus. Neue Interpretationen*, edited by P.M. Lützeler, Stuttgart 1983, page 160.

[103] *Kritische Wälder*, page 178.

Varnhagen not only makes play of imitating the structure and multi-perspectivity of the *Wanderjahre* by casting his review in the form of fragments from a real exchange of letters and from observations made at social gatherings, but also recognises the demands made on the reader by this form. He sets no limits on the possibilities of formal experimentation in the novel but, like Hotho, suggests rather that a necessary concomitant of the multifariousness of the *Wanderjahre* was the destruction or overstepping of all boundaries. In his article on the second version in 1833 Varnhagen does not mention the form but stresses the didactic character and the social agenda of the novel[104]. He compares Goethe and Shakespeare in the sense that he places them both at the crossroads and intersection of two eras. While he feels that the *Wanderjahre* depicts the breakdown of a world that has come into conflict with itself, nevertheless it also reveals Goethe in his old age as forward-looking and able to recognise that the true element of mankind in the future will be 'das Bewegliche' [mobility] [105].

Karl Rosenkranz and his pupil Ferdinand Gregorovius, both followers of Hegel, agree in designating the work a 'Sozialroman' [social novel] and make comparisons with the ideas of St.Simon[106]. Gregorovius uses, like Hotho, Hegel's systematic thought structures to analyse the novel, seeing in it a progression through the three systems of family, education and society. He also isolates movement as the central theme of the novel. He praises the high value placed on work and notes the use of song as a medium of education. Although he criticises the American plans and sees Odoardo's reform plans as an isolated island within the European context, which leads him to characterise Goethe as an unpolitical writer, nevertheless he describes him as cosmopolitan and his 'Weltbund' [universal league] as a forward-looking idea.

---

[104] Klaus Gille suggests that Varnhagen can be seen as 'founder of the so-called "socialist" *Wilhelm-Meister* interpretation', which was then followed by Karl Rosenkranz, Karl Grün, Ferdinand Gregorovius, Hermann Hettner and Alexander Jung. Klaus Gille, page 310.

[105] This is another element of early criticism of the novel which has been taken up again by recent criticism: cf. Gidion, page 103 and also Vaget in *Romane und Erzählungen*, page 160.

[106] Karl Rosenkranz, *Goethe und seine Werke* (1847), extract in Klaus Gille pages 153-7.

In an article written in 1856 Rosenkranz defends the style of the *Wanderjahre* against the reproach of 'Altersschwächen' [enfeeblement], emphasising instead the variety of styles employed by Goethe and the diversity of his language, which can move with ease from the archaic and traditional to the latest neologisms. He compares Goethe's editorial role to that of a modern rhapsode who orders and performs his texts for the modern reader just as the ancient rhapsode did for his listener[107]. Gregorovius is critical of the unrestrained episodic nature of the work and sees it as exhibiting a loss of power in comparison with the *Lehrjahren*. For the language, however, he has praise and makes comparison with Plato's Socratic dialogues.

At the beginning of the present century Max Wundt's comprehensive monograph in the 'Geistesgeschichte' [history of ideas] tradition aims at drawing out the relationship between the *Wanderjahre* and the emergence of a modern world picture[108]. To this end he emphasises the reflective and didactic nature of the work, which he considers to be the work of a thinker as much as of a poet, containing the wisdom of his old age. In the structure of the novel he sees, not formlessness, but rather a development of the traditional epic style, full of digressions and insertions, which he traces back to Homer and he, too, compares the author's editorial role to the role of the rhapsode. Rather than regarding the fragmentary form as a result of 'enfeeblement', he compares the author to Plato creating in his old age a new, original form resulting from a combination of empiricism and mysticism. In particular he picks out the home industry of the spinners and weavers as an intensification of the empirical to a symbol of the spiritual: the craft becomes an art in the description, and such descriptions, he suggests, are a traditional component of the epic style. He insists that the collections of aphorisms in 'Betrachtungen im Sinne der Wanderer' and 'Aus

---

[107] Karl Rosenkranz, 'Über den Vergleich von Goethe's Wanderjahren mit G.Sand's Compagnon du tour de France' (1856) in: Karl Robert Mandelkow, *Goethe im Urteil seiner Kritiker*, Volume 2, page 445.
[108] Max Wundt, *Goethes Wilhelm Meister und die Entwicklung des modernen Lebensideals*, Berlin 1913.

Makariens Archiv' are, by their very nature, an integral component of the novel, both for reasons of style and of content and from this standpoint he refutes, in an appendix, Eckermann's description of how they were introduced into the novel and his claim that they have no real place there.

In his analysis of the techniques of all four of Goethe's novels Robert Riemann makes comparisons with contemporary novels such as Wieland's *Agathon* and *Sophiens Reise* by Hermes[109]. He examines the novels in great detail under the broad headings of structure, character and dialogue. He criticises the 'highly unfortunate mixture of frame-narrative and great novel' in the *Wanderjahre* and sees it as 'in no way an organic continuation of the *Lehrjahre*'. He regards them as representative of different periods of Goethe's production with no closer connection than that between the *Iliad* and the *Odyssey*. Much of the technique of the *Wanderjahre* he feels indicates a falling away from the high point of Goethe's best period.

Eberhard Sarter states in the introduction to his book on the technique of the *Wanderjahre* that he wishes to avoid the usual tendency to attribute the characteristics of the *Wanderjahre* to careless editing and an ageing author[110]. He emphasises Goethe's own tendency towards secrecy as an explanation for much of the play with secrets in the novel; he suggests that the author's awareness of his own fame and role as an author is an explanation for the fictional editor and the intrusive narrator as well as the didactic impulse of the work. He points to the looseness of the form, which embraces the two extremes of fullness of detail - often of the peripheral - and a tendency to summarise. These characteristics he attributes both to an attempt to stimulate the reader and to the awareness of lack of time in an ageing writer. Emphasis is laid on the predominance of reflection over representation; the drive to avoid the ugly while emphasising beauty and order and the narrator's thematisation of his inability to represent the youthful, the

---

[109] Robert Riemann, *Goethes Romantechnik*, Leipzig 1902.
[110] Eberhard Sarter, *Zur Technik von 'Wilhelm Meisters Wanderjahre*, Berlin 1914.

passionate, the dramatic[111]. Sarter's tendency is always, however, to see these elements as a reflection of the author's own character rather than to consider what might be the artistic purpose behind them.

On the centenary of Goethe's death J.G. Robertson, in his *Life and Work of Goethe*, gave an assessment of the *Wanderjahre* for English readers which reiterated the idea that the book is 'a receptacle into which Goethe threw the most varied collection of odds and ends of his work and thought'. While acknowledging Goethe's ability 'to reason wisely (...) on the problems of the nineteenth century, the changes brought about by steam and industrialism and the new horizons opened up by the advance of science', he nevertheless emphasises that the work 'is the most lamentable of Goethe's failures as a creative artist' and only redeems it as a 'book of contemplative wisdom'.[112]

Looking back from the darkest days of the mid-twentieth century Hermann Broch sees Goethe as standing on the threshhold of the modern age with its loss of traditional Christian values[113]. He places Goethe as forerunner, with his 'polyhistoric novel', at the head of a line of modernist writers continuing through Gide, Thomas and Heinrich Mann, Joyce and Musil to Kafka[114]. In his 1936 essay 'James Joyce und die Gegenwart' he suggests that the *Wanderjahre* was misunderstood by Goethe's contemporaries because it was ahead of its times. Broch insists that just as the world is becoming ever more complicated and 'unabbildbar' [impossible to portray] so the work of art, which attempts to reflect it, will of necessity become ever more complicated and inaccessible. He employs the Hegelian concept of totality to interpret the *Wanderjahre* and recognises in

---

[111] Goethe himself, in a letter to Reinhard, claims that both the *Lehrjahre* and the *Wanderjahre* contain equal proportions of representation and reflection, Gräf, 1.2, page 979-80.

[112] J.G. Robertson, *The Life and Work of Goethe*, London 1932, pages 267-73. In characterising the *Wanderjahre* as a 'book of wisdom' Robertson is concurring with a commonly voiced view of critics in the German 'Geistesgeschichte' [history of ideas] tradition.

[113] Hermann Broch, 'Mythos und Altersstil' (1947) in: *Kommentierte Wekausgabe*, edited by P.M. Lützeler, Frankfurt am Main, 1975, Volume 9 *Schriften zur Literatur 2 Theorie*, pages 212-234, here page 222.

[114] Hermann Broch, 'Das Weltbild des Romans' (1933), in: Volume 9, *Schriften zur Literatur 2 Theorie*, pages 89-118, here pages 115-6.

58

both Goethe and in his own generation of modernist writers a common perception of the ethical task of literature to develop the reader's understanding of the world he lives in by presenting him with as complete a reflection of complex reality as possible: 'totality of insight as justification for the existence of literature'. He suggests that Goethe's novel can be regarded as a precursor of the modern novel both in its attempt to represent the totality of life and in the innovative modes of expression incorporated in it. For Broch these two aspects, the originality of form and content, combine with the third, the ethical aspect of the work, to make Goethe the inaugurator of a new age of the novel, the age of the ethical novel[115].

The observations of Thomas Mann on the *Wanderjahre* reveal a much more ambivalent attitude. On the one hand he acknowledges the extent to which Goethe as an old man remained alive to the new social and economic developments of the nineteenth century, even though the roots of his culture lay in the eighteenth century, and points out how this is particularly reflected 'in the epic work of his old age, in the social novel *Wilhelm Meisters Wanderjahre*, in which he anticipates the whole social and economic development of the new century'[116]. On the other hand, in a letter to Hermann Hesse praising that author's own self-reflexive novel *Glasperlenspiel*, he pronounces a very harsh judgement on the form of Goethe's novel: 'a worthy but very tedious and senile farrago', a judgement reminiscent of the accusations of 'enfeeblement' which were common to many of the early reviews of the work[117].

The words of Hermann Broch, which only began to make an impact after 1945, and the work of Erich Trunz, editor of the 'Hamburger Ausgabe', and his students, mark the beginning of a new and more constructive interest in the form and structure of the *Wanderjahre*. In his commentary to the 'Hamburger Ausgabe' of 1950 Erich Trunz uses the model of a frame-narrative with inserted

---

[115] Hermann Broch, 'James Joyce und die Gegenwart' in: Volume 8, *Schriften zur Literatur 1 Kritik*, pages 63-94, here pages 65-66 and 87.
[116] Thomas Mann, 'Goethe als Repräsentant des bürgerlichen Zeitalters' (1932) in: *Gesammelte Werke*, Volume 9, *Reden und Aufsätze 1*, Frankfurt am Main, 1990, pages 297-332.
[117] *Neue Rundschau* 74 (1963), page 227.

novellas and the concept of 'wiederholte Spiegelungen' [repeated reflections] to explain the structure of the work, which he encapsulates in the image of a circle, an image which we will see is Goethe's own internal emblem for the text in the form of the recurring picture galleries within the novel itself[118].

Deli Fischer-Hartmann attempted to prove that the work has an inner unity, which she attributes to the unity of meaning within the open form of the novel. She too highlights the ethical nature of the novel, seeing it as a book of wisdom but also as a novel of the present and future for generations to come. She emphasises the difference between the frame-narrative, dealing with 'renunciation by active and discerning people' and the novellas, dealing with 'renunciation by lovers'. Formally she points out that many of the ethical ideas are both 'demanded in sentences and represented in pictures' and notes the task of the reader to explain for himself the how and why of the individual parts within the whole. She also emphasises that the formal principle of the novel is that of 'repeated reflections'.

Hermann Korff's four-volume work *Geist der Goethezeit* marks a culmination of the 'Geistesgeschichte' tradition of interpretation. Korff misinterprets the social structures described by Goethe in the novel as prescriptive and raises them to an almost metaphysical status as 'ideal images of human communities'[119]. At the same time he sees in the novel an expression of Goethe's sensitivity to the changing times, his awareness that the 'age of Goethe' was at an end, that its values were being questioned and that a new age was dawning. The novel, therefore, represents for him a valiant attempt to engage with the problems of the new age and, in particular, to ensure that as much as possible of the old

---

[118] H.A. Volume 8, page 548: 'the whole composition is geared to bring a circle of different ways of life before our eyes'. These ideas were developed by his students Ernst von Monroy, 'Zur Form der Novelle in *Wilhelm Meisters Wanderjahren*', *GRM*, 31 (1943), pages 1-19; and Deli Fischer Hartmann *Goethes Altersroman. Studien über die innere Einheit von 'Wilhelm Meisters Wanderjahre'*, Halle 1941.

[119] Hermann Korff, *Geist der Goethezeit* Volume 4, Chapter 2 'Der letzte Goethe', Leipzig 1953, page 641. Cf. also Volume 2, page 344, where the social structures described in the *Wanderjahre* are even more resoundingly extolled as 'the eternal laws, the great forms of nature and the archetypes of human community'.

60

culture is kept alive in the new era of socialisation and industrialisation[120]. He feels, however, that this attempt has involved a loss of compositional effectiveness. He criticises the 'too careless composition' of the work and its transgression beyond the boundaries of the novel form, suggesting that the American emigration plans do not arise inevitably from the logical necessity of the novel but are inspired rather by a desire to depict a utopian settlement and as such represent a 'flight from the novel'[121].

Emil Staiger returns more decidedly to the old view that the apparent disunity of the work is a sign of the loss of power which old age brings. He very appropriately uses the imagery of the labyrinth to describe the relationship between the reader and the text, saying, 'We accept that in the attempt to understand the work as a whole no end is to be foreseen in the labyrinth of so many possibilities'. But he uses the image as a way of criticising what he considers to be a defect in the work and does not see that the labyrinth image is an integral part of the work: that it has been deliberately constructed by Goethe as a series of labyrinths of possibility through which protagonist and reader must make their way. He considers it a point of criticism, that the unity of the work lies somehow 'beyond the novel' and must be supplied by the reader, and feels that the novel's formal ambiguity leaves open the possibility of any interpretation whatsoever[122].

In the 1950s several critics interested themselves in an analysis of the symbolic content of the *Wanderjahre*. André Gilg and Wilhelm Emrich both claim a central symbolic significance for the key to Felix's casket. Gilg suggests that the drawing of the key calls attention to that which is beyond the powers of language to express[123]. Emrich sees it as the 'key' to the symbol-interpretation of the whole work and suggests that it functions as the symbol of the symbolic since

---

[120] This aim, which he attributes to Goethe, reflects Korff's own aim for his work as expressed in the preface to the first edition of volume 4: 'to save, for the present and future, what can be saved of the great heritage that the age of Goethe has left us'.

[121] Hermann Korff, Volume 4, page 651.

[122] Emil Staiger, *Goethe*, Volume 3, Zürich 1959, page 137.

[123] André Gilg, *'Wilhelm Meisters Wanderjahre' und ihre Symbole*, Zürich 1954.

it unites within its ambit the various thematic concerns of the novel. He suggests that the form arises from the meaning so that the 'technique of insertions reflects the totality and unity of the novel's substance'. He also sees the novel as 'an anticipation of the multidimensional form of the modern novel'[124].

During the fifties and sixties the concept of 'Entsagung' [renunciation] in the *Wanderjahre* was the subject of monographs by Arthur Henkel and by Bernd Peschken. Henkel understands the novel as first and foremost a didactic work whose secret theme he expresses in a form of words similar to that of Korff: 'the question of how all that is humane in human development, "the old truths", can be held on to and kept alive in an era of collapse and a world of instability and flux'. While neither Henkel nor Peschken takes up Hotho's idea that the text demands that the reader himself join the 'league of renunciation' in his reading practice, Henkel does maintain that the novel requires particularly attentive readers, and suggests that the reader clearly needs to see himself as a pupil. He points to the experimental nature of the novel and describes it as playing games with the form[125]. Peschken excludes consideration of the novellas, aphorisms and poems from his study and concentrates on separating out and unravelling what he calls the 'Erzählstränge' [narrative strands] linked to the five major characters, Wilhelm, Montan, Lenardo, Odoard and Makarie. In choosing the term 'narrative strands' the critic echoes in the very structure of his own work one of the major structuring elements of the text he is discussing, the weaving metaphor. Moreover he puts forward as the key witness for the theme of renunciation the so-called 'Blatt' [sheet of paper] which Wilhelm left behind with Suzanne in the valley of the spinners and weavers. This 'Blatt', he suggests, can be used as a model for the

---

[124] Wilhelm Emrich, 'Das Problem der Symbolinterpretation im Hinblick aud Goethes *Wanderjahre*'. In: *DVjs* 26 (1952), pages 331-352. - Reprinted in: W.E. *Protest und Verheißung* Frankfurt am Main 1960, pages 48-66.
[125] Arthur Henkel, *Entsagung. Eine Studie zu Goethes Altersroman*, Tübingen 1954, pages 22, 15, 10 and 16.

interpretation of the work as a whole. In doing so he has highlighted one of the many self-reflecting elements contained in the work[126].

At the end of the 1960s another new era of criticism of the *Wanderjahre* began. Taking up the ideas of Hermann Broch, critics began increasingly to emphasise the modernity and experimental nature of the *Wanderjahre*, comparing it to Joyce's *Ulysses*, Musil's *Mann ohne Eigenschaften* or to the novels of Samuel Beckett[127]. A new and convincing interpretation of the structure of the *Wanderjahre* is contained in an article by Volker Neuhaus who reads the work, not according to the model of a frame-narrative with inserted novellas and tales which Erich Trunz posits, but rather as comprising the contents of two archives which contain the diverse writings of around twenty fictional characters, not to mention the indeterminable number of writers whose words are contained in the collections of aphorisms[128]. To this variety of texts within one work he gives the name 'Archivfiktion' [archive fiction], thus emphasising the collective nature of the work and its preoccupation with script in all its manifestations[129].

The term 'archive fiction' is adopted by Eric Blackall in his book on all four of Goethe's novels[130]. Blackall, however, makes a distinction between the first version of the *Wanderjahre*, which he considers under the subtitle 'Archive into Novel', suggesting that it is a collective work whose archival form represents the archive of life which it attempts to encompass, and the second version, which he considers under the subtitle 'Counterpoint in the Symbolic Mode'. Taking as

---

[126] Bernd Peschken, *Entsagung in 'Wilhelm Meisters Wanderjahre'*, Bonn 1968, pages 9-10.

[127] For a comparison with *Ulysses* cf. Eberhard Bahr's essay on the *Wanderjahre* in: *Goethes Erzählwerk*, pages 367-374; Adolf Muschg, in *Goethe als Emigrant*, page 123, suggests that the *Wanderjahre* subjects its reader to a test as difficult as that set him by *Mann ohne Eigenschaften*; for a discussion of the aphorism in the *Wanderjahre* and *Der Mann ohne Eigenschaften*, cf. Peter C. Pfeiffer, *Aphorismus und Romanstruktur: Zu Robert Musils 'Der Mann ohne Eigenschaften'*, Bonn, 1990; and for a comparison with the novels of Samuel Beckett cf. Gidion, page 138.

[128] Volker Neuhaus, 'Die Archivfiktion in *Wilhelm Meisters Wanderjahren*', *Euphorion* 62 (1968).

[129] This preoccupation is also emphasised by Klaus-Detlev Müller in his article 'Zum Romanbegriff in Goethes *Wilhelm Meisters Wanderjahre*' in *Deutsche Vierteljahresschrift* 53 (1979) page 283: 'the specific quality of archive fiction is not, therefore, the invention of sources but the demonstration of a variety of forms of writing'.

[130] Eric Blackall, *Goethe and the Novel*, Ithaca and London 1976, pages 236-269, quotation from page 269.

his starting point the report by Eckermann on 11th September 1828 of the revision which Goethe was carrying out for the second version of the *Wanderjahre* he suggests that as a result of this revision the novel was 'transformed from a collective work into a contrapuntal work' and that:

> whereas Goethe had demanded in the first version that the reader himself should see the novel as a collection of separate parts and either respect that or try to provide the connections himself, in the second version he has transformed the whole disparate collection into a highly complex, but nevertheless unitary, contrapuntal structure[131].

He sees the principle of counterpoint not only expressed in thematic polarities such as mobility and stability but also employed as a structural principle of the work through the use of the technique of 'repeated reflections'.

Manfred Karnick places the accent on the theme of the difficulty of communication and sees the disparate form as a result of this theme[132]. He suggests that the form of the novel, which, in its circularity, is simultaneously open and closed, reflects its 'simultaneously open and closed stance on communication'. Heidi Gidion also emphasises the discontinuity of the form which she sees as being underlined by the principal structural units of the novel - the isolated 'Bezirke' [realms] visited by Wilhelm[133]. She suggests that, although it would be nonsense to try to construct 'an ideal reader' out of the various comments of the narrator, nevertheless the reader plays a central role in the work and must be both flexible and able to use his own initiative.

---

[131] 'Everywhere in the manuscript there are gaps of blank paper that still need to be filled out. Here there is something missing in the exposition, here a skilful transition must be found so that it is less apparent to the reader that it is a collective work; here are fragments of great significance, some of which lack the beginning, others the ending: and so in all three volumes there is still very much to be improved to make this important book both agreeable and attractive', Eckermann, page 259.

[132] Karnick, especially page 190.

[133] Cf. especially pages 62-66 for the 'Bezirke'. Like Manfred Karnick (page 102), Heidi Gidion points out the common features of the 'Bezirke', in particular the way in which 'one goes through gates into courtyards, through doors into halls, again through doors into the inner rooms' in a 'movement of uninterrupted entering' - the threshhold imagery suggesting the 'accessibility as well as the isolation' of the 'Bezirke'. Gidion further says, 'The realm does not become a resting place for the one who has been ceremonially initiated; he returns from the inside to the periphery' - a vivid evocation of the characteristics of the labyrinth. It will be suggested in Chapter 4 that these 'Bezirke' can be understood as a series of labyrinths through which the reader must accompany Wilhelm and which reflect in miniature the labyrinth of the text itself.

Another interpretative direction examines the novel within its own historical and cultural context. The East German critic Anneliese Klingenberg seeks to illustrate through extensive research into the sources, that the novel has a close relationship with the reality of its day and she underlines the necessity of reading the novel against the background of its own historical situation[134]. Writing within the context of the East German socialist state she interprets the work as an expression of Goethe's optimistic world view, which has not given up hope of a human society run on socialist lines and governed by reason and good sense. Radically opposed to this viewpoint is the work of Thomas Degering who suggests that the novel embodies Goethe's deeply pessimistic prognostication of the future development of the infant capitalist and industrial society of his day, a forewarning of a 'civilisation' whose main aim is maximum profit and where the individual is no more than a faceless, voiceless cog in the economic machine[135].

Waltraud Maierhofer examines the novel in the context of the evolution of the nineteenth-century German novel[136]. Possibly following Erich Trunz's description of the structure of the *Wanderjahre* as following the principle of 'nebeneinander' [juxtaposition] rather than 'nacheinander' [succession] she takes as her starting point the narrative theory of Karl Gutzkow, who posits the idea of the 'Roman des Nebeneinander' [novel of juxtaposition], and in her analysis of the novel's structure makes comparisons with Gutzkow's own novel *Ritter vom Geiste* and with Immermann's *Epigonen*. She suggests that it is misleading to see the novel as a forerunner of twentieth-century modernist works and that it is more instructive to understand it 'as an attempt to make the whole sense of an epoch tangible in its structure'.

In his latest book on all four of Goethe's novels Stefan Blessin suggests that the application of the term multi-perspectivity to the *Wanderjahre*, and

---

[134] Anneliese Klingenberg *Goethes Roman 'Wilhelm Meisters Wanderjahre oder die Entsagenden' Quellen und Komposition,* Berlin und Weimar 1972.
[135] Thomas Degering, *Das Elend der Entsagung: 'Wilhelm Meisters Wanderjahre',* Bonn 1982.
[136] Waltraud Maierhofer, *'Wilhelm Meisters Wanderjahre' und der Roman des Nebeneinander,* Bielefeld 1990.

indeed to Goethe's narrative technique in general, is misleading and that the term belongs to a later time, when the fragmentary state of the world calls for a correspondingly fragmentary representational method which reflects the world through a series of incomplete and disjointed perspectives[137]. To describe Goethe's narrative technique in all his novels Blessin prefers a more organic image. Each of Goethe's novels, he claims, comprises 'a world made up of little worlds'. He thus suggests that Goethe's technique mirrors nature itself, in that each part is in itself a whole while also forming part of the greater whole. Blessin, too, sees the phrase 'repeated reflections' as the key to understanding Goethe's narrative technique. For this endless reflection of one world within another Blessin uses the image of the Russian doll which contains within it ever more miniature reflections of itself: an image which could equally well be applied to the mise en abyme technique. He then describes how the various episodes converge again and again on one particular 'picture' and then open up again to reveal yet another series of pictures like the corridors and suites of rooms in a fine mansion - a description which suggests exactly that metaphor of the picture gallery which we shall see Goethe himself employing consciously and repeatedly in the *Wanderjahre* as an image for the structure of his novel.

Hans Rudolf Vaget sums up the direction of the most recent criticism of the *Wanderjahre* as 'the enthronement of the reader'. The task of the reader to complete the text and give it meaning is now seen in a positive light. The reader is increasingly regarded as the hero of the novel and the novel as a 'Leseexerzitium' [reading exercise][138]. Ehrhard Bahr has suggested that comparisons can be made between the reader-reception theories of Wolfgang Iser and Goethe's conception of the reader as the re-creator of the author's text. He considers that Iser's

---

[137] Stefan Blessin, *Goethes Romane. Aufbruch in die Moderne*, Paderborn; München; Wien; Zürich, 1996. For the *Wanderjahre* Blessin suggests that its modernity lies in its concern with central issues of the modern world: 'with the indispensable specialisation in a profession, with mechanisation and the different forms of industrialisation, with the role of nature in the development of science and technology'. With Rosenkranz and Gregorovius, Blessin insists that 'work is *the* theme of the *Wanderjahre*'.

[138] Hans Vaget, in: *Romane und Erzählungen* , pages 142 and 144.

description of the programme of the twentieth-century novel - 'to make the reader aware of how he perceives things, how he goes about creating consistency in what he reads, indeed, how his reflective faculties function' - is equally applicable to the *Wanderjahre*[139]. Building upon a notion first expressed by Hotho, Bahr and Vaget extend the idea of renunciation to cover the reader, who must be willing to give up prejudices and presuppositions and also to do without many of the normal signals and aids which he expects in a text[140]. A similar idea is expressed by Adolf Muschg, who sees both the author and the reader as travellers: the author seeks to cross boundaries in his search for a new kind of novel and his task is to draw the reader with him, to help him to step across his own boundaries and to free him from his preconceived assumptions[141].

Several critics have drawn attention to the self-consciousness of the *Wanderjahre* and to its speculative interest in a concept of the novel. Ehrhard Bahr points out the way in which Goethe uses the technique of 'ironic reflection' particularly in those places where he is interested in highlighting the nature of the work as an artistic construct: 'where the novel is concerned with itself as novel'[142]. Eric Blackall describes the first version as 'a novel concerned but also content with the fact of being a novel'[143]. Jane Brown's conception of the work as offering a series of parodies and imitations of various literary, educational and pictorial predecessors also emphasises the primacy of its interest in itself as a work of art within a specific tradition. Klaus-Detlev Müller sees the regular intrusions of the narrator into his own narrative as 'components of a poetics of the

---

[139] Ehrhard Bahr, in: *Goethes Erzählwerk*, page 385. This idea has been developed further by Monica Weber who examines Goethe's concept of the reader and its implications for the *Wanderjahre* in the light of the theories of Iser and H.R.Jauß. Weber ascribes to Goethe a pyramidical view of his readership, reaching from the broad base of the general readership, which was regarded ambivalently by Goethe, to the apex of the discerning reader who acts as inspiration to the writer and for whom Schiller stands as the ideal representative. Monica Weber, *Goethe's Conception of the Reader and its Implications for 'Wilhelm Meisters Wanderjahre'*, (Dissertation for University of Waterloo, Canada, 1986).
[140] See above (footnote 102 in this chapter).
[141] Adolf Muschg, *Goethe als Emigrant*, page 123.
[142] Ehrhard Bahr, *Die Ironie im Spätwerk Goethes*, Berlin 1972, page 110.
[143] Blackall, page 226.

novel' and says in particular of the intervention of the narrator in Book 1, Chapter 10 'that here a poetological programme is actually formulated'[144]. In an article on the 'Noten und Abhandlungen' to the *West-östlicher Divan* Hannelore Schlaffer has suggested that 'gedichtete Theorie' [literary theory incorporated in the literary work] is not an unusual phenomenon in Goethe's work[145]. She claims that just as the 'Noten' contain 'Goethe's history of the philosophy of literature' and 'theory of lyric poetry', the *Lehrjahre* contains the 'history of the theatre' and *Faust* is a 'history and sum total of all types of drama' so the *Wanderjahre* embodies 'his theory of the epic in the modern form of the novel'. Taken together she sees these works as constituting 'the paradox of a philosophy of art in literary form'.

This present study examines the extent to which the *Wanderjahre* represents Goethe's programme for a new form of novel in which practice fuses with theory and the literary work is itself simultaneously a discourse on the construction and interpretation of works of art. While all Goethe's novels are preoccupied to some extent with the processes of constructing and of reading literary texts, this tendency reaches its culmination in the *Wanderjahre*, which represents, within Goethe's own narrative work, a development towards a new post-classical theory of the novel. Paradoxically this new programme links Goethe's narrative work into a continuum of self-conscious or metafictional literature in the western literary tradition[146]. Through an exploration of Goethe's writings on literature and art it is established that he saw the literary work as a process involving a constructive relationship between reader, writer and text and aiming at inculcating in the reader a creative, productive reading practice. An analysis of the various metafictional elements in the *Wanderjahre* itself reveals

---

[144] Klaus-Detlev Müller, pages 280 and 281.

[145] Hannelore Schlaffer, 'Gedichtete Theorie - Die "Noten und Abhandlungen" zum West-östlichen Divan' in: *Goethe Jahrbuch* 101 (1984), page 219.

[146] Steve Dowden has linked the ironic devices used by Goethe in the *Wanderjahre* both backwards to the irony of Lawrence Sterne and forwards to the ironic detachment displayed in modernist fiction. He has coined the term 'kaleidoscopic novel' to characterise the *Wanderjahre* since it attempts to 'expound views and pose questions about many aspects of life'. Steve Dowden, 'Irony and Ethical Autonomy in *Wilhelm Meisters Wanderjahre*', *DVjs* 68 (1994), pages 134-54.

68

the ways in which the novel reflects upon itself and challenges the reader by drawing attention to itself as an artistic construct; and the extent to which it constitutes a discourse on the relationship of text and image and a model of the interaction at every level between the visual and the literary arts[147].

---

[147] What Terry Eagleton has written of 'modernist' texts is also a very apt description of the *Wanderjahre*, 'Many modernist literary works (...) make the "act of enunciating", the process of their own production, part of their actual "content". They do not try to pass themselves off as unquestionable, like Barthes's "natural" sign, but as the Formalists would say "lay bare the device" of their own composition. They do this so that they will not be mistaken for absolute truth - so that the reader will be encouraged to reflect critically on the partial, particular ways they construct reality, and so to recognise how it might all have happened differently', Terry Eagleton, *Literary Theory. An Introduction*, Cambridge 1983, page 170.

CHAPTER 2

Reader, writer and text in Goethe's work

Zum Nachdenken aufzuregen
To make people think

The 'zarte Empirie' [subtle practice] - the inseparability of theory and practice, the fusion of the critical and the creative impulses - is central to Goethe's thought. In *Dichtung und Wahrheit* he wrote, 'Theory and practice always have an effect on each other; from people's acts one can see how they think, and from their ideas one can predict what they will do'[1]. The very title – Poetry and Truth - is an expression of his sense of a similar interdependency between art and life which led him both to question the role of the work of art, whether literary or visual, in relation to life and society and to examine the relationship between writer, reader and text - or, more widely, between artist, artistic product and audience. He insists on the responsibility of art to produce through artifice the illusion of a heightened reality[2]. In a series of observations in the 'Maximen und Reflexionen' he emphasises the role of art in mediating and interpreting the world, 'One to whom nature begins to reveal her open secret experiences an irresistible longing for her most reliable interpreter, art'. Furthermore he highlights the centrality of the human experiencing consciousness both in the primary perception of the world and in its mediation through art:[3].

In Chapter One we saw how Hermann Broch suggested that Goethe, with the *Wanderjahre*, was the initiator of a new literary age, 'the age of the ethical work of art'. In this context we are confronted with the question of how far and in what way Goethe considered the role of the literary work to be didactic or more

---

[1] H.A. Volume 9, page 263.
[2] H.A. Volume 9, page 488.
[3] Goethe, 'Maximen und Reflexionen' Nos. 720 & 725, H.A. Volume 12, page 467.

subtly heuristic. When commenting on the reception of *Werther* he criticises the perception of the public that a printed book must have an obviously didactic purpose and goes on to assert that a really accomplished literary work incorporates a much more subtle educative element, not something merely superimposed on the work but something which springs from the very nature of the work itself: 'it neither approves nor disapproves, but allows attitudes and actions to evolve naturally, and in this way it teaches and enlightens'[4]. In his essay of 1827 'Über das Lehrgedicht' he wrote, 'All literature should be educative, but unobtrusively; it should make one aware of what needs to be learned; one must learn the lesson from it oneself, just as one does from life'. This same perception of the educative aspect of the literary enterprise and the active role of the reader recurs in a letter to Nicolaus Borchhardt in the following year[5]. Much earlier in a letter to Schiller he insisted that the reader's task was to engage in a productive relationship with writer and text[6].

In a letter to Eichstädt the adjective used for this relationship is 'constructive'. Goethe describes the work of art as an artistic construct which the artist has fashioned from an array of diverse elements and which the constructive reader helps to co-produce[7]. In a comment to Kanzler von Müller Goethe emphasises the importance of this constructive-productive relationship between reader, writer and text[8]. Here again the reader is regarded as a re-creator of the text, and as a re-creator who, 'ergänzend' [augmenting], may see more in the text than the author consciously put there and who thereby through his interpretation becomes, in effect, a co-producer rather than a re-producer. The task of the writer is, therefore, to engage the reader through creative participation in the completion

---

[4] H.A. Volume 9, page 590.
[5] 1st May 1828. W.A. 4. 44, page 79.
[6] Schiller/Goethe Briefwechsel. Letter to Schiller of 19th November 1796, page 314.
[7] 15th September 1804. W.A. 4.17, pages 196-7.
[8] 'A work of art, especially a poem, that leaves nothing to puzzle out, is not truly worthy of the name; its highest purpose remains always to provoke thought and only thereby can it become really precious to the viewer or reader, when it forces him to interpret it for himself according to his own way of thinking and, as it were, to recreate and augment it'. *Goethes Gespräche*, edited by Biedermann, Leipzig 1909 (2), 2. 4, page 477.

of the text and to provoke him at every step to exercise his critical faculties. Finally this statement includes the idea of the work of art as a puzzle and enigma, containing within its depths more than it at first reveals, and challenging the reader through its infinite nature to take on the task of interpretation.

The idea of the infinite character of a work of art recurs repeatedly in Goethe's writing and conversation. The first sentence of his essay 'Über Laokoon' stresses this aspect of the work of art:

> A truly great work of art, like a work of nature, always remains boundless to our comprehension; it is viewed, it is experienced, its effect is felt, but it cannot be fully understood, much less can its real essence and excellence be expressed in words[9].

In a conversation with Eckermann on his methods of working Goethe says that he does not take as his starting point an abstract idea but rather the many and varied sense impressions which enter his imagination, and sums up his attitude to poetic creation, 'The more incommensurable and enigmatic a literary work, the better'[10]. For Goethe the works of Homer always represented the exemplary literary work precisely because of their quality of unfathomableness. This idea is set out in 'Maximen und Reflexionen', No. 836 where the profundity and boundlessness, which are the ideal characteristics of a literary work, are emphasised through a comparison with the depths and limitlessness of the universe itself[11].

A further aphorism from this collection underscores this demand that a literary work must say more than the mere surface meaning of the words from which it is composed, 'If a dictionary can keep pace with an author then he is no good' [12]. The concept of the symbol was so essential to Goethe for precisely this reason: it incorporated the potential to carry the word beyond its rational and philological confines into the realms of the unfathomable and the inexpressible:

---

[9] H.A. Volume 12, *Kunst und Literatur*, page 56.
[10] Eckermann, 6th May 1827, page 591.
[11] 'Someone said, "Why do you trouble yourselves with Homer? You don't understand him." My answer was: I don't understand the sun, moon and stars either; but they pass over my head and I recognise myself in them, in that I see them and watch their regular, amazing course and wonder whether something could also become of me'. H.A. Volume 12, page 483, No. 836.
[12] H.A. Volume 12, page 495, No.916. This idea is developed further in No. 917, which implies that the writer's task is to suggest ideas subtly to the reader's imagination rather than to spell out everything in great detail.

> The symbol converts the phenomenon into an idea, the idea into an image in such a way
> that in the image the idea always continues to be both highly effective and unattainable
> and, even when expressed in all languages, remains inexpressible[13].

In the *Tag- und Jahres-Hefte* for 1796 Goethe said of the *Lehrjahre*, 'Therefore this work remains one of the most incalculable, whether one regards it as a whole or in its parts; even I feel the want of a yardstick with which to assess it'; thereby indicating that for the artist, too, his creation may contain more than he consciously put into it[14]. Of the *Wanderjahre* itself he wrote to Rochlitz in 1829:

> But with this kind of book it is the same as with life itself: in the whole complex there are
> necessary and chance elements, priorities and subsidiary elements, now successful, now
> coming to nothing, through which it gains a kind of infinity, which does not quite submit
> to the limits and confines of sensible and reasonable words.

This idea of the work of art as the mediator of the inexpressible is the theme of No. 729 of the 'Maximen und Reflexionen', which goes on to suggest that the act of interpretation is based upon an impossibility: the search for an ultimate meaning; but is also a necessity since it is only through the constant effort to interpret that the powers of judgement can be developed[15]. The work of art, indeed, should not provide answers, but rather should highlight the problems and provoke the reader to ask questions and to seek his own solutions[16]. On this theme Goethe said to Eckermann, 'Human beings are not born to solve the problems of the world, but rather to find out where the problem starts and then to stay within the boundary of what is graspable'[17]. In conversation with Kanzler von Müller about the *Wanderjahre* he acknowledges that it presents a puzzle to the reader and continues, 'everything is just to be taken symbolically, and something else underlies it at every point. Every solution to a problem raises another

---

[13] H.A. Volume 12, page 470, 'Maximen und Reflexionen' No.749. Cf. also page 471, No.752
[14] W.A., 35, page 65. See also Eckermann, page 131, January 18th 1825.
[15] 'Art is a mediator of the inexpressible; therefore it seems to be foolish to want to interpret it again in words. And yet to the extent to which we make the effort there is a gain for the understanding which in turn benefits the faculty carrying it out'. H.A. Volume 12, page 468.
[16] 'A romance is not a trial where there must be a final verdict'. 'Maximen und Reflexionen', H.A. Volume 12, page 498, No.941.
[17] Goethe to Eckermann, page 164.

problem'[18]. In a letter to Zelter in 1828 he wrote of the *Wanderjahre*, 'It will make you think and that is what really matters after all'; and this sentence succinctly expresses the aim of the work[19]. The reader's expectations are not to be fulfilled but he is to be challenged and provoked into abandoning his preconceived ideas and thinking freely.

Goethe describes the positive results of disappointed expectations on his own appreciation of the visual arts: he makes even greater efforts to understand a work of art which displeases him at first sight until he discovers new qualities in it and at the same time new capacities in himself [20]. A particular example of this experience occurs in the *Italienische Reise* when he describes his immediate reaction to the temples of Paestum, which he knew only from architectural drawings and which, with eighteenth-century eyes, he had imagined as much more elegant and slender: 'I found myself in a totally alien world'. Only after an effort on his part to think himself into their historical and cultural world, is he able to approach them and only by immersing himself in their spatial world, by physically moving round them and through them, is he able to begin the interpretative act and gain some idea of the architect's creative purpose[21].

The disappointment of expectations is also an important function of the writer, according to Goethe, and a debt owed to his public. In 'Maximen und Reflexionen' No.984 he says of the relationship between author and public, 'The greatest respect that an author can show for his public is never to provide what is expected, but rather what he himself considers to be appropriate and beneficial at

---

[18] Gräf, 1.2, page 976, 8th June 1821: 'Alles ist nur symbolisch zu nehmen, und überall steckt noch etwas Anderes dahinter. Jede Lösung eines Problems ist ein neues Problem' This sentence seems to suggest the same attitude which H.R. Jauß later described as a 'productive reception (...) which throws up new questions with regard to tradition' and which Jauß illustrates with the example of how Goethe in *Werther* took up the problems which Rousseau was dealing with in *La nouvelle Heloise* and reproblematised Rousseau's answers: in H.R.Jauß, *Ästhetische Erfahrung und literarische Hermeneutik*, Frankfurt am Main 1984, pages 585-647. This idea of a productive reception is very much what Goethe describes as the way in which a literary text should be read.
[19] 'Sie werden euch zu denken geben und das ist's doch eigentlich, worauf es ankommt'. Letter to Zelter, 30th October 1828. W.A. 4.45, page 37.
[20] 'Maximen und Reflexionen', H.A. Volume 12, page 492, No.896.
[21] .H.A. Volume 11, pages 219-20.

each particular stage of his own and others' development'[22]. Already in a letter to Zelter in 1815 Goethe had said that 'the writer's work (...) demands (...) from the reader that he be constantly observing, noticing, interpreting': a formulation which emphasises that the activity of the writer calls forth a reciprocal activity on the part of the reader[23].

The reader is seen as having a very important role to play, even more important than the reading material. Another maxim suggests, 'The most uninspired novel is still better than the uninspired reader, indeed the worst novel shares to some extent in the excellence of the whole genre'[24]. The role is so important because the reader functions as a re-creator, bringing the writer's text to life again in his imagination. This function of the reader is emphasised in a letter from Goethe to Rochlitz on the subject of the *Lehrjahre*: 'and one can thank God, if one has been able to put so much substance in, that thinking and feeling people consider it worth the effort to unravel it again for themselves'[25]. A similar idea of the reader's role is given in the 'Noten und Abhandlungen' to the *West-östlichen Divan* where a productive reading practice for an Arabic poem is described as follows, 'Whoever reads his way into it properly must perceive the events from beginning to end gradually taking shape in his imagination'[26].

In speaking about the *Lehrjahre* Goethe insisted that the created world of the novel 'belonged' in a sense to its creator, 'If we have created a world of our own, then we are also entitled to make its laws', and that 'the visiting reader' must accept the laws of the land or go elsewhere, thus suggesting that the reader does not have any charter for boundless free interpretation[27]. Yet he conceded that 'of course the reader [as a 'visitor'] often sees more clearly, he is open-minded, looks at a picture objectively'. He is careful to suggest the limits of the powers of

[22] H. A. Volume 12, pages 503-4.
[23] Letter to Zelter, W.A. 4. 25, page 266.
[24] 'Maximen und Reflexionen', H.A. Volume 12, No.939, page 498.
[25] Letter to Rochlitz, March 29th 1801. Gräf, 1.2, pages 883-4.
[26] H.A. Volume 2, page 134.
[27] Gräf 1. 2, page 941. A similar idea is expressed in 'Maximen und Reflexionen' No.938. H.A. Volume 12, page 498.

the writer both in the construction of his text, 'since there are always particular instances where one may come upon gaps and breaks' and in its interpretation, since 'an artist who produces excellent works is not always capable of explicating his own or others' works'[28]. He is equally careful to emphasise that 'the enthusiast, the connoisseur, the interpreter has a completely free hand to uncover the symbols which the artist, consciously or unconsciously has buried in his works'[29]. Here again is the idea that the work of art may contain much more than the artist consciously put into it and that the reader can function as producer as well as re-producer. In referring to the *Wanderjahre* Goethe takes the freedom of the reader somewhat further and suggests, if rather light-heartedly, that the reader, given the individual parts, could order them into a whole as well as, if not better than, the author. In a letter to Zelter in 1827 he wrote, 'Only a few rushes are required to finish off the plaiting of the flower-garland, and in the end any good soul could do that, grasping and taking hold of each separate part, and perhaps they would do it better'[30].

Although he insists on the author's right to devise the laws for the fictional work he has created, Goethe is careful to deny any significance to the name of the author. In an anticipation of Roland Barthes argument in his article, 'The death of the author', two aphorisms from Makarie's archive deal with this theme[31]. The first argues that scholars are wasting their energy when they strive to prove the authenticity of a particular text by seeking evidence that will ascribe it to a particular writer rather than concentrating on the interpretation of the text and demands, 'Why should we care about the names, when we interpret a work of art?' Barthes, too, denies that the search for the 'author' is a valid critical exercise:

> To give a text an Author is to impose a limit on that text, to furnish it with a final
> signified, to close the writing. Such a conception suits criticism very well, the latter then

---

[28] Riemer, Volume 3, 20th May 1819, page 117; and 'Maximen und Reflexionen', No.883. H.A. Volume 12, page 490.
[29] Letter to Sulpiz Boisserée, 16th July 1818. W.A. 4. 29, page 239.
[30] Letter to Zelter, 24th May 1827, Gräf, 1.2, page 1031.
[31] H.A. Volume 8, Nos.134 and 135, page 481.

> allotting itself the important task of discovering the Author (or its hypostases: society, history, psyché, liberty) beneath the work: when the Author has been found, the text is 'explained' - victory to the critic.

The second argues likewise that the important thing is not to ascribe a particular work to a particular named author, be it Virgil, Homer or Shakespeare, but to engage in dialogue with the writer without concerning ourselves about his name: 'but we have the writers [die Schreiber] in front of us, and what more do we need?' – 'Schreiber' here being equivalent to Barthes' 'instance writing' in 'The death of the author'. In the *Wanderjahre* a certain distancing of the author is brought about by the device of the intrusive narrator and by the polyphony of narrative voices in the text[32].

Goethe was very aware of the volatile nature of language, of the way in which time can wear down newly-minted expressions into clichés 'so that now every mediocre talent can conveniently make use of the available expressions as ready-made phrases'; and of the 'Wandelbarkeit des Worts' [changeability of the word][33]. In addition he had a keen sense of the ambiguities inherent in the word - of the sheer impossibility of a complete understanding between two people because a particular word could never mean exactly the same to two individuals. In writing of Spinoza in *Dichtung und Wahrheit* he says, 'For I had already all too clearly seen that no one understands another person, that the same words lead to different thoughts in different people, that a discussion or some reading matter gives rise to different trains of thought in different people'[34]. This ambiguity of the word, which on the one hand could lead to misunderstanding, could, on the other hand, offer the richest possibilities for suggesting the subtlest distinctions of meaning. For this reason he proposes as the tutelary god of philologists, 'Apollo

---

[32] Roland Barthes, 'The death of the author' in: *Image-Music-Text.*, essays selected and translated from the French by Stephen Heath, London 1977. In his latest book on the *Wanderjahre* Ehrhard Bahr uses Michel Foucault's essay, 'What is an Author?' (1984), as a starting point to argue that 'Goethe's accomplishment in his *Wanderjahre* was to present a novel in which the fictive is no longer strictly limited by the traditional figure of the author but is put at the disposal of the reader'. Ehrhard Bahr, *The Novel as Archive. The genesis, reception and criticism of Goethe's 'Wilhelm Meisters Wanderjahre'*, Columbia 1998.

[33] 'Maximen und Reflexionen', H.A. Volume 12, No. 1005, page 506 and No. 1024, page 509.

[34] H.A. Volume 10, page 78.

Sauroktonos, immer mit dem spitzen Griffelchen in der Hand aufpassend, eine Eidechse zu spießen' [Apollo the lizard-slayer, with the sharply pointed pencil always in his hand, watching out for a lizard to impale]. The attempt to define and assign ultimate meanings to words is compared to an attempt to pierce a lizard and arrest its darting, iridescent movement, a deadening exercise, for a word which has been defined so exactly that it is no longer allowed its full play of meaning is a word which, like Apollo's lizard, has been deprived of its vital forces. A further series of maxims suggest that sometimes even a literal misinterpretation can provide inspiration, so that 'it becomes a private emendation through which one person [the creative artist] gains for his spirit what another [the philologist, by emending a corrupt passage] gains for the letters'. In such circumstances even a printing error can prove fruitful: 'I always think when I see a printing error, that something new has been found'[35].

The immense possibilities for interpretation are suggested in a passage from the *Italienische Reise* where Goethe compares the study of natural science and the interpretation of works of art saying, 'There is a great deal written about both and yet each individual who studies them can still find a new way of looking at them'[36]. That interpretation is also a continuously changing process is emphasised in the *Farbenlehre* in relation to history:

> There is surely no doubt remaining nowadays that world history must from time to time be rewritten. Such a necessity arises however not because many events have been uncovered later but because new theories are put forward, because the person who lives in a progressive age is led to vantage points from which the past can be viewed and assessed in a new way[37].

---

[35] H.A. Volume 12, 'Maximen und Reflexionen', Nos. 1025, 1026 & 1027, page 510.
[36] *Italienische Reise*, 16th February 1787. H.A. Volume 11, page 171.
[37] *Geschichte der Farbenlehre* '16. Jahrhundert - Baco von Verulam'. H.A. Volume 14, page 93. In Goethe's manner of historical thinking we can perhaps recognise the influence of Herder whose work prepared the ground for an historical way of thinking in Germany. In *Auch eine Philosophie der Geschichte zur Bildung der Menschheit* historical thinking involves 'granting each epoch its own right to exist'. Herder *Werke*, Volume 2, Weimar 1957, pages 279-378.

Here Goethe displays an historical consciousness, which corresponds to the Gadamerian concept of the ever-changing historical horizon of expectations and the concomitant awareness that tradition exists only in constant alteration[38].

This idea of the changing horizon of expectations is also applied to literature in No.145 of Makarie's archive, where Goethe's view of literary history anticipates something of the ideas of the Russian formalists of the origin, canonisation, automisation and decay of literary genres[39]; or the idea of literary history put forward by Hans Robert Jauß: literature as defined and interpreted by its changing reception history: 'the always necessary re-assessing of literary history'[40]. Coupled with this idea in Goethe's maxim is the perception of the writer as part of an historical continuum which represents the only perspective from which it is possible to evaluate the extent of his originality and his literary indebtedness: 'whatever is original to us is best celebrated and safeguarded if we do not lose sight of our forebears'.

The question of originality was of great interest to Goethe. He was very well aware of the high level of intertextuality inherent in the nature of the literary text: 'borrowing' he saw as a natural part of the artistic enterprise, which became from this perspective very much a collective endeavour. A comment on Mirabeau, which Frédéric Soret recorded in his diary, makes this clear:

> What does genius consist in, if not in the ability to take over everything and to make use of whatever strikes us, to appropriate everything and to instil life into whatever material offers itself to us, to take marble from one place and bronze from another and construct a monument out of them? If my belief were not corroborated, that Mirabeau understood to the highest degree the art of appropriating for himself the good ideas of the men closest to him, the whole story of his dominating influence would seem to me very dubious.

Goethe goes on to affirm that this kind of productive 'plagiarism' characterises his own artistic practice too, 'What would I be then, what would remain to me, if this art of capturing booty were regarded as demeaning for the genius? What else

---

[38] Hans Georg Gadamer, *Wahrheit und Methode*, Tübingen 1965 (2nd edition), page 288.
[39] 'In the succession of literary periods what was effective earlier is eclipsed and its successor gains the upper hand; therefore one does well to look back again from time to time', H.A. Volume 8, page 482. See also H.A. Volume 12, 'Maximen und Reflexionen', No. 1000, page 505.
[40] Hans Robert Jauß, *Literaturgeschichte als Provokation*, Frankfurt am Main, 1979 (6), page 170.

have I done?' He insists that many thousands of anonymous people have contributed to his work:

> I collected and made use of everything that came before my eyes, my ears, my senses. Thousands of individuals have contributed their share to my works, fools and wise men, intelligent people and idiots, children, adults and old men, they all came and brought me their thoughts, their skills, their experiences, their life and their existence; so I often harvested what others had sown;

and asserts, 'My life's work is that of a collective nature, and this work carries the name of Goethe'[41].

This same challenge to the concept of originality is voiced in a group of maxims from Makarie's archive (Nos. 174-77), belonging to the series paying homage to that other great borrower, Laurence Sterne; one of which proclaims, 'And so the best sign of originality consists in knowing how to take up an idea and develop it in such a productive way that no one could easily have found out how much lay hidden in it' (486); and even more pointedly in the first aphorism from 'Betrachtungen im Sinne der Wanderer': 'every good idea has already been thought, one must just try to think it through again' (283).

Goethe was quite sure that his work, because of the demands it made on the reader and its refusal to satisfy reader expectations, was not destined for popularity. To Eckermann he said, 'My things cannot become popular', giving as the reason, 'They are not written for the masses, but only for individuals who want something similar and who are going in similar directions'[42]. Indeed he speaks and writes often of his readers as scattered and solitary individuals, as in the introduction to the poem 'Um Mitternacht': 'herewith I most warmly invite my friends scattered throughout Germany to make this poem their own'[43].

His criticism of the general literary public was directed at its unwillingness to be disturbed in its reading habits, at its reluctance, or even

[41] Frédéric Soret, Tagebuch, 17th February 1832. In: *Goethe: Historische Schriften*, edited by Horst Günther, Frankfurt am Main 1982, page 355.
[42] Eckermann, October 11th 1828, page 275.
[43] *Kunst und Altertum*, W.A. 1.41.1, page 370.

80

inability, to grasp something new and unexpected[44]. In a letter to Schiller he wrote regretting this lack of critical awareness on the part of the reading public, who were only willing to accept what they could understand immediately and condemned anything that demanded a little more effort on their part[45]. A similar idea is expressed in a comment to Kanzler von Müller, which refers to both the *Lehrjahre* and the *Wanderjahre*, 'The German people (...) always required a considerable amount of time before they could assimilate a work which diverged from the commonplace, before they could come to terms with it and reflect adequately on it'[46].

Of the public's criticism of the *Lehrjahre* Goethe said, 'But the main criticism is that it is not another *Werther*'; a sadly ironic comment when one remembers that *Werther* became so popular despite its author's intentions: that a book which was intended as a critique of 'Empfindsamkeit' [sentimentality] and a means of overcoming pathological tendencies in the writer's own psyche became, in the popular mind, the handbook of 'Empfindsamkeit' and was criticised for encouraging the pathological tendencies of a whole generation[47]. A verse which Goethe wrote as the book's own imaginary answer to this criticism stresses the problem caused by mis-reading and the importance of developing the ability to read critically:

Der Plumpe, der nicht schwimmen kann,	[The clumsy one, who cannot swim
Er will's dem Wasser verweisen!(...)	He blames it on the water (...)
Und wer mich nicht verstehen kann,	And whoever cannot understand me
Der lerne besser lesen.[48]	He should learn to read better.]

---

[44] Cf. for example No.983 of 'Maximen und Reflexionen', where Goethe makes this point by comparing the reading public to women (!) who are only willing to accept what they want to hear.
[45] Schiller/Goethe Briefwechsel. Letter to Schiller of 7th July 1796, page 235.
[46] January 22nd 1821. Gräf, 1.2, page 953.
[47] To Schultz, January 10th 1829. Gräf 1.2, page1051. Goethe himself attributed the book's effect to the fact that it touched this chord in the psyche of his own generation, 'This way of thinking was so general that *Werther* had such an effect for just this reason, because it struck a universal chord and portrayed the intimate aspects of a sick youthful delusion openly and comprehensibly', *Dichtung und Wahrheit.* 3.13, H.A. Volume 9, page 583.
[48] H.A. Volume 9, page 592.

The public's propensity for mis-reading is also satirised in No. 124 of the 'Xenien':

> Das gewöhnliche Schicksal
> Hast du an liebender Brust das Kind der Empfindung gepfleget,
> Einen Wechselbalg nur gibt dir der Leser zurück.[49]
> [The Usual Fate
> When you have lovingly nursed the child of your imagination at your breast,
> It's just a changeling that the reader gives back to you.]

Goethe's faith in the contemporary reading public was badly shaken by the reception given to *Werther*. In his middle period, however, his faith seems to have been restored somewhat. In 1804 Heinrich Voß reported his appreciative comments on the contemporary reading public which ended with the wish, 'If only I had been able to experience such a thoughtful assessment of my *Götz von Berlichingen* and *Werther* twenty-five years ago!'[50] In the 'Noten und Abhandlungen' to the *West-östlichen Divan*, written between 1816 and 1819, explaining why he considers it necessary to write notes to accompany the poems, he gives a brief outline of the varying reception given to his work by succeeding generations, ending full of praise for the present generation of readers, 'And a second and third generation is compensating me thoroughly for the trials and tribulations which I had to endure from my earlier contemporaries'[51]. At the end of his life the reception of his later works seems to have shaken that faith once more so that he began increasingly to look to future generations for the understanding he missed among his contemporaries, as this comment to Zelter shows, 'The reading public is actually so distracted, insensitive and self-contained that one has more reason than ever to put one's trust in posterity'[52]. He became convinced that the work which was misunderstood in its author's own life-time

---

[49] H.A. Volume 1, page 224.
[50] Gräf, 1.2, page 570. This comment also suggests an appreciation of the concept of the changing 'horizon of expectations' of the public, in the sense in which Jauß uses this term.
[51] H.A. Volume.2, page 126.
[52] Letter to Zelter, October 30th 1828. H.A., Letters, Volume 4, page 307.

might only find interpreters in a later generation; and only much later would it gain widespread accessibility[53].

In spite of this judgement on the wider reading public, Goethe had nevertheless great concern for the reader, as we have already seen, and a strong sense of the importance of the role of the reader. This concern he expressed in a letter as follows, 'And so, in everything that I do, create and compose, I think about how it will reach those friends' [zu jenen Freunden gelangen][54]. The term 'Freunde' is used here not in the narrow sense of personal friends but encompasses all who are 'gleichgesinnt' [like-minded] - the kind of readers who can be assumed to have the capacity to handle the text as interpreters in the same way as the author handles it as generator. These are the readers envisaged in the introduction to the *Propyläen* when he writes, 'He wishes thereby to re-establish his relationship to his oldest friends, to continue it with new ones and in the latest generation to win yet more for the rest of his life' [55].

In his writing practice Goethe translated his perception of the literary work as a form of dialogue between author and reader into a working method. Not only are there constant records of his reading out of parts of so-far-unpublished works to a small circle of friends and acquaintances, but there are also many instances in his letters where he asks for reactions to newly-published or about-to-be-published works[56]. To Wilhelm von Humboldt he wrote requesting such feedback about *Faust II* - 'diese sehr ernsten Scherze' [these very earnest jests] - a work he hesitated to publish in his lifetime because he felt it would meet

---

[53] 'The present moment is a kind of public: one must deceive it, so that it believes one is doing something worthwhile; then it does not stop us but lets us continue in secret with something that will astound its grandchildren', 'Maximen und Reflexionen', H.A. Volume 12, No. 1098, page 518; and No. 985, page 504, 'The appeal to posterity arises from the natural deep feeling that something perennial exists and even if it is not immediately recognised, it will eventually give pleasure not just to the minority but to the majority'.
[54] W.A. 4. 123, pages 1-3.
[55] 'Einleitung in die *Propyläen*', H.A. Volume.12, page 41. These readers correspond to the Model Reader which Umberto Eco describes in *The Role of the Reader*, Bloomington, 1979, page 7, 'The author has thus to foresee a model of a possible reader (hereafter Model Reader) able to deal interpretatively with the expressions in the same way as the author deals generatively with them'.
[56] E.g. Riemer records for November 2th 1808, 'At noon alone with Goethe. On the effect of the "new Melusine" at court'. Gräf, 1.2, page 900.

only with lack of understanding[57]. His letters to friends about the *Wanderjahre* are full of requests for reactions to the work. To Schultz he wrote, 'I hope, my *Wanderjahre* is now in your hands and has given you various things to think about; do not be reluctant to communicate some of them to me'. He repeatedly writes to Rochlitz asking him to give his reactions to the individual parts of the *Wanderjahre* instead of making the attempt to find a key to the whole work. In one letter he gives as the reason for this request, 'It is only by this means that the author achieves the certain knowledge that he has succeeded in arousing emotion and reflection in many different kinds of minds'[58].

In the sixth letter of 'Der Sammler und die Seinigen' the dialogue between author and reader is transposed into a dialogue between the work of art and its recipient - a dialogue which is described in terms of a hermeneutical circle[59], with the interpreter moving from the particular work of art to general principles before returning again to the particular: 'a fine work of art has turned full circle, it is now once more a kind of individual, which we embrace with affection, that we can make our own'[60].

While the literary work is seen as a dialogue between author and reader, the readers whom Goethe envisages engaging in this dialogue are of a very particular kind. He describes them in an earlier letter to Rochlitz where he reports how the *Wanderjahre* has already been received 'von zart aufnehmenden Lesern'

---

[57] 17th March 1832. H.A., Letters, Volume 4, page 481.
[58] To Schultz, June 29th 1829 and to Rochlitz, November 23rd 1829, Gräf 1.2, pages 1057 & 1065.
[59] The theologian Friedrich Schleiermacher was the first to apply the metaphor of the hermeneutical circle to literary studies, in his lectures of 1829 where he describes the interaction between reader and text as circular movements back and forth which continuously spread outwards and reveal the whole and the parts in ever new relationships. Wilhelm von Humboldt, too, describes the way a work of art is to be interpreted in terms sounding very like a description of the hermeneutical circle. 'Aufsatz für Frau von Staël' page 171, in: Kurt Müller-Vollmer, *Poesie und Einbildungskraft. Zur Dichtungstheorie von Wilhelm von Humboldt*, Stuttgart (Metzler) 1967. This circular movement of interpretation is paralleled by Goethe's description, in a letter to Iken in 1827, of his circular method of constructing a text, 'So a long time ago I chose the method of revealing the secret meaning to the alert reader by means of images placed opposite each other and, as it were, reflecting each other'.
[60] 'Der Sammler und die Seinigen, Sechster Brief', H.A. Volume 12, page 84.

[by discerning readers][61]. Elsewhere he describes these readers as 'einsichtig' [thoughtful][62] and 'der echte Leser' [the genuine reader][63]. This reader's task is to re-create or 'relive' the literary work, and in this reliving both sides of the human personality, the two faculties of reason and emotion, must be fully engaged[64]. We saw how Goethe, in a letter to Rochlitz, envisaged the task of the author being to arouse both emotion and reflection in a wide variety of people. The same coupling occurs in the letter to Zelter where Goethe notes, 'The genuine reader will think or feel all this out again'.

This idea that the work of art is a product of both head and heart and should engage both the emotions and the reason, or sometimes the senses and the reason, of the recipient was of great concern to Goethe from the very beginning of his literary career. It is the theme of his letter of 1772 from Wetzlar to Herder in which he describes how his ideas have been affected by his reading of Pindar[65]. In an essay on 'Kunst und Handwerk', unpublished in his lifetime, he sees his own age as one where the balance between the mind and the senses has been disturbed and suggests that it is this balance which produces the conditions necessary for producing true art[66]. In 'Der Sammler und die Seinigen' it is the interaction between reason and feeling which he stresses:

> But the human being is at the same time both an intellectual and an emotional being. He is a whole, a unity of many, intimately connected powers, and the work of art must speak to this human whole, it must satisfy this diverse unity, this united diversity in him [67].

---

[61] September 2nd 1829. Gräf, 1.2., page 1064.

[62] Letter to Boisserée, September 2nd 1829. Gräf, 1.2, page 1062.

[63] Letter to Zelter 19th October 1821. W.A. 4.35, page 146.

[64] 'So may I indeed suggest and hope that people will want to and will actually relive my writing', Letter to Iken, September 27th 1827. H.A. Letters, Volume 4, page 83.

[65] Letter to Herder, c.10th July 1772. H.A. Letters, Volume 1. In the letter Goethe also attributes his new sense of the interaction of body and soul, mind, emotions and senses to his reading of Herder's 'Fragments' i.e. his writing 'Über die neuere Deutsche Literatur. Erste bis dritte Sammlung von Fragmenten' published in 1767 and in particular III.1.6, 'In literature thought and expresson are like soul and body and can never be separated'. *Herders Sämmtliche Werke*, edited by Suphan, Volume 1, 1877, page 398.

[66] 'Since our century has clarified several things in the intellectual sphere, but is perhaps the least skilled at uniting pure feeling with intellectuality, which is the only means of producing a genuine work of art'. In: 'Kunst und Handwerk', W.A. Volume 47, page 56.

[67] H.A. Volume 12, page 81.

The importance of the interaction of these various aspects of human nature, the intellectual, the emotional and the sensory, is also suggested in Wilhelm's programmatic words in the *Wanderjahre*, 'Ich ging aus, zu schauen und zu denken' [I went out to look and to think] (80-1).

Goethe was always conscious of the fact that, for the public, the content of a literary work was much more important than the form. In *Dichtung und Wahrheit*, when writing about the public reaction to *Werther*, he acknowledges that the public cannot be expected to treat a work of literature as an intellectual exercise, since it is only willing to pay attention to the content and material[68]. On several other occasions, however, he laments the fact that the public are only interested in knowing what is fact and what is fiction in *Werther*[69]. In a series of aphorisms in the 'Maximen und Reflexionen' he regrets this tendency of the public to prefer the What to the How and stresses the importance of the form of a literary work, which is more difficult to comprehend than the content. He posits a progression of difficulty in the constituent elements of a literary work whereby everyone can appreciate the material [Stoff] from which it is fashioned, only some can appreciate its substance [Gehalt] and only the smallest minority are able to appreciate the form[70]. This same idea of the primary importance of the form and treatment in a literary work, as in a work of the visual arts, is at the centre of the discussion outlined in the sixth letter of 'Der Sammler und die Seinigen', where it is argued that in Greek tragedy, as well as in sculptural works such as the Laocoon, the 'unbearable subject matter, unpleasant events' chosen for representation were made endurable only by the form and treatment[71].

When contemplating other branches of the arts and sciences, Goethe is also interested in the relationship between form and content. For mathematics and rhetoric he considers the form to be all-important: 'for both, nothing has value

---

[68] H.A. Volume 9, *Dichtung und Wahrheit*, 3.13, page 590.
[69] Cf. for example .HA. Volume 9, *Dichtung und Wahrheit*, 3.13, page 592; and February 1st 1788, Rome, *Goethe: Italienische Reise*, Frankfurt am Main, 1976, page 681.
[70] H.A. Volume 12, pages 471-2. 'Maximen und Reflexionen', Nos. 753-757.
[71] H.A. Volume 12, page 80.

except the form; the substance is unimportant to them' (308); and he regards music as, perhaps, the highest of the arts: 'because it has no material, which must be taken into account. It is all form and substance and elevates and ennobles everything that it expresses' (290). In the light of this comment it is interesting that music has such a symbolic importance in the *Wanderjahre* and runs as a 'leitmotif' through the whole book.

We have seen how Goethe regarded the literary work, to an extent, as a dialogue between author and reader and how he enjoyed reading his work aloud to a small circle. It will be remembered also that two critics made the comparison between Goethe, ordering and performing his work for the reader, and the Homeric rhapsode, ordering and performing his work for the listener. Furthermore it is known that Goethe's favoured method of work, at least with respect to narrative composition, was dictating to a secretary. One of these secretaries, Schuchardt describes such a dictation session in the following way:

> He [Goethe] spoke with a powerful voice, with dramatic expression and sometimes he really made me jump when, as he was dictating the *Wanderjahre* to me, he performed the roles of the characters with great drama or with emotional intensity. As he did so he seemed totally oblivious both of myself and of his everyday surroundings[72].

In a letter to Zelter Goethe tells an anecdote about the origins of the novella 'Wer ist der Verräter?', 'About a year ago I was telling a little story to my daughter-in-law, as we were sitting by ourselves (...). She begged to read it, but I had to tell her that it only existed in my imagination'. Not until a year later does he begin to make a written version of the story[73]. In the 'Nachträge zur Farbenlehre' he ascribes the genesis of the *Wanderjahre* to the year 1810 when he eventually began to write down several of the little stories which had been giving him pleasure for a long time and which he had often recounted at intimate social gatherings[74]. At the end of the tenth book of *Dichtung und Wahrheit* he describes how he first told the fairytale, 'Die neue Melusine', which years later was to find

---

[72] Gräf, 1.2, page 1024.
[73] 7th June 1820. Gräf, 1.2, page 944.
[74] Gräf, 1.2, page.951.

a place in the *Wanderjahre*, to Friederike Brion and the company of young people gathered at Sesenheim and added this comment:

> If anyone should read this fairy-tale in a printed version in the future and doubt whether it could have had such an effect, let that person remember that the human vocation is actually only to have an effect in the present. Writing is an abuse of language, reading silently to oneself is a wretched surrogate for speech. One human being has an effect on another, if he has an effect at all, through his personality.

The comment raises the whole question of the relationship between the written and the spoken word, between the literary work as performance and as text. The collective, multifarious nature of the literary work calls for a collective, collaborative response, which seeks to recreate for the written text the reception conditions of the spoken performance. Therefore Goethe commends Knebel's reading of the 'Helena' scenes of *Faust II* 'in the company of a friend' as a profitable approach, since a literary work is written for many and is in itself many-facetted[75].

Just as the relationship between the spoken and the written word is of concern to Goethe so also is the relationship between the various branches of the arts. The sixth letter of 'Der Sammler und die Seinigen' takes this as its theme and suggests that 'there is a common denominator in which the influences of all the arts, the literary as well as the visual, come together', and that this 'common denominator' is 'the human soul' since 'art is only created by human beings and for human beings'[76]. In the section of the *Farbenlehre*, 'Konfession des Verfassers' Goethe speaks of the 'Verwandtschaft der Künste' [kinship of the arts].

The paradoxical relatedness and separateness of the various arts is the theme of a series of aphorisms and reflections in the 'Maximen und Reflexionen'[77]. The first of these takes up Schelling's description of architecture as 'erstarrte Musik' [solidified music] and expresses the same idea with a slightly

---

[75] 14th November 1827, W.A. 4. 43, page 167.
[76] H.A. Volume 12, page 81.
[77] Nos. 776-785. A selection of aphorisms on the interrelated characteristics of the various arts is also included in the 'Betrachtungen im Sinne der Wanderer' at the end of Book 2 of the *Wanderjahre.*

different image, describing architecture as 'verstummte Tonkunst' [mute harmonisation]. These two images both go back to the ancient practice of accompanying construction work with music and point to the common characteristic of harmony shared by music and architecture. This theme of the relationship between the arts is also a point of discussion in the *Wanderjahre*. Both in the 'pedagogical province' and in the 'artists' province' the interaction of the arts is regarded from both positive and negative perspectives[78].

'Das Gesicht ist der edelste Sinn' [sight is the noblest of the senses] stresses one of the aphorisms in Makarie's archive. Goethe always attached great value to the organ of sight. He regarded it as spiritual rather than material in essence because, unlike the other senses, it does not function through touch[79]. This accentuation of the visual was the source of a deep interest in the relationship between word and image. In his early days Goethe was as attracted towards the visual arts as he was towards literature and, indeed, he suggested that one of his concerns on his Italian journey was to discover whether his real bent lay in the direction of writing or in the direction of painting. He describes how he taught himself the techniques of literary composition by looking at the techniques of the visual arts[80]. From Rome he wrote, 'The fact that I draw and study art, improves my literary ability rather than hindering it'[81]. Forty years later he described to Eckermann how both his artistic and his scientific studies had helped him in his writing[82].

---

[78] In the 'pedagogical province' the theatre is seen as likely to have a damaging effect on the other arts by the educators; while in the 'artists' province' the interaction between the arts is seen in practice in the scene where the sculptural group acts as inspiration to painter, sculptor, poet and architect alike. At the same time the overseer suggests that the widest gulf lies between poet and sculptor.

[79] 'The other four only instruct us through the organ of touch, we hear, we feel, we smell and taste everything through contact; but sight stands infinitely higher, is refined beyond the material and approaches the capacities of the spirit' (480).

[80] 'To achieve this aim I could turn to nothing better than the visual arts'. H.A. Volume 14, *Farbenlehre* 'Konfession des Verfassers', page 252.

[81] *Italienische Reise*, page 587. Letter from Rome, 21st December 1787.

[82] Eckermann, 18th January 1827, page 198.

He was very conscious of the interdependency of the literary and the visual arts. In the Apollo room of the Villa Aldobrandini he is impressed by the way in which Domenichini has translated the *Metamorphoses* of Ovid into the medium of paint; he describes the way Raphael, in his tapestries, creates 'a whole world' in the manner of an epic or a novel; no doubt thinking primarily of the shield of Achilles, he sees the descriptions of works of the visual arts in the *Iliad* as a sign of its modernity[83]. The interaction of word and image is assigned an important function in the *Wanderjahre*, too, where, as we shall see later, works of the visual arts, such as the picture galleries, the complex sculptural group, the ornate medieval book-cover, stand as metaphors for the novel itself.

Metafictional elements in the earlier novels

> Das ist doch wohl der rechte Roman
> Der selbst Roman spielt?
> *That is surely the proper novel*
> *That plays at being a novel*

When we consider the form and techniques of the *Wanderjahre* we can see that they mark not so much an entirely new departure from Goethe's earlier novel-writing practice, but rather an extreme form of a development which can be traced through all four of the novels. Goethe's lifetime embraced almost a whole century, from 1749 to 1832 - a century in which the political, cultural and economic scene in Europe underwent a far-reaching transformation. It was the age of Enlightenment, of the American Declaration of Independence, of the French Revolution, the end of feudalism and the beginning of industrialisation. The four novels not only provide a literary reflection of an age of radical change - an age which saw the beginning of the processes which moulded the modern age - but also cover in an exemplary manner the whole period of Goethe's literary creativity from its beginnings in the wild excesses of 'Storm and Stress' to its complex and often cryptic post-classical close.

---

[83] H.A. Volume 12, 'Maximen und Reflexionen', Nos. 841, 843 and 837, pages 483-4.

The material for *Werther* is an impossible love-story ending in suicide. As well as handling the problem of unattainable love the novel also represents a powerful criticism of social circumstances. Werther commits suicide not only out of hopeless love for Lotte but also because, as a son of the middle-classes and an aspiring artist, he can find no place for himself either in the developing middle-class society or in the still-powerful feudal society. The work is cast in the form of an epistolary novel, with the innovation that Werther's letters have no replies, thus reducing the essentially dialogic nature of the epistolary novel to a monologue. A certain polyphony is reinstated, however through the device of the framing editorial comment. In *Werther* the author takes on the mantle of editor and publisher, and as well as containing the section 'Der Herausgeber an den Leser' [the editor to the reader] the text is also provided with an editorial foreword and, from time to time, with 'editorial footnotes'; the novel consists in the main of letters, but contains also a translation of *Ossian*, incorporates in part a narrative taken from somebody else's pen - Kestner's report of Jerusalem's suicide - and includes stories, such as that of the 'Bauerbursch' [farmhand] and the 'glückliche Unglückliche' [fortunate unfortunate], which reflect on the main action[84].

In the *Lehrjahre* the hero, Wilhelm, attempts to achieve simultaneously the development of his whole personality and his integration into a rapidly changing society. A wide social panorama is spread before the reader with many economic, social, political and ideological contradictions. The enigmatic Society of the Tower, with its echoes of the freemasons and the illuminati, incorporates a utopian element. It strives for a new social order, which is based on a kind of 'concordia ordinum' - the coming together and co-operation of the middle-classes and the nobility. Both Wilhelm and the Society of the Tower are treated with

[84] In his description of his method of working on *Werther* Goethe also endows the work with a kind of background polyphony in that he says that he talked through the content of each of Werther's letters in his imagination in 'ideal dialogues' with a variety of people of his acquaintance of both sexes, different ages and positions and that their imaginary replies have influenced the composition of the letters and given them their 'varied charm'. H.A. Volume 9, pages 577-8.

gentle irony. In spite of the dominant voice of the narrator the *Lehrjahre* gains a certain polyphony through the inclusion of Wilhelm's narrative of his childhood, the maxims of the Society of the Tower, the poems and songs of Philine, Wilhelm, the harpist and Mignon and one whole book containing 'The confessions of a beautiful soul', based on the life of Susanna von Klettenberg, a friend of Goethe's youth. The end of the novel remains open. Wilhelm has not so much reached an end in his union with Natalie as reached the beginning of a new journey. The problem of the relationship between individual and society is handed over to the reader for further consideration.

The *Wahlverwandtschaften* was originally intended as a novella to be included in the *Wanderjahre* but the compelling material expanded to fill a novel. It is a story of love and passions burning just below the surface of 'civilised' society, performed with dramatic power by only four main characters. Its material is an intricate love-story with a tragic ending. It deals with the problems of marriage and adultery and throws a critical light on a section of the nobility which has retreated into private life and dilettantism. Ambiguity holds sway in this novel also. In the figure of Ottilie co-exist a saint and a girl with all the symptoms of anorexia nervosa. Marriage is treated simultaneously as a sacramental and as a problematical realm. Although its form seems more closed, and this story of a failure in communication and its consequences is told by a narrator whose balanced language and smooth and sophisticated tones seek to harmonise the inharmonious, nevertheless in the *Wahlverwandtschaften* other voices can also be heard: in the dramatic dialogues, in the monologues of Mittler, in the novella, in the various letters and in the extracts from Ottilie's diary. In the *Wanderjahre* this polyphony is taken to an extreme and is intensified by an unreliable narrator who constantly disappoints reader expectations, denies responsibility for what he narrates and slips behind the mask of an editor.

All four novels have in common the demand for a subtle and highly developed reading practice. The problem in all four, although treated in very different ways in each, is the antagonism between the needs of the individual and the demands of society. Through a studied ambiguity Goethe aims at the education of the reader - at the development of a reader who is capable of participating actively in the reproduction of the text, or rather, in the production of a textual meaning.

Die Leiden des jungen Werther

> sie billigt nicht, sie tadelt nicht
> *it neither praises nor blames*

As we have seen Goethe was dismayed by the general public's reception of *Werther*. His dismay and disappointment can be explained by the gap between the author's intentions and the public perception of what the book was about. Already in *Werther* Goethe was aiming at a method of presentation designed to provoke the reader into further thought. This aim, however, was thwarted by material, which, on the level of content, fulfilled the contemporary reader's needs and expectations so thoroughly that it invited the reader to identify with the fate of the protagonist and thus made a critical reading more difficult. In *Dichtung und Wahrheit* Goethe comments on the reception, 'Of course, here again it was the nature of the material that was responsible for its influence'[85].

On the one hand it is true that the 'editor's foreword' appears to call for just such an identification: 'und laß daß Büchlein deinen Freund sein, wenn du aus Geschick oder eigener Schuld keinen nähern finden kannst' [and let this little book be your friend, if through fate or your own fault you can find no closer one]; but on the other hand the text itself criticises such an uncritical method of reading which passively treats the text as a mirror, seeking in it only a reflection of the reader's own ideas, convictions and feelings, rather than actively engaging in a dialogue with the text. Lotte provides an example of just such an uncritical

---

[85] H.A. Volume 9, page 588. He goes on to remark on the distortion which ensues through this kind of 'identificatory' reading where the reader pays attention just to the 'story' level of the text and attempts to read as reality what is presented as fiction and, even worse, attempts to imitate that fiction by shooting himself.

reading practice when she says that her favourite kind of author is one whose work most closely mirrors her own life and circumstances[86].

Werther, too, is an uncritical reader who seeks in his reading matter confirmation rather than challenge. In Homer he sees only a reflection of the patriarchal idyll he has constructed around himself at Wahlheim. He says, 'I need lullabies and I have found them aplenty in my Homer' (10). Later, as his mood darkens, Homer is replaced by Ossian (84) and the optimistic light-filled idyll which he sees in the ancient Greek world is replaced by suffering, death and frustrated love in swirling Celtic mists, but his reading practice does not alter: he is still searching for confirmation of his own feelings and moods in his reading matter[87].

This same passive reading practice, which seeks confirmation and identification in the text, is evident in the use Werther makes of *Emilia Galotti*, a copy of which plays an integral part in his stage-management of his own death: '*Emilia Galotti* lag auf dem Pulte aufgeschlagen' (124) [*Emilia Galotti* lay open on the desk]. Just as readers of *Werther* were to find validation for their own suicidal thoughts, and even suicide attempts, in the book, so Werther, the reader, sees in *Emilia Galotti* a validation of his own decision to kill himself. Although the words quoted above are taken almost word for word from Kestner's account of Jerusalem's suicide, Goethe is also very careful within the text to provide justification for it being *Emilia Galotti* which lay open on Werther's desk. In his account of Jerusalem's suicide Kestner notes that he cannot remember which

---

[86] H.A. Volume 6, *Die Leiden des jungen Werther*, page 23. Page references for *Werther* are from this edition. Lotte herself claims to have advanced in her reading practice and looks back indulgently on the time 'when I could sit in a corner on Sundays and share in the happiness and misfortune of a Miss Jenny with my whole heart'. Her reading practice is still, however uncritical and 'identificatory'.

[87] H.R.Vaget suggests also a very calculated use on Werther's part of the reading of *Ossian* on his last visit to Lotte, in spite of all his tears and identification - a calculated bid to rouse and play upon Lotte's feelings: 'it is the hidden intention of this, in spite of all the tears, very calculated act of reading, also to reveal Lotte's love'. H.R. Vaget, 'Die Leiden des jungen Werthers' in: *Goethes Erzählwerk: Interpretationen*, page 54.

scene of the play lay open, although he is sure that he noticed at the time [88]. This comment of Kestner's finds reflection, too, in Goethe's text. He seems to have two scenes in mind, each of which throws a rather different light on Werther's suicide. On the one hand in Werther's letter of 10th May 1771 there is an allusion to Conti's discussion of the conditions of artistic creativity[89]. If the play lay open at this scene it would suggest suicide as a reaction to frustrated artistic aspirations. On the other hand, if Werther had been reading the closing scenes of the play, it would suggest an identification with the figure of Emilia as a sacrificial victim. The possibility of these two scenes suggests the ambiguity and complexity of the reasons for Werther's suicide and leaves a certain freedom of interpretation to the reader.

Werther invests his death, in his imagination, with all the meaning he could not find in his life. It is a strange, gruesome artistic creation, the product of his frustrated aspirations. In life Werther has failed as an artist - he has an artistic temperament rather than true creativity. The creative power, whose loss he mourns, never went outside the world of his imagination. In death he sees himself achieving the union with Lotte which he could not achieve in life, especially after the kiss which he feels has finally made her his; secondly he sees himself as paying for his sins; and thirdly he sees himself as sacrificing himself for his friends. Just as, imaginatively, Werther invests his death with great meaning, so the actual details are very carefully arranged to reflect this - and one of these details is the pistol which he used: Albert's pistol which had been handed to the

---

[88] Kestner's account of Jerusalem's suicide in: Kurt Rothmann *Erläuterungen und Dokumente zu: Johann Wolfgang Goethe: Die Leiden des jungen Werther*, Stuttgart, 1987, pages 98-106.

[89] 'Now I couldn't draw, not one stroke, and have never been such a great artist as in these moments' (9); and Gotthold Ephraim Lessing *Emilia Galotti*, Stuttgart, 1987, Act 1, Scene 4, pages 7-11. Conti laments the difference between artistic vision and artistic achievement, '- Oh! That we don't paint directly with the eyes! On the long journey from the eye, through the arm into the brush, how much gets lost!' The somewhat bizarre question, '- Or do you think, prince, that Raphael would not have been the greatest painting genius if he had unfortunately been born without hands?' finds an answering echo in Werther's letter and self-appraisal.

servant by Lotte herself[90]. Werther's reading of *Emilia Galotti* seems, therefore, to highlight the elements in Emilia's death which he believes that his own death shares: she too could be said to be dying to pay for her 'sin'; she too could be seen as a sacrificial victim; and she too died at the hands of one who loved her. Built into Werther's death scene, therefore, is an implicit criticism not only of those readers of *Werther* who would read the novel in the same 'identificatory' way as Werther reads *Emilia Galotti* but also of the kind of 'reading', whether of a text or of life itself, which seeks only a mirror of its own experience.

As a writer Werther constructs his own story through the letters from which the novel is composed. He creates this story through reflecting himself, not only in the literature he reads, but also in his reading of nature and in the lives of the people around him, such as the 'farmhand' and the 'fortunate unfortunate', in whose stories he sees a reflection of his own. He does not so much reflect upon himself as reflect himself upon others and others upon himself. This 'repeated reflection' is not solely presented as a negative aspect of Werther's own character, however, but is also a comment on the possibilities and limitations of the way in which we see the world. As a 'true Narcissus' Werther, the aspiring artist, is representative, too, of the artistic condition, which creates worlds of the imagination through a process of self-reflection[91].

Hans Robert Jauß has pointed out that Goethe's presentation of Werther's story, without any authorial comment, was a startling innovation at the time which contradicted the practice of Enlightenment writers such as Rousseau, who tended to include didactic passages and moralising digressions in their novels: a practice which was itself an innovation and which, paradoxically, aimed at making the reader think by telling him what to think. In contrast, Jauß says,

---

[90] For Werther's artistic imagination see *Werther* page 85; for his reaction to the kiss and his sense of paying for his sins and sacrificing himself see pages 117 and 123; and for his thoughts about the pistol see page 121.
[91] 'wahrer Narziß', H.A. Volume 6, *Die Wahlverwandtschaften*, page 270. That it is a process of self-reflection is emphasised in Eduard's next sentence, 'He readily sees reflections of himself everywhere and places himself as a background behind the whole world'. Werther says of himself, 'I turn back into myself and find a world!' (13).

96

Goethe's writing practice in *Werther* presupposes, and indeed demands, a reader whose mature and sophisticated reading practice enables him to read with empathy and yet at the same time to go beyond identification in order to make his own moral and artistic judgements[92].

As mentioned earlier, the vast majority of contemporary readers of *Werther* did not rise to this challenge, but either read the book as a mirror reflection of their own moods and feelings or criticised it as a justification of suicide[93]. Only a small minority was capable of the subtle reading, which Jauß suggests that the novel demanded[94]. Reader reaction moved Goethe to add to the second edition of 1775 a verse with an overt moral injunction to the reader, 'Be a man and do not follow in my footsteps'. When he revised the work in 1782, however, he abandoned the verse and chose, instead, to incorporate alterations in the text itself, making implicit the moral commentary explicitly stated in the 1775 verse. In a letter to Kestner he indicates how he intends to achieve this end. Firstly he plans to alter the presentation of Albert in order to give a clearer signal as to how he is to be understood: the reader will see him from perspectives other than that of the volatile Werther and can therefore avoid accepting Werther's misjudgement of him. Secondly he aims to give the novel an added intensity, a

---

[92] H.R. Jauß, *Ästhetische Erfahrung und literarische Hermeneutik*, Frankfurt am Main 1984, pages 630-31.

[93] As an example of the former is the letter from D.Hartmann to Lavater which begins, 'I've devoured it 10 times. The book will remain my friend', in: P.Müller, *Der junge Goethe im zeitgenössischen Urteil*, Berlin 1969, pages 196-7. An example of the latter is the banning of the sale of *Werther* on pain of a fine of ten thalers by the city council in Leipzig at the request of the theological faculty of the university. In Denmark it was also banned, as a work which 'mocks religion, glosses over vice and can ruin good morals', in: Müller pages 129-30. Many Enlightenment thinkers felt that the book should have had an explicit moral commentary, warning young people against following Werther's example. Lessing, for example, in a letter to Eschenburg, a friend of Jerusalem, demanded that the book should have 'a short dispassionate concluding statement' which would give an explicit moral commentary on the text and make it quite clear to the reader how he was expected to react to Werther's fate. Letter of 26th October 1774, in: Müller, pages 159-60.

[94] E.g. Blanckenburg who wrote, 'The writer is not obliged always to present us with a *moral* ideal' (Müller, page 186); and Wieland who wrote in his review of the book in *der Teutsche Merkur* Weimar, December 1774, 'To justify an individual suicide, and also not to justify it, but only to make him an object of pity, to show from his example that an all too soft heart and an ardent imagination are often very pernicious gifts, does not mean writing a justification of suicide', in: Rothmann, page 133.

heightening of effect, which is also designed as a signal to the reader: the heightening of effect is achieved to a large extent by interlacing through the text the complementary story of the 'farmhand', which reflects many elements of Werther's story and illustrates, in a different way, the excesses to which unbridled indulgence of emotions and passions such as Werther's can lead[95].

Wilhelm Meisters Lehrjahre

eine der incalculabelsten Productionen
one of the most incalculable productions

We have seen (page 90, footnote 84) how Goethe described creating for himself an imaginary ideal audience as he was working on the composition of *Werther*, so that the novel became, in a sense, the product of what he calls these 'ideal dialogues', in spite of its essentially monological form. In the latter half of the 1790s, while he was preparing the *Lehrjahre* for publication and as the successive books appeared in print, Goethe converted these imaginary partners in the dialogue about his work into real partners by conducting 'Werkstattgespräche' [workshop discussions] on the work in progress through an exchange of letters and occasional face-to-face conversations with Schiller[96]. The desired polyphony of reaction was achieved by also drawing into these exchanges contributions from Christian Gottfried Körner and Wilhelm von Humboldt[97].

The productive value for Goethe of this kind of interaction, which creates a dialogue between work and reader even in the process of composition, is clear from the frequent appreciative comments in his letters[98]. Early in 1795 he

---

[95] 'To give it {the novel} a few more turns of the screw', and, 'to present Albert in such a way that the passionate youth may well misjudge him, but the reader will not', Rothmann, page 121.

[96] Cf. Klaus Gille, *'Wilhelm Meister' im Urteil der Zeitgenossen. Ein Beitrag zur Wirkungsgeschichte Goethes*, Assen 1971, pages 9-47.

[97] Even earlier he had already created for himself a dialogic working situation. On December 27th 1784 and 17th November 1785 he wrote to Knebel on this theme with relation to the *Lehrjahre*, Gräf, 1.2, pages 721 & 728. From Rome he wrote on the same theme to Karl August on February 10th 1787, Gräf, 1. 2, page 786.

[98] 'Since I have Herr von Humboldt's opinion as well as yours, I will work on even more diligently and untiringly', Schiller/Goethe Briefwechsel, letter to Schiller 10th December 1794, page 75. On 20th May 1796 he wrote in a similar vein during a stay in Jena when he was able to

98

describes how his discussions with Schiller have given him the courage to work out a schema for the fifth and sixth books and explains the value of a reflection which comes from a different perspective, 'How much more advantageous it is to see oneself reflected in others rather than in oneself'[99]. In June 1796 he outlines the kind of two-stage reading, which he hopes for his manuscript from Schiller, 'First of all read the manuscript with friendly enjoyment and then give it a thorough scrutiny'[100].

Later he suggests that the 'desired involvement' of such a reader as Schiller can reveal to the author more about his own work than he himself was conscious of, 'Keep on making me acquainted with my own work'. In the same letter he describes the kind of 'productive reception', which the exchanges with Schiller represent for him and which has a direct effect upon the work in progress[101]. The effect of Schiller's participation, he suggests, is not only to reveal things about his own work to him, but also to widen his horizons and push him beyond his own limits. At the end of this letter Goethe implies that Schiller's involvement in the work could be even more direct since, 'I need only to insert the contents of your letter in the appropriate places and my work would already be improved'; and goes on to say that, if he himself found it difficult to put the finishing touches to the work, 'I would ask you [to do so] with a few bold brush-strokes'[102].

Finally, however, Goethe makes it clear that this kind of productive reception can only be taken so far and that the writer must be free to follow his own creative drive and principles. On the 10th August 1796 he wrote to Schiller, 'I would almost like to send the work to the printer without showing it to you again. It is because of the difference in our natures, that it can never completely

---

discuss the work with Schiller in person. Schiller/Goethe Briefwechsel, page 200.
[99] Schiller/Goethe Briefwechsel, letter to Schiller of 18th February 1795, pages 85-6.
[100] Schiller/Goethe Briefwechsel, letter to Schiller of 25th June 1796, page 213.
[101] Schiller/Goethe Briefwechsel, letter to Schiller of 7th July 1796, page 235.
[102] Schiller/Goethe Briefwechsel, letter to Schiller of 9th July 1796, pages 242 -3.

satisfy your demands'[103]. Already in the letter of 9th July he was intimating that certain characteristics of the work which Schiller pinpointed as faults were a natural result of his own particular type of creativity, 'The fault, which you rightly point out, comes from my deepest nature, from a certain realistic quirk ['einem gewissen realistischen Tic'] which makes me feel comfortable when I conceal my person, my actions and my writings from people'. The 'realistic quirk' which he alludes to here is, in fact, the very medium of his creativity, the veiled and ambiguous presentation in which nothing 'is fully expressed' [rein ausgesprochen wird], a presentation which imitates the ambiguity of life itself and which leaves much to the reader's interpretative skills.

Schiller, von Humboldt and Körner were all agreed that the *Lehrjahre* demanded a reader whose reception of the work was productive and active. In a long letter to Schiller on the *Lehrjahre*, which was published in the 8th volume of the *Horen*, Körner touches on the ambiguity of presentation requiring active participation from the reader[104]. Writing to Goethe at the end of the same month von Humboldt notes with approval the demands made on the reader for a productive reception of the work[105]. Schiller, too, in discussing the presentation of Lothario comments on the necessity of productive reading in the interpretation of this character[106]. He is, however, in general, uneasy about the lack of guidance to the reader and suggests to Goethe that he should not be surprised, 'if there are only a few who have the ability and the skill to understand you'[107]. Like the Enlightenment critics of *Werther* he would prefer more explicit guidance to be given to the reader on how he should interpret the work. In his comments on Book 8 he contrasts Goethe's method of making such guidance implicit in the text

---

[103] Schiller/Goethe Briefwechsel, letters to Schiller of 10th August 1796, pages 271-2 and 9th July, page 242. Goethe reminisces on this period of collaboration with Schiller and on their differences of character in conversation with Eckermann in 1829. Eckermann, 23rd March 1829, page 308.
[104] Körner to Schiller, 5th November 1796. Gräf. 1.2, page 861.
[105] Wilhelm von Humboldt to Goethe, 24th November 1796. Gräf, 1.2, pages 870-1.
[106] Schiller/Goethe Briefwechsel, Schiller to Goethe, 3rd July 1796, page 226.
[107] Schiller/Goethe Briefwechsel, Schiller to Goethe, 2nd July 1796, page 224.

with a more overt form of direction and suggests that the figure of the Abbé might be used for this purpose[108]. Strewn throughout his letters about the *Lehrjahre* are suggestions about where explicit direction to the reader could be given. In the letter of July 8th he wishes there had been a more satisfying exposition of the 'poetic necessity' of the Society of the Tower. In discussing Book 7 he suggests that Jarno, too, is a useful figure for giving explicit direction both to Wilhelm and to the reader[109].

His somewhat conflicting attitude towards the reader - or at least his perception of the difference between the real and the ideal reader - is apparent in his response to Goethe's claim that it is his 'realistic quirk' which impels him to guide the reader through the text by implication rather than by explication. Schiller agrees that explicit commentary only makes it easy for the reader and ideally he should be encouraged towards independence by being thrown on his own resources to interpret the text[110]. Goethe, for his part, recognises the dangers of implicit interpretative direction being completely overlooked by the majority of readers. With regard to the 'Confessions of a Beautiful Soul' in the sixth book he fears that the lack of explicit direction to the reader has weakened the effect of the text on the public[111].

It is clear, however, from Goethe's reaction to Körner's comments on the *Lehrjahre*, that he considered it of the highest importance to foster an active, productive response on the part of the reader. He characterises Körner's own productive reading practice in the following way, 'He deconstructs [dekomponiert] (...) the work, in order to put it together again in his own way'. He deplores the many examples he has experienced of a passive reading practice, where the reader contents himself with repeating the refrain: '*ich kanns zu Kopf nicht bringen!*' [I can't get my head round it]. His reaction is to insist that a work

---

[108] 'As indeed it has happened *implicitly*, but not *explicitly*', Schiller/Goethe Briefwechsel, Schiller to Goethe, 8th July 1796, page 238.
[109] Schiller/Goethe Briefwechsel, Schiller to Goethe, 9th July 1796, page 250.
[110] Schiller/Goethe Briefwechsel, Schiller to Goethe, 9th July 1796, page 245.
[111] Schiller/Goethe Briefwechsel, Goethe to Schiller, 18th August 1795, page 129.

of art demands a response from the whole personality, heart as well as head: 'of course the head can only understand a work of art in conjunction with the heart'[112].

The response of the majority of early readers and critics of the *Lehrjahre* endorsed only too well Schiller's view, 'that there are only a few who have the capacity (…) to understand you'. At the end of 1796 Goethe complained to Meyer about the incoherence and disjointedness of the early verdicts on the book[113]. Some readers followed the path of the early *Werther* reception and were interested in seeking out the truth behind the fiction[114]. The critics generally seemed unable to go beyond a consideration of the content of the work and were willing to take everything at face value. Many overlooked the way in which Wilhelm's long-winded description of his passion for the puppet-theatre was ironised by Mariane's falling asleep in the midst of it and condemned the description as lacking in artistry. The critics scanned the pages for overt didactic elements and believed they had found them in the reflections of the narrator, or even in the reflections of Wilhelm himself, of whom one critic enthused, 'His words are golden'[115]. Others confused the artistic and the moral and condemned the work artistically because of the dubious morals of some of its characters[116]. Jacobi's confession to Goethe that his comments on the last volume of the work are based, not on his own close reading, but on his having listened to it being read

---

[112] Schiller/Goethe Briefwechsel, Goethe to Schiller, 19th November 1796, page 314.

[113] 'And so there is again no bounds to the fragmented verdict after the completion of my novel. You sometimes think you hear the sand at the seaside talking'. Letter from Goethe to Meyer, 5th December 1796. Gräf, 1.2, page 872.

[114] Knebel, for example, wrote to Goethe asking, 'whether anything which actually happened inspired you to write the story of Mignon and her parents?' Letter from Knebel to Goethe of 1st November 1796, Gräf, 1.2, page 854; while Wieland commented on Book 6, 'The confessions of the beautiful soul (...) are from a deceased lady which Goethe just tailored to his own style. You can see the strangeness in every word. Goethe is simply absent from the manuscript'. Conversation with Wieland, November 1795. Gräf, 1.2, page 786.

[115] F.L.W.Meyer in the *Berlinisches Archiv*, in: Gille, pages 89-90.

[116] An example of this kind of criticism comes from Georg Sartorius, History professor in Göttingen, writing in the *Göttingischen Anzeigen von gelehrten Sachen*, who comments thus on the play-actors, 'The sentiments of the troupe of players are never completely pure and natural. This disturbs the reader especially when he remembers what great skill the writer possesses to sketch pure and innocent hearts', in: Gille, page 88.

to him once, become for Goethe a kind of metaphor for the superficial and passive reader, or mis-reader, of his work. His reply to Jacobi makes it clear that nothing less than full, concentrated attention is necessary for the appreciation of a work of art:

> You tell me that you have listened to the fourth volume of my novel with one ear and not entirely to your satisfaction. Heaven grant that it will get a better reception if you should happen to let it take the stage before both your ears, or perhaps, before both your eyes.

This image of the mis-reader remained long in Goethe's psyche so that even as late as 1828 he was referring to Jacobi, in a letter to Boisserée, as the man, 'who believes that you can see better with one eye that with two'[117].

On the other hand, the reviewer in the *Neue Leipziger gelehrte Anzeigen* points out that the book, which he feels may well be Goethe's best work, demands active productive readers, who do not just seek reflections of themselves and their own proclivities in a work of art[118]. And Karl Morgenstern, the professor of aesthetics who later coined the term 'Bildungsroman', in a letter in the *Neue Bibliothek der Schönen Wissenschaften* of 28th August 1795, condemned those critics who were disappointed that Goethe had not offered them 'a second *Werther*' and was one of the first to use the image of Proteus, the Shape-changer, to describe Goethe as an artist and the great diversity of his work[119].

Schiller's oft-quoted formula for Wilhelm's development during the course of the novel: 'er tritt von einem leeren und unbestimmten Ideal in ein bestimmtes, tätiges Leben, aber ohne die idealisierende Kraft dabei einzubüßen' [he steps from an empty and vague ideal into a well-defined, active life, but without giving up the strength of his ideals], has had great influence on the reception of the novel as the exemplary 'Bildungsroman'; the exemplification, in

---

[117] Jacobi's letter to Goethe, 9th November 1796, Gräf, 1.2., page 852-3. Goethe's reply, 26th December 1796, Gräf, 1.2, pages 874-5. Goethe's letter to Boisserée, H.A. Letters 4, page 271.

[118] *Neue Leipziger gelehrte Anzeigen* 1795, page 188, in: Gille, page 83.

[119] 'The great artist breaks the mould after the creation of his magnificent work of art: too proud to produce the same or even something similar twice. Goethe in particular is a Proteus who takes pleasure in the perpetual change of the most varied and diverse shapes', in: *Goethe im Urtheile seiner Zeitgenossen*, edited by Julius W. Braun, 3 volumes, Hildesheim 1969 (Reprographischer Nachdruck der Ausgabe Berlin 1883) Volume 2, page 244.

fact, of Blanckenburg's stricture that 'the essential characteristic of a novel' should be the 'inner history' of the hero[120].

Other comments of Schiller, however, suggest that his view of Wilhelm and his place in the novel was rather less straightforward. He says that Wilhelm is not the most important character in the novel, that one of the peculiarities of the novel is precisely the fact that it neither has nor needs any such central character, and continues, '*An* ihm und *um* ihn geschieht alles aber nicht eigentlich *seinetwegen*' [everything happens to him and because of him but not really for his sake][121]. In making this point Schiller sees himself as contradicting Körner who, he feels, 'has regarded this character too much as the actual hero of the novel: the title and the old custom of considering a hero a necessity in every novel have led him astray'. Körner did, indeed, suggest that the novel's central concern is 'the education of a human being' but he, too, says that 'no *single* character should hold the attention' [122]. His description of Wilhelm as 'a kind of hermaphrodite' has been taken to suggest that he is interpreting Wilhelm according to von Humboldt's criteria in his essay 'Über männliche und weibliche Form' as the 'Ideal reiner Menschheit' [ideal of pure humanity], which von Humboldt describes as 'the figure of (...) a pure being beyond all sexual characteristics'[123]. It could, however, along with the words which precede this image, 'eine mittlere Natur' [an intermediary nature], be taken to suggest that the Wilhelm of the *Lehrjahre* is already to be regarded as a mediator, a figure who encompasses all

---

[120] Friedrich von Blanckenburg, *Versuch über den Roman* (Faksimiledruck der Originalausgabe von 1774), Stuttgart 1965 (=Sammlung Metzler 39), page 392. This conception of the *Lehrjahre* seems also to lie behind Hegel's well-known description of 'das Romanhafte', [the nature of the novel] in his *Aesthetics*. G.W.F. Hegel, *Ästhetik I & II*, Stuttgart 1971, page 659

[121] Schiller/Goethe Briefwechsel, letter from Schiller to Goethe of 28th November 1796, page 319. This idea was taken up by Thomas Mann in his preface to the *Zauberberg*, where he writes, 'The story of Hans Castorps, which we wish to tell, - not for his sake (...), but for the sake of the story (...)'.

[122] This view of the *Lehrjahre* seems to lie behind another definition of the novel by Hegel in *Ästhetik III*, which would also fit the *Wanderjahre*: 'here begins again the wealth and variety of concerns, circumstances, characters, conditions, the broad background of a complete world and also the epic presentation of events'. G.W.F. Hegel, *Ästhetik III*, Stuttgart 1971, page 177.

[123] Gille, page 36.

characteristics within himself, an image of the approach necessary for both writer and reader.

Schiller himself expresses a similar view of Wilhelm when he suggests that part of his function is to give the reader pause for thought and reflection - a quite different interpretation of Wilhelm's 'tendency towards reflection' from that of the early critics who saw in Wilhelm's 'golden' words a didactic element that the reader should take at face value. Here Schiller is attributing to Wilhelm a function very similar to that which we shall see the Wilhelm of the *Wanderjahre* fulfilling: namely acting as a guide to the reader through the text by displaying his own uncertainties and indicating where the reader should pause and think by his own pauses for reflection[124]. That such a role is also Goethe's intention for Wilhelm seems to be suggested by his comments to Kanzler von Müller, firstly where he endorses Schiller's comparison of Wilhelm to 'Gilblas' [sic] and secondly where he describes Wilhelm as 'ein armer Hund' [a poor soul][125].

It seems clear that the view of the *Lehrjahre* shared by all the participants in the 'workshop discussions' with Goethe is closer to what Jean Paul later defined as the 'epic' novel which aims to represent 'die stehende Sichtbarkeit der Welt' [the everyday reality of the world], rather than the 'dramatic novel' which centres on the development of character[126]. Körner says of the novel, 'I see in the *Meister* a world in miniature'; Schiller praises 'the lovely life, the simple abundance of this work'. Von Humboldt, too, sees the novel not as one with a traditional hero, but as one which attempts to present a world in all its complexity, in which Goethe 'portrays the world and life, just as it is, absolutely independent of a particular individual character and precisely because of that open to every

---

[124] 'The reader too needs him [Wilhelm]. His tendency to reflect stops the reader during the most rapid advances in the action and obliges him always to look backwards and forwards and to think about everything that happens'. Schiller/Goethe Briefwechsel, letter from Schiller to Goethe of 5th July 1796, page 229.

[125] To Kanzler von Müller on 29th May 1814, Gräf, 1.2, page 824; and on 22nd January 1821, Gräf, 1.2, pages 953-4.

[126] Jean Paul *Vorschule der Ästhetik*, Hamburg, 1990, pages 251-2. It is also closer to the second definition of the novel by Hegel, where he also aligns it with the epic in attempting to present a total world in all its complexity. G.W.F. Hegel, *Ästhetik III*, page 178.

individual character'[127]. These comments find an echo in Goethe's own later description of the *Wanderjahre*, 'Mit solchem Büchlein ist es wie mit dem Leben selbst' [with such a book it is the same as with life itself][128].

In this context it is interesting, too, that images used by Schiller and Körner to describe the *Lehrjahre* become structuring principles and metaphors for the *Wanderjahre*. Schiller says of the *Lehrjahre*, 'It appears like a beautiful planetary system, everything belongs together, and only the Italian figures, like comets and just as eerie as these phenomena, connect the system to a more distant and greater one'; and in the *Wanderjahre* the planetary system and the individual's relationship to it is one of the great structuring principles of the work. Körner writes, 'All that is worth representing in human nature is merged together here into a vast picture cycle'; and this image becomes, in the *Wanderjahre* (as we shall see in Chapter 3), a metaphor for the technique of the text's construction - the 'cycle of pictures' becomes a series of picture galleries in which every picture can both stand for itself and also offer comment and reflection on all the other pictures.

Friedrich Schlegel's definition of the novel as genre was 'a romantic book' and for him the romantic element was the equivalent of universal - so that romantic literature becomes 'a progressive universal poetry' which unites within itself 'all the separate literary genres' and can embrace everything, both poetic and prosaic, expressed by the written word[129]. What he expected from the novel was exactly this idea that it should be a 'mirror of the whole surrounding world, a picture of the age'. Moreover he claimed that 'the romantic way of writing (...) is always in the process of becoming, can never be completed'; a concept of the novel which is very close to Goethe's aim for the *Wanderjahre*, that it should

---

[127] Letter of Körner to Schiller of 28th October 1796. Gräf page 857; Letter from Schiller to Goethe of 2nd July 1796, Schiller/Goethe Briefwechsel page 220; Letter of 24th November 1796 from Wilhelm von Humboldt to Goethe. Gräf 1.2, page 870.
[128] Letter to Rochlitz of 23rd November 1829. Gräf 1. 2, page 1065.
[129] Friedrich Schlegel, *Kritische und Theoretische Schriften* 'Gespräch über die Poesie', Stuttgart 1978, page 209.

serve as an analogy for 'die Unendlichkeit des Lebens selbst' [the boundlessness of life itself][130].

Schlegel was already interpreting the *Lehrjahre* according to this concept. For him, even more than for Schiller, Körner and von Humboldt, the striking characteristic of the *Lehrjahre* is the replacement of the central hero by a multiplicity of figures[131]. Schlegel also sees already in the *Lehrjahre* exactly that kind of 'zarte Empirie' [subtle practice] characteristic of the *Wanderjahre*, by which the novel itself becomes also a discourse on the novel, a theory of the novel. In his 'Brief über den Roman' he writes that 'such a theory of the novel would itself have to be a novel'[132]. The *Lehrjahre* itself he describes as 'this poetic physics of literature' and writes that 'it was very much the intention of the writer to draw up a comprehensive artistic theory, or rather to depict it in vivid individual instances and viewpoints'[133].

Schlegel picks out in particular the discussions on the staging of *Hamlet* in Book 5 of the *Lehrjahre* to illustrate the way in which the work is at once a novel and a discourse on the nature of the novel. He traces how the reader and Wilhelm are involved throughout the novel in a consideration of artistic practice and theory: 'from the basic perceptions of the rudiments of literature with which the first volume confronts Wilhelm and the reader, to the point where the human being becomes capable of understanding the highest and deepest things'. In the *Hamlet* discussions he sees the culminating instance of this procedure: it is a retarding moment, both a reflection in miniature of the constant retarding impulse of the novel itself which is always attempting to make the reader pause and think, and itself a work which shares this concern to encourage an active, thinking public[134].

---

[130] Schlegel, 'Athenäum-Fragmente', page 90.
[131] 'Firstly that the individuality which appears in it is broken up into different rays of light, divided among several characters', Schlegel, 'Gespräch über die Poesie', 'Versuch über den verschiedenen Styl in Goethes früheren und späteren Werken', page 219.
[132] Schlegel, 'Brief über den Roman', page 211.
[133] Schlegel, 'Über Goethes Meister', page 149.
[134] Schlegel, 'Über Goethes Meister', page 157.

Throughout the novel there are 'retarding moments' such as this, which are designed to stimulate an active participation in the interpretation of the text on the part of the reader, to suggest that the act of reading offers the possibility of a dialogue between reader, writer and text. In Book 1, Chapter 17 Wilhelm discusses his grandfather's paintings with the, as yet unknown, stranger and explains the reasons why he was so attracted to his favourite painting of the 'kranke[n] Königssohn' [the king's ailing son]. Here Wilhelm represents the totally subjective 'reader', such a reader as we have seen already represented by Werther and Lotte, who seeks in a work of art only a reflection and confirmation of his own ideas and feelings. He begins, 'It is the subject which appeals to me in a painting, not the technique'. The stranger's reply to his description of the way in which the painting affected him as a child is, in effect, a criticism of this subjective way of responding to works of art and an indication to the reader as to how he should be responding to the literary work in his hands:

"These feelings are naturally very far from those methods which a connoisseur usually employs to look at the works of the great masters; but probably if the collection had remained in the possession of your family, you would gradually have developed an understanding for the works themselves, so that you did not just always see yourself and your own predilections in the works of art"[135].

In Book 5, Chapter 7 the narrator summarises a discussion between Wilhelm, Serlo and the theatre company on the differences between the novel and the drama without attributing any particular viewpoint to any particular character. His summary of the discussion is, in essence, a description of Wilhelm's role in the *Lehrjahre*. A contrast is drawn between the protagonist in a novel and the hero of a play. The former are expected to be 'leidend' [passive or suffering], whereas from the latter effective action is demanded (307). Since 'the personality of the protagonist must, in whatever way it might be, slow down the development of the action', protagonists in novels, such as, for example, Grandison, Pamela or the Vicar of Wakefield are not so much 'passive' or 'suffering' figures as

---

[135] Goethe, J.W., *Wilhelm Meisters Lehrjahre* H.A. Volume 7, page 70. Page references to the *Lehrjahre* are to this edition.

108

'retardierende Personen' [retarding characters]. Here Wilhelm, the protagonist in the *Lehrjahre*, is made a participant in a discussion which presents a faithful reflection of his own role in the novel and the parallel is drawn with Hamlet, whose characteristics as a hero make the play a suitable analogy for the novel: 'the hero, it was said, is really just made up of convictions; and he is just driven on by events, and therefore the play has something of the protractedness of a novel' (307-8).

In the same chapter Serlo's comments on the talents necessary for, and the task confronting, the actor as mediator between audience and work, reflect also the skills required of both the reader, as interpreter, and the writer, as first producer: 'however easy it may be to set people's imagination in motion, however ready they are to have fairytales told to them, it is nevertheless very rare to find anyone with a kind of productive imagination'. This 'productive imagination' would enable both reader and writer to identify completely with the Other who is represented in the text, rather than merely seeking feelings and ideas similar to their own in that figure; not to make the unfamiliar familiar, but rather to grasp it in all its unfamiliarity. It would enable, therefore, an objective rather than a subjective representation or reading. The result of this 'inner truth of representational skill' would be a fictional truth: 'diese erlogene Wahrheit, die ganz allein Wirkung hervorbringt' [this fabricated truth without which nothing is really effective'] (309-10).

In the following chapter there is a meta-textual element in the form of the 'Theaterfreunde' [theatre-lovers], the description of whose role in the preparations for the performance of *Hamlet* is analogous to the role assigned by Goethe to Schiller, Körner and von Humboldt, the participants in the 'workshop discussions', during the composition of the *Lehrjahre*. Of the 'theatre-lovers' we are told that they were just the kind of enthusiasts an artist would wish for. They present the writer with an ideal audience or an ideal 'readership' as they involve themselves in the production of the work in progress. They are not always in agreement with the writer about his work but their comments represent for him a fruitful exchange during the very processes of production[136].

In Book 8, Chapter 3 there is an example of the way in which a dialogue between text-producer and text-recipient may be incorporated within the text. Goethe thematises an earlier reservation which von Humboldt has expressed about the appropriateness of the epithet 'schöne Seele' [beautiful soul] to describe the 'Stiftsdame' [canoness] of Book 6, using Natalie as his text-internal spokesperson to give an answer to von Humboldt's text-external criticism. Natalie tells Wilhelm that he is 'fairer, yes I may well say more just towards this fine character than some others who have been shown this manuscript': a comment which can convincingly be taken as a covert reference to von Humboldt's privileged view of the manuscript of the *Lehrjahre*. Natalie then continues with a defence of her aunt against the very criticisms, which von Humboldt had levelled against her:

> And yet if a fine nature is far too sensitive and conscientious in its self-formation, there seems to be no tolerance, no forbearance in the world for it. Nevertheless people of this kind are exemplary figures for us in the external world, similar to the ideals in our minds, not to imitate but to emulate (518).

It is a defence which recognises, but makes allowance for, human frailty and indicates that Goethe is not intent on creating patterns of human perfection but in delineating human nature in all its strength and all its fallibility[137].

We have already seen how, in the discussions of *Hamlet*, Goethe has embedded into his text a miniature reflection of the text itself and has set up an analogy between the play and his novel: the analogy that Schlegel described thus, 'Through its tendency to delay the play bears a very close resemblance to the novel whose very essence is delay'. At another point in the text there is a striking image for the novel itself, anticipating even more closely a practice which would become much more pronounced in the *Wanderjahre*. We will see later how the

---

[136] 'They were (...) not in agreement with Wilhelm on every passage; now and then he gave way, but mostly he asserted his own opinion, and on the whole this discussion was very useful to him in the formation of his taste' (310-3)
[137] Cf. Gille, pages 48-50.

image of the picture gallery occurs repeatedly in the *Wanderjahre* as an image for the text itself. In the *Lehrjahre* the uncle's mausoleum constitutes just such a picture gallery, an analogy for the novel itself. The motto of this house of death is *'Gedenke zu leben!' [Choose life!]*; and it is life itself, in all its variety, which the early readers of the *Lehrjahre* like Schiller, Schlegel and Schelling suggested it presented. The novel purports to be a 'mirror of the world' and that is exactly what the picture gallery in the uncle's mausoleum is. But Goethe is careful to point out that here is no haphazard and unplanned reflection of life. Both mausoleum and novel are artistic constructs whose 'erlogene Wahrheit' [fabricated truth] depends on very carefully planned artistic effects. What he writes about the 'Saal der Vergangenheit' [hall of the past] represents his aspiration for the novel itself:

> And certainly if we could describe how felicitously everything was arranged, how there and then everything appeared precisely as it should and no other way, through relationship or contrast, through colourfulness or colour harmony, and produced an effect as complete as it was distinct, we would transport the reader to a place which he would not wish to leave for a long time[138].

Die Wahlverwandtschaften

dieses offenbare Geheimnis
this open secret

During the composition of the *Wahlverwandtschaften* Goethe also followed the practice of drawing others into a dialogue with his work in progress by reading aloud from the manuscript or freely narrating portions of the work to individuals or to a small group of friends and acquaintances. A diary entry for 1st May 1808, before work had begun on the written version, records that he told the first half of the *Wahlverwandtschaften* to Counsellor Meyer during a coach

---

[138] 'Und gewiß, könnten wir beschreiben, wie glücklich alles eingeteilt war, wie an Ort und Stelle durch Verbindung oder Gegensatz, durch Einfärbigkeit oder Buntheit alles bestimmt, so und nicht anders erschien, als es erscheinen sollte, und eine so vollkommene als deutliche Wirkung hervorbrachte, so würden wir den Leser an einen Ort versetzen, von dem er sich so bald nicht zu entfernen wünschte' (553).

journey between Jena and Weimar[139]. In Carlsbad on 24th and 25th of July of the same year, as he was working on the last chapter of the work, Goethe records reading sections of it to Marianne von Eybenberg[140]. In Weimar on 18th April of the following year he notes that he read from the *Wahlverwandtschaften* at court. On 15th September 1809 he sent his wife Christiane a packet from Jena containing the first part of the novel with strict instructions that it should be read in secrecy 'behind closed doors' by the family and that they should inform him of their reactions as soon as possible[141].

His preferred method of committing the text to paper - dictating to his secretary Riemer - also fostered this sense of the work materialising as the product of a dialogue. Riemer describes himself as 'not only a witness, but also an assistant' during the first period of composition in the summer of 1808 in Carlsbad. He emphasises his own involvement with the fictional characters, 'One lived and associated with these invented characters of the imagination, as though they were real'; and describes finding real models for the various characters among the visitors to the spa[142].

The published book, Goethe suggests, is a means of communication with his friends: a category apparently including all those whose open-mindedness and receptivity enable them to respond with sensitivity to the subtleties of the work. To Zelter he wrote in June 1809, in anticipation of the novel's publication, 'I'll probably be able to bring it out during this present year and I'm in all the more hurry to do so, because it is a means of communicating fully once more with my friends in other places'[143]. In a letter accompanying a copy of the newly published novel he writes to Reinhard, 'I actually sent the *Wahlverwandtschaften* as a circular to my friends in order that they should think of me once again wherever they were'. His eagerness to solicit a response to the work is also clear in this

[139] Gräf 1.1, page 365, No. 644.
[140] Gräf 1.1, page 370, Nos. 671 and 672.
[141] Gräf 1.1, page 400, No. 807.
[142] Gräf 1.1, page 366.
[143] Gräf 1.1, page 382, No. 720.

letter, which continues, 'And be so kind as to assure me expressly that I have not made a mistake'[144]. A similar request for a response had already been sent to Rochlitz shortly before the publication date[145]. In a later letter to Rochlitz one can see the clear distinction which Goethe makes between the 'ordinary reader', who does not notice deficiencies in a literary work, and the 'discerning reader', who, 'precisely by making the demands, augments and completes the work for himself'[146]. Again, the emphasis here is on the active and productive participation of the reader.

Goethe repeatedly comments on the inability of the general public to respond adequately to a complex work of art. Just before the publication of the *Wahlverwandtschaften* he wrote to C.G.Voigt, 'Seldom in the world is something received as it is given: unless it is the daily bread from the bakery'[147]. In his diary Riemer refers to 'philistine reviews of the *Wahlverwandtschaften*' and later mentions 'all kinds of nonsense from philistines about the *Wahlverwandtschaften*', which had been reported by Frommann[148]. In November 1809 Goethe writes to thank Charlotte von Schiller for her comments on the novel at a time 'when a lot of nonsense about my work is coming through to me in my hermit's cell'. The following month he tells Marianne von Eybenberg that he is working on the *Farbenlehre* 'while my dear fellowcountrymen struggle to develop an understanding of the *Wahlverwandtschaften* and yet don't quite know how they should begin'[149]. In the letter to Reinhard quoted above he characterises 'the public' as 'a crazy caricature of the *demos*', which sets itself up as an arbiter

[144] Letter of 21st December 1809. Gräf 1.1, page 428, No.863.
[145] Letter to Rochlitz of 28th September 1809. Gräf 1.1, page 404, No.826. Indeed Goethe finishes his sentence with the suggestion that Rochlitz write a review of the work, 'and if it suited you, in print', but, although Rochlitz sent Goethe a letter containing detailed comments on the novel, he was reluctant to write a full-scale review for publication.
[146] Letter of 15th November 1809. Gräf 1.1, page 422, No.854.
[147] Letter of 26th September 1809 to C.G. Voigt, Gräf 1.1, page 403, No. 822.
[148] To Riemer, December 1809, Gräf 1.1, page 427, No. 861; and diary entry for 28th January 1810, page 447.
[149] Letter to Charlotte von Schiller of 24th November 1809, Gräf 1.1, page 425, No.839; and letter to Marianne von Eybenberg of 21st December 1809, Gräf 1.1, page 428, No.862. Marianne von Eybenberg corroborates Goethe's view, 'Never have I heard people speak so enthusiastically, so astutely and so nonsensically and absurdly about anything as about this novel', page 428.

'im Leben und Lesen' [in life and in literature] and attempts to make judgements without the necessary competence to do so. He goes on, however, to suggest more optimistically that the novel is merely ahead of its time and that in a few years a wider audience will be equipped to appreciate its complexities[150].

A striking example of a reading, which overlooks the subtleties and ambiguities of the text, is contained in a letter from Zacharias Werner to Goethe. Werner describes how his conversion to Catholicism came about through reading the *Wahlverwandtschaften*. He singles out a passage in Part Two, Chapter 15 which says of Ottilie, 'only on the condition of a total renunciation had Ottilie forgiven herself, only this condition was mandatory for the whole of the rest of her life'. These words he describes as 'dictated to your pen by the Holy Spirit', as 'illuminated eternal words' and claims that 'it is these words (...) that have made me Catholic'[151] - a truly arresting illustration of a one-sided reading which converts a subtly suggestive text into an overtly didactic piece of work.

Shortly after the novel's publication the old question, which had pursued Goethe in relation to *Werther*, was also raised in connection with the *Wahlverwandtschaften*: 'whether the *Wahlverwandtschaften* is true, whether it is based on fact?' Goethe's answer stresses the importance for him of direct experience as the basis for his art but draws a careful distinction between factual truth and artistic truth, 'Every literary work that does not exaggerate is true and everything that makes a deep lasting impression, is not exaggerated'[152]. Twenty years later Eckermann reported two conversations with Goethe, in February 1829 and February 1830, about the *Wahlverwandtschaften* touching on the same theme. Here, too, Goethe highlights the synthesis of 'poetry and truth' constituting a

---

[150] Letter to Reinhard of 31st December 1809. Gräf 1.1, page 429, No.863.
[151] Letter from Werner to Goethe of 23rd April 1811, four days after his conversion, Gräf 1.1, page 409-10, footnote 1.
[152] Gräf 1.1, page 434, No. 865a, Gespräche 2, 292 - Mit einem Unbekannten [with an unknown person]

literary text: 'he said of his *Wahlverwandtschaften*, that it contains no stroke that had not been experienced, but no stroke exactly as it was experienced'[153].

In the first of these conversations Goethe also underlines the necessity for close and repeated reading of a complex literary text by saying, 'And more has been put into it than anyone is capable of taking in at a first reading' - a point which he also reiterated in connection with the *Wanderjahre*[154]. In the letter to Zelter of 1st June 1809, which was mentioned earlier, he writes, 'I have put a lot into it, hidden some things in it', and uses a favourite paradoxical phrase – 'dieses offenbare Geheimnis' [this open secret] - to characterise a work whose enigmatic nature is designed to present a challenge to the reader[155]. This same idea of the literary work as an enigma which challenges the reader and demands attentive reading is repeated in a letter to the publisher, Cotta, at the time of publication, 'There are a good many things put into it, which I hope will challenge the reader to repeated perusal'[156].

In the case of the *Wahlverwandtschaften,* too, Goethe alludes to the idea that for the artist, as well, his creation may contain more than he consciously put into it or may grow beyond the boundaries he has set for it. From its beginnings as a novella to be included in the *Wanderjahre* it expanded and seemed to take on a life of its own: 'such a work (...) grows under one's hands and imposes on one the necessity of summoning up all one's strength in order to remain master of it and to complete it'[157]. This sense of the work of art going beyond its creator's

---

[153] To Eckermann, February 17th 1830, Gräf 1.1, page 487, No.908. Cf. also to Eckermann, 9th February 1829, page 485, No.906.
[154] Gräf 1.1, page 485, No.906. In a letter to his daughter, Wieland reports Goethe's stricture that the book should be read three times, Gräf 1.1, page 422, No.855a; and it seems likely that Goethe had made a similar comment to Marianne von Eybenberg, since she wrote to him on 24th February 1810, 'And with what pleasure I read this interesting product again for the third time', Gräf 1.1, page 428, footnote 2.
[155] In a later letter to Zelter of 26th August 1809 he uses the image of a veil to express the enigmatic form and the different levels of inscrutability of the work: 'I am convinced that the transparent and opaque veil will not hinder you from seeing right through to the form which is actually intended'. Gräf 1.1, page 393, No.777.
[156] Letter to Cotta of 1st October 1809. Gräf 1.1, page 407, No.833.
[157] The first quotation is from the *Tag- und Jahreshefte* for 1807. W.A. 36, page 28. The second is from a conversation with Abeken of 27th March 1810. Gräf 1.1, page 453, No. 871.

conscious intentions is expressed in a letter to Bettina Brentano at the time of publication, where he writes, 'I cannot myself stand over what it has become'[158].

In form the *Wahlverwandtschaften* conforms to the idea of the dramatic novel, with the action moving swiftly through a sequence of dramatic scenes or tableaux, each of which is commented on by the narrator/director. The dramatic nature of the novel is highlighted by the series of tableaux vivants presented by the characters themselves. On the representational level the novel presents a realistic story of relationships: an account of marital breakdown and adulterous desires. On a meta-textual level it reflects upon itself: it presents an exploration into the fundamental laws governing the construction of a novel (and, more widely, of any work of art) and a consideration of the problems and difficulties encountered in the work of interpretation[159].

Throughout the text there is a great concern for reading and writing, for sign and symbol, figure and image: for all the ways in which mankind makes his mark upon the world and makes sense of the world. The novel is presented from the start as a hybrid form encompassing various different genres and modes of expression. One of the first images is of Eduard grafting cuttings onto young tree-trunks and inserted into the novel itself are letters, diary-extracts and a novella. It also contains accounts of reading aloud and of fresco painting, of music making and of amateur theatricals, of the copying of documents and the drawing up of maps and plans. There are descriptions of paintings and drawings, of buildings and of gravestones, of the architect's collection of artefacts and of Ottilie's collection of aphorisms.

The novel invites reflection upon the relationship between the written and the spoken word. When reading aloud Eduard cannot bear someone looking over his shoulder at the printed word on the page. The narrator explains this firstly as the natural desire 'which the reader has as much as the writer, the actor or the

---

[158] 11th September 1809, Gräf 1.1, page 397.

[159] Cf. J. Hillis Miller's interpretation of the *Wahlverwandtschaften* as a self-reflexive text in the Chapter entitled 'Anastomosis' of his book, *Ariadne's Thread. Story Lines*, New Haven & London 1992, pages 164-222.

116

storyteller, to surprise, to makes pauses, to arouse expectations'[160]. Eduard, himself, suggests a much more intimate relationship between the reader and his material, 'Das Geschriebene, das Gedruckte tritt an die Stelle meines eigenen Sinnes, meines eigenen Herzens' [what is written and printed takes the place of my own thoughts and feelings]. He seems almost to wish to reverse the primacy accorded to the spoken over the written word by Western cultural tradition ever since Plato, when he suggests that the words on the page, which he is reading aloud, are as close to him as his own thoughts[161]. Later, when his close bond with Ottilie makes him eager to believe he can share his most intimate thoughts with her, this desire is made manifest by his allowing, indeed encouraging, her to read over his shoulder.

As well as through the medium of dialogue and in their great set-piece monologues, the characters communicate with each other at various times through the written word in the form of letters. The boundaries between the written and the spoken word are blurred when Ottilie, at the end of the novel, renounces the spoken word and communicates with her friends only through the medium of letters. The written word here, however, does not afford a greater intimacy but rather is a means of evading intimacy, since she writes, 'Aber mein Innres überlaßt mir selbst!' [but my heart you must leave to me] (477). Even more than the letter, the diary, as a confessional medium, raises expectations of confidential communication. The narrator seems to confirm these expectations when he tells us 'that a red thread runs through it all, (...) a thread of affection and devotion' (368). What a disappointment, therefore, when we discover that the contents consist of a mixture of general reflections of her own and 'maxims and aphorisms' copied out from a commonplace book. Paradoxically, however, this

---

[160] H.A, Volume 6, page 269. Page references to the *Wahlverwandtschaften* are to this edition.
[161] 'And would I actually make the effort to speak, if there were a little window installed in my forehead, in my breast, so that the person to whom I want to communicate my thoughts individually, to impart my feelings individually, could already long before, know what I have in mind?' (195)

'portrait of Ottilie' both reveals and conceals[162]; while on the one hand 'her pages reveal what is happening in her soul', those same pages place a veil of words between the world and that very experience[163].

As we shall later see with regard to the *Wanderjahre* this novel, too, contains within itself both textual and pictorial analogues for the whole work. One of the most striking of these is the series of tableaux vivants, imitating real paintings, or rather engravings of those paintings, which are stage-managed by Luciane; and their counterpart, the nativity scene mounted by the architect, imitating no known individual painting but gathering together the various figurative elements characteristic of such paintings throughout the ages. The tableaux vivants are translations of the paintings into another medium and therefore represent interpretations of the original. They are in fact interpretations of interpretations since they are based not directly on the original paintings but on popular engravings of the paintings. As suggested earlier the theatrical nature of the whole production echoes the dramatic nature of the novel itself. The analogy between tableaux vivants and text are hinted at playfully in the case of the last presentation, Terborch's 'Fatherly Admonition'. Luciane stands with her back to the audience, representing the daughter, until their desire to see her from the front becomes so great 'that a lively, impatient character shouted out loud the words that you sometimes write at the bottom of a page: "Tournez s'il vous plait", and aroused general approval' (394). The audience, as 'readers' of the 'text' that the tableau presents, in wanting to see her face, are searching for an ultimate meaning. But Luciane refuses to turn round (and the painting which she represents has, anyway, no face, but only blank canvas behind) and they are denied the reassurance of that ultimate meaning[164].

---

[162] Cf. J. Hillis Miller, page 194.

[163] Rudolf Abeken, 'Über Goethes Wahlverwandtschaften' in *Morgenblatt für gebildete Stände* of 22nd - 24th January 1810, in: *Erläuterungen und Dokumente: Die Wahlverwandtschaften*, edited by Ursula Ritzenhoff, Stuttgart 1982, page 142.

[164] The painting, which was known to Goethe as the 'Väterliche Mahnung', is now interpreted differently and generally considered to be a brothel scene with the 'mother' as procuress, the 'father' as customer and the 'daughter' as prostitute. Cf. Michael Fried *Absorption and*

The risks of misinterpretation are also thematised in the novel. Another visual sign, the glass which is ceremonially thrown in the air by the young mason on the day of laying the foundation stone of the new summerhouse and which miraculously remains unbroken, is taken by the one who picks it up as 'a lucky sign'. Eduard goes further and, because of the 'letters E and O very delicately interlaced' which are engraved upon it, reads into it an indication that he and Ottilie are destined to be happy together. He cries out, 'My destiny and Ottilie's cannot be separated and we will not perish. Look at this glass! Our initials are engraved on it' (356). This reading could equally well be taken as an illustration of his narcissism, since the E and O are both his initials. His misinterpretation is highlighted at the end of the novel when it transpires that the glass, which should have guaranteed his happiness, has long since been broken and a similar one substituted for it. Ottilie, too, performs a subjective misinterpretation when her obsession with and infatuation for Eduard metamorphoses in her mind into a 'feindseliger Dämon' [hostile demon] which she sees as having an objective existence outside of herself and as having gained power over her. She thus objectifies outside of herself her feelings of guilt and self-reproach for the death of Charlotte's child and her own intolerable situation.

The 'topographische Karte' [topographical plan] (266) of the estate which the Captain prepares is a translation of the landscape into the medium of a pictorial representation and a means by which the landscape can be comprehended and reorganised[165]. Eduard converts it, and the landscape he traverses in their company, into a map of the shifting relationships between himself, Charlotte, Ottilie and the Captain. Charlotte's 'Mooshütte' [moss cabin]

Theatricality: Painting and Beholder in the Age of Diderot, Berkeley, University of California Press, 1980, pages 171-3, and especially page 241, note 11, 'By a historical irony that both Goethe and Diderot would have appreciated, the painting is today understood to represent a scene in a bordello'. It is tempting to think that Goethe, especially since he uses the epithet 'sogenannte' [so-called] to qualify the title, was aware of the possibility of other interpretations and chose this painting deliberately for its ambiguity.

[165] We have seen already in *Tristram Shandy* how Uncle Toby's obsessive interest in maps and plans of siege-works is an attempt to come to terms with his traumatic experience at the siege of Namur.

must give way to Ottilie's 'Lustgebäude' [summerhouse] and Eduard makes this graphically clear on the map: 'he took a pencil and drew a really thick and heavy rectangle on the hilltop' (295). The movement of their story through narrative time becomes arrested and spatialised on the 'topographical plan'. The novel presents a fictional landscape of the mind as the scene for the enactment of the drama of human relationships and the map provides a fictional visual representation of this landscape, while the labyrinthine paths through the estate reflect the labyrinthine confusions of the human relationships.

A miniature textual reflection of the novel itself is contained in the poem recited by the young mason to celebrate the laying of the foundation stone for the new summerhouse. The poem as it appears in the novel is itself a translation or interpretation since the narrator gives us a prose rendering of the original verse form, describing how 'a well turned out mason (...) made a charming speech in rhyme, of which I can give only an imperfect idea in prose' (299). The narrator here hints at the provisional, incomplete nature of all interpretation and also at the intrinsic character of the novel form, which must perforce translate the poetic into the prosaic.

A larger scale textual reflection is provided by the interpolated novella. Its subject matter reflects the subject matter of the novel itself and, by altering the register so that tragedy becomes idyll, acts as a commentary on the events of the novel. The novella is a striking example of the mis en abyme technique in that it is highly suggestive of an infinite process of reflection. It is a novella within a novel, which was itself originally intended as a novella within a novel.

The central textual analogy for the text itself within the text is the 'Gleichnisrede' [allegory] of Part 1, Chapter 4 from which the novel takes its name. On the one hand it illustrates the way in which language, which by its very nature is a sign for something else, a representation of something absent, has a tendency to move always towards the figurative and the metaphorical. The book from which he is reading, Eduard explains, is discussing only the inanimate world of 'earths and minerals' (270), but it does so in metaphorical terms, which

120

personify the inanimate in terms of relationships. 'I heard you reading about relationships', says Charlotte, thinking only of human relationships. Eduard and the Captain then attempt to explain the chemical affinities by expressing them in another medium, another sign system - that of letters of the alphabet:

> Think of an A, that is intimately involved with a B, inseparable from each other by many means and by much force; think of a C that is just as closely united to a D; now bring the two pairs into contact: A will throw itself on D, C on B, without one being able to say, which had left the other first, which had first united itself again with the other (276)[166].

The translation of metaphor is then taken one step further when the 'Wahlverwandtschaften' [elective affinities] of the chemicals and minerals is transferred back to the human relationships from which it had originally been borrowed, as Eduard, in a true moment of dramatic irony, applies the formulaic letters of the chemical combinations to his mistaken picture of the future relationships between himself and the captain, Ottilie and Charlotte. Edward's application of the chemical formula to himself and his companions converts the 'Gleichnisrede' into a metaphor for the very way in which a literary text, and most especially a novel, comes into being. Literary texts are created through an act of personification, through the creation of individual characters in the imagination of the writer. The 'Gleichnisrede' represents, therefore, not only on the level of story, a metaphor for the human relations of the four main characters, but becomes also, on the meta-textual level, a metaphor for the basic principle by which novels are constructed[167].

---

[166] Cf. Hillis Miller, pages 213-4. The terms in which this explanation is couched have an echo of Aristotle's discussion of metaphor in the *Poetics*: 'that [Metaphor] from analogy is possible whenever there are four terms so related that the second (B) is to the first (A), as the fourth (D), is to the third (C); for one may then metaphorically put D in lieu of B, and B in lieu of D'. *The Works of Aristotle* translated and edited under W. D. Ross, Volume 11, *De Poetica*, translated by Ingram Bywater, Oxford, 1924, Chapter 21 (1457b). In Aristotle a metaphorical substitution, similar to the chemical substitution of the *Wahlverwandtschaften*, changes the relationships between words and their meanings. This echo reinforces the sense that the *Wahlverwandtschaften*, as well as telling a story, is also engaged in a discussion of the way in which a literary text is constructed.

[167] In a conversation with Eckermann on 6th May 1827 Goethe said, 'The only larger-scale work in which I was conscious that I attempted to present a fundamental idea throughout [durchgreifende Idee] was my *Wahlverwandtschaften*. The novel has thereby become comprehensible to the mind; but I won't say that it has thereby become *better*', and goes on to

At the beginning of the discussion of chemical affinities Eduard explains the personification of the inanimate it exemplifies by saying, 'But the human being is a true Narcissus; he readily sees reflections of himself everywhere, he is the background through which he sees the world' (270). On the diegetic level this designation applies very clearly to Eduard himself. From the first he sees in Ottilie a reflection, a mirror image, of himself. Her headaches on the left side complement his on the right so that he pictures them sitting together, like reflections of each other, 'me leaning on the right elbow, her on the left and our heads on different sides cupped in one hand, what a charming pair of statuettes we make' (281). He is delighted to note that while she is copying a document for him her handwriting has gradually become an exact replica of his own and, when she accompanies his flute playing, her piano-playing accommodates itself to his somewhat defective style. On a deeper level the Narcissus metaphor is a comment on the human predicament, on the Kantian insight that there is no 'Ding an sich': that all human experience is subjective, reflected through the medium of the experiencing individual[168].

On the meta-textual level the Narcissus image represents a comment on the creating and reading of texts. The story from Book 3 of Ovid's *Metamorphoses* of Narcissus, the boy who is consumed with love for his own reflection in the glassy waters of a pool, functions as an exemplary narrative of the artistic condition. The artist is consumed by desire to create an image of the world around him and succeeds only in creating reflections of himself. Similarly the interpreter, in attempting to read the text, must of necessity, project his own subjectivity onto the work with which he is confronted: 'because man's "destiny"

---

stress the necessity of impenetrability and unfathomability for a literary work, Eckermann, page 591. When the 'durchgreifende Idee' is seen to have such resonance on several different textual levels, a hint of the true depths of the work can be glimpsed.

[168] The Narcissus myth was later used by Freud in his paper 'On Narcissism: An Introduction' to describe the 'universal original condition' of man. Its use here by Goethe seems already to express something of this idea.

122

is his predicament as a "true Narcissus", maker and reader of signs that are always his own face in the mirror of the world'[169].

The Narcissus narrative has lately taken on a new resonance as the emblem for the self-reflexive text, the literary work which constantly draws attention to its own status as an artistic construct: 'fiction about fiction - that is, fiction that includes within itself a commentary on its own narrative and/or linguistic identity'[170]. That this is its function, too, in the *Wahlverwandtschaften*, is indicated by the presence of the Narcissus metaphor at the beginning of the 'Gleichnisrede', itself a metaphor for the fundamental principle governing novel construction: its presence there makes it a central element among that series of images which represent the text in infinite reflection.

---

[169] J. Hillis Miller, page 193. We have already seen how applicable to the human and artistic predicament, embodied in the figure of Werther, is Eduard's description of the human being as 'a true Narcissus'.

[170] Hutcheon, page 1.

CHAPTER 3

Reader and writer in the *Wanderjahre*

Wie viel die Menschen schreiben, davon hat man gar keinen Begriff
How much people write, one can't imagine it

At the beginning of his visit to her uncle's estate Wilhelm is informed by Hersilie 'that here we read a lot' (50). Later, in a letter to Natalie he comments on the natural communicativeness of humankind whether by means of the spoken or the written word. He writes, 'Man is a gregarious, communicative being; (...). How often one complains in company that one person doesn't let another get a word in (...)'; and, 'Wie viel die Menschen schreiben, davon hat man gar keinen Begriff' [How much people write, one has absolutely no idea of it]. He goes on to remark about the 'Schreibseligkeit' [writing zeal] of his new friends. In this environment he says, 'You spend almost as much time communicating what is occupying you to your friends and relatives as you have time to occupy yourself with anything' (78)[1]. These comments are true both within the confines of the uncle's estate and for the novel as a whole. Not only does it comprise a multitude of documents of many and various kinds, produced by many different hands, but it also contains within its compass a polyphony of voices: narrators, who may be responsible for a whole story, like the barber relating 'Die neue Melusine', or who may give just a brief outline, such as Angela's account of Makarie's secret gifts in Book 1, Chapter 10 or Makarie's thumb-nail sketch of the young Lenardo at the close of the same chapter; and orators like Lenardo with his great 'Wanderrede' [emigration speech] or Odoardo with his recruitment speech for workers in his province. In addition there are poets: amateur, such as Hilarie,

---

[1] Gonthier-Louis Fink comments that this remark 'also applies to Wilhelm' and therefore can also be regarded as an example of the 'ironic disruption of the portrayal on the part of the author' Gonthier-Louis Fink: 'Tagebuch, Redaktor und Autor. Erzählinstanz und Struktur in Goethes *Wilhelm Meisters Wanderjahre*'. In: *RechG* 16 (1986) pages 7-54, here page 12.

124

Flavio and the Major, or indeed Wilhelm himself, the composer of a 'Wanderlied' [song of emigration]; or professional, such as the poets in the artists' province[2]. What has been said of Cervantes' *Don Quixote* is equally true of the *Wanderjahre*: the majority of its characters can be grouped into overlapping classes of writers and readers, narrators and listeners [3].

When we first meet Wilhelm he is writing his diary and a letter to Natalie. At the first station of his journey, the home of Joseph, he listens as his host narrates his life-story. At the second major station, on the estate of Hersilie's uncle, he receives, from different members of the household, two fictional works and a packet of letters to read. He continues to write a variety of letters in the course of his journey, to Natalie, to the Abbé, to Lenardo, and his travel diary forms one of the most important manuscripts in the narrator/editor's collection. Wilhelm narrates the story of his anatomical studies to Lenardo and Friedrich 'with spirit and enthusiasm' (330), and himself listens to the barber narrating 'with particular skill and artistry' the 'true fairytale' (353) that is 'Die neue Melusine'. As the reader of Lenardo's diary he encounters himself, in the guise of a mysterious traveller, and his own writing, in the form of the sheet of didactic reflections which he had left behind for Susanne and her bridegroom, now carefully copied into Lenardo's diary.

Lenardo writes letters to his aunt, Makarie, to Wilhelm and to the old antique-collector. He is both narrator and recorder of his own story, as he recounts the first half to Wilhelm under the title, 'Das nußbraune Mädchen', and records the rest in the second part of his diary. He describes to Wilhelm and

---

[2] Volker Neuhaus has demonstrated how the *Wanderjahre* comprises 'the collected narratives, poems, reports, diaries, speeches and letters from approximately twenty fictional characters, to which can be added an indeterminable number of authors to whom belong the aphorisms in the two collections', Neuhaus, page 25.

[3] Alter, page 5: 'but it is equally remarkable that the world into which he (Don Quixote) sallies is flooded with manuscripts and printed matter. (...) At times it begins to look as though all mankind were composed of two overlapping classes: readers and writers. It seems as if from behind every roadside bush and every wooded hill another author is waiting to spring out, clutching a sheaf of verse; even a dangerous convict is busy planning the second part of his autobiography as he marches off to the galleys; and the unlooked-for pleasures a traveller may find in the attic of his inn are as likely to be a trunk full of books as the embraces of a hospitable serving girl'.

Friedrich the influences from his childhood and youth, which helped to develop his interest in crafts and technology. These interests find written form in his diary report of the activities of the spinners and weavers, which also contains diagrams and drawings of various technical processes and implements[4]. He both listens to and records in his diary Susanne's narrative of the events in her own life since her father was expelled from his farm. As the leader – 'Das Band' - of the group of emigrants he turns orator and delivers his great sweeping historical and geographical review of human migration.

The lively Hersilie confesses herself an avid reader of French works of fiction 'as long as they are graceful and amusing' (50), and is the fictional translator of the novella 'Die pilgernde Törin' (51). She exchanges letters with her aunt and conducts a one-sided correspondence with Wilhelm, whose answers are not recorded in the text, but which are regarded by Hersilie as no answers, so that she writes, 'A correspondence with you is exactly like a monologue' (319). Makarie, 'the most discreet of all women' (223), exchanges letters with her nieces and with the baroness, who appeals to her to find a solution to the confusions in 'Der Mann von funfzig Jahren'. In conversation she is skilled at the portrayal of character and gives us a preliminary character sketch of her nephew Lenardo. She is convinced of the 'importance of ephemeral conversation' (123) and with the help of her companion Angela she records and stores in her archive 'individual good ideas' which come out of the discussions on a wide variety of subjects held in her salon.

Friedrich, too, who writes with 'a swift, light, legible hand' (334-5), is a chronicler and to him are ascribed the notes which provide the material for Odoardo's story of his broken marriage and Wilhelm's account of his anatomical

---

[4] Lenardo refers to his drawings in the course of his diary, but the editor immediately intrudes into the text to excuse the omission of the drawing (341). The drawing referred to does, however, have a real existence among the illustrations accompanying Heinrich Meyer's account of the Swiss spinning and weaving home-industry written at Goethe's request. The question is raised as to why this drawing could not be included in a text, which does nevertheless include an illustration: that of the enigmatic key to Felix's casket. The explanation may lie in the symbolic importance of the key for the work itself.

studies. As a narrator Friedrich describes to Wilhelm the plans of the emigrants for setting up the various institutions of their new colony in a conversation 'that twisted and turned quite admirably through question and answer, through objection and correction and, with all kinds of delays, moved pleasantly towards its actual goal' (404).

Almost every character has a tale to tell or a discourse to conduct. The three directors of the 'pedagogical province' also become narrators in their explication to Wilhelm of the pedagogical principles according to which their educational province is run. Saint Joseph, the barber and Saint Christopher all convert incidents from their own lives into tales of diverse kinds. Many of the characters then become listeners and readers, recipients of the discourse of others. Dialogue, too, has an important place in the novel and ranges in kind from the dialogue of Julie and Lucidor at the end of 'Wer ist der Verräter?' which is reproduced as a scene from a drama, to the dialogues set down by the narrator in summarised form with introductions such as 'the following proved to be the quintessence of what was discussed' (404). The voice of Montan, as befits a Socratic teacher, is only heard in the dialectic of dialogue, and then often reluctantly and with reserve[5]. Natalie's role in the *Wanderjahre* is that only of reader: she is the recipient of Wilhelm's first three letters, sent in quick succession during the early days of his travels; he begins writing his diary with the intention that it will provide Natalie with a more detailed account of his journey (12); along with letter and diary she also receives various of the manuscripts which are given to him along the way, so that she might gain a more vivid impression of the circles in which he is moving (78)[6]. Finally Natalie is the

---

[5] Wilhelm playfully compares Montan's methods to those of Socrates, 'It seems to me', said Wilhelm, 'that you want to do me the honour of making it clear to me in Socratic manner, of making me confess, that I am extremely absurd and stubborn' (39).
[6] We may perhaps also envisage her in the role of viewer of the paintings brought to her from Lago Maggiore by the artist and listener to his confessional narration of his time spent there with Wilhelm, Hilarie and the beautiful widow (240-1).

recipient of the great labyrinthine letter in which Wilhelm attempts to describe the influences leading him to choose the occupation of surgeon[7].

The fact that so many of the characters are narrators and writers lends the text a multiple perspective, in that the various viewpoints supplement, complement, relativise and sometimes contradict each other. This effect is heightened by the complex perspective of many of the narrative elements. There is hardly a narrative section in the novel, which is unambiguously that which it at first purports to be. The apparent first-person narrative of Joseph's life-story in the first two chapters is revealed in the third chapter to be an account written down by Wilhelm for Natalie 'out of the mouth of an honest, respectable man', filtered through his own consciousness so that not only the language has undergone a change but also the content has been interpreted according to Wilhelm's convictions and way of thinking (28). Here Wilhelm, as recipient, has read into the narrative text an interpretation, which is coloured by his own personal experience and circumstances, since he both identifies closely with Joseph and also feels keenly the contrast between Joseph's happy family life and his own enforced separation from Natalie. This oblique narrative strategy suggests the inherent ambiguity of the narrative act which is so often concerned with the mediated, the indirect statement.

The story of Odoardo's unhappy marriage has its origins in his nocturnal revelations to Lenardo and Friedrich in which he renders 'fragmentary account' of his personal life. This fragmentary discourse is then recorded by the pen of Friedrich (393), and finds its definitive form in the artistically fragmented novella: the series of dramatic scenes into which the narrator/editor shapes his incomplete material.

---

[7] Critics have noted something of a discrepancy in the long delay before Wilhelm informs Natalie about his training as a surgeon, apparently only after 'an interval of some years' and when his training is already complete. Cf., for example, Karnick, page 158 and Gonthier-Louis Fink, page 13. Structurally, however, the letter fits in naturally here at this pivotal point at the end of the second book and before Wilhelm's account in Book 3 of his training.

· The novella 'Die pilgernde Törin' exists in its own right outside the bounds of the novel as an anonymous French novella published in 1789 and translated from the French by Goethe between 1807 and 1808[8]. Within the novel it is translated by Hersilie and given to Wilhelm as bedtime reading. Within the novella the narrative perspective alternates between Herr von Revanne, one of the main characters, and a fairly impersonal narrator who claims to be an acquaintance or friend of Herr von Revanne and to have been told the story by his friend himself (52). Indirectly, too, the voice of the female protagonist is heard in the song through which she covertly tells her own story and in the aphorisms with which she protects her privacy.

The story of Lenardo and Susanne begins as a first person narrative when Lenardo recounts to Wilhelm his last encounter with the nut-brown maiden; it continues as his diary-account of his travels in the Swiss mountains and his search for Nachodine/Susanne. On several occasions the narrator intrudes into the diary and takes over the narrative role, culminating in the depiction of the gathering at the deathbed of Nachodine's father, which is presented by the narrator as a dramatic scene.

In spite of the fact that Makarie has often been seen as 'die höchste Gestalt des Romans' [the highest character in the novel] the female voice is apparently not very strongly represented in the novel[9]. The role assigned to women is superficially a very conventional one. Although Makarie herself has received a wide-ranging education, the girls under her care are provided with a narrowly vocational training, which prepares them only for their role as wife and mother (123)[10]. The female figures who conform to the conventional domestic female role

---

[8] Cf. H.A. Volume 8, pages 568-9.

[9] H.A. Volume 8, page 535.

[10] One of Goethe's correspondents, Göttling (Gräf 1.2, page 1048) mentions this point in his comments on the *Wanderjahre*. In comparing the 'pedagogical province' with Plato's *Republic* he wonders why there is no mention of the education of girls in the former, whereas in Plato girls receive exactly the same education as boys. In conclusion he recommends, 'I think that we should expect in the *Wanderjahre* also a description of female education and finally a union of the sexes which have been educated in this way in a perfectly ideal state, even if only in the blueprint of the three'. That Goethe ignored this suggestion, and indeed, instead described the girls' school under

receive apparently very positive treatment in the *Wanderjahre*. The narrator of
'Wer ist der Verräter?' says of Lucinde that she 'represented those things which
we find desirable for all women' (87). Juliette's uncle says of her, 'She is a fine
girl who has the capacity to learn and understand even more' (70). The blonde
and beautiful Valerine is endowed by the narrator 'with all the advantages that are
typical of blondes' (137). All three are married off to suitable husbands within the
course of the novel. Each of these characters is paired, however, with her more
unconventional counterfoil, whose experience represents a questioning of the
conventional role of woman in society. Within the context of the traditional
fictional happy ending of the novella, 'Wer ist der Verräter?' Julie, the quicksilver
younger sister of Lucinde, can also be provided with a happy ending in marriage,
albeit an unconventional marriage to the world-traveller, Anton, which gives her
the freedom to travel and follow her own inclinations, in a way she could not
within the confines of a conventional marriage. In the novel itself these
unconventional female characters serve to call into question the conventional
female role in society. The brown-haired tomboy Nachodine becomes Frau
Susanne, the successful businesswoman (352), whose relationship with Lenardo
may possibly contain the seeds of a new, more balanced alliance between the
sexes. Hersilie, by her own confession 'a peculiar, madcap girl' (264) in the eyes
of the world, feels that she can find no place among her own generation and, at
the end of the novel, is left in isolation and confusion with her fate unresolved.

It is among these less conventional female characters that a counter-voice
can be heard questioning some of the prevailing patriarchal norms, which the
other characters seem to accept. Hersilie, who exhibits such a great love of both
the spoken and the written word, is the very one to throw doubt upon the
transparency of language when she demonstrates how the conventional wisdom of

Makarie's auspices as he did, gives strength to the idea that he was not so much interested in
producing blueprints for an ideal state, as in producing models which would encourage the reader
to engage in a dialectic with the text, to criticise and to disagree. This idea is further supported by
the way in which Goethe welcomes, in his essay 'Geneigte Teilnahme an den *Wanderjahren*',
Professor Kayßler's criticism of the 'pedagogical province'. H.A. Volume 8, pages 522-3.

the inscriptions above her uncle's doors, 'die Maximen der Männer' [the patriarchal maxims] (66), can also be reversed and reinterpreted to mean the opposite of what they at first seemed to say. Her 'fictional' alter ego, the foolish pilgrim of whom she says, 'If I ever were to go mad, as I sometimes feel like doing, then it would be in this way' (51), highlights, through her ambiguous use of language, the hypocritical value system of the dominant masculine world which is encapsulated in Herr von Revanne's pious wish 'that she were everywhere just as concerned for her reputation as for her virtue' (53), a world in which reputation is far more important than reality.

Susanne makes use of the prevailing language norms for her own ends. When Lenardo expresses surprise at her 'Wohlredenheit' [eloquence], which nevertheless 'sometimes might seem to be not quite natural', she ascribes it in part to her learning to see through the emptiness of the rhetoric of the leaders of her pietistic religious community, and then learning to imitate this language and appropriate it to herself to such an extent 'that if need be I could address a congregation as well as any elder' (421-2). In addition she has learned to imitate exactly, and has appropriated to herself, the opposing rhetoric of her betrothed. We can assume that it was at least in part this ability to manipulate the alien medium of the prevailing language norms, which enabled her to conduct her business so successfully.

Another counter-voice is that of Montan. This Socratic teacher, whose medium is dialectic, is nevertheless deeply sceptical about the power of language and the possibility of genuine communication. At the 'Bergfest' [mountain festival] he does not contribute any of his own ideas to the discussion about the origins of the earth and when Wilhelm presses him for the reason why, he says:

> I have totally convinced myself that each person must keep to himself in the deepest seriousness what is dearest to him, and that is our convictions, each person knows what he knows only for himself and he must keep it secret; as soon as he expresses it dissent becomes active, and as soon as he gets involved in an argument, he loses his own equilibrium, and what is best in him is, if not destroyed, at least disturbed (263).

It is not only a variety of fictional voices and fictional writers, which we hear and read in the *Wanderjahre*. In a work he described as 'an aggregate' Goethe also freely appropriates and assimilates the writings of other real writers[11]. We have seen already that 'Die pilgernde Törin' is a scarcely altered translation from an anonymous French author. Much of the first part of Lenardo's diary consists of sections of the report on the Swiss spinning and weaving cottage industry requested by Goethe from his Swiss friend Heinrich Meyer and included verbatim in the *Wanderjahre* interwoven with the more personal details of Lenardo's travels and the people he met. The two collections of aphorisms echo with other voices since they contain quotations from a variety of sources, from Hippocrates and Plotinus to Laurence Sterne. They also bear witness to the involvement of another hand in the construction of the *Wanderjahre*, since we are told that Goethe entrusted his secretary, Eckermann, with the task of selecting and arranging the aphorisms from a pile of notebooks[12]. This collaboration of Eckermann is quite in keeping with Goethe's playful comment to Zelter when the work was nearing completion that 'any good soul' might finish it off as well as 'and perhaps better' than its author[13]. Moreover it highlights in a very practical way the productive nature of the task which the reader is called upon to perform.

---

[11] 'Das Buch gibt sich nur als ein Aggregat aus' [the book only professes to be an aggregate] in conversation with Kanzler von Müller, Gräf 1.2, page 1067.

[12] Cf Eckermann, 15th May 1831, pages 467-8. Eckermann is convinced that the aphorism-collections have no rightful place in the *Wanderjahre* and were merely included to fill up space when the text proved too short for the three volumes originally planned for it. Many critics have followed Eckermann and argued for the omission of the aphorisms and the accompanying poems and some editors have indeed omitted them. Other critics, however, notably Max Wundt, have argued on the grounds of thematic affinity, style and intention for the retention of both aphorisms and poems. Goethe's own attitude is ambiguous. On the one hand Eckermann, after expressing his own conviction that the aphorisms and poems are out of place in the *Wanderjahre*, reports, 'Goethe laughed at this. "It has already happened," he said today, "and the only thing left now is for you to put the individual pieces where they belong when you edit my unpublished papers after my death". On the other hand Goethe wrote of the aphorisms in a letter to Reichel on 2nd May 1829, 'I don't want the aphorisms from Makarie's archive to be published separately before the work comes out. They only gain their meaning at the end of the work and as part of the whole, separately some could be offensive'. W.A., 4.45, page 261.

[13] Letter of 24th May 1827. Cf. Chapter 2, note 30.

The text-internal narrator

der Sammler und Ordner dieser Papiere
the collector and organiser of these papers

The narrator of the *Wanderjahre* presents himself primarily as the somewhat harassed and confused 'Sammler und Ordner dieser Papiere' [collector and organiser of these papers] (408), as the editor of the large number of the most varied types of manuscripts which, as we have seen, purport to make up the work. Much of his narrative appears to be taken from the diary, which Wilhelm is keeping for Natalie, to which he refers in his first letter, but for the most part transposed into the third person by the narrator. This idea of Wilhelm writing his own story is reinforced by the first image of him in the opening scene of the novel, sitting 'in the shade of a massive rock' as he 'recorded something in his notebook' (7). Some texts come from the papers which are given to Wilhelm, such as the two novellas 'Die pilgernde Törin' and 'Wer ist der Verräter?', the exchange of letters between Makarie and her nieces and Lenardo's diary; some stem from Makarie's archive and some from the emigrants' own archive, much of it preserved by the recording pen of Friedrich.

In almost all of the texts the narrator's voice is somewhere to be heard: sometimes retreating behind the voice of a character and sometimes taking over the narrative reins from the characters themselves. He thematises his own role, sometimes summarising conversations, sometimes suppressing information, sometimes adding information that he has been able to find out for himself. He engages the reader in an intermittent discussion on the nature of fictional narrative, on reader expectations and preferences and on styles and methods of presentation. He first appears in his editorial role in Book 1, Chapter 4, in order to summarise the discussion between Wilhelm and Montan; he is particularly evident in Book 1, Chapter 10, in Makarie's realm, and is the dominating figure in Book 3, Chapter 14 - the narrator's chapter par excellence - in which he orchestrates a complicated interplay between his roles as editor and reporter, commentator and novelist. The voice of the narrator as creative writer is especially obtrusive in some of the novellas, notably 'Wer ist der Verräter?', 'Der Mann von funfzig Jahren' and 'Nicht zu Weit' where he engages the reader in a consideration of the most suitable methods of presenting his material. In these novellas the narrative voice is practically indistinguishable from the narrator of the Wilhelm/Lenardo action. This seepage of the narrative voice from one level of the narrative to another highlights the fact that distinctions such as 'frame-story', 'fairytale' or 'novella' are narrative artifices; emphasises the instability of their defining characteristics, which can be blurred or overturned at the whim of the narrator, and suggests that fantasy and reality are overlapping categories which are not always so easy to hold apart.

In his first direct intervention in the narrative in Book 1, Chapter 4 the narrator says of the conversation between Wilhelm and Montan, 'This conversation, which we pass on only in outline, carried on almost until sunset' (37), suggesting that he possesses a much more detailed account of it which he has summarised for the reader. He refers in the same way to the pedagogical theory expounded by the three directors of the 'pedagogical province', 'whose content we will however summarise briefly' (154); and to Friedrich's account to Wilhelm of the principles by which the leaders of the emigrants will organise their new colony: 'the following proved to be the quintessence of what was discussed' (404). So, also, he indicates that he possesses a wealth of material on the conversations between Makarie and Wilhelm, from which he is only able to select a sample: 'a good many pleasantly instructive topics were discussed, from which we choose the following' (127). As editor, too, he is careful to give the origin of any written or spoken words which he introduces into his text: 'through later communications of the astronomer we are in a position to relate, if not sufficient as least the gist, of their conversations on such important points' (444); and to avoid authenticating any text of doubtful validity: 'unfortunately this essay was only written down from memory a long time after the contents were communicated and is not, as would be desirable in such a remarkable case, to be regarded as completely authentic' (448-9). He frequently repeats this sense of

134

himself as an editor, whose job it is to select and summarise, endorse and verify, choose and reject from an immense body of manuscripts, which increasingly threaten to overwhelm him as he nears the end of his task. Time and space are limiting factors, which control his efforts. They prevent him both from indulging in protracted personal reminiscences (258), and from presenting his material to the reader in a more gradual and detailed manner (404). When speaking with this editorial voice he portrays himself as an earnest and conscientious worker, aware of the seriousness of his task and dedicated to assembling and ordering his documents for publication[14].

This narrator/editor, however, does not restrict himself to an editorial role, but speaks with several different voices and plays a number of contradictory roles within the course of the narrative. Sometimes he appropriates the persona and characteristics of Goethe himself: he confesses his reluctance to include in his text the pedagogues' harsh criticism of the theatre, 'And yet may the editor of these papers himself confess here: that he let this strange passage go through with a certain amount of reluctance' (258) [15]; and he plays, on several levels, with the existence of the *Lehrjahre* as a work whose characters and situations will be well-known to the readers of the *Wanderjahre*. Wilhelm, Felix and Montan move on as main characters into the *Wanderjahre* as though it were a straightforward sequel to the *Lehrjahre*. Several minor characters are assembled at the eleventh hour by the narrator, when he ostentatiously purports to tie up the loose ends of his 'story', and he refers cursorily to the present situation of others, notably Natalie and Lothario. Like the editor of the fictitious 'manuscripts' comprising the

---

[14] Even in this editorial role, however, the narrator is not an entirely passive recipient of already existent manuscripts, but seeks out extra information where he feels it necessary for the enlightenment of his readers. So, for example, he introduces details of the uncle's earlier life with the phrase, 'The following is what we could find out by asking questions' (81). The description of the artist's pictures 'Urteil eines Kenners' (235-6) and the explanation of the word 'Wildheuer' (237) would also seem to be additions of this kind, included for the information and edification of his readers.
[15] Here is a threefold play upon the relationship of fiction to reality: firstly a reference to the fictional Wilhelm's former love of the theatre, then the fictional narrator's confession of a similar passion and finally an allusion to Goethe's own continuing ambivalent attitude towards the theatre.

Wanderjahre Goethe, too, as he prepared the two versions of the novel for publication in the 1820s, was acting literally as 'editor' of his own manuscripts, many of which had been completed up to twenty years previously[16]. By this device the literary work draws attention to its own origins and to its status as an artistic construct.

Parallel to his role as editor the narrator assumes the role of novelist, with a relationship to his material and sources which is creative rather than documentary. To this end he sometimes draws the reader into a consideration of the type of texts suitable for inclusion in a novel. During his account of the discussions in Makarie's salon, for instance, he intervenes abruptly to prevent the astronomer from reading his mathematical paper with the excuse that he is afraid of trying the patience of his readers further since it is not the kind of material they expect in a novel. The important thing in a novel, he suggests, is to get on with the story (118)[17]. With reference to the accounts of the extraordinary gifts of Makarie and the 'Gesteinfühlerin' [rock diviner], the narrator once again raises the question of reader expectations of the material suitable for a novel. The paranormal elements of both the 'ätherische Dichtung' [ethereal poetry] and the 'terrestrisches Märchen' [terrestrial fairytale] lead him to describe them as exactly the sort of material normally considered suitable for a novel (445).

In his introduction to the novella 'Der Mann von funfzig Jahren' he touches on the growing appetite of the reading public for fictional works published in instalments, which was a topical question in the first half of the nineteenth century since the enormous increase in the number of periodical

---

[16] In the 'Zwischenrede' of the 1821 version of the novel the role of Goethe, the author, as editor of his own manuscripts is more explicitly thematised, 'In the course of the present editing, although undertaken with due care and courage, we nevertheless come up against all the difficulties which have delayed the publication of this volume for twenty years'. This reference constitutes a play on the fictionality of the editor-role: Goethe was editor of many papers in his work on the *Wanderjahre*, but not of the fictional archives of the novel itself. Author and fictional editor are not identical, but the temporary and partial assumption of the Goethe persona by the fictional editor on the one hand problematises the relationship between fiction and reality and on the other hand highlights the non-identity of author and narrator.

[17] An ironic reference to reader expectations from an author who, like Laurence Sterne and Jean Paul, so often complained of the conventional reader's craving for the 'story'.

publications had greatly encouraged this reading habit. After saying that he, at first, had planned to satisfy this preference of his readers, he then suggests that this particular story is more suitable for continuous narration. In the event, however, he does not totally keep to this intention. The novella itself consists of one continuous narration but includes a metaleptic element at the end when Makarie enters from a different narrative level like a 'deus ex machina' to resolve the confusions. Further instalments are then added and the narrative metalepsis is intensified in the Lago Maggiore episode and in Book 3, Chapter 14, when the characters from the novella break the frame and enter the level of narrative occupied by Wilhelm and his associates[18]. This intermingling of different narrative levels is a means of drawing attention to the fictionality of the whole text, of breaking the illusion and encouraging the reader to reflect on the relationship between fiction and reality.

This play with the fictionality of the text is especially apparent in the Lago Maggiore episode[19]. The narrator introduces his 'real' artist as a routine stereotype from the world of fiction, 'He [Wilhelm] found himself together with a painter, many of whose like roam about in and haunt the real world and even more in novels and plays' (226). A further level of fictionality is superimposed on the text when the artist is said to have read about Mignon in the *Lehrjahre* and become enchanted by her as a fictional figure (227). Mignon thus enters the world of the novel as a character out of a previous fiction who has already become well-known as a focus for romantic sentiment. The tension between fiction and reality is highlighted all the more, since the *Lehrjahre* as a novel was published over twenty years before the *Wanderjahre*, but as a sequence of fictional events what

[18] This question of frame-breaking belongs to the discussion of the extent to which the structure of the *Wanderjahre* can be regarded as a frame-story with embedded tales, according to the model favoured by Erich Trunz or the model of an 'archive fiction' preferred by Volker Neuhaus and Gonthier-Louis Fink among others. Both of these models contribute elements to the structure of the *Wanderjahre* but neither model alone can adequately describe its protean nature.
[19] Elsewhere Hersilie draws attention to her own fictionality and that of her fellow characters through her suggestion that her household – 'unser Personal' (67) - resembles the stock characters from a comedy or a work of light fiction.

takes place in the *Wanderjahre* can only be separated by a matter of months from the events of the *Lehrjahre*, scarcely time for Mignon's story to have been committed to print.

In his role as creative writer the narrator calls attention to the fact that the text is an artistic construct. He repeatedly makes the reader aware of the mechanisms of his craft. After introducing 'Wer ist der Verräter?' directly with Lucidor's first impassioned monologue he comments drily, 'But it would cost many words to explain this short, passionately sincere monologue' (86), before he proceeds to outline Lucidor's past history. At the end of this section he again turns to the reader with a direct comment, 'But there is need of a short statement in order to explain this also, and how the intensity of such eloquence fits with what we already know of him' (90), before giving a quick sketch of Lucidor's character. Later he draws attention to the writer's absolute authority over his material when he abruptly cuts off the old house-guest in the midst of his history lesson with the comment, 'How Lucidor would have liked to interrupt the good old man, if it had been polite to do so, as the narrator can with impunity' (102).

In the novella 'Nicht zu Weit' the narrator lays bare even more fully the techniques of his narrative. In introducing this novella he regrets having 'only incomplete and unsatisfactory knowledge' of Odoard's lifestory and unhappy marriage, which he owes to Friedrich's recording skills. He then goes on immediately to speak of the 'visualising of interesting scenes', which seems to refer more appropriately to his own creative shaping powers than to Friedrich's skills as a recorder, since he proceeds to shape out of the sketchy record at his disposal a highly dramatic and artistically disjointed representation of a fragmented relationship, of the disintegration of a marriage. He orchestrates a presentation alternating between his own third-person narrative and the contrapuntal voices of Odoard and the old nurse, marking each shift in perspective clearly with a word to the reader. The narrator makes explicit his own role as creative writer in relation to this novella when he comments on his 'modus operandi' with regard to his material by saying that he is working according to the principles of storytelling and has begun his account abruptly 'medias in res' (395). In the last scene of this dramatic novella the narrator casually takes back the fiction that it is based solely on Friedrich's record of Odoard's 'fragmentary account'. With the introductory words, 'Yet it now becomes necessary as well to give more immediate news of the lady herself and of the rustic celebration that seemed to go so badly' (402), he goes on to recount the wretchedness and humiliation suffered by Albertine on this same night with a detail and an empathy which could hardly have come from Odoard's account.

In 'Der Mann von funfzig Jahren' the narrator confronts the reader repeatedly with evidence of how the text has been constructed and engages him in consideration of narrative techniques. His own general reflections on the action are often highlighted by an introductory comment such as: 'at this opportunity we make the following remark' (193); with a rhetorical question he doubts the possibility of representing particular circumstances adequately (205); and he indicates when he is passing over material, which would make his story too long-drawn-out, with such phrases as 'to describe how this could be achieved would be too long-winded' (202). He discusses with the reader the different modes of narrative and involves him in a consideration of the best way of presenting a particular situation, posing the question of when dramatic presentation should give way to narration or reflection:

> Our readers have probably convinced themselves that from this point on in the presentation of our story we must not proceed any longer by representation but by narration and observation, if we want to penetrate into the states of mind on which everything now depends, and visualise them for ourselves (215)[20].

At several points in this story the narrator evokes the time-honoured topos of the poet confessing his own inadequacy. As he reaches the point where he wants to describe the developing affection of Hilarie and Flavio for one another

---

[20] The narrator's distinction between 'darstellend' and 'erzählend' corresponds precisely to the basic distinction made in twentieth century narrative theory. Cf. Franz K. Stanzel, *Theorie des Erzählens* Göttingen 1979, pages 70-1. Stanzel distinguishes between 'two basic forms of narration' which are 'reporting narrative' and 'scenic presentation', which are variously labelled by different theorists: e.g. 'actual' and 'scenic narrative' (O. Ludwig); 'panoramic' and 'scenic presentation' (Percy Lubbock); 'showing' and 'telling' (N. Friedman).

he suggests that he lacks the capacity to describe such a delicate love story adequately and that it would be better depicted by the hand of a female writer (208); of the final parting scene between Flavio and the beautiful widow he comments that he does not have the courage to depict it since it may become apparent that he lacks the youthful fervour necessary for such a task (209)[21]. He also confesses to a sense that he lacks the delicacy of expression to give an adequate account of Hilarie's misgivings about the sudden change in her affections (220).

This concern with style and manner of presentation also extends to comments on the manner of delivery or on the poetic style of various characters within the work. After summarising the 'fairytale' version of Anton Reiser's life made up by Julie's wild young brother for Lucidor he describes the boy's long-winded and rather naive narrative style (98). He comments on the unusual warmth and liveliness with which Wilhelm delivers his account of his anatomical studies (330). In 'Der Mann von funfzig Jahren' he delivers an appraisal of the major's hunting poem (198); and later presents a contrasting picture of his son Flavio's rather mediocre poetic talents, which require passion to spark them off (208). His consciousness of artistic style can also be seen in his inclusion of the critique of the painter's work at Lago Maggiore, the 'Urteil eines Kenners' [verdict of a connoisseur].

Through his introductory comments to 'Der Mann von funfzig Jahren' the narrator lets us know that he is well aware of the conventions which govern fiction-writing and of reader expectations and preferences, even if he is not always willing to indulge them. Throughout the work he makes us feel that he is attempting to create an air of suspense by withholding information, often playfully and usually with a hint of mystification. Implying that it is not within his power to reveal the secret of Wilhelm's case of surgical instruments he says,

---

[21] This comment can only be regarded as tongue-in-cheek since he has already depicted an earlier passionate scene between Flavio and the beautiful widow, albeit through the words of the young Flavio himself. It could also be seen as a playful allusion to the wide register of styles of the *Wanderjahre* itself, which exploits all the possibilities of script.

'What it was however, we may not confide to the reader at this point' (40); and of Wilhelm's rescue work as a surgeon among the miners he claims, 'Of what kind this was however we may not yet reveal' (264). Although he ostensibly refused to gratify the public taste for fiction by instalments in the case of 'Der Mann von funfzig Jahren', he does exactly this with the story of 'Das Nußbraune Mädchen': he allows it to develop gradually through many sections, from its indirect beginning in Book 1, Chapter 7 with the exchange of letters between Makarie and her nieces and nephew to its indefinite conclusion in Book 3, Chapter 14: 'what cannot be decided remains in the balance' (447); and creates suspense at the moment of climax by breaking off the fictional 'manuscript' of Lenardo's diary just at the point where Lenardo was about to find Nachodine/Susanne again: 'here the manuscript ended and, as Wilhelm asked to see the continuation, he discovered that it was not at present in the hands of his friends' (352).

In the 'Zwischenrede' in the middle of Book 2 the narrator excuses himself for introducing 'an interval of several years' at an inappropriate moment and regrets that typographical reasons prevent him from placing it at the end of a volume. In this way he once more pierces the illusion of the fictional world and reminds the reader of the print and paper and binding, which is the factual reality of a work of fiction. At the same time he comments on the discrepancy between fictional time and real time, between narrative time and narrated time, and draws an analogy with the conventions of the contemporary stage which is even less concerned with a true-to-life reproduction of time-spans than narrative fiction:

> And yet the space between two chapters will surely be enough to leap over the extent of imagined time, since we have long been accustomed to allow the like to happen in our own presence between the falling and the raising of the curtain (244).

Although he repeatedly pays lip service to the conventions of fiction writing, he pointedly highlights instances when he flouts them to suit his purpose. When, for example, a new character is introduced at the eleventh hour in order to tie up some loose ends the narrator comments, 'In order to explain (...) this anomaly, we are obliged at the last moment to introduce a new player into this wide-ranging drama' (445). Sometimes novellas and other insertions are carefully introduced, as when Hersilie gives Wilhelm her translation from the French of 'Die pilgernde Törin' to read. At other times the scene changes are abrupt and without introduction, reminiscent of the changes of scene in a film, as, for example, when Wilhelm goes straight from his conversation with Makarie at the end of Book 1, Chapter 10 to an encounter with Lenardo, the subject of his conversation with Makarie, at the beginning of Chapter 11.

In Book 3, Chapter 14 the thematisation of the role of narrator and of the process of narration becomes particularly pronounced. The organising voice hovers between his role as novelist parading his characters before us for the last time and editor selecting what should be published from a mass of material. Both these sides of his activity are encompassed by his description of his task as 'the duty of communicating, presenting, explaining and drawing to a conclusion'. On the one hand the editor sees with relief 'the serious task of a faithful reporter, which we have undertaken', coming to an end; while on the other hand the creative writer – 'from our narrating and portraying side' (436) - considers the fates of his characters and how best to draw his novel to a conclusion. This chapter offers simultaneously a suitable novel-conclusion exaggerated to the point of parody with many more than the required two marriages of light fiction and comedy; and a retraction of this happy ending, as the fate of many of the main characters is left hanging in the balance and the 'ending' becomes a 'non-ending' as the book continues for a further four chapters, followed by aphorisms, a poem and the ambiguous phrase 'ist fortzusetzen' [to be continued][22].

In the 1821 version the narrator is a rather more obtrusive figure whose utterances tend to make explicit what, in the second version, has become implicit

---

[22] Ambiguous because it is uncertain whether the phrase refers to the poem 'Im ernsten Beinhaus' which directly precedes it, or to the work as a whole. Editors of different editions have dealt with the various components of the *Wanderjahre* in different ways depending on their interpretation of the work: E. Bahr, in the Reclam edition includes all the poems that accompanied the 1821 version, the aphorisms, and the two poems 'Vermächtnis' and 'Im ernsten Beinhaus' as well as the phrase 'ist fortzusetzen'; E. Trunz, in the Hamburg edition omits all the poems and the phrase 'ist fortzusetzen'; while the Aufbau edition omits the introductory poems.

in the his relation to his material and to his readers. We have seen how in the 'Zwischenrede' he is much more closely identified with the Goethe who was himself editing his own, often twenty-year-old, manuscripts for the novel. Here, too, there is a very explicit comment about his conception of the reader as an active participant who is to be encouraged by the indeterminacies in the text to recreate it for himself:

> And so we will give here several chapters, whose full realisation would indeed be desirable, just in cursory form, so that the reader not only feels that something is missing here, but that he is more directly informed of what is missing and fashions for himself that which, partly because of the nature of the subject and partly due to the present circumstances, cannot come before him fully formed or supported by the proper authentication (1821. 107)[23].

He is more explicit in his reference to his use of the techniques expected in a novel, such as suspense and mystification. After alluding to the characters of the *Lehrjahre* he withholds more detailed information on their present circumstances with the words, 'because mystery and reservation are indeed befitting for a book such as ours' (1821. 173). When introducing Wilhelm's account of his vision of Natalie on a neighbouring mountain peak, which was replaced in the 1829 version by the 'ätherische Dichtung' of Makarie, he is more openly sceptical than his later counterpart about his 'fairytale' and unsure about its inclusion, suggesting that it is exactly the kind of unlikely tale that is included in a novel, only to be later explained away as a dream:

> What throws us into complete disarray, in historical terms, is the strange circumstance that directly following on all this is the most unlikely narrative, in kind like those fairytales by which one tantalises the curiosity of the listener for a long time with marvels and at the last minute explains that what one was talking about was a dream. Nevertheless we will pass on word for word what we have in front of us. (1821. 139);

and returning with relief to the 'firm ground and earth' of a more realistic narrative.

Although Chapter 12 is preceded by a long 'Zwischenrede' in which the narrator thematises his role as editor and makes explicit the active role he has assigned to the reader, nevertheless he feels the need to pause again at the

---

[23] Page numbers for the 1821 version refer to: Goethe, J.W., *Wilhelm Meisters Wanderjahre oder die Entsagenden*, Urfassung von 1821, Bonn, 1996.

beginning of Chapter 13 to excuse his lack of detailed information about the education in the various branches of the arts practised in the 'pedagogical province' (1821.123). Here he also draws the attention of the reader to his problems as editor with the calculation of time and to the vagueness and uncertainty of time in his text, comparing the fictional world of the novel to the real world of historical events in this respect: 'just as happens in world history' (1821. 123). Immediately after his account of Wilhelm's visit to the 'artists' province' he once more directly confronts the reader with his problems as editor, complaining that there is no record of the conversation when Wilhelm rediscovers Jarno as one of the leaders in the 'pedagogical province': 'on this point our manuscripts have abandoned us'; that he has found reference to a meeting of Wilhelm with Lothario and the Abbé, but without the reassurance of an exact date; he mentions that among the papers there are also several references to 'Entsagung' [renunciation] but nothing that constitutes a detailed exposition. Even the map with its arrows and dates, which seems to be giving exact details of Wilhelm's intended journey for the following few months and which at first reassures the narrator that he is 'once again in the real world' (1821. 139), proves to be covered in mysterious figures and signs which suggest a hidden significance. In this way the narrator stresses his own confusion, lack of knowledge and uncertainty and his floundering attempts to make sense of the various papers he has received.

In the 1821 version of the *Wanderjahre* the novellas tend to be more carefully introduced into the text than is always the case in the later version. Rather than being introduced directly by the narrator, as in the second version, 'Der Mann von funfzig Jahren' is, in the first version, a manuscript sent to Wilhelm by Hersilie. In her accompanying letter she sows confusion as to the elements of truth and fiction in the story, writing to Wilhelm, 'What is true and what is fictional in it, you must try to find out for yourself' (1821. 86), while at the same time asserting the real existence of the characters in the story and hoping for a meeting between them and Wilhelm, a meeting which does then subsequently take place at Lago Maggiore. 'Wer ist der Verräter?' and 'Die pilgernde Törin' stem not from the young civil servant and Hersilie, as in the second version, but from 'Lenardo's Archive' and are read to Wilhelm by Friedrich, in the case of the former 'bringing the story engagingly to life with a great deal of natural energy and vivacity' (1821. 192). 'Wo steckt der Verräter?' is introduced, not as fiction, but as a story concerning 'excellent members' of the association; while 'Die pilgernde Törin' is used by Friedrich as a negative example of a pointless pilgrimage in contrast to the well-thought-out plans of the association:

> So that one might fully register what a difference there is between a foolish pilgrimage, on which a good many people roam around in the world, and a well-thought-out, successfully launched enterprise such as ours (1821. 174).

There is an interesting change of function for 'Die pilgernde Törin' between the two versions. In the 1829 version it is introduced much more positively, by Hersilie, as the way in which she herself would like to be 'foolish' if she ever were, and through her introduction the voice of the protagonist becomes a much stronger counter-voice in the text questioning and throwing doubt upon its implicit norms and assumptions.

In both versions of the *Wanderjahre* it is a function of the narrator-persona to prompt the reader to reflect on the relationship between fiction and reality, by the way in which he constantly confuses the boundaries between the two and by the way in which he allows the different levels of fiction in his narrative to overlap and cross over into each other. He functions as an alienation factor, keeping the reader in a state of alert confusion, as he paradoxically draws him into sympathetic identification with the characters and stories while at the same time constantly puncturing the bubble of illusion of the fictional world and forcing the reader to distance himself from the 'story', to recognise the text as a literary construct and to enter into an active dialectic with it.

Wilhelm

als Repräsentant von allen
as representative of all

In the protagonist, Wilhelm, the roles of reader and writer coincide. He is the generator or the recipient of most of the texts that go to make up the *Wanderjahre*. It is in the role of reporter or correspondent that we first encounter him: 'he was just writing something down in his notebook' (7). The first scene is framed by his writing activities. At the end of the scene we are told, 'Then [he] withdrew to his room, where he straightaway took up his pen and passed part of the night in writing' (11). He is, in fact, recording his own story, in the form of a diary to be sent to Natalie along with his letters and other manuscripts collected on his way. 'You will only hear what the wanderer encounters' (13), he promises Natalie. Volker Neuhaus has shown how the novel is made up of Wilhelm's writings - diaries and letters - along with other manuscripts which have either been entrusted to him or to which he has had access, many of which, including Wilhelm's own diary extracts, have been filtered through different perspectives or worked on by the 'editor' before they have entered the novel[24].

This image of Wilhelm at the very beginning of the novel, as he sits 'in a fearsome, imposing place' and writes, is reminiscent of 'the artist himself at work' whom Goethe mentions in his essay 'Ruisdael als Dichter'. In this essay Goethe describes three paintings by Jakob Ruisdael from the Royal Saxon Collection. In the second of these paintings, commonly known as the 'Kloster' [monastery], the old half-ruined monastery buildings could well have provided a model for the home of Saint Joseph whom Wilhelm is just about to meet:

> A ruined, indeed devastated monastery-building, close behind which however one can see well-preserved buildings, probably the dwelling place of an official or toll-keeper, who still collects local tolls and taxes, although they are no longer the lifeblood of the community they once were [25].

---

[24] Neuhaus, page 25.
[25] H.A. Volume 12, 'Ruisdael als Dichter', page 139. Joseph's home is described as 'a large monastery building, half in ruins and half well preserved' (13).

The link between past and present whereby, on the one hand, the old ruined monastic buildings take on a new life as home and work-place and, on the other hand, the disintegrating creations of the hand of man are given new life by the creative power of nature, is common to both scenes. The Ruisdael scene, we are told, allows us the opportunity of contemplating past and present, 'which interweave so delightfully with each other'. In the ruins of the church, which was the companion building to Saint Joseph's chapel, we are told that centuries-old trees have grown up, rooted in the remains of the walls and 'in company with various kinds of grasses, flowers and mosses gave the impression of hanging precariously in the air' (16).

The artist is himself depicted in the Ruisdael painting sitting in the foreground working at a drawing and his position, like that of Wilhelm in the opening scene of the *Wanderjahre*, is described in the essay as 'bedeutend' [imposing]. Of this undoubtedly rather clichéd pictorial element Goethe notes, 'And with emotion we catch sight of this so often misused motif here in its rightful place, as imposing as it is effective', and he goes on to suggest that the artist here both represents himself as producer of the work of art and his future viewers or recipients as reproducers or co-producers by their work of interpretation. The artist sits at his work 'as representative of all those who gladly would become engrossed with him in the contemplation of the past and the present that weave together so delightfully'. There is the suggestion here of the work of art as a continuum, as a link through time from past to present and future[26]. In the story of Saint Joseph, too, art is seen as having the role of

---

[26] This sense of the work of art as a continuum, which links its individual recipients through time, is also expressed in the *Lehrjahre* by Wilhelm when contemplating the works of art in the 'Saal der Vergangenheit' [hall of the past]. Here, in anticipation of the subject matter of the *Wanderjahre*, Wilhelm sees an art which presents a totality of life: 'it was a world, it was a heaven'; and begins to understand something of the continuum that art represents and the relationship of the transience of the individual human life to the permanence of life and its representation in art when he exclaims, 'Nothing is transient except for the one who looks on and appreciates'. This understanding of the function of art is encapsulated in Wilhelm's comment, 'You could equally well call it the hall of the present and the future'; and is also expressed by Goethe in the poem 'Im Gegenwärtigen Vergangenes' -

providing a link and a sense of continuity between past and present, in that the deep impression made on him by the medieval paintings around the walls of the chapel influences the way in which Saint Joseph lives his life in the present: 'for if something inanimate has life it can also bring forth something with life' (15). This vivid pictorial and thematic link between the painting in the essay and the monastery buildings in the *Wanderjahre* highlights the connection between the artist depicted in Ruisdael's painting and Wilhelm. Wilhelm's role, too, is that of representative. He is both artist and public, reader and writer. He leads the reader out on a journey through time and space, beyond what is expected within the confines of a novel; he himself embodies the attitude: 'ich ging aus zu schauen und zu denken' [I went out to observe and to think] (80-81), which Goethe suggests is necessary for both reader and writer. Through the course of the novel, he is presented with different models of the reading process as well as with different texts and situations on which to practise his reading, and while himself learning to 'read' more accurately, he is nevertheless still described at the end of the novel as 'problematical', and much is left unresolved.

Wilhelm is, then, marked out from the beginning as one with a high degree of interest in textual matters. Although his initial appearance as recorder can be explained by the exigencies of the renunciation theme, which entails separation from his beloved Natalie and the resulting need to communicate through letters and diaries, nevertheless he continues to display the same degree of interest in the word in all its forms throughout the novel. In the first scene he enters into a discussion with his son Felix on the naming of things and the dubious nature of names, the ambivalent relationship of appearance to reality[27]. When Felix asks him the name of a stone he at first does not know, but then recalls, 'daß es die Leute Katzengold nennen'. [that people call it mica, or cat's

---

'Was ihr sonst für euch genossen,   [What you used to appreciate yourselves
Läßt in andern sich genießen"   Continues to be appreciated by others]
                                    (H.A. Volume 2, pages 15.)

[27] Cf.Birgit Baldwin, '*Wilhelm Meisters Wanderjahre* as an Allegory of Reading', in: *GYb.* 5 (1990), pages 213-232.

gold] (7). Wilhelm's explanation of the name 'Katzengold' to his son, 'Probably because it is false and cats are also thought to be false' (7), highlights the way the name contains within it both the stone's deceptive appearance as gold and its false reality. The pinecone, too, is deceptive in appearance, it 'doesn't look like a cone, it's round, after all' (7). This theme is then immediately taken up again and re-explored on a deeper level with the arrival of 'a strange apparition' in the form of Saint Joseph the Second and his family who appear to be a reincarnation of the holy family on the flight into Egypt and provoke Wilhelm into wondering 'whether you are real travellers or whether you are only spirits'. The whole episode of Saint Joseph plays with the idea of the relationship between appearance and reality: Joseph has modelled his life on the paintings on the walls of his chapel-home and the paintings in turn record and preserve for him the story of his life. Both Wilhelm and Joseph express a sense of confusion at the ambiguities of what is appearance and what is reality. In this opening scene Wilhelm is not sure whether he is seeing real human travellers or just 'spirits'; of his momentous first meeting with Marie, Joseph recalls, 'This heavenly figure, (...) now seemed to me like a dream, generated in my soul by those paintings in the chapel. Soon those paintings seemed to me to have been only dreams, which here were resolving themselves into a lovely reality' (23). At the end of his account Joseph assures Wilhelm, however, that his family's imitation of the holy family is not simply superficial appearance but has been internalised and has become the determining factor of their spiritual lives: 'but the virtues of that archetype of fidelity and purity of mind were reverently kept alive and practised by us' (28).

In his subsequent meeting with Jarno, now renamed Montan because of his newly developed (or rather reawakened) interest in geology, Wilhelm becomes involved in a discussion about the 'book of nature' since Montan has rejected human communication as inadequate and turned instead to the 'mute teachers' which are the rocks and stones[28]. He praises the language of nature for the apparently contradictory reasons that it is both inscrutable [nicht zu begreifen] and yet simple: 'nature has only one alphabet'. The discussion revolves around the theme of the impossibility of complete communication: the necessity of something remaining inscrutable and the banality of most human communication. Wilhelm here is a naive and optimistic believer in the possibilities of human communication while Montan has chosen the script of nature precisely because of its impenetrability. This language is not easily comprehended, perhaps, but at least, according to Montan, it is not so open to ambiguity and misinterpretation as human script or indeed human language in all its forms - 'the poor stuff of empty words' (34) - which is so full of ambiguities that it is open to endless misinterpretation.

When Wilhelm arrives at the next station of his journey, the estate of Herslie and Juliette's uncle, he is first of all attracted by the maxims inscribed in 'goldenen Buchstaben' [golden letters] above the doors in all the rooms, which lead to a discussion of the ambivalence of the word. The laconic words appear more as icons than as concepts since the flow of words has been frozen into the static pose of a picture through the decorative form of the golden letters, until they have become, according to Hersilie, like the maxims from the Koran on the walls of Muslim buildings which their believers 'more revere than understand' (68). Two opposing methods of interpretation are offered by the two nieces in their role as hermeneuts explicating the maxims for Wilhelm's benefit. Juliette interprets the enigmatic words according to the enlightened, rational, optimistic spirit prevailing on her uncle's estate, smoothing out the apparently contradictory elements in an attempt to reconcile the paradox. Her method of interpreting embodies what Wilhelm later, with the total agreement of her uncle, sums up as the value of such laconic maxims: that they can provide a stimulus 'to consider opposite opinions and find a resolution' (70). Thus in her explication of 'Property

---

[28] H.A. Volume 12, 'Maximen und Reflexionen', No.678, page 460.

and Common Ownership', individual ownership is allowed validity only insofar as it furthers the common good. She and Wilhelm then vie with each other to find more and more extravagant examples to illustrate this thesis. While Juliette's method of interpretation is referred to as 'auslegen' [to lay out], what Hersilie is aiming at is something much more radical. She describes her method of interpretation as 'umkehren' [to turn upside down]. She attempts to read the sayings against the grain and look at what they might really be saying behind their smooth unproblematical appearance. She focuses on the ambiguity of such seemingly unproblematical 'truths': the way in which one person's truth can quite often be somebody else's falsehood. She does this by illustrating how 'the patriarchal maxims' assume quite a different aspect when viewed from the perspective, and through the experience, of a woman. The journey 'from the useful through the true to the beautiful' may not always be so gratifying when made in the opposite direction. Her irreverent interpretations suggest the possibility of inverting received and canonical truths in order to see them with fresh, unbiased eyes. Hersilie's is a counter-voice in the rational, enlightened world of her uncle, a voice which questions, like Montan's, whether knowing and comprehending must always be regarded as an undisputed 'good'. She mischievously asserts, 'I would gladly forget what I know and what I have understood is also not worth much' (70).

In her role of providing a counter-balance to the unrelieved rationality of her uncle's world Hersilie offers Wilhelm a work of fiction, a novella, to read. This novella, 'Die pilgernde Törin', has as one of its major themes also the idea of the ambiguous and deceptive nature of words. The heroine uses conventional language as a cloak to preserve her privacy in that she counters any questions about her past and personal life with seemingly straightforward and 'truthful' general aphoristic sayings; but at the same time she reveals her personal history indirectly through the unconventional means of an apparently fictional and also highly explicit folk-song. Her behaviour, although unconventional, far from being foolish, is notable for its circumspection. On the one hand she insists that the dangers to which a lone woman traveller is exposed are often imaginary rather than true, but on the other hand she describes the care she takes to avoid any possibility of danger:

> Moreover she travelled only at times and on paths, where she believed herself to be safe, did not talk to everybody and stayed sometimes at suitable places where she could earn her keep through the kind of service which she had been brought up to offer (53).

In the apparently safe haven of the Revanne household she escapes from her impossible position as the object of desire of both father and son by means of ambiguous words which tell no lie but which allow the two men to jump to a false conclusion, by deluding them into a misreading of the situation which accords with their own prejudices. Her parting admonition to them - 'Learn from my example how to depend on the steadfastness and discretion of your beloved. You know whether I am unfaithful and your father knows too' - is nothing less than an exhortation to learn the art of reading perceptively.

The second work of fiction offered to Wilhelm on the uncle's estate, the novella 'Wer ist der Verräter?', is given to him to read by the 'younger official' with the words, 'If you have been able to appreciate the refinement of an aristocratic and wealthy French eccentricity, I hope you will not reject the simple, dependable respectability of German ways' (85). This novella offers an opposing view of literature from that embodied in 'Die pilgernde Törin'. That novella ended on a question and in uncertainty. Here, the novella progresses from the initial agonised confusion of Lucidor's monologues to the clarity of the concluding dialogues and the resolution of an almost fairytale happy ending: 'the honourable man's cheeks were suffused with colour, his features lost their wrinkles, his eye became moist and a handsome, imposing young man emerged from the husk' (114).

Not only is Wilhelm the recipient of a variety of texts during the course of the novel, but he is also marked out as one who is open to new experience and ideas, to that which at first may appear strange and disconcerting. Joseph is happy to tell Wilhelm his life-story because he feels that he recognises in him one who is capable 'of taking a miracle seriously too, when it has a serious basis' (17). Hersilie informs him 'that we read a lot here' (50) and assumes that in him they have encountered a kindred spirit: 'I'm sure you read too before going to sleep?' (51). The younger civil servant, in his accompanying note to the manuscript of the novella poses the question, 'Who is so gifted then, that he can appreciate many different kinds of things?'; and in the following paragraph answers it himself, saying of Wilhelm, 'But you, my passing friend, appeared to me as such a person' (85). In her salon Makarie suggests he be included in the discussion on mathematical ethics because 'he seems the kind of person who would be happy to take part in it' (116), and even the astronomer concedes him 'a certain freedom of spirit' (117). This openness gives him access not only to the word in all its variety, whether written or spoken, but also to other branches of the arts which had previously been closed to him. Under the influence of the artist in the surroundings of Lago Maggiore he begins really to grasp for the first time the value of the pictorial arts and he learns 'receptive as he was, to see the world with the artist's eyes, and as nature unfolded the open secret of her beauty one felt an uncontrollable longing for art as the truest interpreter' (229)[29]. In the company of the singing emigrants he even discovers within himself a 'singing daimon' (312) and composes a 'migration song', which is then used as a basis for variations by his companions. This aspect of Wilhelm, his receptivity, corresponds to the 'subtly receptive readers' of whom Goethe spoke in his letter to Rochlitz[30].

In Lenardo's diary we encounter Wilhelm for the first time described entirely from outside, rather than experiencing the regions he traverses either partially or totally from his perspective. Here the effect has a certain similarity to the effect of Aeneas suddenly encountering a depiction of his own experiences in

---

[29] Here is an explicit statement of a theme, which is implicit throughout the novel: the role of art as an interpreter of the world. It is not, however, the first time Wilhelm has shown receptivity to works of the visual arts. In the *Lehrjahre* we learn that he was not only deeply affected as a child by the painting of the sick prince, but most particularly in the 'hall of the past' in Natalie's house (Lj. 552-4) he experiences a moment of deep insight brought about by his contemplation of the paintings.

[30] Gräf 1.2, 2nd September 1829, page 1064.

the ruins of Troy, on the walls of the temple of Juno in the city of Carthage[31]. The reader, with the protagonist, is an external observer of the scene in which the protagonist has already taken part and is simultaneously drawn into the scene and distanced from it. Wilhelm is now represented from quite a different perspective through Susanne's description of the encounter. He arouses confidence in the people he meets: when he goes 'it was as if with him all good spirits had disappeared' (423), and his departure leaves a noticeable void in the community he has left. He is no longer a 'Wanderer' [wanderer] but a 'Reisender' [traveller] (422). The figure of Wilhelm here represents the role of the writer or artist in society[32]. He is seen as a guide and leaves behind a manuscript, a single sheet of observations ['ein Blatt'] (423 & 425), intended to offer guidance through the complexities of life to Susanne and her betrothed. At the same time this manuscript is one of the many miniature reflections of the text within the text itself, not only highlighting its themes, construction and form, but also indicating a productive way in which it may be read[33]. The first observation emphasises the limitations of the individual in the face of the enigma of life and depicts the individual life as an erratic journey through the labyrinth of the world, a journey reflected in the circuitous wanderings of Wilhelm and the reader through the pages of the text: 'so he only gropes his way, acts quickly, lets go, stands still, moves, hesitates and rushes and all the errors, which bewilder us, arise in so many ways' (426). The second emphasises the impossibility of certainty in earthly life and, by extension, in the reading of texts: 'even the most level-headed is obliged in the daily life of the world to be wise for the moment'. The third observation describes the attitude of constant reflective activity and the openness to

---

[31] *Aeneid* Book 1, lines 456ff.

[32] In the 'Noten und Abhandlungen' to the *West-östlichen Divan* the writer wishes 'to be regarded as a traveller', and he further assigns to the writer 'the role of a pedlar, who lays out his wares pleasingly', with a neat play on the various meanings of the word 'auslegt' - the merchant displaying his wares and the writer interpreting his material.

[33] Cf. Bernd Peschken, 'Das "Blatt" in den *Wanderjahren*' in: *Goethe* 27 (1965), pages 205-230. See especially page 205: 'Since the "Blatt" does not form, but discusses, it could announce what the form of the novel is'.

inspiration which are necessary both for the reading of texts and for the reading of life experience: on the one hand, the careful close work implicated 'in direct attention to the duty of the day' and, on the other hand, the receptivity to sudden insight which 'a proper attitude towards the sublime' implies. These two essential constituents of a constructive reading practice are repeatedly proposed in the *Wanderjahre* and are most clearly articulated in that 'synthesis of world and spirit' outlined in aphorism 123 in 'Betrachtungen im Sinne der Wanderer':

> Everything that we call invention or discovery in the higher sense, is the serious exercise or activation of an original feeling for the truth, developed in secret for a long time, which suddenly in a flash leads to a fruitful insight (302).

Through Wilhelm, both in his capacity as reader and as writer, hints are given of a fruitful way of reading texts. In Makarie's castle he shows himself just as enthusiastic about pithy aphorisms as he was on the uncle's estate and obtains permission to copy out as many of these maxims as he wishes. Although these sentences, we are told, at first appear paradoxical when we are unaware of their origin, nevertheless they can provoke us to an inventive kind of close reading which resembles the passage through a labyrinth or maze and 'obliges us to go backwards by means of a reversed procedure of uncovering and discovering and, wherever possible, to visualise for ourselves the lineage of such thoughts, from the distant past right up to today' (125). It is just this labyrinthine reading and interpretative method, which Wilhelm advocates in his letter to Natalie, where, as we have seen in Chapter 1, the spirit of Laurence Sterne is invoked to justify the construction of digressive texts.

In his programmatic words to the custodian on the uncle's estate Wilhelm describes his purpose as a combination of close observation and reflection: 'I went out to observe and to think' (80). He has been described because of this as a passive hero but Goethe's concept of 'schauen und denken' was rather of an active participation in the world. This 'schauen und denken' of Wilhelm's is not so much to be seen as a mark of passivity, but rather to be taken in the same spirit as Gadamer's insistence that 'reading expressly involves action'[34]. In the context of his researches into the possibility of the existence of an 'Urpflanze' [primordial plant], Goethe asks the question in the botanical garden in Verona, 'What is observation without thought?' and suggests that the experience of the great variety of new plants helped to stimulate his thought processes and foster creativity[35]. 'Schauen' and 'denken' are seen as active, creative processes.

His very choice of profession, too, links Wilhelm with the creative person, and therefore with the writer[36]. He is drawn to the healing profession of surgeon through his appreciation of the beauty of the human form, which has its roots in his friendship with the drowned fisher-boy: 'so beautiful was the human form, of which I had had no idea' (272). This love of human beauty further attracts him to the work of the artificial anatomist since he cannot bring himself to dissect the arm of the young girl who drowned herself through unhappy love: 'for when he removed the covering the most beautiful female arm, that had ever wrapped itself around a young man's neck, lay revealed' (324-5); in the final scene, during his attempt to save the life of his own son Felix, it is again the beauty of the human form which strikes him: 'there he lay then stretched out on his father's greatcoat, the most charming youth' (459). He also describes how 'ein gewisses Vorgefühl' [a certain intuition] had helped him in the beginning of his anatomical studies. This 'Vorgefühl' is similar to the 'Ahnung' of the world, which Angela attributes to the poet in Book 1, Chapter 10 and, by analogy, to Makarie in her relationship to the solar system.

The skills which Wilhelm learns from the artificial anatomist are described as a cross between an art and a craft, a creative exercise which the

[34] Hans-Georg Gadamer 'Bildkunst und Wortkunst', in: *Was ist ein Bild*, edited by Gottfried Boehm, München, 1994.
[35] H.A. Volume 10, page 60.
[36] The link between artist and healer is made explicit in the 5th letter in 'Der Sammler und die Seinigen' when the uncle invokes the figure of Apollo with the words, 'Apollo, in so far as he concerns himself with doctors and artists', H.A. Volume 12, page 78. The connection is also highlighted in *Faust II* in the figure of Chiron who is both 'the noble pedagogue' (7337) and the 'doctor who can name every plant' (7345).

anatomist compares to the creative activities of Ezekiel in the Old Testament, collecting and reassembling bones (327), and later to divine creative powers, transforming clay into sentient beings (329). They are skills which allow him to exercise his talents in making connections and joining together, rather than the traditional anatomist's skills of dissection: 'connecting means more than separating, reproducing more than looking' (328). 'Nachbilden' and 'Verbinden' [reproducing and making connections] are also characteristic activities of both the writer and the reader. In combining the skills of the artificial anatomist with those of the surgeon; in becoming the physical healer, 'der liebvolle Wundarzt' [the caring surgeon] (459), whose craft is described by Montan as the 'most divine of all occupations' (282), Wilhelm becomes a symbol of the spiritual healer, the poet, and his role in society[37].

Lenardo

> eigentlich keine Geschichte
> *really no story*

Lenardo, like Wilhelm, is the narrator and recorder of his own story. The first half takes the form of a narration to Wilhelm and it is then continued in two diary-instalments which are entrusted to Wilhelm and which he, as the text-internal reader, reads along with us. This device enables us to see the narration both from Lenardo's point of view and also from Wilhelm's, especially as the latter is directly invoked in the text, when Lenardo expresses his annoyance at Wilhelm's attempt to speed up the wedding of Susanne and her fiancé: 'since it had already caused me secret annoyance, to learn from that story, that Wilhelm had hastened the union' (425); and also appears in person in Susanne's own narration as the mysterious traveller: 'during these days a traveller spent some time with us, probably under an assumed name' (422).

Although Lenardo denies that what he is about to narrate is a story - 'Ich darf Ihnen wohl vertrauen und erzählen, was eigentlich keine Geschichte ist' [I

---

[37] Cf. Brown, pages 73-4.

can no doubt tell and confide to you, something that is really no story] (129) - it contains some of the most 'novel-like' elements in the whole work: a mystery surrounding the identity of a vanished girl and a protracted search, culminating in the discovery of her whereabouts. In form, too, it imitates some of the elements expected of a novel, beginning 'medias in res' with the exchange of letters between Lenardo, Makarie, Hersilie and Juliette and continuing in instalments spread throughout the work to create the required suspense. Although Lenardo denies that it is a love-story (129), that is exactly what it becomes, as the diary of a technical observer, travelling on a commission from the 'league of emigrants' through the mountains to study a cottage industry necessary for its American project, develops gradually into the story of the reunion of two 'lovers' and ends with the narrator taking over the reins of narration from Lenardo to present the dramatic scene at the death-bed of Susanne's father, in which the dying man effectually unites the two in a spiritual union. Indeed, it is seen as such from the beginning by Makarie, who characterises it as 'Leidenschaft aus Gewissen' [passion caused by conscience] (448), and by Hersilie, who, in the 1821 version, refers to Lenardo as 'der Leidenschaftliche' [the passionate one] (1821. 85). And yet Lenardo, too, is right. It is 'no story' in the sense of a conventional novel, since, in spite of the reunion of Lenardo and Susanne and the moving scene at the death-bed of Susanne's father, there is no happy ending with an exchange of wedding vows, but rather a fading away into the uncertainty of 'what cannot be decided remains in the balance' (447): a demand that the reader consent to the lack of a resolution and give thought to the possibilities which this uncertainty proclaims.

Lenardo's story in many ways reflects Wilhelm's own story. Lenardo, too, is a traveller: not only has he made 'the traditional tour through civilised Europe' (129), but he also embarks upon his fact-finding mission among the spinners and weavers of the Swiss alpine valleys which leads him back to his beginnings, to

Susanne/Nachodine[38]. For, as with Wilhelm, Lenardo's development exhibits a retrospective teleology. The 'image of the supplicant girl' (133), which he carries with him burnt into his psyche, leads him forward into a past which becomes his future. Lenardo has tried to deny the past, to say that he has 'really no story', to assert the possibility of a completely fresh beginning - 'his principal inclination, to begin right from the beginning' (242) - but his own story demonstrates the impossibility of this denial of the past, and by implication, the impossibility of a denial of the historical and narrative continuum. His very aspiration to emigrate to America is a confirmation of this continuum, since it is an inheritance from his grandfather, who did exactly that two generations previously. The situation of Lenardo, his uncle and his grandfather embodies the contradictory and complementary strivings of different generations: first the striving from Europe to the simplicity and naturalness of America, then the striving from America to Europe's old culture and then back again to the 'primeval conditions' (142) of America.

Just as Lenardo's story is a reflection of Wilhelm's, so the stories of Joseph and of Montan also offer different reflections of the same basic pattern. Joseph has in common with Wilhelm and Lenardo the determination of his future trade through the tools of that trade, which are early idealised in his mind. He possesses in his memory and in the paintings on the walls of his chapel-home the image of those very tools. Wilhelm possesses in concrete reality the case of surgeon's tools, which partly helps to determine his future. Lenardo possesses in his memory the image of the tools of various crafts, which for him were the beloved toys of his childhood. In a similar way Montan partly explains his choice of geology as a return to a childhood activity when he wielded the geologist's hammer along with the 'Pochjungen' [pit-lads] of his uncle's mines.

A second factor, which plays an important role in determining the life's way of these characters, is an image of ideal womanhood, which is impressed

---

[38] Or more evocatively in the 1821 version: 'the great travel-adventure through civilised Europe' (1821. 51).

upon their memory. For Joseph it is the ideal image of Marie, as a virgin-mother figure gazing down on him from the donkey. For Wilhelm it is a similar vision of Natalie as the ideal maiden, an Amazon-like figure on horseback, gazing down on him, as he lay wounded on the ground. An extra factor for Wilhelm is the earlier vision from his childhood of the transfigured and idealised figure of the fisher-boy both in life and in death. For Lenardo the vision of the female figure is reversed and it is the image of the 'supplicant girl' gazing up imploringly to him from the ground at his feet, which imprints itself on his memory and helps to determine his future course: his renunciation of his feudal origins and participation in a movement which seeks to find a place in the new world for the dispossessed and displaced of the old world. In each case the imprinting of the image on the memory is accompanied by the real or metaphorical sensation of physical pain, of a wound. Wilhelm is lying wounded on the ground after being attacked by a band of robbers when Natalie comes to his rescue and appears to him as a heavenly vision; Marie, too, has been attacked by marauding robbers and her husband has been fatally wounded; Lenardo describes how 'that image of the supplicant girl' (133) has made such a vivid impression on his imagination that it lingers there like a wound that refuses to heal: 'a vivid impression is like another woumd; you don't feel it when you receive it. Only later does it begin to hurt and to fester' (133).

The sections of the novel which tell the story of Lenardo and Susanne - that is the two parts of 'Lenardos Tagebuch', 'Das nußbraune Mädchen' and the exchange of letters between Makarie and her nieces and nephew - represent a complex and wide-ranging mise en abyme for the whole book. The content, form, and construction of Lenardo's story reduplicate the construction, form and content of the whole work. Klaus-Detlef Müller has described the way in which the form represents a mirror image in miniature of the novel as a whole. Purporting to have been constructed from the contents of one or more archives the novel contains within itself a representative spectrum of all the possible types of text. Lenardo's story, too, is presented through a variety of diverse text-sorts reflecting in miniature the diversity of written forms which is the distinguishing characteristic of the work as a whole:

> The events are introduced by an *exchange of letters* between Makarie, her nieces Juliette und Hersilie and Lenardo (1,6). Next come Wilhelm's *conversations* with Makarie about Lenardo (1,10) and with Lenardo about Nachodine/Valerine (1,11) and finally the *novella-like narrative* "The nut-brown maiden" (1,11). The next records are again *letters* (Wilhelm to Lenardo and to the Abbé, the Abbé to Wilhelm (II,6 und 7)), then follow the two parts of Lenardo's *diary* (III, 5 und 13) and finally the *authorial report* of the editor (III,14) [39].

The content of this non-story of Lenardo and Susanne, too, reflects the wider content of the novel itself. Lenardo's wanderings through the Swiss mountains reduplicate, on a smaller scale, Wilhelm's wanderings through the whole landscape of the text; Lenardo carries within himself, as a guiding light, 'that image of the supplicant girl' (133) which has made just as deep an impression on his soul as the internalised image of Natalie has upon Wilhelm's[40]. Both Natalie and Susanne - the 'schöne Seele' [beautiful soul] and the 'Schöne-Gute' [good and beautiful one] represent for Wilhelm and Lenardo as much an ideal as a reality. Both men are on a quest, searching for a purpose in life and in the course of this search learn skills, which will be of use both to themselves and to the community. As Lenardo hands over his diary to Wilhelm to read, he says of it, 'I will not claim that it is especially pleasurable to read; it seems to me to be always enjoyable and to an extent instructive' (338). Here are thematised the difficulties, which the text presents to the reader, and the twin aims of the writer to entertain and, at the same time, to educate, echoing the Horatian formula 'aut prodesse volunt aut delectare poetae' [poets want to either please or profit]. Lenardo's description of his diary functions as a covert commentary on the nature of the whole work.

---

[39] Klaus Detlef Müller, pages 280 and 296.
[40] In his first letter to Natalie Wilhelm writes, 'How could I have torn myself away, if the imperishable thread had not been spun, which will unite us for all time and for eternity' (11).

Makarie

ein seliger Geist
a blessed spirit

The figure of Makarie has elicited conflicting critical response throughout the reception history of the novel. The overwhelming majority of critics have seen her as a positive figure but there is also a middle ground, which casts a more ambiguous light upon her, and an undercurrent of criticism, which sees her in a more negative light. The early commentators of the Hegelian school emphasised her social and moral role. Heinrich Gustav Hotho regarded her as a 'judge' and 'representative of the purest, most sensitive morality', while Ferdinand Gregorovius saw in her an embodiment of the ideal of humanity[41]. The opposite pole is represented by the Young German writer, Theodor Mundt, who says of her, 'The most bizarre phantom of all is surely Makarie', in a novel where he regards all the characters as 'nebulous'[42]. Julian Schmidt considers the figure to be the climax of a celebration of eccentricity, which he blames on Goethe's lack of clarity about his own intentions[43].

In the twentieth century the positive view of Makarie is represented by Erich Trunz who describes her as 'the highest figure in the novel'; and by Albert Fuchs for whom she is 'the living symbol of spiritual integration in the cosmos'[44]. The negative view has been taken up by twentieth-century critics in a more radical way and has been attributed to Goethe's intentional aims. Jane Brown, whose interpretation emphasises the elements of literary and artistic parody in the novel, suggests that, while Makarie may appear to be 'one of the most sublime examples of Goethe's mythmaking', this sublimity is 'repeatedly undercut and

[41]Fambach, page 323; and Gregorovius, page 114.

[42] Mandelkow, Volume 1, page 461.

[43] Julian Schmidt '*Wilhelm Meister* in Verhältnis zu unserer Zeit': in *Die Grenzboten* 14.1, Volume 11, Leipzig, 1855. He writes, 'So as a result of intensified eccentricity the spiritual element evaporates into a strange play of nature, which is just as foreign to poetry as it is to real life'.

[44] H.A., Volume 8, page 542; and Albert Fuchs 'Makarie': in *Goethe-Studien*, Berlin 1968, pages 97 -117.

162

corrected' by the author. She feels that Makarie's ill health suggests an imbalance between the earthly and spiritual parts of man's being. Brown emphasises the 'mystifying theatricality' of the figure as she appears in Book 1, Chapter 10 and contrasts her with Wilhelm whom she considers the real 'spiritual and physical healer' in the novel and the sole representative of the 'role of the poet in society'[45].

The most radical view of Makarie is expressed by Thomas Degering[46]. He interprets the whole book as a prognosis of an industrialised society, where the principal aim of maximum profit will entail an increasing tendency towards totalitarianism and the attendant restrictions on individual freedom. Like Brown he feels that Goethe presents the figure of Makarie in an ironic manner and sometimes with a humour bordering on the Dickensian. He states categorically, 'Goethe does not believe in her'. For him Makarie is less a 'schöne Seele' than a mentally, as well as physically, sick old woman, deceived and used as an unwitting pawn on the chess-board of a sinister secret society who not only gain from her the necessary financial backing for their enterprises but also see her as a means of lending their economic ventures a spiritual dimension by raising her to the status of a living saint. Degering sees Makarie as representing the love which has no place in the new social order, but also suggests that she is blind rather than a 'seer': that her often-praised 'mirror-images' of people's inner selves are literally the wrong way round and that people who come to her for advice always end up doing exactly the opposite of what they really want.

These widely diverging interpretations of Makarie can all be read out of a text whose very coin is ambivalence. The ambiguity, which surrounds her, is brought out by Adolf Muschg who observes that it is a characteristic shared by many of the female figures to whom Goethe gives the epithet 'heilig' [saintly],

---

[45] Brown, pages 69-75. A similar view was also expressed by Bernd Peschken in *Entsagung in 'Wilhelm Meisters Wanderjahre'*, Bonn, 1968, pages 201-11.
[46] Degering, pages 241-275.

from the 'schöne Seele' of the *Lehrjahre* to Ottilie in the *Wahlverwandtschaften*[47].
He suggests that Makarie represents no fixed 'Wahrheit für alle' [universal truth],
but is rather a very subjective ideal, a saint for the modern world, a symbol of the
'Heiligen in ihnen [den Menschen] selbst' [whatever is saintly in themselves],
who represents different things for each individual.

The figure is presented from a multiplicity of perspectives and on various
levels - personal, social, literary and symbolic. For the most part our view of her
is reflected through the words and images of others; only very rarely do we hear
about Makarie in her own words. The most sustained first-person account of her
is the exchange of letters with her nieces, on the subject of her nephew Lenardo's
return home. Here Makarie is presented in her most everyday guise and we are
given, on the simplest personal level, a compelling psychological study of a
lonely, unmarried elderly woman who has invested much of her reservoir of love
in her seemingly neglectful and undeserving nephew. The sickness, which, we are
later told, she uses to disguise from an incredulous world her unique relationship
to the cosmos, here appears as a psychosomatic headache. Makarie has received,
after three years silence, a letter from Lenardo, who is on a grand tour of Europe.
She wants to answer it and satisfy his desire for information about the situation at
home, but cannot bring herself to write to him after three years of neglect and so
retreats behind a headache and a request to her nieces to send the necessary letter
for her. In the replies of her nieces, especially of Hersilie, there is a mixture of
loving sympathy and slight impatience at this retreat of their aunt behind a
headache and at her blind love for the spoilt Lenardo: 'Sie machen andere viel
leiden, indem Sie leiden und blind lieben' [you cause others a lot of suffering,
since you suffer and love blindly] (77). Makarie accepts Hersilie's criticism of her
incorrigible love, but at the same time suggests that her love is not blind, but
rather unconditional, that she loves in spite of the hurtful behaviour of her
nephew: 'Lenardo with all his idiosyncrasies deserves our trust' (77). Here, in this

---

[47] Adolf Muschg, pages 115-6.

164

small personal vignette, a wider question is raised with the word 'blind'. Makarie is later described as a 'Seherin' [seer] and the reader is left to wonder about her clear-sightedness. Is this spiritual 'seer' in fact blind when it comes to more earthly things? Does she see the true nature of each individual, as it seems to Wilhelm in Book 1, Chapter 10: 'the sympathetic goodwill of the inestimable woman had removed the husk and enhanced and invigorated the sound kernel' (116); does she transfigure each one into an ideal creation of her own; or does her transfiguring picture reveal the potential hidden within each individual?

On a social level Makarie represents the phenomenon of the wealthy aristocrat to whom privileges and possibilities are open, which were not available to the vast majority of women of her time. We are given a realistic picture of a wealthy and aristocratic woman with intellectual interests both artistic and scientific who regularly holds a kind of salon in her castle where discussion ranges over art, literature, philosophy and mathematics. In the astronomer she has her own resident academic with whom to conduct learned discussions[48]. Like the 'beautiful soul' in the *Lehrjahre* she enjoyed an education as a child which was not restricted to the usual 'female' areas and as a wealthy woman in her own right she is able to lead an independent life and pursue her intellectual interests without the material worries to which the majority were exposed. At the same time she shows a loving and caring interest in those around her and concerns herself with the education of girls. In spite of Makarie's own wide-ranging education, however, in the school for girls organised on the estate by Angela under Makarie's auspices, the education provided is narrowly vocational, and is intended, as in a similar description in the *Wahlverwandtschaften,* to lead 'for the most part to marriage' (123).

This element in the two novels reflects an on-going debate at the beginning of the nineteenth century about the kind of education most suitable for

---

[48] A historical prototype for Makarie has been suggested by W.Foerster (quoted in Bauer's article 'Makarie' in *GRM* 25 (1937), pages 178-197) in the Herzogin von Gotha, wife of Ernst II and her astronomer Franz Xaver von Zach (1754-1832).

girls and indeed the whole area of women's involvement in public life. Friedrich
Kittler has shown how the new education laws in fact made it more difficult for
women to matriculate and gain a university education in comparison with their
sisters of a few generations previously, such as Dorothea Christina Leporin, who
gained her doctorate in 1742, and who wrote a study examining the reasons why
more women did not follow her example[49]. Many of the voices raised in the early
years of the nineteenth century on the subject of women's education (including
the voices of the very women who were organising schools) were united in the
belief that a girls' school ought to be run like a family, because the private, family
sphere was the arena where the girls would pass their adult working lives. The
Luisenstiftung, founded in Berlin in 1811, for example, was intended to be like 'a
large family'. (...) The principal is called father and the female principal and
supervisors are called mothers'; and the poet and teacher Carolina Rudolphi is
described as being 'a loving mother' to her pupils in Heidelberg. The aim of these
schools was to educate girls for their role as wives and mothers. This is exactly
the aim of the ideal girls' school described by the assistant in the
Wahlverwandtschaften when he contrasts the education suitable for boys with that
suitable for girls, whom 'one should bring up to be mothers' (*Wvw.* 340). Here we
see, therefore, a reflection of a popular contemporary view on the subject of
women's education and, as suggested previously, a provocation to the reader to
reflect for himself upon the subject.

It is, however, on the symbolic level that the Makarie-figure performs its
most central function. Goethe said of both the *Lehrjahre* and of the *Wanderjahre*
that their real level of functioning lay on the symbolic level: 'everything is just to
be taken symbolically, and everywhere there is something else behind'[50]. Of the

---

[49] Friedrich Kittler *Aufschreibesysteme 1800.1900*, München, 1995; and Dorothea Christina
Leporin 'Gründliche Untersuchung der Ursachen, die das Weibliche Geschlecht vom Studiren
abhalten, Darin die Unerheblichkeit gezeiget, und wie möglich, nöthig und nützlich es sey, Daß
dieses Geschlecht der Gelahrsamkeit sich befleisse', Berlin, 1742. Reprinted, Hildesheim/New
York 1975.
[50] Conversation with Kanzler von Müller, 22nd January 1822: 'that the whole novel is completely
symbolic, that behind the surface characters something general, something higher certainly lies

symbol he said, 'That is true symbolism, where the particular represents the more general, not as dream and shadow, but as a living, momentary revelation of the unfathomable'[51]. In the Makarie-figure the personal and social personae are this particular which serves as a vehicle for the symbolic level of the figure.

We have already seen that many critics have regarded Makarie as an embodiment of Goethe's ideal of humanity. Erich Trunz writes of her that 'the supreme example of human advancement portayed by Goethe is the figure of Makarie'[52]; and in his comparison of the Makarie- and Faust-figures Ernst Loeb says that Makarie 'unites in herself the highest potentialities of truth, goodness and beauty (...) in the purest representation of the eternal feminine (...) which the writer has achieved'[53]. In this figure the two ideals of womanhood and of humanity seem both to complement and to contradict each other. In a conversation with Eckermann in 1827 on the subject of Lord Byron's presentation of women Goethe said that women were 'the sole receptacle, that still remains to us moderns, into which to pour our ideals', since Homer had exhausted all the possibilities of the male ideal 'in Achilles and Odysseus, the Bravest and the Shrewdest'[54]. Riemer reports a conversation with Goethe on a similar subject in 1809 during which Goethe made what Riemer described as a 'remarkable comment on himself'. The comment, 'that he conceives the ideal in a feminine form or in the form of a woman', is perhaps not so remarkable as Riemer suggests when one considers how many of Goethe's contemporaries in the late eighteenth and early nineteenth centuries were expressing similar ideas.

In an article written for the *Horen* in 1794, 'Über den Geschlechtsunterschied' [On the difference between the sexes], Wilhelm von Humboldt asserted, 'And so everything feminine has particular effect on those powers, which are characteristic of the whole human being at the stage of unspoilt

hidden', Gräf, 1.2., page 953; and conversation with Kanzler von Müller, 6th June 1821, Gräf 1.2, page 976.
[51] W.A. 42(2), pages 151-2.
[52] H. A. Volume 8, page 588.
[53] Ernst Loeb 'Makarie und Faust': in *ZfdPh* 88 (1969), pages 583-597, here page 596.
[54] Eckermann, 5th.July 1827, pages 236-7.

simplicity', and in 1795 he wrote in 'Über die männliche und weibliche Form' [On masculine and feminine form], 'For even in the highest degrees of perfection the epitome of femininity is clearly comparable to the epitome of pure humanity'[55]. In the same year, in 'Über die Diotima', Friedrich Schlegel suggested that the figure of the priestess Diotima in Plato's *Symposium* 'shows us an image not only of beautiful femininity, but rather of perfect humanity'[56]. Both these writers were interested in working out a set of contrasting characteristics for the masculine and the feminine according to the principle of binary opposition. In his two articles von Humboldt contrasts feminine 'suffering receptivity' and masculine 'productive independence'. The feminine is associated with 'warmth', 'feeling', 'abundance of material', 'calm', 'imagination', 'nature', 'contact' and the masculine with 'light', 'art', 'form', 'effort', 'reason', 'will'. Friedrich Schlegel endows masculinity with the 'energy of the definite' and femininity with the 'beauty of the indefinite'. He associates women with 'passivity' and with nature: 'in the bosom of human society only women have remained children of nature'. The eponymous heroine of his novel *Lucinde* is described as a 'priestess', a 'lovely Madonna', and a 'mediator between my disjointed self and indivisible eternal humanity'[57]. Diotima, too, is assigned the role of mediator between the ideal and the real: 'she was the priestess of the immortal seer, and graciously proclaimed to mortals, what the divine youth entrusted to her pure soul'[58].

This same constellation of feminine characteristics is apparent in the presentation of the figure of Makarie. In the novella 'Der Mann von funfzig Jahren' she is described as 'the confessor of all troubled souls' and in Book 3, Chapter 14 she is contrasted with Lydie and Philine in a tableau of saintliness, which portrays 'the two sinners at the feet of the saint' (441). In his dream in the

[55] Wilhelm von Humboldt, 'Über den Geschlechtsunterschied und dessen Einfluß auf die organische Natur', page 286; and 'Über weibliche und männliche Form', page 322 in: *Werke I, Schriften zur Anthropologie und Geschichte*, Darmstadt, 1960.
[56] Friedrich Schlegel, 'Über die Diotima' in: *Kritische Ausgabe I, Studien des Klassischen Altertums*, Darmstadt 1979, page 71.
[57] Friedrich Schlegel, *Lucinde*, Reclam, Stuttgart, 1965, pages 96, 35, 72, 87 and 94.
[58] Friedrich Schlegel, 'Über die Diotima', page 82.

168

observatory Wilhelm sees Makarie as 'in almost clerical garb' and the climax of these images is reached in this dream when she is transfigured before his eyes into the image of the Madonna, mother and saint merging into the holy mother. Makarie is also close to nature; is indeed, in the 'ätherische Dichtung' represented as being a part of nature in her harmonious participation in the movements of the solar system: '[she] did not just observe it, but was at the same time a part of it' (449). In the exchange of letters with her nieces she is characterised as one who 'suffers and loves blindly' (77). She is physically sick, confined to a wheelchair, but her suffering is also caused by the pain she feels at the seemingly neglectful and uncaring behaviour of her nephew Lenardo, a mental pain which manifests itself physically in headaches. Her love, which Hersilie describes as blind, is unconditional. Although not a mother in the literal sense she is a mother figure in her capacity for unconditional love and in the care that she offers to all who come to her for help.

Friedrich Kittler has suggested that, for writers around 1800, 'nature, love, woman' are synonymous and that the function of this constellation of characteristics, which come together in the figure of the mother, is to act as an inspiration to the writer; although she can express herself neither through the spoken nor the written word. As 'eine schriftlose Stimme' [a voice without writing] she has 'the right to be a voice, but not the right to have a voice'[59]. The first words spoken about Makarie - 'as if the voice of a Sibyl from ancient times now gone from sight were uttering in all simplicity pure divine words about human affairs' (65) - links her with Diotima as a mediator between the divine and the human, but could also suggest that she does not so much have a voice of her own but rather is a channel for the voice of 'Gott-Natur' [God-Nature], of inspiration for the masculine creative mind[60].

---

[59] Kittler, pages 84-88.
[60] Cf. 'Im ernsten Beinhaus', H.A. Volume 1, page 366:
Was kann der Mensch im Leben mehr gewinnen   [What more can the human being win in life
Als daß sich Gott-Natur ihm offenbare?   Than that God-Nature reveals itself to him?]

In her salon Makarie does seem to fulfil the function described thus by Kittler: 'the mother does not write, but inspires others to speak'. She is the initiator or instigator of much discourse on a variety of subjects. We are told about the astronomer and Montan, 'The discussions which they conducted in Makarie's presence were extremely interesting' (442); but her own voice seems curiously silent. Both Makarie and her opposite pole, the 'Gesteinfühlerin' [rock diviner] seem to represent to their male counterparts, the astronomer and Montan, raw material for their scientific enquiries and experiments; or rather they are described in terms of implements, 'eine so bereite Wünschelrute' [a very ready divining rod] (452), or machinery, 'eine lebendige Armillarsphäre, ein geistiges Räderwerk' [a living armillary sphere, a spiritual mechanism] (451), for the furtherance of these enquiries. On the other hand, one of the aphorisms from Makarie's archive concerns itself with the same idea and emphasises that the human being, through his potential for harmony with the universe has the possibility of a greater understanding of natural phenomena than would be possible for any man-made machine[61]. This would suggest that the emphasis in the 'armillary sphere' comparison is being laid on Makarie as a symbol for this human potential for harmony with the universe.

When Wilhelm has his dream-vision of Makarie transfigured to a star she represents for him a symbol of the human being in complete harmony with the cosmos. The dream is both an echo of his own thoughts of the previous evening and an anticipation of the mystical description of Makarie in the 'ätherische Dichtung'. As Wilhelm gazes at the stars he is at first overwhelmed by the insignificance of the human being in relation to the cosmos, but then, in a moment of 'Kantian' insight, he formulates for himself a satisfactory explanation of man's place in the order of things by drawing an analogy between the physical laws

---

[61] 'The human being in himself, insofar as he makes use of his sound senses is the greatest and most accurate physics apparatus, that there can be; and that is precisely the greatest disaster of the newer physics, that one has separated the experiments, as it were, from the person and is only willing to recognise nature in what artificial instruments show and wants to limit and prove what nature can achieve through these instruments'. H.A. Volume 8, page 473.

which create order in the universe and the ethical laws which create order within the psyche of the individual: 'can you even think of yourself in the centre of this eternal living order if you do not at the same time discern inside yourself a constant motion circling round a pure midpoint?'(119)⁶². His epiphanic dream of Makarie is, then, an ekphrastic moment in which his thought impresses itself deep in his consciousness through a powerful image. The vision is ekphrastic in the sense that it is described in terms which are reminiscent of a religious painting and has many features in common with Raphael's painting of the Sistine Madonna, a painting with which Goethe would be familiar from the Dresden art gallery.

It is not surprising that Wilhelm's new insight should take this form. His moments of insight have often come through visions of this epiphanic nature. The earliest such experience he records is in his childhood when he was awakened to the value of sensuousness, love and friendship through his vision of the naked fisher-boy whose drowning was to have such a profound effect on the later course of his life:

> And as he climbed out, stood up straight, to dry himself in the strong sunshine, my eyes seemed to be dazzled by a triple sun, so beautiful was the human form, of which I never had an inkling (272).

In another sense, too, the vision of Makarie's transformation is a highly personal, subjective experience of Wilhelm. In its presentation of his ideal as a holy, madonna-like figure it is reminiscent of the language he uses in describing Natalie, who represents for him the ideal of human potential. He describes Natalie, too, as a 'priestess' and as a 'saint'. During his first encounter with her, as he lies wounded on the ground, her caring and comforting presence causes her to appear to him as an almost supernatural vision 'as if her head were crowned with an aureole and gradually a radiant light spread over her whole image', and

---

⁶² In the *Kritik der praktischen Vernunft (Abschnitt 'Beschluß')* Immanuel Kant wrote, 'Two things fill the soul with ever new and increasing admiration and reverence (...): the starry sky above me and the moral law inside me...'

she seems to disappear just as mysteriously as he sinks into unconsciousness
(*Lj*.231).

In Natalie, however, Wilhelm does not just see the feminine
characteristics of a Madonna. She is, as well, an androgynous figure, on
horseback and clad in her uncle's greatcoat, the 'Amazon', incorporating a
harmonious balance between the masculine and feminine sides of humanity. As
followers of Plato both Friedrich Schlegel and Wilhelm von Humboldt insisted
that the human ideal was only attainable through such a harmonious balance of
masculine and feminine attributes[63]. In *Lucinde* the exchange of sexual roles
during intercourse is seen by Friedrich Schlegel's protagonist, Julius, as 'a
marvellous and meaningful allegory for the perfecting of the masculine and
feminine into full and complete humanity'[64]. In 'Über die Diotima' Schlegel asks
rhetorically, 'What is uglier than the overloaded femininity, what is more
revolting than the overdone masculinity, which predominate in our conventions,
in our judgements, and even in our better art?' and continues, 'But precisely the
overbearing forcefulness of the man, and the selfless devotion of the woman are
in themselves exaggerated and ugly. Only independent femininity, only gentle
masculinity is good and beautiful'[65]. Wilhelm von Humboldt stresses repeatedly,
'Only the combination of the characteristics of both sexes brings forth
perfection'[66]. He is convinced that both the ideal of artistic beauty and the ideal of
ethical humanity demand a perfect balance of masculine and feminine attributes:

> But the highest and most perfect beauty demands not only union, but *the most precise
> balance* of form and material, of artistic restraint and freedom, of spiritual and sensory
> unity, and this is achieved only when the characteristics of both sexes are fused in the
> imagination, and from the merging of pure masculinity and pure femininity, humanity is
> forged[67].

---

[63] In Plato's *Symposium* the comedian Aristophanes relates a myth to account for the two sexes.
Primeval man united within himself both male and female characteristics but, as punishment for a
planned assault on the gods, was divided by Zeus into two separate halves - the male and the
female. Love between the sexes represents the yearning of mankind to regain its lost original
unity.
[64] Schlegel, *Lucinde*, page 11.
[65] Schlegel, 'Über die Diotima', pages 92 and 93.
[66] Von Humboldt, 'Über den Geschlechtsunterschied', page 287.
[67] Von Humboldt, 'Über die männliche und weibliche Form', pages 296-7.

Makarie, too, has an element of androgyny in her portrayal. As a child she enjoyed an education, which was not restricted to the usual 'female' areas, and her interests have remained as much 'masculine' as 'feminine'. In her knowledge of astronomy she unites scientific enquiry with intuitive 'Anschauungen' [visualisations][68]. To balance these two complementary aspects of human nature is the aim of the harmonious human being. It is the purpose and aim of Wilhelm's journeyings: 'I went out to observe and to reflect'; it is the same problem and challenge for the human being in this world that Goethe first set out in Faust's 'Zwei-Seelen' [two souls] speech: to achieve a balance between the spiritual and material aspects of his nature; the challenge which is laid out in programmatic form in Book 3, Chapter 14 of the *Wanderjahre*: 'to balance these two worlds against each other, to demonstrate the characteristics of both in transitory phenomena, this is the highest form towards which the human being has to advance himself' (445); and, as we have seen in Chapter 2, it is, according to Goethe, the necessary prerequisite for both the effective artist and the productive reader who must combine the activities of 'fühlen' and 'denken', of intellect and intuition in their creative and interpretative work.

On a symbolic level, Makarie represents the ideal embodiment of the creative person, whether writer, philosopher or figurative artist. She is characterised by Hersilie in her letter as blind, in the 'ätherische Dichtung' of Book 3, Chapter 15 she is described as a 'seer'; this combination of the blind seer has been an epithet traditionally ascribed to the creative artist since the time of Homer. Angela compares her intuitive 'knowledge' of the universe to that of the poet: 'that nothing in the world comes to his notice, that he has not already experienced in his intuition' (126). A similar idea about Shakespeare is expressed by Goethe in the essay 'Shakespeare und kein Ende': 'that very few were as aware of the world as he was, that very few, who gave expression to their inner

[68] 'For she did not deny that she had diligently studied astronomy from her earliest youth, that she was well-instructed in it and that she had missed no opportunity to gain a clear picture of the universe from books and instruments'. H.A. Volume 8, page 450.

perceptions, allowed the reader to share to such a high degree their understanding of the world'[69]. In the *Farbenlehre* Plato, too, is endowed with this intuitive knowledge: 'he is not so much concerned to get to know the world, because he already surmises it'[70].

The influence of the creative person continues after death in the products of his creativity, which survive him. Goethe expresses this sense of the immortality of the writer metaphorically to Falk on the death of Wieland:

> I would not be in the least surprised, indeed I must find it completely in accord with my views, if some day I should meet this Wieland again after centuries as a world monad [Weltmonade], as a star of the first magnitude, and saw and was witness to the way he refreshed and illuminated everything that came anywhere near him with his lovely light. Truly, to capture the nebulous essence of some comet in light and clarity, that might be called a pleasing exercise for the 'Monas' of our Wieland [71].

This rather playful suggestion bears a marked resemblance to Wilhelm's dream of Makarie's transformation to a star and to the idea in the 'ätherische Dichtung' of her possible influence on future generations:

> But we hope that such an entelechy does not completely depart from our solar system, but when she reaches its boundary, that she will long to return again in order to involve herself once more in earthly life and philanthropy to the benefit of our great-grandchildren (452).

The figure of the star as an analogy for the poet is also used in *Faust II* when Euphorion, the offspring of Faust and Helena and an embodiment of the poetic principle, is represented as a star:

> Holy Poetry
> May it rise heavenwards!
> Shine, the loveliest star,
> Far and farther on![72]

Later, in his Icarian flight through the air, he is described as a comet: 'he throws himself into the skies, his garments bear him up for a moment, his head is radiant,

---

[69] H. A. Volume.12, page.288.
[70] H.A. Volume 14, pages 53-4.
[71] Conversation with Falk, 25th January 1813. Biedermann, *Goethes Gespräche*, Volume 3, page 67.
[72] *Faust II*, lines 9863-6.

174

behind him streams a tail of light'[73]. In his 'Epilog zu Schillers Glocke' Goethe similarly celebrates Schiller after his death as a radiant comet:

> Er glänzt uns vor, wie ein Komet entschwindend,
> Unendlich Licht mit seinem Licht verbindend.
> [He gleams ahead of us, disappearing like a comet,
> Combining light unceasingly with his own light][74].

There is also a great similarity between the portrayal of Makarie in the 'ätherische Dichtung' and the description in the historical section of the *Farbenlehre* of Plato's relationship to the universe; his influence on his surroundings: 'he penetrates the depths, more to fill them up with his essence, than to explore them'; and his influence on his fellow men: 'everything that he utters refers to an eternal unity, good, truth, beauty, whose challenge he strives to awaken in every heart'. Makarie's name is the feminine form of the Greek word for blessed. Plato, too, is described as, 'ein seliger Geist' [a blessed spirit]; his metaphorical movements through the cosmos are similar to Makarie's: 'he moves upwards into the air with longing to be part of his origin once more', and the complete description suggests a similar harmony between microcosm and macrocosm[75]. Both Wieland with his 'lovely light' and Plato with his desire 'to communicate kindly' seem also to share Makarie's unconditional love for mankind which is as much the precondition of the artist as a 'feminine' characteristic.

As befits a metaphor for the artist and writer Makarie is established from the start as a figure with a high degree of interest in words. We approach her realm through the uncle's estate where, as we have seen, words have an important role. Apart from the two novellas, which Wilhelm is given to read, all examples of the word on the uncle's estate are factual and the pictures, too, in the gallery are portraits of historical figures: 'in the whole castle there was no picture which

---

[73] *Faust II*, stage direction after line 9900.
[74] H.A. Volume 1, page 259.
[75] H.A. Volume 14, pages 53-4. Compare also the description of Shakespeare in 'Shakespeare und kein Ende': 'Shakespeare is akin to the world spirit, he pervades the world as it does; nothing remains hidden from either of them', H.A. Volume 12, page 289.

touched even distantly upon religion, tradition, mythology, legend or fable' (65). Portrait and biography are for the uncle the highest forms of art and a collection of examples of the authentic handwriting of the figures in his portrait gallery, he says, are 'my kind of poetry' (80). It is in this prosaic world that we first hear of Makarie, the subject of the 'ätherische Dichtung'. She is introduced to us indirectly through her nieces' description of her as an 'Ursibylle', a wise woman, whose words represent a mediation between the metaphysical and physical worlds. In early Roman legend a sibyl was the guardian of the books of wisdom, which she offered to the last king of Rome at an ever-increasing price, and another guided Aeneas through the terrifying realms of the underworld.

In Makarie's castle the word dominates in all its forms. The spoken word is highly prized in conversations at all levels, from Makarie's transfiguring descriptions of her relatives to the discussions which range over literature, art, philosophy and mathematics. The written word is equally important. Here the passionate horseman Felix leaves aside his riding and is initiated into the gentler art of writing. Angela's task is to make a written record of the most valuable thoughts, which emerge from the discussions and reading in Makarie's salon. As befits her name she is a messenger who records the spoken word and passes it on to posterity. These records are then preserved in Makarie's archive.

At the beginning of Wilhelm's visit to Makarie we are told of her descriptive talents. Through her 'discerning benevolence' the people, whom she describes, 'stand as if transfigured before his [Wilhelm's] soul' (126). This reads like an example of the interaction between reader and writer described by Wilhelm von Humboldt in his essay for Madame de Stäel: 'to this end he must appeal to our imagination and compel it to produce spontaneously the image of whatever he intends to show'[76]. At the end of Wilhelm's visit we are given an example of Makarie's talent in her loving portrayal of Lenardo whose faults and virtues are viewed from all sides until a living word-picture illustrates the

---

[76] Kurt Müller-Vollmer, *Poesie und Einbildungskraft. Zur Dichtungstheorie Wilhelm von Humboldts* Stuttgart 1967, page 159.

aphorism with which Makarie begins: 'nature has ensured that we possess no fault that cannot become a virtue, no virtue that cannot become a fault' (127).

Makarie's ability to reveal a person's inner qualities to others, and more importantly, to himself, is exactly what she displays during her intervention in the tangled relationships in the novella 'Der Mann von funfzig Jahren', when the major, grateful for her intervention, describes how:

> That excellent woman, by holding up an ethical-magical mirror [sittlich-magischen Spiegel], through the outer confused form of some unfortunate one has revealed his pure and beautiful heart and suddenly reconciled him to himself and inspired him to a new life (223).

In her 'geistreicher Schilderung' [discerning portrayal] Makarie's talent as an artist comes together with her talent as a reader. Her 'sittlich-magische Spiegel' is both the artistic product and an interpretative tool, which enables her to read and understand both the macrocosm of the universe and the microcosm of the individual human being. Here the roles of reader and writer coincide in that of interpreter.

These themes of the link between an understanding of the macrocosm and an understanding of the microcosm and the role of the poet in society are treated also in the poem 'Vermächtnis', which stands between Books 2 and 3 of the *Wanderjahre*. Here, too, the human being is related to the external sun of the macrocosm:

> Verdank es, Erdensohn, dem Weisen,   [Thank the wise man, son of the earth,
> Der ihr die Sonne zu umkreisen   Who showed her and her siblings
> Und dem Geschwister wies die Bahn   The way to circle around the sun]

and to an internal sun of the microcosm:

> Denn das selbständige Gewissen   [For the independent conscience
> Ist Sonne deinem Sittentag,   Is the sun that guides your ethical life]

and the role of the poet is that of interpreter and guide:

> Denn edlen Seelen vorzufühlen   [To seek out the way for noble souls
> Ist wünschenswertester Beruf.   Is a most desirable calling]

The poet's role as guide is expressed in the first aphorism in Makarie's archive: 'es gibt Steine des Anstoßes, über die ein jeder Wanderer stolpern muß.

Der Poet aber deutet auf die Stelle hin' [there are obstacles, over which every traveller must stumble. But the poet indicates where they are] (460). It is a role also assigned to Makarie. This is hinted at in the epithet 'Ursibylle' which recalls the Sibyl of Cumae who guided Aeneas through the terrifying labyrinth of the underworld. She is several times described as a guiding spirit by other characters in the novel. Associated with her are the words 'schlichten' [to smooth out] and 'entwirren' [to disentangle]. This image is reinforced at the end of the novella 'Der Mann von funfzig Jahren' where she is again described as a guiding spirit: 'the confidante, the confessor of all troubled souls, all those who have lost themselves, wish to find themselves again and do not know where' (223). She is endowed with the talent of helping others to find their true selves. In her presence, we are told, the individual gains the freedom to be wholly himself: 'only to bring to light the good, the best that was in him' (448). Through the 'ethical-magical mirror' of her words she enables those who have lost their way to perceive the possibilities and potential within themselves and challenges them to make the potential into a reality.

It has been suggested that a real-life model for Makarie, as for the 'beautiful soul' in the *Lehrjahre* was Susanne von Klettenberg, the friend of Goethe's youth[77]. Certainly there are passages describing Susanne in *Dichtung und Wahrheit*, which, in several striking details, bear a strong resemblance to the portrayal of Makarie. Goethe describes how one evening at sunset he seemed to see Susanne and her surroundings transfigured before his eyes. He attempts to make a drawing of the scene and in the accompanying poem which he sends with the drawing to a friend he calls the scene 'a dream' and pictures Frau von Klettenberg as resting under God's wings and surrounded by 'Himmelsluft' [heavenly air]. In Book 15 of *Dichtung und Wahrheit* he explains that, 'I could easily have noticed that from time to time her health failed, but I concealed it from myself and was all the more able to do it since her good spirits increased

---

[77] J.M.Lappenberg, *Reliquien der Fräulein Susanna Catharina von Klettenberg nebst Erläuterungen zu den Bekenntnissen einer schönen Seele*, Hamburg 1849.

with her illness' (198). Later in this book he describes her ability to solve other people's problems thus:

> For when that woman cast a serene, indeed a blissful glance over earthly things, whatever entangled us other children of earth, disentangled easily in front of her, and she was usually able to point out the right way just because she looked down into the labyrinth from above and was not herself trapped in it[78].

This metaphor of someone of harmonious vision raised above the labyrinthine confusions of earthly life is also used by Goethe to describe the poet. In a letter to Schiller he described the effect of Homer's poetry as follows: 'for one is always lifted up above everything earthly, as if in a Montgolfier, and finds oneself truly in that intermediate sphere in which the gods move to and fro'[79]. In Book 13 of *Dichtung und Wahrheit* he writes of 'true poetry', 'Like a hot air balloon it lifts us up, along with the ballast that is fastened to us, into higher realms and allows the tangled maze of the earth to lie unrolled beneath us from a bird's eye view'[80].

Just as Makarie functions as interpreter and mediator between the individual and the problems of the world with her 'ethical-magical mirror' so she functions as a mediator between the generations with her archive. The archive is a 'memory-building' which represents the collective memory, no longer held within the head of mankind as in oral cultures, but preserved and recorded in script with the intention of passing it on to future generations. The function of the archive is the preservation of script and its transfer to posterity. In the 'Betrachtungen im Sinne der Wanderer' we hear that 'literature is the fragment of fragments'. The archive represents the fragmentary way in which tradition is preserved and passed on. It is one of the concerns of the writer, just as it is one of Makarie's concerns, to preserve and pass on this tradition to future generations. The epithet 'Angel on Earth' used of her and the name of her amanuensis, Angela, point to this function of messenger and mediator between the generations. The first aphorism in the 'Betrachtungen im Sinne der Wanderer' - 'every wise thought has already been

---

[78] H.A. Volume 10, pages 41 and 57.
[79] Schiller/Goethe Briefwechsel, letter to Schiller, 12th May 1798, page 629.
[80] H.A. Volume 9, page 580.

thought, one must only try to think it out again' - also suggests the continuity of thought through the generations and the futility of the pursuit of complete originality.

If Makarie's archive represents a kind of compendium of human thought and ideas in the realms of art, literature, science, religion and philosophy, there are indications in the novel of two ways in which this library of human thought can serve as an inspiration for following generations. In Book 1, Chapter 10 the narrator reports on the careful, analytical, labyrinthine process by which Wilhelm pursues meaning backwards through the paradoxical and often contradictory collection of aphorisms:

> They were conclusions which appear paradoxical, if we do not know their genesis, but compel us to go backwards by means of a reversed procedure of uncovering and discovering and, wherever possible, to visualise for ourselves the lineage of such thoughts from a great distance, from their starting-point onwards (125).

In the same chapter Angela describes how, when reading aloud from the aphorisms to Makarie at night, the words suddenly take on a magical inspiring life of their own so that 'a thousand details leap out in a remarkable way, just like when an amount of quicksilver falls and divides itself up in all directions into countless beads of the most varied shapes' (124). It had seemed as though Makarie was no more than a passive source of inspiration for the astronomer and Montan when we recalled their conversations in her presence, in Book 3, Chapter 14. Here, however, we see Makarie in an active role as reader/writer/interpreter. Angela had previously described the potency of the word, how 'individual good ideas (...) from a stimulating discussion (...) leap out like seeds from a many-branched plant' (123), an evocation of the Platonic 'logos spermatikos' which Socrates claims can only be generated through the spoken word, through dialogue:

> When one employs the dialectic method and plants and sows in a fitting soil intelligent words which are not fruitless but yield seeds from which there spring up in other minds other words capable of continuing the process forever, and which make their possessor happy, to the farthest possible limit of human happiness[81],

---

[81] Plato, *Works*, Volume 1, *Phaidrus*, Loeb Classical Library, edited by G. P. Goold, translated by

and not 'through a pen with words which cannot defend themselves by argument and cannot teach the truth effectually'. Goethe attributes this generative power to the written word as well. But here the written words are being read aloud again and are placed in a situation of dialogue with the listener and with the other aphorisms in Makarie's collection. These two ways of attaining insight are brought together in aphorism 123 from the 'Betrachtungen im Sinne der Wanderer'[82]. In the 'Konfession des Verfassers' of the *Farbenlehre* Goethe describes his own method of poetic production in a similar way, saying of a theme that interested him, 'After I had developed it in secret for years, at last all of a sudden, I set it down on paper extempore and instinctively, as it were'[83].

The sudden inspiration is a result of long practice and preparation, of the internalising of the necessary principles and rules. This again is a bringing together of the two activities of 'observing' and 'reflecting'. Makarie's understanding of the solar system comes about through a similar combination of intuition and careful study leading to 'a very well-ordered imagination' (451). What the astronomer suspected at first of being the result of 'a hidden guile' turns out to be just that combination of observation and reflection which is a necessary prerequisite for creativity, whether it be creative production or creative reproduction.

The figure of Makarie incorporates, too, something of the ambiguity of the writer's role. The magic mirror, which she holds up to the individual, may transfigure but it may well be deceptive. The images, which it reveals, are reverse images. One of the last aphorisms in Makarie's archive warns of this:

> It is not easy to reproduce anything totally objectively. You could say that the mirror is an exception to this, and yet we never see our appearance quite correctly in it; indeed the mirror reverses our image and makes our left hand into our right. This could be a metaphor for all reflections about ourselves (486).

Harold North Fowler, Harvard & London 1982, pages 569-70.

[82] 'Everything that we call invention or discovery in the higher sense, is the serious exercise or activation of an original instinct for the truth, for a long time developed in secret, that suddenly, in a flash leads to a fruitful insight' (302).

[83] H.A. Volume 14, page 252.

And in Book 3, Chapter 14, the farewell scene at Makarie's castle, when the narrator attempts to tie up the loose ends, in a parody of a conventional novel ending, we seem to see not so much a guiding figure helping others to find their true selves, but rather a representation of the tyranny of the great over lesser mortals as Philine and Lydie deny their former selves and, in a tableau with Makarie, are reduced to nothing more than stereotypes of penitent 'sinners at the feet of the saint' (441). There is something ineradicably banal about much of this scene, with the solutions Makarie provides to the relationships she disentangles suddenly appearing very conventional, while much that is more complex remains 'im Schweben' [in the balance] (447). Here is an indication of the paradox of the simultaneous limitlessness and limitation of the writer's role and an invitation to the reader to take on the role of creative re-producer.

Excursus: 'Die neue Melusine', a paradigm of misreading.

At the end of the tenth book of *Dichtung und Wahrheit* Goethe recounts how he told his fairytale 'Die neue Melusine' for the first time as a student of twenty to the Brion sisters and other members of the household in Sesenheim. He is pleased with the success of his narration and, as he describes its effect on his listeners, he delivers a short and light-hearted, but nevertheless seriously intended contribution to narrative theory. The rewards of the successful storyteller lie in the reactions of his audience. His aims are to entertain, move and engage the sympathies, and then, to provoke interpretative efforts on the part of his audience, to force them to think and to stretch this thought further by confusing and disappointing expectations, summed up finally in the twin aims of 'profit and pleasure': 'to bequeath, to the imagination, the stuff of new images and, to the reason, matter for further contemplation'[84].

---

[84] His achievement is 'to arouse the curiosity, to capture the attention, to provoke the listener into the overhasty solving of impenetrable mysteries, to disappoint the expectations, to bewilder with a progression of ever stranger happenings, to arouse pity and fear, to cause anxiety, to move and finally by converting apparent gravity into witty and amusing levity to

Goethe carried this story around in his head for many years before it found its final place as one of the narratives in the *Wanderjahre*. It had been published previously in two instalments with an interval of two years between in the *Taschenbuch für Damen*. He refers to his first attempt to compose a written version in a letter to Charlotte von Stein in 1782 but says that other pressures have hindered him from getting very far[85]. There is a further mention of an attempt to capture the tale in written form in a letter of 1797 to Schiller who was looking for contributions to his journal, *Die Horen*[86]. Later that year, as he travelled towards Switzerland, he wrote to Schiller from Frankfurt, comparing himself as a traveller to the protagonist of his fairytale and hoping that he would succeed in committing it to paper during his journey, 'I'll probably be able to scribble down that little travel tale for you during the journey'[87]. Not until 1807, however, do a series of diary entries indicate that Goethe, during a visit to Jena, had succeeded in his long-cherished aspiration. Over a period of ten days from 21st to 31st May the progress of the work is recorded from beginning to end[88]. Already at this stage Goethe intended the fairytale for the *Wanderjahre*, which he had been working on for some years. As the years passed, however, and the *Wanderjahre* seemed to defy completion, Goethe contemplated including 'Die neue Melusine' in *Dichtung und Wahrheit* in 1812 and then, in 1817 and 1819, brought it out in the two instalments in the *Taschenbuch für Damen*.

Katharina Mommsen has posited a close connection between Goethe's original telling of the tale, his attempts to produce a written version and events from his own life[89]. She sees him, in the first instance, as identifying with the

---

satisfy the soul, to bequeath to the imagination the stuff of new images and to the reason matter for further contemplation'. H.A. Volume 9, page 446.

[85] Letter to Charlotte von Stein, September 1782. H.A., Letters, Volume 1, page 406.

[86] Goethe writes, 'The tale with the little woman in the box also sometimes smiles at me again, but it won't come to proper fruition yet'. Schiller/Goethe Briefwechsel, letter to Schiller, 4th February 1797, page 353.

[87] Schiller/Goethe Briefwechsel, letter to Schiller from Frankfurt, 12th August 1797, page 436.

[88] Tagebuch - 21st May and 31st May 1807. W.A. 3. 3, pages 211-17.

[89] *Goethes Märchen*, edited by Katharina Mommsen, Frankfurt am Main 1984, 'Zur Deutung der Neuen Melusine', pages 152-162.

protagonist in his attempt to escape from the narrowness and limitations of the dwarf-world. She suggests that the original inspiration for the tale might have been, on the one hand, Goethe's sense of guilt at his abandonment of Friederike and, on the other hand, his fear of the restrictions and narrowness of the life at Sesenheim, for all its attraction, and his presentiment of the restricted life that marriage to Friederike would impose upon him. She attributes the unattractive character of the hero partly to an attempt by Goethe to disguise this autobiographical element and his sense of identity with him. His renewed interest in the story, in 1782, came at the time when he was beginning to fret under the restrictions of life in Weimar and was first thinking of an escape to Italy. In 1797, when he describes to Schiller his vain attempts to write the story, he was thinking of a second trip to Rome, once more to escape the restricted life of Weimar. At this stage Mommsen sees Goethe as identifying with Melusine, too, as a figure who must leave her beloved because he has not fulfilled certain conditions, just as Goethe felt in Weimar that the original conditions of his collaboration in government there had not been observed.

In the context of the *Wanderjahre* 'Die neue Melusine' is introduced, in keeping with its oral origin, as a tale told by the otherwise reticent barber to Wilhelm and the leaders of the emigrants - a tale, moreover, which the barber claims, despite its striking fairytale elements, is autobiographical and, therefore, based on memories of his own past. 'Die neue Melusine' is often interpreted as one of the tales in the *Wanderjahre* acting as exemplifications of behaviour lacking self-restraint, where the protagonist eventually learns to comply with the demands of renunciation and emerges into the frame-story. According to this interpretation the barber, as protagonist of the fairytale, is the epitome of immoderation. He breaks all the conditions imposed upon him by Melusine, but is nevertheless still granted the opportunity of marriage to her and life in the world of the dwarves. He throws away this last chance also, however, and ends up exactly at his starting point without having learned anything at all from his experience. The figure of the barber/narrator, who emerges from the realm of the fairytale into the world of the frame-story, is often seen an example of someone who has eventually learned self-restraint and reaped the rewards of this lesson. He has been enabled to develop one special talent - 'the gift of storytelling' (353) - by controlling his natural garrulousness and accepting the imposition of a vow of silence in everyday life in order to be able to channel his drive towards communication into effective storytelling[90].

The barber may well have made the important step from unrestrained licence to renunciation by the time he comes to tell his tale, but he remains nevertheless a highly paradoxical figure. Not only is there a certain paradox in the idea of a vow of silence leading to the development of an outstanding talent for storytelling, but the stories he tells are also described paradoxically as 'wahrhafte Märchen und märchenhafte Geschichten' [true fairytales and fairytale stories], and, although he claims that the story which he is about to launch upon really happened to him, it turns out to have all the characteristics of a fairytale, moving from the human world to the world of dwarves and back again and full of purses with inexhaustible supplies of money, magic keys, caskets and rings[91]; while the barber himself is also referred to by Wilhelm as a character from the realm of fairytale, as 'Rotmantel' [Redcoat] (315)[92]. There is paradox, too, in fairytale which is autobiography and which is told by a first-person narrator.

Although a consummate storyteller, the barber is, by his own admission, inadequate as an interpreter of his own story and still carries it with him so vividly in his memory precisely because he has not been able to interpret it

---

[90] Cf., for example, H. A. Volume 8, pages 650-1 or Klingenberg, pages 131-4.

[91] Not only does it have all these fairytale elements but the story is, in fact, as the title implies, an adaptation of an older fairytale, that of the water-nymph, Melusine and Count Raimond. Oskar Seidlin has commented on the way in which the older tale is allowed to shine through the newer in spite of all the changes which Goethe made: 'not unlike a palimpsest, in which the old text can be read at the same time behind the new one' (page 151). This technique has the effect that, as with a palimpsest, the text contains a sub-text, and is thus able to say more than its apparent surface meaning. Oskar Seidlin, '*Melusine* in der Spiegelung der *Wanderjahre*' in: Fs. V.Lange pages 146-162. Reprinted as 'Coda. Ironische Kontrafaktur: Goethes "Neue Melusine"' in: O.S. *Vom erwachenden Bewußtsein und vom Sündenfall*, Stuttgart 1979, pages 155-170.

[92] 'Rotmantel' refers to a fairytale, 'Stumme Liebe', from Musäus' collection *Volksmärchen der Deutschen* in which a ghostly barber in a red coat appears to the protagonist in a haunted house and silently shaves him.

satisfactorily to himself so that it is lodged there as an irritant awaiting further explication. It is a story he says, 'which, although it happened to me some years ago, still makes me uneasy when I remember it, indeed even holds out the hope of a final resolution' (354). The barber exhibits many characteristics in common with Wilhelm. As 'derber Wundarzt' [doughty surgeon] (353) he shares the calling for which Wilhelm has spent so many years training; he too is the narrator of his own story, at the centre of which is an ideal and ultimately unattainable woman. Like Wilhelm and Lenardo this narrator is also a traveller but, unlike them, his travels do not bring him progress and development but are completely circular in motion so that he ends up exactly where he started out. He ends his tale, 'And so I came finally, although by a considerable detour, back to the stove and to the cook, where you first got to know me' (376); and moreover he ends up there without having learned anything from his experiences on the way. He describes himself as 'much more foolish and inept'. In the course of telling his story, the barber consistently misapprehends and misconstrues the evidence of his own senses. Whereas Wilhelm, with his characteristic attitude of 'observation' and 'reflection' represents a fruitful way to approach the task of interpretation, the barber serves as a representative model of the mis-reader, the mis-interpreter.

At the centre of the barber's narrative is Melusine's magical, dwarf-crafted travelling casket, a reduplication of the mysterious casket discovered by Felix in the underground cavern. Like this 'Prachtbüchlein' [ornamental book-cover] Melusine's casket is also a work of art. It has been crafted by dwarves, who are the archetypical artist-craftsmen of Nordic mythology and have an understanding of the labyrinthine subterranean world of underground passages (367); it has the property of unfolding itself from a casket into a magnificent summer palace for dwarves (369); and the process whereby it does so is compared to the intricate mechanisms of a writing desk constructed by Röntgen, a technically complex and highly skilled work of craftsmanship:

> Whoever has seen a writing desk manufactured by Röntgen, in which with one pull a great number of springs and compartments start to move, writing surface and writing

implements, compartments for letters and money open out at the same time or shortly
after each other, will be able to form an idea of how that palace opened out (372).

In his letter to Schiller from Frankfurt on his way to Switzerland, at the time when
he was planning a written version of the tale Goethe makes an allusion to
Melusine's casket and particularly to its essential quality as a work of art, a
container of ideals. He too, he suggests, is carrying with him a metaphorical
Melusine's casket, containing his ideals[93].

This work of art that is the casket opens up for the narrator of the tale, the
barber, to experience the mixture of 'poetry and truth' which is his narrative: a
narrative which he claims is a true story, but which, in reality, belongs firmly in
the world of art among his 'true fairytales and fairytale stories'. The barber, like
Wilhelm, is at the same time protagonist, narrator and interpreter of his tale. As
interpreter he stands outside his text and acknowledges both the impossibility and
the necessity of the search for ultimate meanings but within the text he also plays
the role of mis-interpreter or mis-reader who overlooks every textual clue offered
to him.

As we have seen, the barber in his tale, like Wilhelm in the *Wanderjahren*
embarks on a labyrinthine journey. The barber comments at the end of his tale
that he has returned to his starting point 'although by a considerable detour'
(376); Wilhelm, in his letter to Natalie explaining his decision to become a
surgeon, claims that his goal of full communication is to be reached 'only by a
detour' (279). Unlike Wilhelm, who follows, both in the letter and in the
Wanderjahre, a multicursal labyrinth with many dead ends and false starts but
gains in enlightenment and development through his journey, the barber follows a
unicursal labyrinth whose single path leads him straight to its centre, the mystery
of the casket and the new world which it opens up to him. Although he fails all
the tests, which are set for him along the way, he is nevertheless allowed to reach

---

[93] 'What ideals I still have are carried with me enclosed in a little casket, like that little undine
pygmy-woman'. Schiller/Goethe Briefwechsel, letter to Schiller from Frankfurt, 12th August
1797, page 436.

this centre, but he then returns to the outside without having recognised the mystery at the centre of the labyrinth.

As the barber moves through his maze Melusine acts for him as an Ariadne-figure, guiding him through the labyrinth, offering him the clues which will enable him to pass the tests she has set him and reach the goal: 'a happiness (...) that is very close to you, but that can only be embraced after several tests' (356). She warns him successively against 'wine and gaming', 'wine and women' (358) and 'wine and anger' (363). The barber misses each of these clues and does exactly what he should have avoided. His distorted vision, fixed as it is on the material world, can envisage the casket only as a container of money or jewels. He reckons, 'Since it was just not heavy enough to contain money, still there could be jewels in it' (359); and a little later speculates again upon its contents, saying, 'My thoughts were again busy with the jewels, I suspected that a carbuncle lay in the casket' (361). Even his love for Melusine is inextricably bound up with his love for the riches she can provide for him. He recounts, 'My yearning for her redoubled and I believed that I couldn't live any longer without her and without her money' (357). In spite of the gift of a 'Hauptschlüssel' [master key] (356), which will open all doors, his mind remains obdurately closed as to the true nature of the casket's treasure. Even when the waiter unwittingly gives him a hint that this treasure is of a different kind from the gold and jewels of the commonplace treasure-chest, saying, 'We suspected that you had a lot of money and valuables with you; now however we have seen your treasure going down the stairs and it appeared in every way to merit safekeeping' (358), his mind remains fixed on exactly such material treasure. Ultimately the casket takes on the banal character he has conceived for it and becomes a mere treasure-chest. Instead of the interpretative 'master key' he receives a 'Schlüsselchen' [little key] which is suitable for opening this material treasure-chest: 'in place of the money, which seemed to have run out, I found a little key; it belonged to the casket, in which I found a considerable amount of compensation' (376). The real treasure, however, is Melusine, who offers him the possibility of widening his horizons and opening his mind to a world beyond that of his own limited experience.

This casket, as a work of art is, like Felix's 'ornamental book-cover', an analogy for the literary work which opens up to the reader to allow entry into another world and, through the experience of otherness, offers the possibility both of an appreciation of that otherness and of a deeper understanding of his own selfhood[94]. At the heart of the casket is Melusine who introduces the protagonist to a new world, the world of the dwarves, which has its own genesis and creation myths. It is a world whose strangeness may sometimes appear ridiculous, especially as it is associated with diminutive size: the dilemma of the dwarf-race which gradually diminishes in size through the generations culminates in the birth of a prince who is so small 'that the attendants even let him slip out of his nappies and no one knows where he has got to' (369). The dwarves are also, however, a race of craftsmen with outstanding artistic talents who, in addition, have the capacity to construct magical rings with the power of altering the laws of dimension; but the protagonist cannot see beyond the indignity of their small size and finds his feelings for Melusine inevitably changed when he discovers the secret of her origins. When he enters the world of the dwarves with her he admits, on the one hand, to the enhanced sensations and perceptions which he experiences in this world, but at the same time he cannot forget the dimensions and standards that are part of his former experience: he is unable to develop the capacity to step outside of himself and to appreciate the value of otherness.

---

[94] Oskar Seidlin comments on the way in which a relationship is suggested between the two caskets by the fact that Goethe follows 'Die neue Melusine' immediately with Hersilie's letter in which she reports the reappearance of Felix's casket 'as if it had glided across from secondary story, which had just been heard, into the main story', page 159. Birgit Baldwin is more emphatic that it was Goethe's deliberate intention to suggest the gliding across of the casket from the fairytale into the 'real story' and maintains that this blurring of boundaries is part of Goethe's technique of calling attention to, and calling into question, narrative artifices such as 'fairytale' and 'frame-story'. Cf. Baldwin, pages 218 and 231. The juxtaposition of the two caskets also emphasises, however, their common characteristic as works of art and their symbolic significance as analogies for the literary work itself.

In a parody of Wilhelm's Kantian experience in Makarie's observatory the barber has his own 'Kantian experience' in the dwarf-world, which leads him to believe that he carries within himself a standard of ideal dimension, a revelation which strengthens his resolve to return to his own world[95]. Wilhelm's experience led him to see a relationship between the laws governing the macrocosm of the universe and the microcosm of man, so that he draws a parallel between the physical laws, which create order in the universe, and the ethical laws, which create order within the psyche of the individual. The barber, on the other hand, experiences no ethical revelation but only a false sense of the superiority of one material yardstick over another: 'I felt inside myself a yardstick of my former size, which made me uneasy and unhappy'. His 'ideal' is no more than a matter of physical measurement, quantitative rather than qualitative: 'I had an ideal of myself and sometimes appeared to myself in a dream like a giant'.

The barber's distorted perception of the world is emphasised by the contrast between himself and Melusine. Melusine embodies balance and harmony: the words 'Anmut' [grace] (362) and 'Würde' [dignity] (355) are characteristically used to describe her. She is associated with the harmony of music, singing and playing the lute, and her musical talent is a means of drawing people together in convivial entertainment. The barber, on the other hand, lacks all balance and harmony. He is warned against excess of various kinds by Melusine and particularly against 'sudden eruptions of passionate desire' (356). Associated with him are the words 'Ungeduld' [impatience] and 'Übermut' [arrogance] (355), 'Verwegenheit' [recklessness] (355) and 'Verzweiflung' [despair] (356). He is 'inclined to make rash decisions' (371). His attitude to music is negative. He says, 'I will just confess, that I have never been able to make much of music, it had, rather, an unpleasant effect on me' (364). And later declares even more emphatically that music 'seemed to me (...) the most hateful

---

[95] Cf. Henkel, page 92.

thing on earth' (373). Where others experience harmony he perceives only disharmony.

From a very early age Goethe was keenly appreciative of the mixture of truth and fiction, which constitute the essential nature of the fairytale. As a nineteen-year-old he wrote to Friederike Oeser, 'A fairytale has its truth, and must have it, or else it would not be a fairytale'[96]. In the 'Maximen und Reflexionen' 'Märchen' is defined in the following way, 'Fairytale: which portrays to us events that are impossible as possible, in possible or impossible circumstances'[97]. In a reference to the 'Die neue Melusine' itself he speaks of the 'certain humorous grace, which can arise from the combination of the impossible with the ordinary, the incredible with the everyday'[98]. In his comment on the story in *Dichtung und Wahrheit* Goethe emphasises that it is the interplay of 'Ernst' [gravity] and 'Scherz' [levity] which enables the storyteller simultaneously to entertain and to educate his listener. With its combination of the familiar and the fantastical, its synthesis of 'gravity and levity', 'Die neue Melusine' functions as a light-hearted vehicle for a parodistical reflection in miniature of the theme of understanding and interpretation which is a major concern of the work as a whole.

---

[96] 13th February 1769. W.A. 4. 1, page 198.
[97] H.A. Volume 12, No. 935, page 498.
[98] In an unpublished essay of 1827, as he ponders the possibility of composing further such fairytales. Mommsen, *Goethes Märchen*, page 151.

CHAPTER 4

'A very intricate work of art'
'Ein merkwürdig verschlungenes Kunstwerk'

The *Wanderjahre* as a paradigm of 'world literature'

das Fragment der Fragmente
the fragment of fragments

The novel itself, according to its narrator, purports to be constructed from a selection of texts entrusted to him to edit. In the 'Zwischenrede' of the first version of the novel the narrator describes his task thus:

> For we have to find a solution to the dubious task of choosing from the most heterogeneous papers what is of the most benefit and significance, so that it can be appreciated by thoughtful and educated minds and refresh and support them at various stages of their lives (1821.106-7).

These most varied texts include practically all forms of writing: novellas and fairytales, letters and diaries, poems and songs, factual reports and learned articles, translations and works of other people's hands. It was this variety of texts within the one work, the collective nature of the novel, which led Volker Neuhaus to coin the term 'archive fiction' in order to designate the form of the *Wanderjahre*. The library and archive in Makarie's castle represents a concrete image within the novel for this form of collective work.

At the time when he was working on the *Wanderjahre* Goethe was very interested in the concept of 'Weltliteratur' [world literature]. His first recorded usages of the term stem from 1827. In a conversation recorded by Eckermann on 31st January 1827, in which the literature under discussion ranged from Chinese romances to the novels of Richardson, to Manzoni and back to the tragedians of ancient Greece, Goethe insisted, 'National literature doesn't mean very much now; the age of world literature is at hand, and everyone must play his part to accelerate this age'[1]. By the term 'Weltliteratur' Goethe did not intend to imply an inflexible, exclusive canon of master-works, of works of great literature, but rather a body of texts which was in a continuous process of growth and change, embracing 'script' in all its variety: the concept included, for Goethe, journalism as much as belles-lettres, the topical as well as the traditional[2].

Fritz Strich has offered the following definition for Goethe's idea of 'Weltliteratur':

> World literature is the literature mediating between nations and making them acquainted with each other, the intellectual space in which the different peoples meet each other and exchange their intellectual wealth[3].

This definition brings out Goethe's fondness for the metaphor of trade and commerce to describe the intellectual exchange between people of different nations[4]. It also makes clear the importance for Goethe of the spoken word in this context. World literature embraces for him not only the exchange of written texts, but more importantly, represents a direct spoken discourse between the nations. This idea is stressed in words he addressed to a gathering of natural scientists in Berlin, 'No! Here it is rather a question of living, working authors getting to know each other and finding themselves inspired through inclination and public spirit to work in cooperation'[5].

---

[1] Eckermann, page 211. A diary entry for 15th January 1827 reads, 'Dictated to Schuchardt regarding French and world literature'. In volume 6.1 of *Über Kunst und Altertum* (1827,) Goethe wrote in a review of *Le Tasse,* a drama by Duval, 'I am convinced that a universal *world literature* is developing, in which an honourable role is reserved for us Germans'. W.A. 41(2), page 265.

[2] In *Über Kunst und Altertum* Vol.6.2. (1828) Goethe wrote of the *Edinburgh Reviews*, 'These periodicals, as they gradually win a larger readership, will contribute most effectively to a hoped-for universal world literature', W.A. 41(2), page 348. To the editor of the Italian journal *L'Eco* he wrote on 31st May 1828, 'The first forty-seven pages of your periodical, which you have launched in Milan, have given me a most pleasant surprise; through their content and the pleasing form, which you are so well able to give them, they will certainly contribute in the most pleasing way to the universal world literature, which is disseminating itself ever more vigorously and I can honestly assure you of my interest'. W.A. 4.44, page 108.

[3] Fritz Strich, *Goethe und die Weltliteratur*, Bern 1957 (2), page 322.

[4] E.g. 'The spirit gradually developed the desire also to be admitted into the circles of more or less free intellectual commerce'. In: 'Einleitung zu Thomas Carlyle, Leben Schillers', W.A. 42(1), page 187.

[5] 'Die Zusammenkunft der Naturforscher in Berlin. 1828', W.A. 2. 13, page 449.

The growth of a world literature is a development for the most part welcomed by Goethe as a means of fostering understanding between the nations. He suggests that the merits of a particular author can often be seen much more clearly by someone from outside:

> Carlyle has written the Life of Schiller and really evaluated him in a way a German would not easily do. On the other hand we have a clear understanding of Shakespeare and Byron and can perhaps appreciate their merits better than the English themselves.[6]

With regard to his own work he is pleased to note the variety of perspectives contained in reviews by critics of different nations. In 'Helena in Edinburgh, Paris und Moskau' (1828) he comments:

> Here the Scotsman strives to penetrate the work; the Frenchman, to understand it; the Russian, to take possession of it. And so Carlyle, Ampère and Schewireff, totally without prior agreement, have gone through all the categories of possible participation in a work of art or of nature[7].

On a more general level he suggests that through an intellectual exchange, through an understanding and appreciation of each other's literature in its widest sense, the nations, while preserving their diversity and individuality, can learn to understand and accept their differences:

> I only wish to repeat, that there can be no question that the nations should think the same, but that they should become aware of each other, understand each other and, if they cannot love each other, at least learn to tolerate each other[8].

Goethe regards the concept of world literature also, however, as somewhat ambivalent. One of the aphorisms for Makarie's archive warns, 'Now, since a world literature is inaugurating itself, the German has, if we look closely, the most to lose; he will do well to think about this warning'. Elsewhere he emphasises in a light-hearted image the immensity, limitlessness and uncontrollability of the power he has invoked, 'Then notice, that the world literature that I have conjured up is streaming towards me to engulf me like the sorcerer's apprentice'[9].

---

[6] Eckermann, 15th July 1827, page 243.
[7] W.A., 41(2), page 358.
[8] *Über Kunst und Altertum.* 6.2. 1828, W.A. 41(2), page 348.
[9] Letter to Zelter, 21st May 1828. H.A., Letters, Volume 4, page 277.

Within the ambit of 'Weltliteratur' Goethe used another term, 'Weltpoesie' [world poetry], to distinguish a smaller, more specialised category. Fritz Strich gives it the following definition:

> World poetry is the universal human poetic gift granted to all nations and ages by nature, which can emerge completely independent of rank or education and that is why it manifests itself particularly clearly in what one calls folk literature.

'Weltpoesie' represents for Goethe, on the one hand synchronically, the geographically all-embracing 'Volkspoesie' [folk poetry] of all nations, but is also, on the other hand, diachronically inclusive, covering all literary works which through the ages have exercised and still continue to exercise an influence over the human imagination: works such as those of Homer, Plato, Shakespeare or the Bible, whose international status belies their national origins.

Although Goethe's employment of the term 'Weltliteratur' dates from the 1820s the nucleus of his concept of world literature had begun to develop in the first decade of the new century. In June 1808 Professor Niethammer, an official of the Bavarian state education system, sent Goethe a copy of a lecture in which he outlined his idea of a 'National-Buch' [national book] for Germany. In this lecture he regretted what he saw as the low level of German culture in comparison to her European neighbours and suggested that such a 'National-Buch', which would in effect be a compendium of the best of 'classic' German literature of all kinds, could provide the German people not only with enjoyment and education but also with a standard for the judgement of literature. Such a book could be to Germany what Homer had been to the Greeks or what the Bible had been to Christendom. Niethammer suggested the names of Goethe and Voß as two people who would be ideally suited for such an undertaking since 'one had given Homer to the Germans and the other had given them so much that was Homeric'[10]. Niethammer sent a copy of his lecture to Goethe accompanied by a letter requesting him to involve himself in the preparation of such a 'National-Buch'.

---

[10] W.A. 42 (2), page.407. He is referring to the German translation of Homer by Voß.

Goethe received the idea enthusiastically and began a series of sketches and notes for the project, although nothing eventually came of it. It is clear, however, from these notes that already Goethe's ideas were reaching beyond the idea of a national literature and towards the idea of a world literature. In a note under the heading *Unde* (whence) he suggests that the content of such a book should comprise 'what is good and authentic from all times and peoples'. He goes on to stress the important contribution of other nations to German literature, noting that 'translations are an essential part of our literature' and under the sub-heading 'Deutsches Fremdes' [German borrowings] he suggests that an important part of any 'National-Buch' would be 'the literature from all ages and places which was important to human beings of all times and kinds'.

Goethe suggests that the Bible can be taken as a symbol of the form of such a book[11]. In *Dichtung und Wahrheit*, describing his perception of the collective and polyphonic nature of the Bible he emphasises that it is the work of many hands covering a long time-span: 'the Bible as a cumulative work which came into being little by little and was reworked at different times'[12]. In a passage in the *Farbenlehre* he emphasises the infinite variety of interpretative methods which the Bible has attracted to itself, a whole chorus of interpreters who 'want to interpret and to explain, to connect or to supplement, to systematise or to apply'; and suggests that this variety is the result of its vast scope and unfathomability: 'because of the independence, the wonderful originality, the many-sidedness, the totality, indeed the immensity of its content, this work brought with it no yardstick by which it could be measured'[13]. In the 'Noten und Abhandlungen' to the *West-östlichen Divan* the same idea occurs of 'das Buch aller Bücher' [the book of all books] as a symbol for all literary texts, through which the reader wanders as through a labyrinth and from which he learns to develop his 'reading' skills and gains new insights: 'and so the book of all books was able to

---

[11] 'Die höchste Form einer solchen Sammlung finden wir in der Bibel' [we find the highest form of such a collection in the Bible] W.A. 42 (2), page 421.

[12] H.A. Volume 9, page 508-9.

[13]*Goethe. Historische Schriften*, edited by Horst Günther, Frankfurt am Main 1982, page 187.

demonstrate book by book that it was given to us so that we might test ourselves in it as if in second world, so that we might lose our way in it, so that we might enlighten and educate ourselves'[14].

In the *Wanderjahre* the Bible is used as a symbol for the ideal form of the novel itself. It is 'das Buch aller Bücher', the exemplary book per se and its various components are characterised in the following way:

> They combine together so happily that from the most diverse elements a remarkable unity emerges. They are complete enough to satisfy, fragmentary enough to stimulate; sufficiently barbaric to offer a challenge, sufficiently tender to bring calm; and how many other contradictory characteristics there are to praise in these books, in this book! (160)

This is a description which serves equally well for the *Wanderjahre* itself, a novel that is, at one and the same time, both complete and fragmentary, constructed as it is from a collection of the most diverse texts and in a wide variety of tones, both tender and barbaric - from the dry formality of the academic article, to the graceful lightness of the most delicate of love stories or the irreverent coarseness of the comical tale.

Goethe's suggestions for the content, themes and form of the proposed 'National-Buch' bear a remarkable resemblance to the content, themes and form of the *Wanderjahre*. In considering the 'Gehalt' [substance] of the 'National-Buch' Goethe suggests that it should be on three levels:

> In such a collection there would be a highest level, which would perhaps be beyond the comprehension of the majority. They should develop their imagination and understanding through it. They should learn to venerate and respect; to see something unattainable above them; something which would draw at least some individuals upwards to the higher levels of culture. Then there would be a middle level, and this would be what one wanted to educate them towards, what one would wish to see them gradually comprehend. The lowest level would comprise what is immediately acceptable to the majority, what satisfies and attracts them[15].

These diverse levels are also a feature of the *Wanderjahre,* whose contents range from 'Schwank' [comical tale] to 'ätherische Dichtung' [ethereal poetry]. In the *Wanderjahre,* as in the plan for the 'National-Buch', the suggestion is made that

---

[14] H.A. Volume 2, pages 128-9.
[15] W.A. 42 (2), page 415.

literature must attempt to satisfy the needs of the whole human being. As well as the spiritual element - the 'Oberstes' [highest level] -

> The imagination would be stimulated by events, myths, legends and fables. For the sensory nature the unmediated passion of love, with its weal and woe, naïve humour, extraordinary situations, pleasantries and uncouth pranks would be presented.

The first word in the notes for the 'National-Buch' under 'Nähere Form' [detailed form] is 'Neben einander' [juxtaposition]. Under the influence of Erich Trunz the word 'Nebeneinander' has become a commonplace to describe the construction of the *Wanderjahre*[16]. In the novel itself the recurring motif of the picture gallery serves as a metaphor for the way in which the text is constructed by a method of juxtaposition, an attempt to suggest that all the elements making up the work should be regarded as standing simultaneously side-by-side. The second phrase used by Goethe to describe the form, which the 'National-Buch' should take, is 'Gleichniß von der Mosaick' [image of the mosaic]. Here again is a similarity with the form of the *Wanderjahre*, which Goethe himself described as 'an aggregate' and the image of the mosaic too suggests the careful piecing together of the most diverse of elements[17]. Finally the third phrase in Goethe's list is 'Verbindung auch Apop[h]t[h]egmatisch' [connection also apophthegmatic], a phrase which neatly describes the *Wanderjahre* with its contradictory drives towards making connections and creating disjunctions, a work in which, on the one hand, the recurring image of weaving suggests the way in which the various threads of narrative are woven together to create a unified whole and which, on the other hand, is forever threatening to fall apart into a series of aphorisms and whose second and third parts do in fact end with an unmediated collection of maxims[18].

---

[16] H. A. Volume 8 page 529, 'The images do not stand in temporal succession, but in spatial juxtaposition. They should all be there at the same time and be compared with each other'.

[17] In conversation with Kanzler von Müller in 1830, 'The book only claims to be an aggregate', Gräf, 1.2, page 1067. In conversation with W.J. Tomaschek on 16th August 1822 Goethe refers to, 'What was earlier scattered, now strung together'. Gräf, 1.2, page 996.

[18] These contradictory drives towards connection and separation are repeatedly reflected in various sections of the work. For example the anatomical sculptor says, 'Connection means more than separation' (328); in 'Der Mann von 50 Jahren' the question is put, 'And should not loving and

In Goethe's imagination the idea of a 'National-Buch' has been transformed into a 'Welt-Buch' [world book] and in the *Wanderjahre* he creates a literary image of what such a 'Welt-Buch' might contain. Much of his later work can be regarded as collectives or compendia. In the *West-östliche Divan* he journeys east and attempts a synthesis between the lyric of east and west while at the same time offering a spectrum of the possibilities of lyric and, in the 'Noten und Abhandlungen', engaging the reader directly in the consideration of the problems of lyrical production. In *Faust II* the most varied possibilities of dramatic creation are rehearsed, from classical drama to masque and at the same time, in the union of Faust and Helena, a synthesis is attempted between the spirit of north and south, the medieval and the classical, whose progeny, Euphorion, embodies not only the spirit of poetry for all times - 'heilige Poesie' [holy poetry] - but also serves as a memorial for Goethe's own contemporary, Lord Byron[19].

In 1829 Goethe was noting, 'Europäische, d.h. Welt-literatur', [European, i.e. world literature] but in fact he had already gone far beyond this, as the breadth and inclusiveness of the articles in the volumes of *Kunst und Altertum* indicate; the contents of one volume for instance ranging from articles on Homer, Euripides and Aristotle's *Poetics* to articles on Indian and Chinese literature. In 1827 he was already saying to Eckermann, 'The age of world literature is at hand'. In the *Wanderjahre* the Abbé suggests that 'Hausfrömmigkeit' [domestic piety] must now be replaced by 'Weltfrömmigkeit' [world piety] and the possibilities for Europe and for the wider horizons of the New World are explored in the plans of the migrants and the emigrants. The novel itself incorporates many of Goethe's ideas on 'Weltliteratur'. He stressed the importance of the role of the

---

abiding have just the same rights as sundering and shunning?'; it is said of Flavio and Hilarie as they skate together that they were 'now together, now separate, now divided, now united' (212); in the same story the effects of floods and of ice are contrasted, 'Then the spectacle of the world changed suddenly; what was previously separated by floods, was now connected by dry land' (211); during the episode at Lago Maggiore we are told, 'Several days were spent in this peculiar way between meeting and parting, between separation and being together; in the enjoyment of the most delightful company departure and deprivation always hovered in front of their distraught souls' (233).

[19] 'One thought one glimpsed a well-known figure in the dead youth', *Faust II*, lines 9691-9938.

translator. In his review of Thomas Carlyle's anthology, *German Romance,* he writes, 'So every translator is a prophet to his own people'[20]. In the *Wanderjahre* there is a story translated from the French, 'Die pilgernde Törin', and the various members of the uncle's household represent in themselves a kind of society of European literature. Hersilie says of them:

> That in our house a lot of reading is done and that we have divided the different literatures amongst us by chance, through inclination, also no doubt out of a spirit of opposition. Uncle is fond of Italian literature, the lady here doesn't take it amiss if you take her for a genuine Englishwoman, but I am true to the French writers, as long as they are amusing and elegant. Over here Papa Land-agent enjoys early German literature and the son can then, as is appropriate, devote his attention to the newer, more modern authors (50).

The major, in 'Der Mann von funfzig Jahren', translates and paraphrases poems from Horace and Ovid. In the collections of maxims and aphorisms are selections from Plotinus, from Hippocrates and from the Koran and references to Byron, Shakespeare, Calderon, Laurence Sterne and Lessing. Represented too is direct spoken intellectual exchange. In Makarie's castle discussion covers a wide range of intellectual spheres and reflects perhaps something of the intellectual exchange in Goethe's circle in Weimar. To the discussion on the uses and misuses of mathematics the astronomer introduces a translated article with the words, 'And so I've brought some written material with me, more precisely translations: for in such matters I trust my countrymen as little as myself; agreement from foreign and distant parts seems to me to provide more certainty' (117-8).

With the 'archive fiction' of the *Wanderjahre* Goethe has gone some way to reproducing in a literary work an image of his concept of 'world literature' - fragmentary, unfinished and infinite, it contains everything that has been stored up in the human memory and that still has an influence on the human imagination. It embraces texts as old as Homer or Plotinus and articles from the latest journals such as the Italian *Eco* or the French *Globe*. This fragmentary and yet infinite aspect of literature is the subject of a group of maxims from the

---

[20] H.A. Volume 12, page 353. In this review he also says of translation, 'For whatever one might say about the shortcomings of translation, still it is and remains one of the most important and useful tasks in general worldwide communication'.

'Maximen und Reflexionen'. No. 911 says, 'Literature is of its very nature fragmentary, it contains only monuments of the human spirit, insofar as they have been set down in writing and in the end have survived'[21]. The libraries and archives contained in the *Wanderjahre* represent human memory recorded as script, 'monuments of the human spirit', while the novel itself, in all its aspects, represents all the diverse possibilities of human verbal interchange, spoken as well as written - 'world literature' - the very thing which is described in one of the maxims from 'Betrachtungen im Sinne der Wanderer' as 'the fragment of fragments' (294)[22].

The interaction of text and image

in goldnen Buchstaben
in golden letters

The novel contains not just a compendium of text-types but also a kaleidoscope of art-forms. It is full of examples of ekphrasis, from the cycle of pictures illustrating the life of Saint Joseph to the picture galleries in the 'pedagogical province' and on the uncle's estate, from the ivory crucifix and the illuminated book-cover to Melusine's casket and the beautiful widow's embroidered wallet. With a spectrum that runs from ekphrastic descriptions to collections of aphorisms it raises the whole question of the interaction of text and image and the relationship of the successivity of the literary text to the simultaneity of the visual arts.

The question of the relationship between image and word, between the visual and the literary arts has interested thinkers since ancient times. Cicero relates the story of Simonides of Chios, to whom was attributed the invention of that mnemonic technique which relies on the making of a picture in order to retain things in the memory, a technique of invaluable assistance to the orators for

---

[21] H.A. Volume 12, 'Maximen und Reflexionen', Nos. 910-12, page 494.
[22] The maxim continues, 'The smallest part of all that happened and was said, was written down and from what was written down the smallest part has survived'. This maxim is also No. 910 in the 'Maximen und Reflexionen'.

whom Cicero's handbook was written[23]. Lessing quotes, in the introduction to his *Laokoon oder über die Grenzen der Malerei und der Poesie*, the dictum attributed to Simonides 'that painting is mute poetry and poetry is voiced painting', only to qualify it by insisting that even the ancients limited this comparison to the effect only of these two sister arts, while asserting that in choice of subject matter and mimetic techniques they were quite different. Lessing takes Plutarch as his authority for this statement and uses the quotation -"Ὕλῃ καὶ τρόποις μιμήσεως διαφέρουσι [they differ in subject matter and in mimetic techniques] - from Plutarch's work, *De gloria Athenarum*, as the motto for his *Laokoon*[24].

We have already seen Goethe's interest in the 'Verwandtschaft der Künste' [sisterhood of the arts], and how, while not suggesting that the techniques employed by the visual artist were identical to those employed by the writer, he felt that his knowledge of the techniques of the visual arts helped him to acquire the techniques of literary composition[25]. This concern with the mutuality of the visual and the literary is a recurrent preoccupation in his work. No.907 of the 'Maximen und Reflexionen', in the section on 'Literature and Language', contains a reflection on the relationship between word and image. Beginning with the declaration, 'Word and image are correlates, which constantly seek each other', it considers the way in which word and image both complement and supplement each other and the way in which words have a tendency to convert

[23] Cicero *De Oratore* Book 2 (para 352). The story goes that Simonides was dining with Scopas, a rich and influential citizen of the town of Crannon in Thessaly. Simonides recited a poem in honour of Scopas, however he also included in his poem praise of the twin gods Castor and Pollux. When he was finished Scopas shabbily declared that he would only pay Simonides half of the agreed amount for the poem - the other half Simonides should seek from his beloved Tyndarides whom he had praised so fulsomely. Shortly afterwards Simonides was summoned from the banqueting hall by two young men standing outside the door. At this point the banqueting hall collapsed and Scopas, with all his retinue and guests, was buried in the ruins. When the relatives came to bury the victims they could only be identified because Simonides could remember the seating order of the banqueters around the table. This event gave him the idea of the memory technique whereby the mind is imagined as a wax-tablet on which a picture of the things to be remembered is inscribed, with each item assigned to its own particular place. Cicero, *Works*, Volume 3.1, Loeb Classical Library, London and Cambridge (Mass.) 1967, pages 464-7.
[24] Gotthold Ephraim Lessing, *Laokoon oder über die Grenzen der Malerei und Poesie*, Stuttgart 1964, page 4.
[25] Chapter 2, pages 87-9.

202

themselves into images by turning into tropes and metaphors. It reflects on how traditional forms of script, whether religious or secular: 'Gesetzbuch und Heilsordnung (...) Bibel und Fibel' [code of law and order of salvation (…) Bible and primer], usually combined a delicate balance of word and image and how the disturbance of the balance between what could be expressed in words and what could be expressed in images would result in the production of textual monstrosities.

In the poem 'Gedichte sind gemalte Fensterscheiben' Goethe uses a metaphor from the visual arts - stained glass windows - to describe poetry. Just as the stained glass window is dark and opaque from the outside and only reveals its true colours and splendour to the initiated who have entered the church, so it is with the interpretation of poems. On the surface they appear opaque and impenetrable and only reveal their true nature to one initiated in the skills of interpretation, one who can enter 'die heilige Kapelle' [the sacred chapel]. Then they will provide exactly that combination of delight and profit, which Horace says is the aim of the poet: they will 'educate you and delight the eyes'[26]. This poem finds its echo in the *Wanderjahre* in the house of the 'collector', whose stained glass windows present a dark and impenetrable face to the world, but nevertheless hold out the promise of both pleasure and enlightenment within: 'sombre windowpanes, intricately framed, suggested a delightful glow of colour within' (144).

---

[26] H.A. Volume 1, page 326:

Gedichte sind gemalte Fensterscheiben!
Sieht man vom Markt in die Kirche hinein,
Da ist alles dunkel und düster;
Und so sieht's auch der Herr Philister:
Der mag denn wohl verdrießlich sein
Und lebenslang verdrießlich bleiben.

Kommt aber nur einmal herein,
Begrüßt die heilige Kapelle;
Da ist's auf einmal farbig helle,
Geschicht und Zierat glänzt in Schnelle,
Bedeutend wirkt ein edler Schein;
Dies wird euch Kindern Gottes taugen,
Erbaut euch und ergetzt die Augen!

[Poems are stained glass windows!
Look into the church from the marketplace,
Everything is dark and gloomy there;
And this is how the philistine sees it:
He may well be morose then
And remain morose his whole life long.

But if you only come inside,
Become acquainted with the sacred chapel;
Then suddenly it gleams with colour,
Story and ornament instantly shine forth,
The exquisite glow lends significance;
This will be fitting for you children of god,
Will educate you and delight the eyes!]

During his stay in Italy Goethe formed a plan with Wilhelm Tischbein of collaborating on a project for a joint work, in which paintings by Tischbein of idyllic scenes would be accompanied by poems of Goethe on the same themes. The original idea came from Tischbein but was enthusiastically taken up by Goethe, as he described in the *Italienische Reise*[27]. The plan remained no more than a plan, however, and apart from a few sketches from Tischbein nothing more was done. Years later, when Tischbein had returned to Germany and was working as court-painter in Eutin he sent Goethe a folder of water-colour copies of a cycle of oil-paintings on idyllic themes which he had painted for Herzog Peter Friedrich of Oldenburg, the final fruits of those far-off dreams in Italy. Inspired by the paintings Goethe, too, was moved to take up the old plan once more and produced the essay 'Über Tischbeins Idyllen' which he published in the journal *Über Kunst und Altertum* in 1822. The essay consisted of precise descriptions of the paintings accompanied by more general reflections on the themes of the pictures. Each description then culminated in a poem inspired by the painting. Goethe had arranged the single illustrations, which he received from Tischbein, into a cycle, which represented a 'Steigerung' [ascent] from the natural and earthly world to the spiritual, returning full circle to the natural world with the last picture, 'Berge, Wasser und Wolken' [mountains, water and clouds][28]. When he received a copy of Goethe's text Tischbein commented in a letter to Rennenkampff on the way such an interchange between artist and poet offered the possibility of ongoing mutual inspiration, 'I just received it a few days ago and Goethe's poetry has reawakened ideas in my mind that I would now like to draw to accompany his words'[29]. In his turn Goethe described the interaction of painting, poetry and prose on his imagination in an accompanying letter to Tischbein when he sent him a

---

[27] 20th November 1786, H.A. Volume 11, page 139.
[28] Cf. Erich Trunz, 'Über Goethes Verse und Prosa zu Tischbeins Idyllen' in: *Studien zu Goethes Alterswerken* edited by Erich Trunz, Frankfurt am Main 1971, 'Similarly our series of idylls goes from troglodyte Fauns to hovering sylph-figures, (...). In this way Goethe groups Tischbein's motifs into a cosmic symbol-world', page 46.
[29] Tischbein in Eutin to Rennenkampff in Oldenburg, 10th August 1821. Trunz *Studien*, page 29.

204

printed copy of the essay, 'Then I was inspired to add prose commentaries to my verses, just as I previously accompanied your drawings with stanzas'[30].

In the *Italienische Reise* Goethe often describes how he saw real-life scenes through the eyes of the art-lover. In Venice he writes of 'my old gift of seeing the world through the eyes of that painter whose pictures I have just been studying'. He ends his description of the countryside and its inhabitants between Bozena and Triente, 'Everything formed a living, moving Heinrich Roos'. Of ball-players in Verona he says they took up 'the loveliest positions, worthy of being modelled in marble'; while of Palladio's house in Vicenza he says 'Canaletto should have painted it'[31]. These frequent comparisons perhaps express a similar view to that put forward later by Oscar Wilde in his essay 'The Decay of Lying': that the human being in an advanced state of culture is bound to see nature filtered through the medium of art[32].

Goethe also compares the work of the visual artist to that of the writer. Palladio's power as an architect is 'exactly like the power of a great writer, who forms from truth and lies a third thing whose borrowed existence enchants us'[33]. He sees the visual artist as creating a work which is also a narrative text to be 'read'. Already the titles of two essays, 'Ruisdael als Dichter' [Ruisdael as poet] and 'Rembrandt der Denker' [Rembrandt the thinker], suggest this idea. In the Ruisdael essay three landscape paintings of Ruisdael are discussed 'as a text with a great deal of substance', and the artist's achievement is described as follows:

> The artist has grasped with admirable intelligence the point where creativity coincides with intellect and delivers to the viewer a work of art which, in itself pleasing to the eye, also engages the mind, stimulates the memory and finally expresses a concept without being limited by it or losing its emotional appeal[34].

---

[30] Goethe in Weimar to Tischbein in Eutin, 20th December 1821. W.A. 4. 35, page 211.
[31] H.A. Volume 11, pages 86, 26, 45, 55.
[32] Oscar Wilde, *Complete Works* Collins, London & Glasgow 1970, 'The Decay of Lying', page 983, 'And the true disciples of the great artist are not his studio-imitators, but those who become like his works of art, be they plastic as in Greek days, or pictorial as in modern times; in a word, Life is Art's best, Art's only pupil'.
[33] H.A. Volume 11, page 53.
[34] H.A. Volume 12, 'Ruisdael als Dichter', page 318.

Again the combination of 'Gefühl, Verstand und Einbildungskraft' [emotion, reason and imagination], the investment of the whole complex of human capacities, is insisted upon for the production and for the reception of a work of art.

In the essay 'Über Laokoon' Goethe notes that the static product of the sculptor can attain the dynamic of a text 'through the representation of a single moment'. When the right 'punctum temporis' is chosen, 'a passing moment', then the work of art will achieve a sense of constant dynamism and 'because of this will be gain life ever anew for millions of viewers'[35]. A curious little anecdote told by Riemer in relation to 'Die neue Melusine' indicates the strength of the connection between the visual arts and literature in Goethe's mind. Riemer relates:

> Last night Goethe saw his fairytale of Melusine shimmering out under an architectural framework. In his dream he believed it to be beauty and truth and wanted to write it down; but when he awoke the nonsense vanished[36].

The progressive, temporal nature of the literary work has become, in the dream, a static, framed picture, a spatial work.

In the *Wanderjahre* this interest in the relationship between text and image finds expression through the many examples of ekphrasis contained in the text. The particular characteristic associated with ekphrasis by the Greeks and Romans was 'enargeia' or perspicuity with its connotations of 'clearness', 'vividness', 'in bodily shape', 'manifest to the mind's eye'. The term has come to be used of a textual image described with a vividness, which creates in the reader or listener such an intense experience of the object described that he seems to see it with the distinctness of a real object before his mind's eye.

The archetypal ekphrasis is the 'Shield of Achilles' from Homer's *Iliad*. Hephaestos had forged the shield for Achilles at the behest of the goddess Thetis, mother of the Greek hero, after Achilles' weapons and armour had been lost when

---

[35] H.A. Volume 12, 'Über Laokoon', page 60.
[36] Gräf, 1.2, pages 889-890.

Patroclus was killed by Hector. On the shield Hephaestos depicted the whole living cosmos: in the middle sun, moon, stars, earth, sea; in the next circle a series of scenes from the human world: city and countryside, war and peace, work and festival; and surrounding the whole the flowing waters of the all-embracing Oceanus. In a footnote in *Laokoon* Lessing said of the description, 'With a few paintings Homer made his shield into the embodiment of all that happens in the world'[37]. The shield description represents a retarding moment in the action of the poem before Achilles returns to the battle and there is renewed description of the slaughter. The terrible slaughter of battle is both relativised and intensified by being set in the context of the cyclical order of nature and of human life depicted on the shield. As Achilles shoulders this artefact, with its depiction of the whole living cosmos, it is also a reminder both of what Achilles is fighting for, and of what he is about to sacrifice as he returns to battle and to certain death.

In an article on Achilles' shield Wolfgang Schadewaldt suggests:

> Goethe has come closest to the spirit of Homer – not with the description of a piece of equipment made of bronze but with the description of a building and although he does not bind himself to Homer, perhaps indeed did not consciously think of him, nevertheless his words form the finest, most universal commentary on the shield of Achilles[38].

The building in question is the 'Saal der Vergangenheit' [hall of the past] in *Wilhelm Meisters Lehrjahre* in which, as on the shield of Achilles, the 'unzählige Bilder' [countless pictures] present an image of the timeless cycle of human activity in all its diversity. The sight of it provokes Wilhelm to cry out, 'What life (...) in this hall of the past! One could just as well call it the hall of the present and of the future' (*Lj*.551). And indeed the motto of this mausoleum - it is the burial place of Natalie's uncle and will become also the burial place of Mignon - is '*Gedenke zu leben!*' [*Choose life!*] (*Lj*.550). Like the shield of Achilles this description also represents a retarding moment in the action, before the dramatic incident of Mignon's death, and an opportunity for calm and reflection on the

---

[37] Lessing, *Laokoon,* page 135.
[38] Wolfgang Schadewaldt, 'Der Schild des Achilleus' in: *Homer, Die Dichtung und ihre Deutung,* WdF 634, edited by Joachim Latacz, Darmstadt 1991, pages 173-199.

human condition governed as it is by the constant tension between the two poles of life and death.

Of the relationship between word and image encompassed by Homer's shield-description Erika Simon writes, 'The simultaneity of painting and the succession of writing here coincide for the listener and the viewer', and suggests that in this fusion the distinction between the visual and literary arts, which has presented modern aesthetics with a problem since Lessing's 'Laokoon' essay, is cancelled out[39]. It is this very problem which also greatly concerned Goethe. In a conversation with Riemer he described the disadvantage of literature, as opposed to the visual arts, as being, 'That it is not eusynopton', and gave this as the reason why the works of Homer, for example 'must be performed in the manner of a rhapsode', in order to be properly appreciated[40]. This reproduction of the advantages of the simultaneity of the plastic arts in a work of literature while, at the same time, retaining the dynamic progression of the text is exactly what Goethe was aiming at in the *Wanderjahre*.

This intention is indicated meta-textually in the novel through the repeated metaphor of the picture gallery. On the level of content the picture galleries, the 'Heiligtümer' [sanctuaries], which form the centre of the various labyrinths of experience through which Wilhelm and the reader are led, reinforce through repetition the guiding principles of the different realms of experience in which they are to be found. The cycle of frescoes representing the life of Saint Joseph have provided the second Joseph with the prototype on which to model his own life; the portraits of exemplary public figures in the uncle's gallery point up the enlightened rationality of the ideas and the principles by which he runs his estate; and the biblical and mythical themes of the cycles of paintings in the galleries of the 'pedagogical province' reflect the ethical convictions which form the basis of

---

[39] Erika Simon, 'Der Schild des Achilleus' in: *Beschreibungskunst - Kunstbeschreibung: Ekphrasis von der Antike bis zur Gegenwart*, edited by Gottfried Boehm and Helmut Pfotenhauer, München 1995, page 124.
[40] Gräf 1.2, page 926. Conversation of March 26th 1814. By 'eusynopton' Goethe means 'easily seen at a glance' and with the term 'rhapsodienweise' he intends to convey 'in an episodic way', representing the amount which a rhapsode could recite in an evening.

the educational principles of this region. On a meta-textual level the picture gallery serves as a metaphor for the way in which the text itself is constructed and should be read. The picture gallery, where every picture both stands for itself and reflects and comments on all the other pictures, combines the simultaneity of the visual arts with the dynamic progression of the literary text. The many picture galleries in the text are, for the reader, a visual pointer to the technique of the text's construction, a technique which Goethe, in a letter to Iken, described himself as favouring, 'And so long ago I chose the method of revealing the hidden meaning to the attentive reader through episodes that confront and at the same time reflect each other'[41].

This technique of reflecting the whole text in miniature within the compass of the text itself finds echoes in Thomas Mann's *Zauberberg,* where the central '*Schnee*-Kapitel' [Snow Chapter] has been described as a miniaturised model of the whole novel[42]. We have seen already how Wilhelm's letter to Natalie, describing his reasons for wishing to train as a surgeon, can be regarded as a miniaturised textual reflection of the whole work in its aims, effect on the reader and method of construction. We have seen a textual analogue for the collective nature of the whole work offered by one of the elders in the 'pedagogical province' in his description of the Old Testament. We have further noted the way in which the construction, form and content of Lenardo's story reduplicate and reflect in miniature elements of the whole work. Similarly the picture galleries represent in a visual form a repeated use of the mise en abyme

---

[41] Letter to Karl Jakob Ludwig Iken, September 27th 1827, H.A. Letters 4, page 250. Goethe's description of this favoured technique of constructing a text is reminiscent of Wilhelm von Humboldt's description of the way a work of art is to be interpreted, 'That in the contemplation of works of art (in contrast to philosophical and historical works) one does not pursue a developing series of ideas, but frequently retraces one's steps, describing an endless circle, and in the analysis of the composition of the individual parts one is over and over again led back from the one to the others'. 'Aufsatz für Frau von Staël', in: Kurt Müller-Vollmer, page 171. Müller-Vollmer comments that this is a 'clear formulation of the hermeneutic circle to be overcome by the interpreter of a work'. Goethe too could be said to be reflecting in his work the hermeneutical circle to be described by both author and interpreter.

[42] Kindlers Literatur Lexikon, Volume 7, 'Im zentralen *Schnee*-Kapitel (dem verkleinerten Modell des gesamten Romans')' [in the central Snow-Chapter (the miniaturised model of the whole novel)], page 1391.

technique, endlessly reflecting the text from within through a series of reduplications. This series of reduplications or reflections of the text within the text can be seen as another literary manifestation of the phenomenon of 'wiederholte Spiegelungen' [repeated reflections], which Goethe discusses in his essay of the same title. There, in response to having received a handwritten copy of his reminiscence, 'Wallfahrt nach Sesenheim', [pilgrimage to Sesenheim] from Professor Näke of Bonn, Goethe was discussing how the image of Friederike Brion worked through time and affected many people and had finally returned through Professor Näke's work to have an even more powerful effect on Goethe himself, the original creator of the image. The intensifying effect is compared to that of entoptic colours, which do not fade when reflected from mirror to mirror but rather ignite[43]. In the novel the many reflections of the text within the text have the effect of distilling and intensifying the impression made by the text.

The image of the mirror, along with the mirror image, has a central significance within the text. One of the aphorisms in Makarie's archive (No. 179, 486) takes as its theme the paradoxical attributes of the mirror both to reflect accurately and to distort reality. We shall see later how this idea is manifested in the mirror images in the novella 'Wer ist der Verräter?'. The 'ethical-magical mirror' associated with Makarie is a richly ambiguous metaphor. Firstly it is an image, which is made up of words, as Makarie reflects the people she describes through the medium of word-pictures. Secondly it is left to the reader to weigh up the extent to which Makarie's mirror images are accurate reflections of the people she describes and the extent to which they represent distortions or transfigurations of the essence of these individuals. Lenses of all sorts, reading glasses and telescopes, too, are depicted as sharing this paradoxical quality of simultaneously clarifying and distorting what is seen through them: in the observatory Wilhelm's rather pompous diatribe against these artificial means of sharpening one's sight is

---

[43] H.A. Volume 12, 'Wiederholte Spiegelungen', pages 322-3.

gently ridiculed but at the same time raises the serious problem of man's relationship to technology.

Halfway between text and visual work of art, the mysterious 'casket' (43) or 'ornamental book-cover' (44) which Felix discovers during his wanderings through underground caverns and passages has exercised the interpretative skills of a large number of critics[44]. The mystery surrounding its discovery; its reappearances at various crucial moments in the text; its reflections in the other caskets which appear in the work - Melusine's travelling casket and the actor's cosmetic casket - have led to it being regarded as the central symbol of the novel or, indeed, as a symbol of the symbolic 'per se'. On one level the casket, with its lock and key, has been interpreted as having erotic connotations and functioning symbolically in the developing relationship between Felix and Hersilie[45]. Wilhelm Emrich, however, warns against one-dimensional interpretations of the casket and its key and makes the suggestion that it should be regarded as the 'Symbol des Symbolischen' [symbol of the symbolical]. He sees it as positing an inner relationship between all the different spheres of the novel: geology, love problems and social problems, religious and educational problems. The casket is both a visual and a literary work of art, 'no larger than a small octavo volume, in appearance ornate and medieval, it seemed to be made of gold, decorated with enamel' (43). On a meta-textual level, precisely because it is halfway between word and image, it functions as the representative work of art and in its key lies the pointer to its interpretation. In the hands of the reckless and impetuous Felix the key breaks off in the lock and the secrets of the casket remain undisclosed.

---

[44] For example: Eric Blackall, Stefan Blessin, André Gilg and Birgit Baldwin; and also Volker Dürr, 'Geheimnis und Aufklärung: Zur pädagogischen Funktion des Kästchens in *Wilhelm Meisters Wanderjahren*', *Monatshefte* 74. 1 (1982); Wilhelm Emrich, 'Das Problem der Symbolinterpretation im Hinblick auf Goethes *Wanderjahre*' in: *Protest und Verheißung: Studien zur klassischen und modernen Dichtung,* Frankfurt am Main 1960; Friedrich Ohly, 'Goethes Ehrfurchten - ein ordo caritatis', *Euphorion* 55, 1961, pages 113-45 and 405-48; 'Zum Kästchen in Goethes *Wanderjahren*' ZfdA 91, 1961-2; A.G. Steer, *Goethe's Science in the Structure of the "Wanderjahre"* Athens (Georgia) 1979; and Joseph Strelka, *Esoterik bei Goethe* Tübingen 1980.
[45] Hersilie asks Wilhelm of the drawing of the key included in her letter, 'Doesn't it remind you of an arrow with barbs?' (321) - a reference to the arrows of the Greek love-god Eros. It is then all too easy to see the lock and key as phallus and vagina.

Only in the hands of an expert - 'an elderly goldsmith and jeweller whom the uncle valued very highly' (458) - does it become obvious that the key is not broken but consists of two magnetically joined parts, which 'are strongly bonded together, but only open up for the initiated' (458). The secrets of the work of art will not reveal themselves to the impatient and overhasty interpreter. Only one who is willing to take time and work patiently at acquiring the skills of interpretation can expect to penetrate its mysteries. The action of the expert in immediately closing the casket again suggests that it is not so much the content of a work of art which is intrinsically important, but rather the effort which the artist has put into its construction which calls forth a similar investment of effort on the part of the interpreter in seeking to understand it.

The key, which accompanies the casket, is represented in the only illustration in the text. André Gilg has suggested that this drawing of the key, as pure image, draws attention to the limits of language[46]. The key, while appearing to have all the supposed straightforwardness of a visual sign is in fact as ambiguous as any textual sign and has called forth many competing interpretations. Within the text itself Hersilie asks, 'Doesn't it remind you of an arrow with barbs' (321), but this is not, in fact, the idea that the drawing would immediately bring to mind and is merely her interpretation. Many critics have endorsed her view and interpreted it as a symbol of erotic love, relating it to the triangular relationship between Hersilie, Felix and Wilhelm. Others have interpreted the drawing as depicting freemasonic symbols. This key may playfully be offering itself as a solution to the enigma of the text, but in reality it is calling attention to the impossibility of the search for ultimate meanings. The casket, when opened, does not yield up an ultimate secret but must immediately be closed again to allow for further attempts to penetrate its mysteries. The reader must be willing to forego the possibility of an ultimate meaning, while retaining the readiness to continue with the work of interpretation.

---

[46] Gilg, page 135.

Within the text there are reduplications of Felix's mysterious casket in the magical, dwarf-crafted travelling casket from 'Die neue Melusine' and in the rejuvenating cosmetic casket from 'Der Mann von funfzig Jahren'. We have seen already how Melusine's casket provides an analogue for the art of misinterpretation. The cosmetic casket, on the other hand, reinforces on a different level the suggestion that the development of understanding is a slow and gradual process, demanding much patience. A correspondent in the exchange of letters which makes up 'Der Sammler und die Seinigen' refers to 'the magnificent edifice of art with its different levels'- even the art of the cosmetician is made up of 'Stufen und Grade' [stages and degrees], which can only be learnt gradually, and still has 'secrets for the initiated' (177)[47].

In the 'artists' province' we are offered a metaphor for the text in the form of a sculpture, an example of the great work of art as a labyrinth of infinite possibilities. The sculpture - 'Dieses merkwürdig verschlungene Kunstwerk' [this remarkably intricate work of art] - proposes for the text a metaphor which, like the picture galleries discussed above, is spatial and three-dimensional: '[it] presented an equally favourable impression from every angle' (253). The adjective 'verschlungen', which can equally well refer to a winding path or the intertwining threads of a woven fabric, encompasses the intricacies of both the labyrinth and weaving metaphors. The sculpture reproduces a battle between Amazons and heroes and is reminiscent in its complex intertwinings of the Laocoon statue. In his essay 'Über Laokoon' Goethe discusses two types of sculpture. The first type consists of a single figure: 'Jupiter with a thunderbolt in his lap, Juno resting on her sovereign dignity, Minerva lost in contemplation'. This type of work of art he describes as 'geschlossen' [closed]. The second type are works of art which comprise 'smaller circles, where the individual figures are conceived and sculpted in a relationship with others' - an image which calls to mind both the recurring picture galleries of the *Wanderjahre* and Goethe's

---

[47] W.A. 47, page 144.

description of his method of constructing texts 'by means of episodes which contrast with and reflect each other'. Goethe assigns the Laocoon group a place amongst this second type of sculpture because it shows 'the movement together with its cause'. In this statue is encompassed the paradox of a moving stillness or a static motion. Important is the 'representation of the moment', the choice of that elusive 'punctum temporis' which sums up the climax of the action. Goethe suggests that by standing in front of the statue with closed eyes one can, by the sudden opening and closing of the eyes, create the illusion of movement and set the whole sculpture in motion; or that the same effect can be achieved by viewing the statue by torch-light. Here again the paradoxical problem is addressed that the visual arts are constantly striving from static representation towards narrative movement while the literary arts constantly seek to freeze their temporal dynamic into the simultaneity of the visual image.

Just as Goethe describes the Laocoon group as 'unendlich' [infinite], so the statue group in the 'artists' province' in the *Wanderjahre* is also 'unendlich': it provides inspiration for the painters and artists as well as for the poet whose words set the static group in motion 'so that the frozen group really seemed to revolve on its axis and the number of the figures appeared to double and treble' (254). Like the Laocoon statue it focuses attention on the problematic relationship between the visual and the literary arts, the former always trying to break the bounds of its static space and become movement, while the latter is ever attempting to impose static form upon its temporal movement. In this sculpture, then, we can see again a metaphor for the novel as a whole, the work of art as a challenge and difficult process: 'the more incommensurable and incomprehensible to the mind a poetic production, the better'[48].

This same tension between the visual arts and the textual arts is reflected in the complex interplay of word and image constituting the story of 'Saint Joseph the Second'. In these narratives Joseph expresses a sense of confusion, a sense of

---

[48] Eckermann, 6th May 1827, page 591.

hovering between dream and reality, 'Soon those pictures seemed to me to have been only dreams, which here dissolved into a lovely reality' (23). This sense of confusion is conveyed to the reader by the transition from the living picture of the family's progress down the mountainside: 'to his astonishment our friend to came face to face in reality with the Flight into Egypt which he had so often seen in paintings' (9); to the wall-paintings: 'he saw the on wall a repetition of yesterday's living painting' (15); to the fictional reality of the family itself. Joseph's narration of his life-story wakes the still pictures into flowing time, while being itself punctuated and frozen for an instant into the 'puncta temporis' of the pictures which are reflected in the titles of the narrative sections, 'Die Heimsuchung' [The Visitation] and 'Der Lilienstengel' [The Lily Stem]. The narrative flow of 'Die Heimsuchung' freezes momentarily at the point where Marie enters Frau Elisabeth's house as Joseph cries out, 'Frau Elisabeth, you're being visited!' (24). There is a similar halting of the narrative flow in 'Der Lilienstengel' as Joseph, in the midst of his narrative, specifically recalls one of the paintings on the wall of his chapel with the words, 'And straight away I recalled the lily stem which rose from the ground between Mary and Joseph in the painting as witness to a pure relationship' (26).

The paintings in the chapel serve as a kind of 'memory-temple' preserving the past for Joseph - or the story of the past he wishes to remember - in vivid present images[49]. The fact that the narration, as we discover later, is not entirely Joseph's and has been filtered through Wilhelm's consciousness, emphasises again the partiality and perspectivism of script[50].

---

[49] A similar function is performed by the 'memory-temples' constituted by Tristan's hall of statues in Thomas von Bretagne's Tristan-novel, where the statues preserve for Tristan the memory of his love for Isolde; or the room where Lancelot is imprisoned by Morgan le Fay in the prose-Lancelot, which he transforms into a picture gallery commemorating for himself his love for Guinevere. The difference is that both Tristan and Lancelot are preserving the memory of a guilty secret love whereas for Joseph his pictures represent both the model for his 'imitatio Josephi' and the record of his fulfilled love for Marie, still a present reality to him.

[50] 'If it is not entirely in his words, if here and there I have expressed my own convictions in place of his'. H.A. Volume 8, page 28.

In Joseph's temple to memory one picture is treated differently from the others. It is the painting of the medieval legend of Herod's carved throne. This picture, with its representation of the carpenter's tools and the intricate carvings of the throne, had inspired in the child Joseph the desire to emulate his namesake in following the carpenter's trade. It embodies a kind of idealisation of the craft of woodworking in that the intricate carvings would be impossible to achieve in reality and are only possible through the medium of paint. Unlike the other paintings in the chapel, this painting does not so much act as a preserver of memory but on the contrary is itself preserved in Joseph's own memory: it has almost disappeared from the wall through the ravages of time and is indecipherable to the uninitiated, but comes alive in Joseph's narration - not as a static 'punctum temporis' creation of paint but as a narration in time. We must pick for ourselves the moment that is actually represented from the flow of Joseph's narrative. The lack of realism in the depiction of the carving, 'that admittedly must have been easier for the painter to produce than it would have been for the carpenter' (19), leads only to Joseph valuing his chosen craft more highly, since the painting gives him an ideal picture of the possibilities of the craft and brings it nearer to an art.

Joseph's way of life is only possible because he lives in an isolated mountainous district, cut off to a certain extent from the latest social developments and is still integrated in a traditional, largely patriarchal and feudal society that is based on self-help and help for one's neighbour and community[51]. 'Einseitigkeit' [specialisation] is not yet a necessity but what is needed is rather the ability to play many roles: 'the worker, the messenger and the carrier all are united in one person' (18). The kind of society depicted here is like the society which Goethe describes in his notes and poems to accompany 'Wilhelm Tischbeins Idyllen' where the holy family is seen as the ideal community; or in

---

[51] 'A steward lives in that place, who takes care of the administration and collects the taxes and tithes which have to be paid here from far and wide'; 'The person is more dependent on his own resources, he must learn to trust his own hands and feet'; 'each one is closer to the other, meets him more often and lives with him in pursuit of common goals'. H.A. Volume 8, pages 14 & 18

the 'Epochen Geselliger Bildung' where the 'idyllische Epoche' [idyllic age] is described in the following way: 'the circles close themselves off from the outside and must do so since they have to safeguard their existence in the rough elements' - except that for Joseph the circle is not only the narrow circle of his family but embraces the wider circle of the whole mountain community[52].

The 'Saint Joseph the Second' episode has been interpreted very positively. For instance Erich Trunz says of it, 'This first image of life presents the normal, the exemplary', and goes on to compare it to a painting by Raphael, saying, 'There is something of the harmony of Raphael in this prose'[53]. Indeed, he proceeds to comment on the word-pictures of the Joseph narrative as though they were actually paintings by Raphael: 'the vivid clarity and purity of the figures the luminosity of the colours, the devout sincerity of the convictions, combined with great representational skill' (556). Other critics, however, offer a more negative interpretation of the Joseph episode as a criticism of the imitative, nostalgic art of the Nazarene school of painting, a school of painting sharply criticised by Goethe at about the same time as he was composing this episode[54]. This interpretation of the episode as constituting an unambiguous parody of the Nazarenes is hard to sustain, however, in the face of the textual evidence. Joseph's imitation of his patron saint is not merely a detailed imitation of the outer manifestations of Saint Joseph's life in the paintings. Indeed he recognises the absurdity of this outward imitation and himself half laughs at the 'imitatio Josephi' of his outward appearance. Hannelore Schlaffer cites the use of the word 'wunderlich' [strange] to describe Joseph in order to prove Goethe's parodistic intention here but, in fact, Joseph uses the word ironically against himself to indicate that he is himself well aware of the somewhat strange figure he cuts along with his family: 'for people happily allow charity to have a strange exterior' (22).

---

[52] Aufbau, Volume 11, page 447.
[53] H.A., Volume 8, page 556.
[54] Cf. Anneliese Klingenberg, pages 30-37 and Hannelore Schlaffer, *Wilhelm Meister. Das Ende der Kunst und die Wiederkehr des Mythos*, Stuttgart 1980, pages 26-33.

What interests him, however, is not so much the 'outward appearance' (28) as the fact that it 'fits so well with our inner selves' (28). The imitation of the outer details is just an accompaniment and an outward sign of the imitation of the 'virtues of that archetype of fidelity and purity of thought' (28). Joseph is not inwardly fixated on a mere outward imitation of the holy family but concentrates on imitating the spirit of the holy family, which results in an outward effect on the community in which he lives. Both in his job and in his voluntary activities he has a beneficial influence, if not exactly a 'Wirkung in der Ferne' [a far-reaching effect], at least an effect in the neighbourhood on his own community.

In contrast to the situation described by the educators of the 'pedagogical province', where 'Ehrfurcht' [reverence] is something that must be inculcated into their students, Joseph is accredited with a natural 'Ehrfurcht'. He describes how his dealings with Frau Elisabeth 'aroused in me a special reverence for her, and her house, which was extremely well-kept, seemed to me to be like a kind of small shrine' (21).

In Joseph's environment man, nature and art exist together in harmony. Although Wilhelm's guide exclaims, 'It's a terrible shame about the lovely church', (13) on seeing the ruined buildings, rather than provoking this reaction the buildings present the idea of the interaction of nature and art on each other throughout the centuries, an interplay which is also reflected in the *Novelle* and which represents a natural cycle of change[55]. Joseph's chapel is also his living quarters - both 'Heiligtum' [shrine] and a natural part of his everyday life - as are the paintings decorating its walls. Rather than being unaware of the transitoriness of human life, as Hannelore Schlaffer claims, Joseph is deeply aware that change

---

[55] In the *Novelle* too this interplay of art and nature is seen filtered through a variety of media as the princess sees the ruins first through the lenses of a powerful telescope and then as drawings in the portfolio of the court artist. The natural cycle of change is described thus, 'It is a wilderness like no other; a locality made unique by chance, where the traces of long-vanished human energy allow themselves to be seen in the most earnest conflict with eternally living and constantly productive nature'. *Goethe. Novellen*, edited by Katharina Mommsen, Frankfurt am Main 1979, page 201. The same interplay is noted by Goethe in the first of Tischbein's idylls (Trunz *Studien* pages 8-9) in which ancient ruins return to nature and gain a new life as they are overgrown by vegetation - an idea carried through in his accompanying poem.

is part of the natural cycle of life[56]. He exclaims, 'Life belongs to the living and whoever is alive must be ready for change' (27); but is also aware of the rhythm of change, of the necessity of a fitting time and season and says, 'One sees the flowers withering and the leaves falling, but one also sees the fruit ripening and new buds developing' (27). He is also conscious - or Wilhelm, as his interpreter, attributes to him the thought - of the possible influence of art on human susceptibilities: that art can continue to have an influence and to affect the life of future generations: 'for when that which is lifeless is full of life, it can also bring forth new life' (15).

The word-pictures of the cycle of Joseph's life, which form the opening narrative of the *Wanderjahre*, cannot be interpreted one-dimensionally, whether in a positive or a negative way. They are as ambiguous as their flickering, unstable nature, hovering between dream and reality, at once living pictures, fictional narrative and narrated pictures and all are images realised through the medium of word. On the one hand we are aware that the idyllic life which Joseph leads, like the life of the spinners and weavers in their remote valleys, is doomed to extinction or, at least, to change, through the forces of industrialisation and social development. It is a life which is fading as rapidly as the painting of Herod's throne in Joseph's chapel, only kept alive in the imagination of those upon whom it has exercised an influence. It is a life which has to be left behind but which also poses a question to the reader: what of value from this dying way of life can and should be carried over by the traveller into the future of the technological age?

The reader is again confronted with a series of paintings in the episode around Lago Maggiore when Wilhelm goes on his pious pilgrimage to visit the scenes of Mignon's early childhood and meets up with Hilarie and the beautiful widow, characters from the novella 'Der Mann von funfzig Jahren'. The relationships between levels of fiction and between word and image are here

---

[56] Hannelore Schlaffer, page.27.

again very complex. Wilhelm encounters a painter, whose reading of the *Lehrjahre* has led to an intense interest in the figure of Mignon and her fate. The levels of fiction and reality are confused as the *Lehrjahre*, describing Wilhelm's earlier life, is here introduced into the text of Wilhelm's continuing life-story, as a recently published work of fiction[57]. In the 1829 version of the *Wanderjahre* the reader is left to make this tacit assumption, whereas in the 1821 version the reader is explicitly referred to the *Lehrjahre* in order to appreciate Wilhelm's feelings as he makes his pilgrimage: 'how he felt in those circumstances, we do not find expressed, but anyone who can recall the end of the *Lehrjahre*, will no doubt conjure up similar feelings in his own heart and mind' (1821. 108). The painter's own fictional status is highlighted, too: he is described as a type 'of which there are many wandering and roaming around in the real world and even more in romances and dramas' (226).

The episode begins with the artist translating Mignon's song 'Kennst du das Land?' [Do you know the land?] into the medium of paint. His first painting is a representation of the second verse of the song where 'she stood beneath the lofty colonnaded doorway of a fine country house, gazing pensively at the statues in the entrance hall' (227). The scene is not described in detail but referred to along with other scenes from Mignon's childhood painted by the artist. The first verse of the song with its lemons and oranges is referred to even more indirectly, not as a painting but as part of the actual landscape which the friends recognise with a wistful smile, 'when they caught sight of the bay-tree standing high, the pomegranate turning red, orange- and lemon-trees unfolding their blossoms while at the same time the fruit glowed amongst the dark leaves' (229). The third verse, on the other hand, is represented in the text by a vivid ekphrasis, which brings the painting to life so that we not only see Mignon in the midst of the wild and colourful gypsy-band surrounded by desolate and dramatic mountain scenery, but

---

[57] A similar device in *Don Quixote* causes Quixote to encounter characters in the second book of his adventures who have read stories from the first book of his adventures.

also feel the spray from the waterfalls and hear the clang of the musical instruments with which the pack-animals are laden.

A further form of interaction between word and image is evoked in this episode. The narrator introduces into the text the 'Urteil eines Kenners' [verdict of a connoisseur] (235) in order to provide the reader with a more expert, technical assessment of the artist's work. This digression gives Goethe the opportunity to introduce a further writing genre into his text, the description of works of the visual arts, and also to consider a problem that was of great interest to himself and his contemporaries, in an age before mass reproduction and the consequent easy access for all to visual reproductions of paintings and sculptures: the necessity and the inadequacy of 'Buchstabenbilder', or verbal descriptions of works of the visual arts. The parody of such 'word-pictures' in the 'connoisseur's verdict' thematises both the value and the deficiencies of this genre.

Apparently at opposite ends of the spectrum which runs from concept to image are, on the one hand, the depiction of the key to Felix's casket and, on the other hand, the collections of aphorisms in Makarie's archive and the 'Betrachtungen im Sinne der Wanderer': the one being pure image and the others, pure concept. Paradoxically, however, these two extremes come together in their effect in the text. Both halt the flow of the narrative and provoke the reader to thought and reflection[58]. The seemingly unambiguous visual sign and the inherently ambiguous linguistic sign both point to the necessity for unceasing interpretative effort and to the futility of the demand for conclusive meanings.

Many of the aphorisms are gathered together in Makarie's archive. The archive, like the picture galleries, is a spatial, timeless image, representing a halting of the flow of both time and language. Like Joseph's chapel it is a temple to memory, but whereas the chapel is the personal memory of an individual, the archive comprises the collective memory of mankind, a whole tradition of thought

---

[58] André Gilg (page 135) suggests that the drawing of the key calls attention to something that is beyond the powers of language to express. Birgit Baldwin draws parallels between 'the sleek, impenetrable visual sign' and 'the ambiguous linguistic sign' (page 224) in their capacity for insisting upon interpretation.

preserved in script. It 'helps to root the human being in the time-continuum and is the best antidote against the loss of a historical sense'. Angela says of it, 'In this way we come to the contemplation of that harmony which is man's vocation and to which he must often become reconciled against his will, since he is only too eager to imagine that the world makes a new beginning with him' (123). It is literature in its widest sense – 'the fragment of fragments' (294) - at one and the same time all embracing and incomplete. The archive functions both actively and passively. On the one hand it is a store-house, which preserves passively the ideas of the past; on the other hand it encourages the active seeking out of these ideas and the discovery of connections between them and 'compels us to go backwards by means of a reversed procedure of uncovering and discovering and, wherever possible, to visualise for ourselves the lineage of such thoughts, from the distant past right up to the present day' (125); furthermore it can make possible new inspiration through a sudden insight into hitherto un-thought-of connections and distinctions 'just as when an amount of quicksilver falls and divides itself up in all directions into countless little beads of the most varied shapes' (124)[59].

The role of both the key and the aphorisms within the text is the subject of the first aphorism in Makarie's archive:

One may not and cannot reveal the secrets of life's pathway; there are obstacles over which every traveller must stumble. But the poet indicates the spot (460).

They are stumbling blocks which halt the smooth flow of the narrative and force the reader to slow down long enough to become aware of the ambiguities and ambivalences of the text. Appropriately the aphorism which thematises this function is itself a metaphor, a textual image.

---

[59] Cf. Chapter 3, pages 154 and 179.

Weaving the labyrinth of the text

sich verflechtend und entwindend
weaving in and out

Included within the *Wanderjahre* are various metaphors for the work itself as an artistic construct and metaphors for ways of pursuing its meaning. The metaphors of the labyrinth and of weaving run throughout the text on the levels of content, of symbol and of discourse. On the level of discourse they are used both to suggest the method of construction of the text and to offer a way of reading it. Both ideas are contained in the 'Zwischenrede' of the second version of the novel which, at a central point within the novel itself, 'lays bare the device' of the work's composition[60]. The narrator says of his characters:

> Erwarten wir also zunächst, einen nach dem andern, sich verflechtend und entwindend, auf gebahnten und ungebahnten Wegen wiederzufinden (244).
> [We can expect them, therefore, to reappear shortly, one after the other, weaving in and out, on well-trodden and untrodden pathways]

It could be argued that both the labyrinth and weaving have become worn-out metaphors, so much part of the everyday currency of speech that they have long ceased to have any figurative potency. It is perhaps rather the case, however, that they are archetypal metaphors, which retain their potency precisely because they are so universal[61]. Both weaving and the labyrinth are metaphors used commonly for life itself in such phrases as 'the rich tapestry of life' or 'the labyrinth of the world'. The primordial image for man's life is the image of the fates - Lachesis, Clotho and Atropos - spinning, measuring and cutting the thread of life as described by Plato in Book 10 of the *Republic* in the Myth of Er[62]. The weaving image occurs in the Old Testament: 'I have cut off like a weaver my life'

---

[60] Cf. Terry Eagleton, page 170, on modernist literary works.

[61] The metaphors have gained a new resonance with the development of the communications labyrinth that is the Internet and the World Wide Web.

[62] Plato *Republic* translated by Desmond Lee Penguin Classics 1974 page 451. These figures - 'die Parzen' - describe their role in the 'Mummenschanz'-scene of *Faust II*: '... to count the hours, to measure the years, /And the weaver takes up the thread', lines 5305-5344.

(Isaiah 38.12); and in Martin Luther's translation of the New Testament: 'Denn in ihm leben, weben und sind wir' (Apostelgeschichte 17.28)[63].

Both the labyrinth and weaving are also metaphors used to describe the work of art or, more particularly, the written text. The word 'text' itself is derived from the Latin word 'texere' - to weave[64]. In Ovid's *Metamorphoses* weaving and storytelling are brought explicitly together as Athene and Arachne contend with each other to prove who is the better weaver and each weaves tales of human and divine transformations into the fabric of her tapestry:

> illic et lentum filis inmittitur aurum,
> et vetus in tela deducitur argumentum[65].

The labyrinth has been regarded since ancient times as a symbol for the complexities of the difficult text or discussion, both as an image for the discovery of a way through ignorance to understanding and as an image for impenetrability and unnecessary complication.

Both the labyrinth and the intricately woven fabric are ambivalent images, suggesting both order and chaos, harmony and threat. Weaving can create an intricate ordered whole out of a multitude of threads, but it can also create a net to entrap the unwary. The labyrinth motif includes within itself very different perspectives. From the point of view of the labyrinth-walker it is ambivalent, either a dynamic and exciting pursuit of a goal or a confusing loss of orientation. From the perspective of the privileged viewer from above it offers a satisfying prospect of unity in complexity. Manfred Schmeling has pointed out how important the role of the labyrinth is as a medium of cultural communication. He notes not only its importance for disciplines such as philosophy, psychology, art

---

[63] [For in him we live and move and have our being (Acts of the Apostles, King James' version)]. There is an allusion to this passage in the *Lehrjahre* where it is said that Wilhelm 'lebte und webte (...) in der Shakespearischen Welt' (Lj. 187) [Wilhelm lived and moved (...) in the Shakespearian world].

[64] The use of 'textus' to refer to a literary text, which is common in medieval Latin, can be traced as far back as Quintilian. In passing it might be noted that the family name of Goethe's mother was Textor.

[65] Ovid *Metamorphoses*, Book 6, lines 68-69, 'Pliant gold thread, too was interwoven/ As old stories were pictured on the looms'. Penguin Classics, page 136.

history and religion, but also how widespread it is in the recreations and discourses of everyday life: in games, toys, drawings, dances, halls of mirrors and mazes. He attributes its durability to the quality it possesses:

> to represent the inner and the outer world not only in its individual aspects, but also in its total complexity. The term 'labyrinth' embraces both structurally and conceptually everything that the world contains of both chaos-causing and ordering elements[66].

At the very end of his life in a letter to Wilhelm von Humboldt Goethe described the weaving image as 'an image that I am so fond of using' and in 1826 he wrote in *Über Kunst und Altertum*:

> The fabric of our life and work is composed of different threads, since the essential and the coincidental, the arbitrary and the positively desired weave themselves together, each of the most contrasting kind and often impossible to differentiate[67].

Werner Keller suggests that it represents for Goethe an 'Urtropus' [archetypal image] and that it offers the writer so many rich possibilities because it is an image:

> which appears both as a verbal and as a nominal metaphor and has a wide range of connections at its disposal, which befit the various possibilities of the simile; the unceasing activity of God-Nature; the movement of supernatural powers; the intertwining of human fates and also the structure of works of art - the self and the world are captured in Goethe's universal and central metaphor, in the weaving metaphor[68].

It is a metaphor used by Goethe to describe the diversity and varying significance of the human biographies making up world history[69]. The bewildering multifariousness of the works of the encyclopaedists, which he describes in *Dichtung und Wahrheit*, is caught in the image of a huge and noisy weaving factory[70].

The weaving metaphor is used in the *Lehrjahre* at the fateful point of Mignon's death when Wilhelm, in a moment of insight sees his own destiny, the fabric of his life, woven together with the lives of those around him:

---

[66] Manfred Schmeling, *Der labyrinthische Diskurs,* Frankfurt am Main, 1987, page 13.
[67] H.A. Letters, Volume 4, 17th March 1832, page 480.
[68] Werner Keller, *Goethes dichterische Bildlichkeit*, München 1972, pages 193-206.
[69] H. A. Volume 12, 'Maximen und Reflexionen', No.1103, page 519.
[70] H.A. Volume 9, page 487.

> There are moments in life, when events move to and fro in front of us like winged weaving shuttles and inexorably complete a fabric which we have more or less spun and set up on the loom ourselves (556).

In *Faust 1* the 'Erdgeist' [earth-spirit] describes its own activity as weaving, 'And so I work at the whirring loom of time/And weave the living garment of the Godhead' (lines 508-9). The same idea of the creative power of nature encompassed in the weaver-image – 'natura textor' - is the theme of the poem 'Antepirrhema'[71]. This poem takes and develops several lines already used by Goethe on a different level in *Urfaust* when Mephisto, in the guise of Faust, is advising the student and satirises the work of the philosophers in the following way:

Zwar ist's mit der Gedankenfabrik	[Indeed it's just the same with the ideas factory
Wie mit einem Webermeisterstück,	As with a masterpiece of weaving
Wie ein Tritt tausend Fäden regt,	How one tread moves a thousand threads
Die Schifflein 'rüber hinüber schießen,	The shuttles shoot back and forth,
Die Fäden ungesehen fließen,	The threads flow unseen
Ein Schlag tausend Verbindungen schlägt.	One stroke creates a thousand connections]

(lines 353-358).

As said above, the reverse side of the weaving metaphor is the metaphor of the net, which presents a threat to the rash and the unwary. In Ovid's story in the *Metamorphoses* Arachne was punished for her challenge to Athene's weaving skill by transformation into a spider, condemned to spin forever her beautiful but deadly web. In *Faust II* the choir, in mourning Euphorion, sing of him, 'But you ran unstoppably/Of your own accord into the impassive net', (lines 9923-4). In *Die natürliche Tochter* the governor asks Eugenie, 'How should I now/ Undertake

---

[71] H.A. Volume 1, page 358:

Antepirrhema	
So schauet mit bescheidnem Blick	[Look with a modest glance
Der ewigen Weberin Meisterstück,	At the masterpiece of the eternal weaver
Wie *ein* Tritt tausend Fäden regt,	How *one* tread moves a thousand threads,
Die Schifflein hinüber herüber schießen,	The shuttles shoot back and forth,
Die Fäden sich begegnend fließen.	The threads flow to meet each other.
Ein Schlag tausend Verbindungen schlägt,	*One* stroke creates a thousand connections
Das hat sie nicht zusammengebettelt,	She hasn't patched this together,
Sie hat's von Ewigkeit angezettelt,	She has generated it from eternity,
Damit der ewige Meistermann	So that the eternal craftsman
Getrost den Einschlag werfen kann.	Can work in the weft with confidence]

to loosen, the perplexing coils/Of the extraordinary knot that entangles you?';
while her father uses the same image to describe the effect that news of her death
has on him, 'Let me tear to shreds the tangled death-nets/Of a dark and gloomy
dream-web!'[72].

Goethe also uses the weaving image explicitly to describe the creation of
works of both the literary and the visual arts. In a letter from Rome he records his
pleasure at finishing the revision of *Claudine*, which he describes in terms of a
piece of embroidery cloth, 'The material which is to be embroidered, must have
an open weave, and for a comic opera it must be woven exactly like Marli'[73]. In
his essay 'Über das Lehrgedicht' he comments on 'how difficult it is to weave
together a work from knowledge and imagination: to join together two opposing
elements in a living body'[74]. In the *Wanderjahre* itself the image is used in the
'Künstlerlied' [artists' song] of the whole field of artistic creation, which is
compared to the creativity of nature:

Wie Natur im Vielgebilde	[Just as the manifold variety of nature
Einen Gott nur offenbart,	Reveals only one God,
So im weiten Kunstgefilde	So in the wide realm of art
Webt ein Sinn der ew'gen Art. (255).	One spirit of eternal art is weaving away]

A reflection in the 'Maximen und Reflexionen' suggests that a complex
literary work can be regarded as a weaving together of a diversity of plots, time-
scales and settings: 'there is nothing to be said against the three unities, when the
subject is very simple; but occasionally three times three unities, pleasingly
intertwined, have a very agreeable effect'[75]. The idea of the text of the
Wanderjahre itself as a weaving or threading together of heterogeneous materials
recurs often in Goethe's comments on the novel. Of the year 1807 he noted:

> This season was rich in shorter tales devised, begun, continued and completed. They
> should all form a wonderfully attractive whole, strung together on a romantic thread
> under the title *Wilhelm Meisters Wanderjahre*[76].

---

[72] H.A. Volume 5, pages 285 and 264.
[73] *Italienische Reise,* Insel, Frankfurt am Main 1976, letter from Rome of 6th February 1788, page
682.
[74] W.A. Volume 41.2, page 227.
[75] H.A., Volume 12, No.923, page 496.
[76] *Tag- und Jahreshefte,* 1807. Gräf, 1.2, pages 998-9.

In May 1810 he wrote to thank his friend Heinrich Meyer for his account of the spinners and weavers in the Swiss mountains with the words, 'These days after your introduction I have studied the cotton industry well, and am now trying to prepare a sufficiently realistic warp to go with a poetic weft'[77].

Within the novel itself weaving is used both as a metaphor and occurs as part of the content of the novel. As part of the content, weaving occupies a singular position. It is the subject of Lenardo's factual report in his diary on the technical aspects of the spinning and weaving industry. This report incorporates large sections which are in reality a factual report taken by Goethe from somebody else's pen: the report sent to Goethe at his request by Meyer. Interwoven with this factual report are the narrative strands which tell of Lenardo's travels through the region, of the people he meets and in particular the continuation of the story of his subconsciously driven search for the 'nut-brown maiden': a subtle interweaving of factual and fictional, of poetry and prose. In 1829 Goethe wrote to Göttling about this section of the work:

> I am especially pleased that direct observation of the reality caused you to be favourably disposed towards my spinners and weavers. For I was always concerned whether this interweaving of strictly scientific technical elements with elements of an aesthetic and emotional nature could create a good effect[78].

This observation on the construction of the 'diary' is reminiscent of the comment already quoted above from the essay 'Über das Lehrgedicht' and is also an apt description of the whole work and its technique of weaving together the most disparate of elements into a unified whole. The passage also suggests the care with which Goethe undertook this interweaving process and contradicts the idea that the novel consists of merely carelessly thrown together 'materials for a book'.

On a metaphorical level the spinning and weaving with their beauty and harmony of movement, resulting in the creation of an ordered whole, are a

---

[77] Gräf, 1.2, pages 902-3.
[78] Letter to Göttling, 17th January 1829. H.A., Volume 8, page 524.

symbol of the idyllic order of the life of the spinners and weavers themselves in their remote and secluded mountain villages. This very order is, however, itself threatened by the possibility of impending chaos to be brought about by the ever-advancing 'Maschinenwesen' [mechanisation].

The weaving motif occurs again in miniature in the novella 'Der Mann von funfzig Jahren' in the form of the 'Brieftasche' [letter-case] which the beautiful widow is making and which is also a tiny symbol of human harmony since woven into it is the memory of all the thoughts, 'about people, about situations, about joy and sorrow' (189), which came to her during the process of making it. This harmony too, however, carries with it its own rather playful disharmony and threat: the major, on receiving the letter-case as a gift, attempts to show his gratitude to the beautiful widow in a suitably poetic way with a translation from Ovid's *Metamorphoses*. Suddenly realising that the verses in the *Metamorphoses* are spoken by Arachne, he sees the beautiful widow for a moment as a spider 'in the centre of a web that she has spread' (198), a predatory female threat to the harmony and order of masculine lives. Here, on this playful level, is the only example in the *Wanderjahre* of the reverse side of the weaving metaphor, the woven fabric as a dangerous and threatening net or spider's web.

Frederick Amrine has suggested that the text has many of the formal features which are characteristic of the romance mode of narrative, including multiple narration and a 'multifoliate' plot: 'the prolific and apparently disorderly inclusiveness, the way in which events engender a whole range of disconnected happenings whose connections are yet felt though never pointed'; and the tendency for story to grow out of story creating a complexity which is close to that of life itself[79]. Amrine attributes to the *Wanderjahre* a unity similar to that of medieval romances, arising from the interweaving of a number of different themes or stories into a complex tapestry of text: a formal principle that has analogies in the basic patterns of Romanesque and early Gothic ornament,

---

[79] Frederick Amrine, 'Romance Narration in *Wilhelm Meisters Wanderjahre*', in: *GQ* 1982. The quotations stem from Gillian Beer, *The Romance*, London Methuen 1970, pages 76-7.

especially interlace and coiling spiral patterns. Amrine points to Goethe's strong interest in Romance in his later years in support of his thesis: to his admiration for Scott's historical romances and Johnson's *Rasselas*, for Chinese Romances and for *Daphnis and Chloe*. Wilhelm Emrich, too, points out the meta-textual function of weaving as an analogue for the text's construction[80].

The way in which, on the level of discourse, the metaphor of weaving is used to 'lay bare the device' of the text's construction is emphasised within the novel by the 'Geschirrfasser' [loom-mender] who describes weaving as 'the oldest and most glorious art, which above all distinguishes the human being from the beast' (347). This description is even more appropriate for language, the art which, in a much more radical way, distinguishes the human being from other animals.

The idea of the text as an intricately woven fabric has been closely related since ancient times to the idea of the text as a labyrinth. Lucretius uses a labyrinthine image for the tongue: 'cunning crafter of words' [verborum daedala lingua][81]. Virgil, in the *Aeneid*, speaks of the labyrinth of Crete with its 'woven path'[82]. Both elements are contained in the archetypal myth at the origin of these metaphors: the story of Daedalus and Theseus, of Ariadne and the Cretan labyrinth. Ariadne's thread brought Theseus safely out of the labyrinth; and later Daedalus, after escaping from imprisonment in his own labyrinth, was rediscovered by Minos when he solved the puzzle of how to run a thread through all the intricate windings of a complex seashell. He tied the thread to an ant and allowed the ant to carry it through all the complexities of the shell, which form a natural labyrinth. The tracery of the thread, the spider's web, weaving, the woven fabric, the network of pathways in the labyrinth create a spatial pattern which represent and transform the temporal linear nature of the narrated word.

---

[80] Wilhelm Emrich, *Die Symbolik von 'Faust II'*, Bonn 1957 (2), page 35.
[81] Lucretius, *de rerum natura*, Book 4, line 549.
[82] Virgil, *Aeneid*, Book 5, lines 588-91.

230

The labyrinth motif has had an incomparable fascination for artists and writers from ancient times to the present day. It offers, in a sense, the ultimate delusion: the illusion of endless, limitless wandering, but within a tightly controlled, limited space. It is at one and the same time a symbol of chaos and a symbol of cosmos. On the one hand the labyrinth-walker runs the risk of losing himself in the tortuous meandering paths of the labyrinth. It symbolises both the subjective confusions inside the human mind and also the difficult path through the objectively existing world around us. On the other hand the labyrinth represents a complex order in diversity - a cosmos, for those who view it from outside, from a bird's eye perspective.

Both these aspects of the labyrinth, as chaos and as cosmos, are used frequently as metaphors by Goethe throughout his writing[83]. Cities become labyrinths for the visiting traveller. In the *Italienische Reise* he describes how, in Venice he threw himself without a guide 'into the labyrinth of the city, which, although completely cross-cut by canals of all sizes, is reconnected by bridges both big and small': an image which balances neatly both the chaotic and the ordering elements of the labyrinth. In Sicily he experiences the city of Palermo as a labyrinth from which the stranger can extricate himself only with the help of a guide and on a visit to the ancient theatre at Taormina the thickly-growing agave plants form a labyrinth which must be penetrated in order to return to the city[84]. Unfinished or fragmentary buildings, too, reveal maze-like aspects. In Rome he describes how the visitor, on passing the arch of Titus, becomes entangled 'in the labyrinth of the Palatine ruins'[85]. On visiting Cologne cathedral he attempts to comprehend the intentions for the whole from its unfinished state and regrets the lack of a guide who could lead him through its complexities[86].

---

[83] We have already seen (in Chapter 3, page 178) these two contradictory/complementary aspects of the labyrinth brought out in Goethe's description of Susanne von Klettenberg and in his comment on 'true poetry'.

[84] H.A. Volume 11, pages 68, 230 and 297.

[85] *Italienische Reise*, Frankfurt am Main 1976, 'Zweiter Römischer Aufenthalt', page 689.

[86] H.A. Volume 10, pages 32-3.

Museums and libraries, dictionaries and encyclopaedias all display labyrinthine qualities. In *Dichtung und Wahrheit* Goethe describes how the 'Antikensaal' [hall of antiquities] in Mannheim became for his younger self 'a forest of statues, through which one has to thread one's way'; while at an even younger age he became embroiled in the works of the encyclopaedists and lost himself 'in an even bigger labyrinth, as I found Bayle in my father's library and became absorbed in it'[87]. The natural sciences are labyrinths whose penetration depends on the Ariadne's thread furnished by long hours of careful study of the physical laws combined with practical experience. Of his interest in meteorology Goethe writes, 'But my real intention was to point experimentally to a ball of thread with whose aid one could extricate oneself from the bewildering labyrinth of our standard meteorological tables'. In a poem celebrating the opening of the salt-works at Stotternheim a similar image is used of the study of geology, while the diverse forms of animal life lead him to see the study of anatomy, too, in terms of a labyrinth for which one must find a guiding thread[88].

The arts, too, constitute a labyrinthine world for those who study them. An article in the *Edinburgh Review* on German art is described as 'an essay which occupies itself with journeying through and describing the labyrinth of the German way of thinking and German art'[89]. The study of painting and the visual arts is a maze whose confusions can only be overcome with much practice: 'despite the state of confusion in which I find myself, I already feel that practice, knowledge and inclination are already coming to my aid in these mazes'. In Catania, on a visit to Prince Bescari's collection of antiquities Goethe casts Winckelmann in the role of Ariadne, as guide to the complexities of classical art: 'I learnt again and helped myself forward quite well with that thread of Winckelmann, which leads us through the different artistic epochs'[90]. During his

---

[87] H.A. Volume 9, pages 501 and 239.
[88] W.A. 2.12, page 68, 'Meteorologie'; W.A. 4, page 285, 'Die ersten Erzeugnisse der Stotternheimer Saline'; 2.8, pages 16-17, 'Einleitung in die vergleichende Anatomie'.
[89] W.A. 42 (2), 'Edinburgh Reviews', page 350.
[90] H.A. Volume 11, pages 107 and 291.

second stay in Rome he has recognised that the human body represents just as much of a labyrinth for the aspiring artist as for the anatomist: 'without a thread, which one only learns to spin here, one cannot find one's way out of this labyrinth. Unfortunately my thread is not growing long enough, but at least it is helping me through the outer passageways'[91]. In the introduction to the *Propyläen*, he uses the same image to argue that, since the most important subject of art is the human body, the artist needs just as firm a grasp of the laws of nature as the scientist in order to be able to represent its complexities[92].

In the literary works, too, labyrinthine metaphors of order and disorder proliferate. In the poem 'Zueignung', which serves as a preface to *Faust*, the old manuscript brings back to the poet the sorrows of 'the wild, labyrinthine course of life'; while in the 'Prolog im Himmel' the idea of the labyrinth lies behind the image of erring man; and the chaotic world of 'Walpurgisnacht' is reflected in the 'labyrinth of valleys' through which Faust and Mephisto approach the Brocken and through which they are 'guided' by an 'Irrlicht' [will-o'-the-wisp]. In *Faust II* the mountainous landscape with its mineral wealth challenges the skill of its inhabitants, the gnomes, with its labyrinthine complexities and harbours in its subterranean recesses spirits long fled from the lower-lying regions who 'carry on their secret work through labyrinthine chasms'. Helena describes her journey from the realm of Greek myth to the medieval world as an 'Irrfahrt' and on arrival her companion Phorkyas vanishes 'in the labyrinth of the castle'; while Faust envisages his own journey in the opposite direction back to the mythical archetypes - 'zu den Müttern' [to the mothers] - as a voyage of exploration through 'this labyrinth of flames'; and the Trojan women feel themselves, since the sack of Troy, to be trapped on a nightmare, labyrinthine journey of suffering[93].

Werther uses the image of the labyrinth in his altercation with Albert over suicide to represent the 'Krankheit zum Tode' [mortal illness] of the suicidal

---

[91] *Italienische Reise*, page 626.
[92] H. A. Volume 12, 'Einleitung in die Propyläen', page 43.
[93] *Faust I & II*, lines 14, 328-9, 3841, 5898-901, 10429, 9145, 7079 and 9590-2.

condition: 'nature finds no way out of the labyrinth of confused and contradictory forces and the human being must die'[94]; while in the poem 'An Werther' the poet looks back in old age on a lifetime of entanglement in the labyrinth of passions from which his literary creation escaped by suicide and suggests that words - his literary compositions - are the only thing that can offer him the possibility of a way out: 'Geb ihm ein Gott zu sagen, was er duldet' [may a god give him the means to say what he suffers][95]. In his commentary on the poem 'Urworte, Orphisch' in *Über Kunst und Altertum* Goethe links together ῎Ερως · 'Liebe' [love] - and Τύχη · 'Das Zufällige' [chance] - with the image of the labyrinth, using it to suggest the endless aberrations of the passions: 'it lures the confused into new labyrinths, here is no limit to the going astray: for the way is an error'. The poem 'An den Mond' also concerns itself with the internal labyrinth of the human heart - 'das Labyrinth der Brust'[96].

In *Die natürliche Tochter* there is a rich vein of labyrinthine imagery. As a work in which Goethe attempts to come to terms with the upheavals of the French Revolution the play is full of images, not only of threatening nets and ordered weaving, but also of labyrinths of order and of disorder. Eugenie's father pledges to celebrate his daughter's survival after her first plunge into the ravine by creating a labyrinthine order out of the labyrinthine chaos of the landscape. Later, when he once more mistakenly thinks her dead, he conjures up her ideal image in his imagination to be a guiding light to him on his further way through the world:

> Schwebe vor,
> Wohin ich wandle, zeige mir den Weg
> Durch dieser Erde Dornenlabyrinth!
> [Hover ahead
> Wherever I walk, show me the way
> Through this earth's labyrinth of thorns!]

[94] H.A. Volume 6, page 48.
[95] H.A. Volume 1, page 380.
[96] W.A. 41 (I), pages 219 and W.A.1, page 101, line 35.

The first image of Eugenie is a pointer both to her impetuous, adventurous nature and to her impending fate, as her father describes how he lost sight of her - 'die Amazonentochter' [the Amazon-daughter] - 'in the labyrinth of the headlong chase'. The metaphor recurs in the fourth act to indicate how she has become entrapped in the labyrinthine network of court intrigue:

> Und so umschlang ein heimlich Labyrinth
> Verschmitzten Wirkens doppelt ihr Geschick
> [And so a secret labyrinth of malign intrigue
> Entwined itself doubly around her fate][97].

Since ancient times the labyrinth has been used as a metaphor for the difficult text or discussion, both in a pejorative sense, to denote arguments which were unnecessarily complicated and positively, for the dialectic by which the wise teacher leads the student through the necessarily winding paths towards knowledge and understanding. In Plato's *Euthydemus* Socrates uses the image playfully to describe the wordplay of two verbal conjurers with whom he is involved in a discussion. The discourse, he says, 'seemed like falling into a labyrinth; we thought we were at the finish, but our way bent round and we found ourselves as it were back at the beginning, and just as far from that which we were seeking at first'[98]. In the *Consolations of Philosophy* Boethius, while eager to learn, complains to Philosophy about the difficult circular argument she has involved him in:

> "You are playing with me," I said, "by weaving a labyrinthine argument from which I cannot escape (inextricabilem labyrinthum texens). You seem to begin where you ended and to end where you began. Are you perhaps making a marvellous circle of the divine simplicity?"[99]

In *On Christian Doctrine* Augustine suggests, 'What is sought with difficulty is discovered with more pleasure'[100]. Jerome, in his commentary on the prophet

---

[97] H.A. Volume 5, pages 233, 264, 219 & 266.

[98] Plato, *Euthydemus* 291B.

[99] Boethius, *Consolations of Philosophy* translated by Richard Green, Indianapolis 1962, page 72. Latin: Boethius *Philosophiae consolatio* edited by Ludwig Bieler C.C.S.L. 94 Turnholt. Brepols 1957.

[100] 'Nemo ambigit (...) cum aliqua difficultate quaesita multo gratius inveniri', *On Christian Doctrine* 2.8.(13).

Ezekiel, uses the image of the labyrinth as a metaphor for the holy scriptures, 'So also I, entering the ocean of those scriptures and so to speak, the labyrinth of the mysteries of God'; and the same image occurs in the preface to Book 2 of his commentary on Zacharias, 'We endure labyrinthine errors and guide our blind footsteps by the thread of Christ'[101]. The metaphor was also used of the work of poets. Sidonius Apollinaris (431-487AD) uses it to praise the poetry of a man he names only as Peter, 'We have the completed work; weaving (texens) it with art in the dimeter, he has run a hard journey and labyrinthine ways'[102]. In the Middle Ages the term 'Aristotle's labyrinth' was used to describe the complexities awaiting those who embarked upon a study of Aristotle's writings and dialectic methods[103].

Goethe, too, uses the image of the labyrinth to denote the difficult philosophical text. In the essay 'Einwirkung der neueren Philosophie' he describes how, when he read Kant's *Kritik der reinen Vernunft,* he experienced for the first time the attraction of a theoretical work: 'but now for the first time a theory seemed to smile at me'; but nevertheless he felt unable to enter fully into the labyrinth of the text: 'it was the entrance that pleased me, I couldn't venture into the labyrinth itself'[104]. We have seen already (Chapter 3, page 178) how Goethe makes use of labyrinth-imagery in order to describe the effect that literature can have upon the recipient. In the letter to Schiller quoted there he claims, with the startlingly modern image of the hot-air balloon, that the poetry of Homer has the power to give one a bird's eye perspective, an overview on the world. In addition we have seen how this idea of the power of literature to offer

---

[101] Jerome introduces this image by quoting from the *Aeneid* Book 5 (see above) and Book 6. 27: 'hic labor ille domus et inextricabilis error [here is the toil of the house and the inextricable wandering]'. Jerome, *Commentariorum in Ezechielem prophetam PL,* 25 447- 449. Jerome, Preface to Book 2 *Commentary on Zacharias,* 'Labyrinthos patimur errores, et Christi caeca regimus filo vestigia'.

[102] Sidonius Apollinaris, *Epistulae et carmina* edited by Christian Luetjohann, *MGH Auct. antiq.,* 8, page 65, lines 88-91.

[103] Cf. for instance Arnulf of Milan (d.1077) *PL.* 147, 289, 'Meagre wit has narrowed me so that I see with difficulty the entrance to Aristotle's labyrinth'.

[104] W.A. 2. 11, page 49.

236

the bird's eye perspective is repeated in Book 13 of *Dichtung und Wahrheit* combined with the image of the labyrinth[105]. Goethe also uses the image to describe both the writer's experience in constructing literary texts and the reader's task of interpretation. Writing to Schiller about the *Lehrjahre* he says, 'In the end I have simply kept to my idea and I will be pleased if it leads me out of this labyrinth'[106]. In the novel itself, Shakespeare's *Hamlet* is experienced as a labyrinth by its would-be interpreter, Wilhelm, who says, 'I struggled in this maze for a long time in vain, until I hoped finally to reach my goal in a very particular way'[107]. In a letter to Frau Fromann in 1820 Goethe explicitly refers to the manuscript of the *Wanderjahre* as 'die Irrgänge des Wanderers' [the wanderer's maze][108].

The labyrinth, in the form of the 'domus daedali', functions generally as a symbol for the complex work of art or the magnificent artefact whose greatness appears at first as confusing complexity but gradually reveals to the viewer the order inherent in its diversity. The labyrinth is also a sign of difficult process, of the laborious process of artistic creation, of the careful interweaving and ordering of circuitous paths. It serves at the same time as a model for the artist's intention and as a pattern for the interpreter's 'modus operandi'. It is the epitome of duality: incorporating at the same time artistry and confusion, order and chaos, the work of art and the process of its creation. It emphasises both the role of the artist and the role of the reader or interpreter: on the one hand the most careful craftsmanship; on the other hand the most painstaking interpretation. When artist and interpreter discharge their task effectively they achieve an important objective and rise above the perplexities of the labyrinth. The labyrinth can also however function as a sign of impenetrability. Here is emphasised the never-ending

---

[105] H.A. Volume 9, page 580.
[106] Schiller/Goethe Briefwechsel, letter of 10th December 1794, page 75.
[107] H.A. Volume 7, page 217. Cf. *Wilhelm Meisters theatralische Sendung,* where it is also said of Wilhelm's preoccupation with *Hamlet,* 'He exerted himself for a long time in this labyrinth in vain', Book 6, Chapter 17. W.A. 52, page 223.
[108] Letter to Frau Fromann, 9th December 1820. Gräf, 1.2, page 949.

imprisonment that complexity and diversity can create. Trapped in the labyrinth, the wanderer pursues in vain the desired goal[109].

Literary labyrinths are to be found in all literary periods. Manfred Schmeling cites the ancient Greek world, the late medieval period, the renaissance, the baroque period, the romantic period and the twentieth century as high points and names Homer, Ovid, Comenius, Hoffmann, Hugo, Zola, d'Annunzio, Joyce, Kafka, Borges and Robbe-Grillet as important authors of literary labyrinths[110]. Penelope Reed Doob analyses Virgil's *Aeneid*, Boethius' *Consolations of Philosophy*, Dante's *Divine Comedy* and Chaucer's *House of Fame*, pointing out elements of their structure and imagery which indicate that they too function as literary labyrinths[111]. Marianne Thalmann looks at the Romantic writers from the perspective of their tendency to create labyrinths and suggests that this tendency to write labyrinthine literature comes on the one hand from their attempt to cope with the growing complexity of contemporary life, particularly city life: 'wenn die Welt Chaos ist, wird das Labyrinth seine künstlerische Ordnung' [when the world is chaos, the labyrinth becomes its artistic ordering]. On the other hand they are influenced by a type of popular bestseller found in the lending libraries, the 'Bundesroman', itself an off-spin of the eighteenth century interest in freemasonry and other secret societies such as the Illuminati whose aim was the education of mankind towards a fuller humanity[112]. The freemason 'topos' is used both by Mozart in the *Zauberflöte* and by Goethe in the Wilhelm Meister novels[113].

---

[109] Cf. Penelope Reed Doob *The idea of the Labyrinth from Classical Antiquity through the Middle Ages*, Ithaca & London, 1990, Chapter 3.

[110] Manfred Schmeling, page 15.

[111] Penelope Reed Doob, Part 3.

[112] Marianne Thalmann, *Romantik und Manierismus* Stuttgart 1963, page 55.

[113] Cf. Scott Abbott, 'Des Maurers Wandeln/Es gleicht dem Leben'. The Freemasonic Ritual Route in *Wilhelm Meisters Wanderjahre*, in: *DVjs* June 58, 2 (1984), pages 262-288. Goethe's ambivalent attitude to the freemasons, of whose Weimar lodge he was for a while an enthusiastic member, is reflected in his ambivalent presentation of the 'Society of the Tower' and its successors.

Manfred Schmeling traces some of the main motifs which are connected with labyrinthine narrative: labyrinthine gardens and city- or landscapes; labyrinthine buildings, particularly towers and libraries; metaphors of flying, dreams and time travel; labyrinthine thought processes[114]. In the later middle ages the labyrinth's metaphorical dimension as a labyrinth of love, fate or spiritual progress was emphasised. The labyrinth idea is closely connected with art, love and death. The renaissance and baroque periods revelled in fantastical labyrinthine constructions of all kinds: hedges, lawns, waterways, walls, buildings, texts and musical scores.

Labyrinthine narrative is pre-eminently a self-reflexive form. It often makes use of the device of ekphrasis: the writer describing buildings, paintings, frescoes, sculptures with an important function in the text. Structurally the text is marked by interlacing and repetitions, by affinities and antinomies. Stylistically the narrative discourse is characterised by a high degree of repetition (variations on a theme), by contradictions and by the suggestion of different possibilities. Along with the narrative that he tells, the narrator himself and his reader become part of the fiction. The plot and the discourse co-exist in a highly complex relationship to one another, whereby the element of discourse tends to dominate over the element of plot so that the process of the production of the text becomes itself part of the discourse. In other words there is a continuous analysis of the narration during the process of narration. The reader is kept constantly aware of the selective processes which have gone into the construction of the text, the partial, particular views of reality which it represents and so is encouraged to think critically, to fill in the gaps and to consider alternative possibilities.

In his 'Vorwort zum deutschen Gil Blas' Goethe distinguishes between two kinds of narrative. The first is the conventional novel, novella or tale, a closed structure, from which its readers expect 'an internal consistency, which, however many labyrinths we are led through, should emerge again and bring the

---

[114] Schmeling, page 226.

whole thing to a close within itself'. The alternative is a narrative form which tries to present a model of life: 'Das Leben des Menschen'. This second type of narrative is open-ended like life itself and does not round everything off neatly by tying up all the loose ends or by loosing all the entanglements and knots:

> Das Leben des Menschen aber, treulich aufgezeichnet, stellt sich nie als ein Ganzes dar; den herrlichsten Anfängen folgen kühne Fortschritte, dann mischt sich der Unfall drein, der Mensch erholt sich, er beginnt, vielleicht auf einer höheren Stufe, sein altes Spiel, das ihm gemäß war, dann verschwindet er entweder frühzeitig oder schwindet nach und nach, ohne daß auf jeden geknüpften Knoten eine Auflösung erfolgte[115].
>
> [But human life, faithfully recorded, never represents itself as a whole; fearless progress follows upon the most glorious beginnings, then accident interferes, the person recovers, he begins, perhaps on a higher level, his old game, that was appropriate to him, then he either disappears prematurely or fades away gradually, without a resolution occurring to every knot that has been tied.]

It is noteworthy that the imagery both of the labyrinth and of the entangled thread is used to present these two alternative models of narrative fiction.

The second alternative is a programme for a new concept of the novel, a programme which can be applied to Goethe's intention for the *Wanderjahre*, a novel of which he wrote to Johann Friedrich Rochlitz in 1829:

> But with this kind of book it is the same as with life itself: in the whole complex there are necessary and chance elements, priorities and subsidiary elements, now successful, now coming to nothing, through which it gains a kind of infinity, which does not quite submit to the limits and confines of sensible and reasonable words[116].

This programme for a new conception of novelistic narrative, which attempts to reflect the confusion, uncertainty and variety of life itself, is not so far removed from the narrative programme expressed by André Gide a century later in *Les Faux-Monnayeurs* where the protagonist delivers the following critique of the conventional paradigm of the novel and with it an indication of how narrative form must fit itself to the new uncertainties of life:

> C'est affaire à vous, romanciers, de chercher à les [les situations fausses] résoudre. Dans la vie, rien ne se résout; tout continue. On demeure dans l'incertitude; et on restera

---

[115] W.A. Volume 42.1, page 91. The book in question, the 'German Gil Blas' was the autobiography of a library attendant in Weimar, Johann Christoph Sachse, which Goethe recommended to Cotta for publication in 1822.
[116] 23rd November 1829. H.A., Letters, Volume 4, page 356. (Cf. Chapter 2, page 72)

jusqu'à la fin sans savoir à quoi s'en tenir; en attendant, la vie continue, continue, tout comme si de rien n'était[117].

[It is your job, novelists, to try and resolve them [false situations]. In life nothing resolves itself; everything continues. One lives in uncertainty; and one will remain right to the end without knowing what it's all about; in the meantime, life continues, continues, just as if nothing has happened.]

Manfred Schmeling emphasises that for the twentieth century writers of labyrinthine discourses such as Gide, Joyce, Kafka or the French 'nouveau roman' writers like Robbe-Grillet the labyrinth no longer serves as a pattern of possible order in the universe. The loss of a sense of centre means that for these writers the labyrinth has come to symbolise principally the sense of imprisonment and hopelessness, the inner and outer confusion in a world that has become more and more incomprehensible. These new uncertainties did not, however, first begin in the twentieth century. Already in the early nineteenth century the classical norm, with its claim to unity and integrity of form, had become problematical. The end of the eighteenth century and the beginning of the nineteenth century had seen upheavals which had brought about a changed European world order. Feudal Europe was fast disappearing; the French Revolution had brought dreams of equality and nightmares of terror; the restoration period was attempting to return to former certainties with repressive measures while the Industrial Revolution was to ensure that the old order could never return. Looking back over the previous sixty years in one of the *Zahme Xenien* of 1821, Goethe sees labyrinth upon labyrinth of confusion proliferating and wonders where a new Ariadne's thread will be found:

Seit sechzig Jahren seh' ich gröblich irren	[For sixty years I've seen all go far astray
Und irre derb mit drein;	And have myself strayed with the rest;
Da Labyrinthe nun das Labyrinth verwirren,	Since labyrinths without end confuse the labyrinth,
Wo soll euch Ariadne sein?[118]	Where will you find a new Ariadne?]

---

[117] André Gide, *Les Faux-Monnayeurs*, Librairie Gallimard Paris 1925, page 406. Manfred Schmeling, pages 23-4, quotes only the first part of Goethe's comment, his description of the 'closed' work of fiction, and draws from it the conclusion that it was not until the twentieth century with the works of the modernists and later the post-modernists that a narrative model of the kind outlined by Gide was conceived.

[118] W.A. 3, page 253.

In a letter to Zelter in 1825 he characterises the new age as an age of mediocrity and delivers a commentary which sums up many of the likely effects of the coming industrialisation:

> Young people become excited too early and then are swept away in the maelstrom of time. Wealth and speed are what the world admires and what everyone strives after. Railways, express deliveries, steamships and all kinds of resources of communication are the things that the educated world is intent on, to overeducate themselves and thereby remain in mediocrity[119].

Some of the aphorisms in Makarie's archive and in the 'Betrachtungen im Sinne der Wanderer' reinforce this view. In the new age everything is 'veloziferisch' [very rapid] (288); it is characterised by 'the briskness of trade, the lightning spread of paper money, the escalation of debts in order to pay debts' (289). There is a danger that a young person might be swept away in the 'Zeitstrom' [flow of time] (288). This speed and complexity is accompanied by an increasing specialisation and fragmentation in many aspects of life. Modern science is characterised by increasing 'Vielfachheit und Zerstückelung und Verwickelung' [multiplicity and dismemberment and complication] (467). In a letter to Wilhelm von Humboldt in March 1832 about *Faust II* Goethe sums up the sense of confusion brought about by this increasing complexity and fragmentation, 'Verwirrende Lehre zu verwirrtem Handel waltet über die Welt' [confusing teaching about confused dealings rules over the world][120]. Already at this time there was doubt about the validity of traditional categories of order - the 'Zeiten des Wertzerfalls' [times of disintegration of values] as Hermann Broch designates the centuries from the eighteenth to the twentieth - had already begun[121]. In the *Wanderjahre* the labyrinthine form of the text and the many labyrinths within the text both express this sense of a chaotic world and at the same time embody an attempt to control and order that chaos: 'for that very reason the rudder is put into the hand of the human being in his fragile craft, so that he does not obey the caprice of the waves but the purpose of his own insight'

---

[119] 7th June 1825. H.A., Letters, Volume 4, page 146.
[120] H.A., Letters, Volume 4, page 481.
[121] Hermann Broch, Volume 9. 2, page 222.

(288). In the attempt to challenge the reader and make him think there is also the intention to put into his hand the 'rudder' - his own insight - which will help him to steer his way through the confusing complexities both of the narrative text and of life itself.

Two different types of labyrinth representation have been distinguished: more common from ancient times up to the medieval period was the unicursal or simple pattern, a single winding path leading inevitably to the centre and then back out again; from the renaissance onwards the more dominant form was the multicursal pattern offering a choice of different paths and dead-ends. Penelope Reed Doob suggests that two kinds of multiple narrative correspond to these two labyrinthine patterns. The unicursal labyrinth is analogous to a complex story where many disparate elements and episodes are linked together by some feature such as a common protagonist; the multicursal labyrinth is analogous to interlaced stories like the French cyclical romances where the 'complexity is augmented by the sheer number of linked but divergent episodes that may have little in common'[122]. The *Wanderjahre* has characteristics of both these types of narrative, having a protagonist and eponymous hero, whose story is traced through the whole text, but also containing many disparate elements whose only connection with the hero is that they belong to texts he has either read or heard.

In her analysis of the *Aeneid* Doob suggests that it displays the following characteristics of the labyrinthine narrative: the geographical wanderings of the hero trace a pictorial labyrinth of error; the narrative begins 'medias in res' and constantly winds back and forth in time not only describing a linear progress but also incorporating cyclical patterns of retold histories, prophecies and fulfilments, while lexically and syntactically the style often relies on ambiguity, on a double viewpoint, the frequent ambiguities demanding multiple interpretation[123]. The *Wanderjahre*, too, describes the hero's linear progress through time, but also contains cyclical patterns of retold histories. Examples of such retold histories are

---

[122] Penelope Reed Doob, page 206.
[123] Penelope Reed Doob, page 246.

Wilhelm's childhood trauma at the drowning of the fisher-boy; his account of his anatomical studies; and Lenardo's account of his encounter with Nachodine and his diaries of his travels in the Swiss mountains. The text also contains an element of the possibly prophetic in Wilhelm's dream of Makarie's apotheosis; and the cyclical element of Wilhelm's physical movement through geographical space is repeated in Makarie's metaphorical movement through cosmic space.

The combination of linear and cyclical movement is contained in the image of the spiral; a pattern intimately connected with the labyrinth. The simple unicursal labyrinth is indeed a spiral pattern, winding in towards the centre and back out again. Karl Kerenyi says that the spiral - 'a never-ending line, the simplest and oldest form of the labyrinth, a never-ending progression' - is representative of infinity and therefore immortality: that the spiral movement represents 'its [being's] capacity to wind itself endlessly through death' - the movement inwards towards the centre-point representing the movement towards mortality and death and the movement outwards towards the periphery representing the return to life and immortality[124]. In the poem 'Weltseele' Goethe explicitly associates the image of the labyrinth with the cyclical courses of the planets and stars in the solar system: 'the labyrinth of the suns and planets'[125]. The 'ätherische Dichtung', with its account of Makarie's cyclical movement outwards towards the periphery of cosmic space brings together spiral and labyrinth and suggests metaphorically the possibilities of human immortality[126].

Several critics have used labyrinthine metaphors to describe the way in which the *Wanderjahre* functions. Erich Trunz combines both labyrinth and weaving-imagery in his description of how the theme of renunciation is

---

[124] Karl Kerenyi, *Werke*, Volume 1: *Humanistische Seelenforschung*, Wiesbaden 1966, pages.260 and 262.
[125] H.A. Volume 1, page 248.
[126] This passage has been interpreted as representing Goethe's 'belief in the immortality of the active human being': Anneliese Klingenberg, page 445; or as a 'myth of immortality and the after-life' after the manner of Plato in his dialogues: Georg-Karl Bauer, page 181. It has been described as 'poetry of vision' in which 'Makarie (...) embodies the immortal in mankind': Hannelore Schlaffer, 1980, page 185.

244

incorporated into the structure of the novel: 'the straight and tortuous paths before one becomes a renunciant are particularly depicted in the numerous novellas which are woven into the novel'[127]. He also compares the aphorism-collections to a labyrinth of learning experiences for the reader. Of the 'Betrachtungen im Sinne der Wanderer' he writes, 'These 177 sentences are like a large, unfamiliar park in which one goes astray, discovers new things over and over again, learns to see the well-known with afresh and repeatedly wants to break into cries of delight, amazement and empathy'[128]. Emil Staiger uses the metaphor to criticise a text which he feels leaves open too many possibilities of interpretation and leaves too much to the reader[129]. The image is used by these critics, however, in an almost subconscious echoing of the text itself without taking into account how consciously Goethe has embedded the weaving and labyrinth motifs into his text and used them as a model for the structure of the work[130].

The two aspects of the labyrinth, chaos and order, are presented metaphorically in the *Wanderjahre* through a description of the landscape. Wilhelm, who has met up again with Jarno/Montan in the mountains, grows dizzy at the sight of the chasm below and Montan assures him:

"There is nothing more natural (...) than that we grow dizzy when we glimpse a breathtaking scene that we come across unexpectedly, and then feel simultaneously our importance and our insignificance. But there is no true pleasure except where one first must grow dizzy" (31).

The 'Schwindeln' [dizziness], referred to here, is analogous to that 'Erstaunen' [amazement] which the poem 'Parabase' affirms as the vital response to the study of the natural world: 'Zum Erstaunen bin ich da' [I am here to be amazed][131]; and to the 'Schaudern' [shuddering] which Faust, as he contemplates the fateful journey 'to the mothers', describes as 'humanity's best part' (line 6272). It is the

---

[127] H.A. Volume 8, page 529.
[128] H.A. Volume 8, page 638.
[129] Cf. Chapter 1, page 60.
[130] Unlike Friedrich Amrine and Wilhelm Emrich (see notes 80 and 81 above) who explicitly comment on the meta-textual function of the weaving image in the *Wanderjahre*.
[131] H.A. Volume 1, page 358. In the 'Ausgabe letzter Hand' this poem, together with 'Epirrhema', 'Antepirrhema', 'Metamorphose der Tiere' and 'Metamorphose der Pflanzen' forms a cycle whose theme is the study of nature. Cf. Manfred Karnick, pages 22-5.

necessary human reaction of a-mazed wonder, the labyrinthine bewilderment, which precedes all true learning. As they stand on the mountain peak together Wilhelm and Montan see, to one side of them, the landscape laid out in an orderly pattern, 'several peaks (...) a range of hills (...) visible in the distance the lakes and rivers and a fertile region seemed to spread out like a sea'. On the other side their gaze is drawn 'in schauerliche Tiefen, von Wasserfällen durchrauscht, labyrinthisch miteinander zusammenhängend' [into horrifying depths, tortuously linked together, with waterfalls gushing through] (32): on the one hand nature is ordered, clear and comprehensible, on the other hand chaotic and impenetrable. This use of the word 'labyrinthisch' is one of only two explicit uses of the word 'labyrinth' in the text: here it is used in a spatial context to describe a wild and threatening landscape. The second use of the word occurs in the introduction to the novella 'Nicht zu weit' where it is used to describe the inner space of the confusions in the human mind: 'they stayed together until deep in the night and entangled themselves ever more inextricably in the labyrinths of human fortunes and convictions' (393). Although the word occurs within the text only twice, the text itself is a proliferation of both spatial and spiritual labyrinths.

The 'Bergfest' [mountain festival] offers another metaphor for the tension between chaos and order in the novel. The subterranean flames produce a magnificent harmonious display which is a reflection of the cosmic harmony of the stars and planets, as experienced by Makarie on her mystical journeyings through space. This harmony however is disturbed by human quarrelsomeness as the scientists argue over the process of the formation of the earth and ends in a humorous hyperbole which nevertheless sadly contains uncomfortably too much of the truth: 'and so the marvellous festival might almost have ended with fatal deeds' (262). The effect on Wilhelm of this clash of rival scientific explanations for the creation of the world vividly illustrates the disorientating effect on the individual in the modern world of the loss of the 'centre' of traditional theological doctrine. In the face of the competing theories the ordered world collapses into chaos in his bewildered imagination:

> Our friend, who still from time immemorial cherished in his inmost mind the spirit that
> hovered over the waters and the deep flood that stood fifteen ells above the highest
> mountains, felt very confused and depressed and it seemed to him, on hearing these
> strange discourses, that the so well ordered, cultivated and populated world collapsed into
> chaos in his imagination (262).

Wilhelm's letter to Natalie, in which he attempts to set out his reasons for becoming a surgeon, makes clear that the model for the construction of the whole text is the labyrinth of difficult process which in turn provokes labyrinthine interpretative methods on the part of the reader[132]. Not only is the text itself a labyrinth of many different narrative strands and types of text, not only is the reader treated as a maze-walker who must go through the textual labyrinth in order to gain insight; but also the many and various types of labyrinth in the text complement and provide analogies for the labyrinth of the text. Makarie's archive and the 'Betrachtungen im Sinne der Wanderer' are library-labyrinths full of contradictory and complementary statements challenging the reader directly, without any mediating narrative, to use his combinatory and interpretative skills. The reader accompanies Wilhelm on his journey through the labyrinth of life through a variety of miniature labyrinths each constructed on the principle of a small, enclosed world[133]. This labyrinthine movement is exemplified when Fitz leads Wilhelm, Montan and Felix to the clearing in the woods to spend the night with the charcoal-burners: 'und so folgten sie ihm alle durch wundersame Pfade zum stillen Ort' [and so they all followed him along strange pathways to the secret place] (37). Heidi Gidion characterises these small, enclosed worlds with the designation 'Bezirke' [realms]. Each is approached through a well-ordered landscape; each is to be entered through a 'Pforte', 'Tor' or 'Tür' [portal, gate or doorway] suggesting both the enclosed nature of the area and the possibility of access, of passing through to a new realm of experience; each contains a well-

---

[132] Cf. Chapter 1, pages 23-4.

[133] In the first version of the *Wanderjahre* this method of construction is explicitly thematised when Montan describes the 'pedagogical province' in the following terms, 'Points of active instruction sown, as it were, over a large space. In each place you find a little world, but so complete in spite of its restriction, that it must reproduce and represent every other world, even the great one' (1821.36).

constructed building, which in turn contains a hall or gallery, often lined with pictures, an inner sanctum or 'Heiligtum'[134]. This construction is repeated in ever-varying ways from Joseph's cloister to the uncle's estate, from the house of the collector to Makarie's castle, in the pedagogical province and in the house of the anatomical sculptor. Each of these areas represents an attempt to give order, pattern and meaning to a chaotic world. Each is also intended to be 'a model in nothing and in everything a guide and stimulus'[135]. Each must be read against the other and also be seen to contain its own contradictions. The idyllic world of Saint Joseph appears to flicker between reality and dream and has a 'peculiar old-world atmosphere' (16); the orderly lifestyle of the spinners and weavers is threatened from outside by the 'Maschinenwesen' [mechanisation], corresponding to the monstrous minotaur in the centre of the traditional labyrinth. The enlightenment rationality, which is the guiding principle on the uncle's estate, can only exist by denying the imagination and fantasy a place (65); it is criticised from within by the counter-voice of Hersilie and must protect itself from the chaos without by means of prison-bars. In the 'pedagogical province' Wilhelm's repeated 'stutzen' [stopping short] suggests to the reader where he should pay close attention and consider the ideas expressed with extra care; the leaders themselves suggest that, for all their careful planning and cultivation of the children's talents, 'on occasion it all develops better of its own accord' (154), and they have no better way of dealing with children who do not conform than sending them home to their parents[136].

---

[134]. Heidi Gidion, page 62 and page.65. Cf also Scott Abbott, pages 262-288, where he draws analogies between the ritual routes of the Freemasons and Wilhelm's progress through the various realms of experience.

[135] The comment on Laurence Sterne in Makarie's archive, No. 171 page 485.

[136] Goethe's own ambiguous attitude to the principles embodied in the 'pedagogical province' can be gauged from his wry reaction in the article 'Geneigte Teilnahme an den *Wanderjahre*' to Professor Kayßler's criticism of the institution: 'He is not completely satisfied with my institutions, which I hold against him so little that I immediately wrote on his thoughtful pamphlet: "Il y a une fibre adorative dans le coeur humain [there is a thread of adoration in the human heart]." Through this confession I meant to express total agreement with such an honourable man'. H.A. Volume 8, pages 522-3.

248

Other labyrinths are to be understood as initiation labyrinths: Felix's descent into the underworld of the 'Riesenschloß' [gigantic castle] awakens him to a new awareness of life and, with the mysterious casket discovered in its innermost recesses, comes to light a concrete symbol for the enigma of the text containing it. Here Fitz warns of the dangers, 'For no one ever finds his way out of these caverns and chasms again' (42); and Wilhelm, with his ball of thread, acts as a guide to help Felix return to the outside world. Wilhelm's account of his childhood visit to the country, with its maze-like wanderings through meadows, woods and gardens, combines in one day initiation into the secrets of friendship, love and death and awakens in him an appreciation of the beauty of the human form.

In 'Der Mann von funfzig Jahren' the corridors and halls of the beautiful widow's house represent for Flavio the dangers of love, as 'she paces up and down alone in her enchanted halls, when the spirits, that she held spellbound there, are released' (186). Here the emphasis is on the confusion of feelings caused by love. The poem composed by Flavio and answered by Hilarie reflects the inner chaos that is caused by unbridled passion as he writes, 'I experience night and death and hell'; and the order that can be restored by a love based on empathy and friendship, as she replies, 'Come into the brightness and heavenly radiance of friendship' (206). In this story too the landscape presents pictures of order and chaos. The floodwaters bring danger and chaos; but order is restored as the waters freeze bringing safety and renewed communication. The frozen landscape also brings the opportunity for Flavio and Hilarie's moonlit skating-dance, which, with its intricate weaving of meeting and of 'Scheiden und Meiden' [parting and avoiding], imposes a pattern on the chaos of love[137]. This pattern is then again disturbed by the appearance of the major, and the inner feelings of the three are mirrored in their outer circumstances as they stray disorientated on the

---

[137] Here can perhaps be seen echoes, too, of Theseus' 'geranos' in which the boys and girls he rescued from the labyrinth repeated the intricate movement through the labyrinth in a ritual dance in the safety of the island of Delos; and also of Ascanius' intricately weaving 'Trojan ride' in the *Aeneid.*

slippery expanse of the frozen lake in the moonlight. A similar metaphor for the dangers and temptations of love is played out on Lake Maggiore where the water provides a mobile element for the interweaving of the boats of the four participants as 'several days were spent in this peculiar way between meeting and parting, between separating and being together' (233), and the trance-like state of these few days is converted to chaos as reality intrudes and 'now paradise was changed as if by the stroke of a magic wand into a complete wasteland' (240).

The confusion of the major's inner feelings in 'Der Mann von funfzig Jahren' is presented with great psychological vividness in the image of the circle of the labyrinth revolving inside his psyche as he hopelessly seeks a way out: 'so it was during sleepless nights when all sorts of hateful things, forever changing shape, kept whirling round in his inmost mind in a very unpleasant circle' (222).

The most striking representation of the chaotic labyrinth of inner feelings is the story of Odoard and Albertine's unhappy marriage in 'Nicht zu weit', introduced with the sentence, 'They stayed together until deep in the night and entangled themselves ever more inextricably in the labyrinths of human fortunes and convictions' (393). Here the various elements - the open fragmentary structure of the story; the movements of the protagonists to and fro through physical space; the joyfully organised birthday party which is reduced to chaos - all reflect the despair and chaotic inner feelings of a couple chained together in a loveless marriage.

The 'Lustspielnovelle' [comedy-novella] 'Wer ist der Verräter?' offers a total contrast to the open-endedness and fragmentary nature of 'Nicht zu weit' and of the novel as a whole. We will see in the next section how it serves as a model of the 'conventional' narrative form which Goethe outlines in the first part of the quotation from the 'Vorwort zum deutschen Gil Blas' and highlights, by its very closed nature the experimental, open-ended and questioning form of the novel itself.

In Lenardo's great 'Wanderrede' [migration speech] the world itself becomes a labyrinth, crossed and re-crossed by the most varied groups, so that the earth 'is flooded with a teeming race of ants that crosses and re-crosses each other's paths' (386). Lenardo describes a chaotic movement through time and space and attempts to impose an order upon it with his picture of the contemporary world made clearly comprehensible and penetrable to all, because of the overview created by modern researchers and explorers:

> The time is past, when we rushed adventurously out into the wide world; through the endeavours of scientific world travellers who have described their discoveries perceptively and reproduced them artistically we are well enough acquainted with all places to know roughly what is to be expected (390).

In the same way he attempts to impose order on the chaos of the emigrants' inner feelings, expressed in the farewell verse, 'For the bonds are broken,/The trust is violated' (317), with the counter-verse, 'Head and arm with cheerful energy,/Everywhere they are at home' (318).

This same pattern of an apparent chaos, which is really a controlled disorder, whose underlying order can be restored at will, is also evident in the 'pedagogical province'. The customary ordered pattern of life in the province is disturbed only in the place 'where the great market-day was held'. Of this locality we are told, 'an incredible turmoil was milling around there and one could not distinguish whether the wares or the buyers were raising more dust' (245). In this carnivalesque atmosphere, however, the pupils can be controlled at will through whistle-signals, as the 'Aufseher' [supervisor] demonstrates to an anxious Wilhelm[138].

Each of the small, enclosed worlds in the text has its own guide, sometimes also a counter-guide or perhaps a mis-leader. On the uncle's estate Juliette helps Wilhelm to interpret the inscriptions while Hersilie provides a counter-interpretation and also offers Wilhelm a fictional text to stimulate his

---

[138] This pattern of controlled chaos is also emphasised by Goethe in his descriptions of the gathering on the Corso in *Das römische Carneval*. He begins with a description of 'the crush, the turmoil, the noise and the boisterousness', which gradually rises to a crescendo as the day progresses, until 'no one will let the right be taken from him to turn away from order as night falls'. But this carnivalesque chaos is limited not only spatially by the narrow confines of the Corso but is also limited temporally so that as the night progresses 'this confusion disentangled itself, if somewhat later, nevertheless usually without harm'. Goethe *Das römische Carneval*, Frankfurt am Main 1995, pages 27 and 41-2.

imagination. Wilhelm and Felix are led astray by Fitz, who is described in the first version of the *Wanderjahre* as a 'will-o'-the wisp', to enter the uncle's estate through forbidden paths and end up in the prison. In the 'pedagogical province' Wilhelm is passed from the guiding hand of the 'supervisor' to be initiated into the secrets of the 'Heiligtümer' [inner sanctums] by the three leaders themselves. Montan acts as a Socratic or maieutic educator to Wilhelm with his metaphor of the charcoal kiln when he takes Wilhelm through a question and answer session in order to make him think. Wilhelm describes this somewhat flippantly as a lesson 'auf sokratische Weise' [of a Socratic nature] (39) but it can also be understood as a metaphor for the way in which the writer plays the role of midwife helping the reader to give birth to his ideas[139].

In Chapter 3 we have seen how the role of the poet as guide is also a role assigned to the sibylline Makarie. In his representational role as reader and writer Wilhelm is both trapped within the labyrinth of the text and acts as a guide to its complexities. Like Daedalus he is a craftsman/artist who was both a prisoner within the labyrinth, which was his own creation, and a rescuer and guide who directed others on the way through its intricacies. The novel begins 'medias in res' with Wilhelm in doubt and confusion as he repeatedly answers Felix's questions with: 'ich weiß nicht' [I don't know] (7). There is an overt allusion to the Daedalus analogy in the episode early in the novel when Wilhelm draws from his pocket an Ariadne-thread - 'einen Knaul Bindfaden' (43) to help him in his search for Felix in the subterranean, labyrinthine corridors of the gigantic castle. Much later, in Susanne's valley, he appears as a guide and leaves behind a 'leitendes Zeichen' [guiding sign] in the form of the 'Blatt' [sheet of paper], a text intended as a guideline through the complexities of life. In his choice of profession Wilhelm becomes also the craftsman/artist whose goal is to benefit mankind.

Daedalus is a figure espousing the middle way, who warns his son:

---

[139] Cf. Manfred Karnick, page 38.

'medio,' que, 'ut limite curras,
Icare,' ait. 'moneo ne, si demissior ibis,
unda gravet pennas; si celsior, ignis adurat.
inter utrumque vola (...)
me duce carpe viam[140].

Felix is something of an Icarus figure, like Euphorion in *Faust II*[141]. His passionate nature drives him to fly too high - or in his case to ride too wildly - and he plunges into the water. Wilhelm, on the other hand, like Daedalus, is a proponent of the middle way. During the course of his epiphanic experience in the observatory in Makarie's castle he gains the insight that man must find a balance between the inner and outer worlds, between the microcosm and the macrocosm and between the spiritual and earthly demands of human existence. This insight is prefigured at the beginning of the novel when we see Wilhelm placed physically between heaven and earth: 'the stars of heaven (...) illuminated him again, (...). Again he was gladdened by the sight of the great mountain range', (11); and it is summed up programmatically near the end of the novel: 'to move these two world in conjunction with one another, to manifest the characteristics of each one in each transitory episode of life, that is the highest form towards which man has to educate himself' (445). But even for a craftsman/artist who has gained such insight the way does not lose any of its complexities. Daedalus loses his son; the end of Wilhelm's story remains open and offers us no conclusion. We do not know whether Wilhelm's newly acquired skills will enable him to save Felix or not. In the last chapter we are told only that 'he seemed to be already fully recovered' (460). The image of Castor and Pollux is also ambiguous, suggestive as much of death as of immortality[142]. Felix's life is not necessarily saved at the

---

[140] Ovid, *Metamorphoses*, Book 8, lines 203-8: "'I warn you, Icarus," he said, "you must follow a course midway between earth and heaven, in case the sun should scorch your feathers, if you go too high, or the water make them heavy if you are too low. Fly halfway between the two (...): take me as your guide, and follow me!'" Penguin Classics, page 184.

[141] As Euphorion attempts to fly and plummets to the ground at the feet of his parents the chorus cries out, 'Ikarus! Ikarus!' *Faust II*, line 9901.

[142] When the mortal twin Castor was killed his immortal brother Pollux persuaded Zeus to allow Castor to share in his immortality. Zeus stipulated, however, that the two should have the gift of immortality alternately, so that it entailed eternal separation and death for one as long as the other lived. The ambiguity of the Castor and Pollux symbol for Goethe is highlighted by the Ildefonso

end, but the suggestion remains that the questing human spirit which he represents is at the same time both supremely vulnerable and unquenchable: "but you will always be created anew, marvellous image of God!" he cried out, "and you will straightaway be harmed again, injured either from inside or from outside" (460). Wilhelm and Felix incorporate the circularity of the text, which begins with them - with Wilhelm's concern for his son's education - and after inscribing the circles, the 'Irrgänge', of Wilhelm's wanderings, ends also with them. It is arguable that this ending is on a higher plane and that the circles which Wilhelm inscribes represent an upward spiral movement, a 'Steigerung' [progression]. At the end, however, Wilhelm remains 'problematical' (455), an embodiment of Goethe's stricture about the literary text: 'every solution to a problem raises a new problem'[143].

On the level of discourse the reader's guide through the text is the narrator. But this is no omniscient narrator providing the reader with a clear account of a sequence of events. The narrator takes the reader into a labyrinth of confusing possibilities without putting into his hands the ball of thread which will lead him safely through. He is saying in effect that the guiding thread has been broken and the reader is thrown back on his own resources - with only hints of broken threads from the narrator - in order to map the labyrinthine complexities of a text which aims to simulate 'das Leben selbst' [life itself] - and which reflects all the confusions of the rapidly changing and developing social, economic and cultural life of the early nineteenth century, the thresh-hold of the modern technological age.

---

bronze statue-group which stands in the entrance hall of his house in Weimar. The fraternal pair, with arms entwined, was variously explained by Goethe as representing Castor and Pollux or as representing Thanatos and Hypnos, the gods of sleep and death.
[143] Conversation with Kanzler von Müller, 8th June 1821.Gräf, 1.2, page 976.

Excursus: 'Wer ist der Verräter?'

eine innere Konsequenz
an internal consistency

The novella 'Wer ist der Verräter?' contains and continues many of the themes and images of the other novellas and of the novel as a whole, but in its closed form it also offers a total contrast to the experimental, open-ended and questioning form chosen by Goethe for the novel itself and for many of its component parts. It serves as a model of the 'conventional' narrative form, which Goethe parodies in *Faust I*, 'Vorspiel auf dem Theater'[144]; and whose characteristics he outlines in the 'Vorwort zum deutschen *Gil Blas*':

> For from them [novel, morality tale, novella and such like] as moral artistic productions we rightly demand an internal consistency, so that no matter how many labyrinths we are led through, it emerges again and the whole thing should come to a conclusion within itself[145].

A function of 'Wer ist der Verräter?' is, therefore, to highlight by its very contrast the open-ended and questioning form of the novel itself.

'Wer ist der Verräter?' can be characterised as a 'Lustspielnovelle'[146]. It uses some of the stock characters of comedy: two sisters of contrasting character, a confused lover, a rascally younger brother, two more or less tyrannical fathers, an old family friend and a mysterious stranger; and its end is that of the usual comedy: 'the goal of the action is as usual two weddings'[147]. Goethe then takes variations on this set of stock characters and plays on them in all different registers, from the light-hearted comedy of 'Wer ist der Verräter?' right through to tragedy.

---

[144] Zufällig naht man sich, man fühlt, man bleibt,
Und nach und nach wird man verflochten;
Es wächst das Glück, dann wird es angefochten,
Man ist entzückt, nun kommt der Schmerz heran,
Und eh' man sich's versieht, ist's eben ein Roman

[By chance we grow close, we feel, we stay,
And gradually we become entangled;
Happiness grows, then it's challenged,
We are in rapture, then the suffering comes,
And before we realise it, it's a novel.]
Faust I, lines 158-165.

[145] W.A. Volume 42.1, page 91.

[146] In discussing Tieck's *Zauberschloß*, Friedrich Sengle defines a 'Lustspielnovelle' [comedy-novella] in the following way: 'for the opposition to the engagement lies only in a harmless, comical obstinacy that is either overcome by decisive action or suddenly collapses of its own accord'. Friedrich Sengle, *Biedermeierzeit*, Volume 2, Stuttgart 1972, page 1040.

[147] Cf. Friedrich Sengle, pages 433-5, particularly page 433.

Hersilie emphasises the kinship of herself and her family with this set of stock characters, when she describes them to Wilhelm as:

> the usual set eternally repeated in novels and plays: an eccentric uncle, one docile and one lively niece, a wise aunt, the usual guests; and if the nephew would only come back, he would make the acquaintance of a wayward traveller, who perhaps might have brought an even more unusual companion with him, and so the tiresome piece would have been devised and set in motion (67).

This device is used, on the one hand, to draw attention to the fictional status of Hersilie and her fellow characters; on the other hand it is used to contrast the fate of Hersilie, in her relationship to Wilhelm and Felix, with the normal 'happy ending' of comedy. Another variation on this set of stock characters provides the 'dramatis personae' for the novella 'Der Mann von funfzig Jahren'. Friedrich Sengle has also described this novella as a 'Lustspielnovelle' but, although it does end eventually in the expected two marriages, this only happens outside the framework of the novella itself, when its characters have emerged into the main narrative, and are included in the strange parody of a happy ending in Book 3, Chapter 14 amongst the several marriages with which the narrator/editor pretends to round off his story[148]. The characters of Hilarie and Flavio, too, suffer a sad transformation when they emerge from the fiction within a fiction of the novella into the cold light of novel 'reality'. From poetic personifications of young love they are flattened out into the banal figures of a flighty and fickle bride and a boring would-be poet, who is grudgingly described as 'likeable enough' (437).

In 'Die pilgernde Törin' a similar set of characters, a father and son in rivalry in a love relationship, is used to call into question the usual assumptions about the roles of male and female in society. In *Die Wahlverwandtschaften*, which was originally planned as a novella to be included in the *Wanderjahre,* there is another variation on this set of stock characters and the deepest register of all is sounded as the love-entanglements across barriers of age and convention seem destined to lead inexorably to tragedy.

---

[148] Sengle, Page 571.

Hersilie's own story offers a contrast to that of Lucidor as she moves in the opposite direction from him. At the beginning she sees herself and her family as characters from a comedy but she goes from cheerful dialogue to desperate monologue, from comedy to tragedy, until she writes to Wilhelm, 'My situation seems to me like a tragedy by Alfieri; since confidants are completely lacking, in the end everything has to be conducted in monologues' (319). Nothing about her situation is resolved at the end of the book; she simply disappears from view. Makarie, 'the confidante (...) of all troubled souls', seems unable to offer her any help and neither she nor Felix nor Wilhelm are present at Makarie's castle when the narrator makes his pretence of tying up the loose ends. Hersilie is left at the end of the novel caught up in a labyrinth of confusion and isolation with her future an open question.

The scene of action in 'Wer ist der Verräter?', the buildings and parkland of a wealthy estate, provides a miniature reduplication of the setting of the whole novel, with its various and diverse realms; and Lucidor's wanderings through this scenery reflect in miniature and parody Wilhelm's course through the novel[149]. Images from the novel have slipped over into and are reflected in the novella. The mysterious casket discovered by Felix becomes in the novella an ordinary jewellery casket, supposedly a gift from Antoni to his betrothed. The image of the mirror plays a more important role; emphasised is its dual aspect as a true reflector and as a distorter of reality - the ambivalence of which the maxim from Makarie's archive warned[150]. At first the emphasis is placed on the power of the mirror to reflect reality, to reproduce nature on its surface. The focal point of the gardens is a hall which contains a mirror, positioned in such a way as to reflect the finest view; the effect on those entering the hall is to surprise them with the identity of reality and reflection: 'no one stepped inside without looking back and forth with pleasure from the mirror to reality and from reality to the mirror' (94).

---

[149] The same setting, a wealthy country estate, is the backdrop both for the comic confusions of 'Wer ist der Verräter?' and for the tragic entanglements of *Die Wahlverwandtschaften*.

[150] H.A. Volume 8, page 486. The aphorism is quoted on page 180 of Chapter 3 to illustrate the ambiguity in the representation of Makarie.

The next mention of the mirror emphasises its potential for distortion. After searching in vain for his beloved Lucinde through the maze-like pathways of the park, Lucidor enters the hall and is dazzled by the reflection of the setting sun in the mirror. In the confusion of his mind he misinterprets the scene, apparently being played out before his eyes, as a love scene:

> The setting sun, reflected back out of the mirror, dazzled him to such an extent that he could not recognise the two figures who sat on the couch, but he could make out that the hand of a female was being kissed in a very ardent way by a male sitting next to her (99).

Once he has been united with Lucinde he sees himself in her arms reflected in the mirror: 'but now, as he opened his eyes again his rapturous gaze fell on the mirror. He saw her there in his arms, and himself clasped in her arms' (107). The reflected landscape forms a suitable backdrop for his happiness, and is itself transfigured by that happiness. The last mention of the mirror reiterates once again its ambiguity, its power both as a reflector and as a distorter, when Julie says of it, 'Now when we stand right here we are reflected above in the wide expanse of the glass surface, there we can be distinguished really clearly, but we cannot recognise ourselves' (110).

The novella has a very clear structure and moves forward logically to its conclusion. There is confusion aplenty, but only within the mind of Lucidor himself. Contrary to the usual comedy plot he does not have to struggle against opposing external forces in order to win his true love. Instead the opposing side, which comprises the rest of the 'cast', must struggle against his inner confusions in order to ensure a happy ending. From the beginning of the novella the reader follows Lucidor, through all the confused labyrinths of his monologues, each coming up against a dead-end as he is successively prevented from confiding in his father by his sudden departure, in the old house-guest by his sickness and in Lucinde by her household duties. The inner confusion, revealed by his monologues, is reflected in the spatial labyrinths of the corridors and park he traverses. He is led 'through the long, rambling corridors of the old castle' (104); he himself 'roved along every one of the pathways of the park' (99). All ends, however, in the clarity of dialogue with Julie as Lucidor's confusions are cleared up and the well-rounded ending complies with the expectations for this kind of narrative that 'the whole thing should come to a conclusion within itself'. The labyrinthine landscape, viewed from above, becomes in Julie's description once again the labyrinth of order which it was at the beginning, 'How clear the flat land lies at the foot of the mountains! (...) Now you see below on the left, how beautifully everything has unrolled itself!' (109).

A metaphor for the progress from chaos to order, which marks the development of this story, is the fairground. At the beginning it stands with 'all kinds of machinery piled up in confusion' (95); at the end 'all the machinery was brought to life and set in motion' (113), creating its own pattern of order. As mentioned above the novella comes to a 'proper' conclusion with the expected two marriages and nothing left unresolved. As the main characters are sorted out into suitable couples even the age difference is overcome and there is a 'fairytale' element in the ending as Anton is transformed 'and a handsome, imposing young man appeared out of the husk' (114). This 'fairytale' element on the one hand contradicts the young civil servant's description of the story as a realistic tale portraying 'the simple honest respectability of German circumstances' (85); and on the other hand suggests that real life, and the literature which attempts to reflect real life, is much less orderly and well-rounded, reaching no 'satisfactory' conclusion but going ever onwards 'without there being a resolution for every knot that has been tied'.

EPILOGUE

The aesthetic of the open work

ein Unendliches in Bewegung
an infinity in motion

The novel comes to its inconclusive conclusion with the poem 'Im ernsten Beinhaus', and with the enigmatic words 'ist fortzusetzen' [to be continued]. The poem, entitled in different editions 'Bei Betrachtung von Schillers Schädel' or 'Schillers Reliquien' and also referred to as the 'Gedicht auf Schillers Schädel', was written in 1826 when clearance-work in the 'Jakobsfriedhof' [cemetery] in Weimar meant that for a time Goethe took Schiller's skull for safe-keeping into his own house[1]. The poet imagines himself in the vault where the skulls, laid in orderly rows, and the dead bones in disarray, disconnected and bereft of all function, are about to be brought up into the light of day. The skull - 'die dürre Schale' [the dry shell] - at first seems to be as meaningless and devoid of purpose as the rest of the bones, but then it is transformed by the poet's imagination into a precious container - 'geheim Gefäß' [mysterious vessel]. The transformation comes about because the poet's skill as an interpreter enables him to read the difficult 'text' offered to him:

> Doch mir Adepten war die Schrift geschrieben,
> Die heil'gen Sinn nicht jedem offenbarte.
> [But the text was written for me, the initiate,
> The solemn significance not revealed to everyone]

This interpretative ability translates the dry and lifeless skull into a living metaphor - receptacle and dispenser of new meanings. The skull of the dead poet, erstwhile container of the mind which created literary works, becomes a solid

---

[1] Riemer and Eckermann gave the poem the title 'Bei Betrachtungen von Schillers Schädel' [On Looking at Schiller's Skull] in the 'Nachlaß'. The 'Jubliäums-Ausgabe' of 1902, taking up a reference by Goethe to the poem in connection with the 'Reliquien Schillers' in a letter to Zelter on 24th October 1827, gives it the title 'Schillers Reliquien' [Schiller's Relics]. Diary entries for 25th and 26th February 1826 record Goethe's work on the poem. Cf. H.A., Volume 1, page 571.

symbol for the text which demands interpretation: 'Geheim Gefäß! Orakelsprüche spendend' [mysterious vessel! pouring forth oracular sentences] - one more of the many reflections of the text within the text and one which this time implies a continuous process of interpretation stretching out beyond the text itself. And the message, which this enigmatic text communicates, is equally ambiguous: in art, as in life, the only constant is change, nothing remains fixed and immutable. As in Spinoza's formulation 'deus sive natura' - 'Gott-Natur' [God or nature] - apparent polar oppositions can dissolve and melt into each other:

> Wie sie das Feste läßt zu Geist verrinnen
> Wie sie das Geisterzeugte fest bewahre[2].
> [As she makes solid matter dissolve into spirit
> So she turns the creation of the spirit to solid matter]

The words 'ist fortzusetzen' have provoked discussion about what exactly was to be continued. They have been understood to refer to the collection of aphorisms that constitute Makarie's archive. They have been interpreted as having reference only to the poem 'Bei Betrachtung von Schillers Schädel'. This view is strengthened by the fact that in the 'Ausgabe letzter Hand' they stand in brackets at the end of the poem and in the same Roman print as the poem itself, while the rest of the text of the *Wanderjahre* is printed in Gothic script. It has been argued that the words refer not so much to a continuation of the poem itself as to a cycle of poems taking up the themes intimated in the four aphoristic closing lines[3]. The phrase has been taken as pointing to a sequel to the novels - the 'Meisterjahre' [The Master Years] - which would create a trilogy corresponding to the three stages in the training of a master craftsman and provide a satisfactory conclusion to the sequence. Certainly Goethe seems, at the time of the publication of the first version of the *Wanderjahre*, to have had such a sequel in mind. In a conversation with Kanzler von Müller on 8th June 1821 he spoke of a 'trilogy'

---

[2] H.A. Volume 1, pages 366-7.
[3] Cf. the exchange of articles by Karl Viëtor, Franz Mautner and Ernst Feise in *PMLA*, 49 (1944), pages 142-183 and 1156-1172.

and of the difficulties that the realisation of the third part - the 'Meisterjahre' - would entail[4].

The words 'ist fortzusetzen', however, seem to point not to the sort of resolved closure that a sequel would imply, but rather to the possibility of an 'unendliche Fortsetzung' [never-ending continuation] - that very infiniteness which Karl Kerenyi ascribes to the spiral movement. The formula 'ist fortzusetzen' was first used by Goethe at the end of the fragments of *Faust II* in volume 12 of the 1828 edition of his works. Two contemporary reactions to the words when they appeared there are suggestive of how they may be interpreted in the *Wanderjahre*. Zelter wrote to Goethe on 8th June 1828, '*To be continued – and I pray that it will be so! But: by whom?*'; while Reinhard declared, 'I appreciate that there should be a continuation of Faust; for there is always something to add to it; it cannot and should not be finished off'[5]. The question is not so much what is to be continued as who is to do the continuing and the implication, with such open works as *Faust II* and the *Wanderjahre,* must be that the responsibility for the continuation is handed over to the reader and interpreter - Goethe's comment on Jean Paul's work, is equally applicable to his own texts: 'such a text could be a temptation to a boundless interpretation'.

This reading is reinforced by the formulation of the phrase itself. Extolling the Greek language Goethe once said:

> The way of speaking through verbs, especially through infinitives and participles, makes every expression undefined; nothing is really determined, circumscribed and fixed, it is only an intimation, in order to evoke the object in the imagination[6].

In contrast to the more definite formulations 'Wird fortgesetzt' [will be continued], 'Fortsetzung folgt' [continuation will follow] and 'Die Fortsetzung nächstens' [the continuation next time] used at the end of articles in the *Propyläen* and in *Über Kunst und Altertum* the passive, gerundive form of the verbal phrase 'ist fortzusetzen' creates an indefiniteness, uncertainty and

---

[4] Gräf, 1.2, page 976.
[5] Cf. Viëtor, page 1170.
[6] W.A. 2. 3, page 202.

ambiguity similar to that which Goethe appreciated in the Greek language[7]. The phrase thus enables him to offer no more than the merest intimation that the most appropriate continuation of the text is the reader's creative interpretation[8].

Just as the spiral is suggestive of infinite movement, so too its cognate, the labyrinth, delineates an apposite image for the open work of art: an artificial construct which offers within an enclosed and limited space the illusion of unbounded and limitless motion - a metaphor of infinity encompassed by finiteness. Umberto Eco has examined the labyrinth as the metaphor for the voyage of discovery through the universe of semiosis or of human culture. He has set up a contrast between, on the one hand, the medieval 'dictionary' idea of knowledge whose representation is the Porphyrian tree, where definition branches out by genera and species and, on the other hand, the encyclopaedic knowledge envisaged by Diderot and d'Alembert in the Enlightenment for whose representation the image of the rhizome has been suggested. Eco converts both tree and rhizome into the metaphor of the labyrinth and traces a cultural journey from the classical unicursal labyrinth as traversed by Theseus in which 'one *cannot* get lost; the labyrinth itself is the Ariadne thread'; through the multicursal labyrinth of the Mannerist maze which is exemplified by the tree 'in which certain choices are privileged in respect to others (...) and only one among them leads to the way out'; to the encyclopaedic rhizomic labyrinth where there is no single way out because there is no single correct interpretation, no ultimate meaning. The rhizomic labyrinth posits a conception of human culture structured according to a network of multiple, variable and infinite interpretations[9].

---

[7] Cf. Karl Viëtor, '"Ist fortzusetzen": zu Goethes Gedicht auf Schillers Schädel' in: *PMLA*, 49 (1944), pages 1170-1171.
[8] Cf. Ehrhard Bahr in *Goethes Erzählwerk Interpretationen,* page 388. Bahr comments, 'In this sense the last sentence of the novel "To be continued" (525) can be applied to the maximum liberation of the reader from the text'; although it is not so much a 'liberation of the reader from the text' which is suggested by the phrase as an unlimited engagement with the text.
[9] Umberto Eco, *Semiotics and the Philosophy of Language*, Macmillan, London, 1984, Chapter 2, 'Dictionary vs. Encyclopedia', quotations pages 80 and 81.

An explicit identification of the literary work with the labyrinth is made in Jorge Luis Borges' short story, 'The Garden of the Forking Paths'. The protagonist's ancestor Ts'ui Pên, a Chinese philosopher, has withdrawn from the world supposedly to write a novel and construct a labyrinth. Book and maze turn out, however, to be identical. The novel is his labyrinth, functioning on many diverse time-levels, capable of multiple interpretations and created as a riddle to challenge the interpretative skills of the reader. The phrase used to describe it - 'this diaphanous mystery' - echoes the phrase favoured by Goethe to describe his own literary work - 'dieses offenbare Geheimnis' [this open secret] [10].

Eco's own novel, *The Name of the Rose*, is structured as a labyrinth encompassing a fictional and a metafictional quest. The fiction describes the search for an elusive and subversive text - the lost book of Aristotle's *Poetics*, a treatise on comedy; the arena of this search is a labyrinthine library - the mysterious and menacing 'Aedificium'. Both book and library are metaphors for the fictional work itself, whose metafictional search, like that of the *Wanderjahre*, is an investigation of its own conditions of being and its status as a cultural product. It is an illustration of the necessary and all-pervasive intertextuality of the literary text; an exploration of the way in which the interaction of the fictional text with the reader produces the configuration of its own distinct cosmos and an assertion of the provisional and inconclusive nature of all interpretation. Eco's postscript to the novel highlights these ideas: 'the labyrinth of my library is still a Mannerist labyrinth, but the world in which William realizes [by the end of the novel] he is living already has a rhizome structure: that is, it can be structured but is never structured definitively' [11].

---

[10] Jorge Luis Borges, *Labyrinths. Selected Stories and Other Writings*, edited by Donald A. Yates and James E. Irby, Penguin, 1970, page 50.
[11] Umberto Eco, *Postscript to 'The Name of the Rose'*, translated by W. Weaver, San Diego, 1984, page 58. Cf. also page 23, 'Writing a novel is a cosmological matter, like the story of Genesis (...) What I mean is, to tell a story, you must first construct a world'; and page 20, 'Books always speak of other books, and every story is a story that has already been told'.

In evolving a poetics of the open work Eco posits a kind of hierarchy of artistic 'openness'. He first examines a narrow category of works which he designates 'works in movement' which 'are characterized by the invitation to *make the work* together with the author'. Examples are drawn from musical works and from plastic artefacts. In the field of literary production Eco cites Mallarmé's experimental *Livre* in which the author 'set out to validate a specific poetic principle: "un livre ni commence ni ne finit; tout au plus fait-il semblant" [a book neither begins nor ends; at the most it is all pretence]. Even in these most open of works Eco makes clear that what the performer, addressee or interpreter is offered is the 'chance of an oriented insertion into something which always remains the world intended by the author'. On a wider level he suggests that there are works, like Brecht's plays or Joyce's novels, 'which, though organically completed, are open to a continuous generation of internal relations which the addressee must uncover and select in his act of perceiving the totality of the incoming stimuli'. Finally on the widest level of all he maintains that openness is the essential underlying condition of every work of art:

> *Every* work of art, even though it is produced by following an explicit or implicit poetics of necessity, is effectively open to a virtually unlimited range of possible readings, each of which causes the work to acquire new vitality in terms of one particular taste, of perspective, or personal performance.

Eco quotes Luigi Pareyson as evidence of the extent to which twentieth-century aesthetics has been concerned to point out the essential openness of every work of art and the resultant paradoxical definitive and provisional nature of every performance or interpretation of a work: 'the work of art (...) is a form, namely of movement, that has been concluded; or we can see it as an infinite contained within finiteness'[12]. Eco suggests that in response to the inescapable openness of the work of art per se the tendency today is for the artist to subsume this openness into a positive aspect of his artistic production.

---

[12] Umberto Eco, 'The Poetics of the Open Work' in: *The Role of the Reader*, Bloomington, 1979, pages 47-66, quotations from pages 62 and 63.

Goethe, too, was preoccupied by this essential quality of the work of art and responded in the composition of the *Wanderjahre* by incorporating this openness into the structure and organisation of the work. It is a text which makes the disclosure of this intrinsic openness part of its aesthetic programme and which exhibits an engagement with all three levels of openness described by Eco. The whole organisation of the work is predicated on and designed to illustrate the idea that openness is the essential condition of all works of art. The use of analogy and reflective devices indicates a conscious openness to the 'continuous generation of internal relations'. The involvement of Eckermann in the selection of aphorisms for the text; the comment to Zelter that 'every good soul' might order the parts of the text into a whole as well if not better than the author himself and the injunction 'ist fortzusetzen' are suggestive of an incipient 'work in movement'.

The organic image of the rhizome labyrinth with its insistence on continuous growth and change and multiple interconnection is in accord with Goethe's sense that organic change - decay and growth - is the essential characteristic of the natural world and therefore of life itself. This perception pervades both his literary and scientific works. In *Faust* the spirit of nature - the 'Erdgeist' [earth spirit] - describes its own work as unending movement and change:

> In Lebensfluten, im Tatensturm
> Wall' ich auf und ab,
> Webe hin und her! (lines 501-3);
> [In the tides of life, in the storm of deeds
> I surge up and down,
> I weave back and forth]

Werther's fevered brain converts this 'Geist des Ewigschaffenden' [spirit of the eternally creating] into 'ein ewig verschlingendes, ewig wiederkäuendes Ungeheuer' [a continually devouring, continually regurgitating monster][13]. The phrases 'So gestaltend, umgestaltend' [fashioning and refashioning] in the poem 'Parabase' and 'Und umzuschaffen das Geschaffene' [to recreate the created] in

---

[13] H.A. Volume 6, page 53.

266

'Eins und Alles' capture this kaleidoscopic movement which is the essential feature of nature:

> Es soll sich regen, schaffend handeln,
> Erst sich gestalten, dann verwandeln,
> Nur scheinbar steht's Momente still[14].
> [It should work hard, act creatively,
> First form itself, then transform,
> Only apparently does it stand still for a moment]

On the one hand, in his study of cloud-formations Goethe notes the confusion that can be caused by the proliferating terminology for these most transitory of natural phenomena: 'because the variety is so great, that no terminology can define such things and just confuses the imagination more, rather than helping it'[15]. On the other hand, in his essay 'Über den Granit' [On Granite] he demonstrates how, in the 'observation of the oldest, firmest, deepest, most unshakeable son of nature', the changes wrought by time even on this oldest form of rock lead him to a contemplation of the processes of evolution and natural change[16]. In the *Wanderjahre* we have seen the central significance of mutability encapsulated in Joseph's words, 'Life belongs to the living and whoever lives must be ready for change' (27).

This sense of nature's limitless capacity for change is translated by Goethe into an aesthetic concept which stresses movement, change, infinitude as the essential element of art. In his essay on Winckelmann he stresses Winckelmann's good fortune in being in Rome at the time when the excavations in Herculaneum and Pompeii were bringing forth the most priceless artefacts to enrich museums and private collections alike. Museums and art galleries to which nothing new is added, he claims, are merely vaults to house the dead and the ghosts of the past. They are characterised by closure and limitation: 'in such a limited circle of art-works, one gets used to regarding such collections as a completed whole'. He insists, on the contrary, that such art collections must be living, growing,

---

[14] H.A. Volume 1, page 358 and 368.
[15] 'Wolkengestalt nach Howard'. W.A.II.12, page 37.
[16] H.A. Volume 13, page 255.

changing entities: 'one should be reminded by a continuous flow of new acquisitions, that in art, as in life, it is not a matter of the preservation of a finished product, but that an infinity is in motion [ein Unendliches in Bewegung sei]'. Art denies all closure and embraces instead unlimited movement. It is this concept of art which motivates the recurrent metaphor of the picture gallery in the *Wanderjahre*: the galleries represent an attempt to recreate, through their endless reflections upon each other, something of the infinite mobile continuum of art and to invest the single, finite work of art, which is attempting to encompass the infinity of both art and life, with a sense of this 'infinity in motion'[17].

The metaphor of the picture gallery, therefore, offers an important pointer to the structure of the work. Just as each picture in a gallery is an analogue of all the others and each reflects on and contributes to the interpretation of the others, so in the novel the various parts are arranged in a relationship of analogy to each other, so that the interpretation of each of the parts is influenced by its relationship to the others. Like the metaphor of the labyrinth this arrangement highlights the possibility of multiple, variable interpretations within a framework which has been organised by the author. Many of the aphorisms in the 'Maximen und Reflexionen' are concerned with the use of analogy, including a series (23-36) which emphasises the lack of finiteness and closure of the analogy: 'the analogy has the advantage that it does not conclude anything and really does not want any finality'; and its capacity to generate openness and allow for a plurality of meanings:

> The analogous case does not want to impose itself nor to prove anything, it sets itself off against another without combining with it. Several analogous cases do not join together into closed ranks, they are like good company, which always inspires rather than gives[18].

Some of these aphorisms are repeated in the 'Betrachtungen im Sinne der Wanderer' and the last aphorism in Makarie's archive returns to the subject: 'whoever lives for a long period in serious society admittedly does not encounter

---

[17] H.A. Volume 12, page 116.
[18] H.A. Volume 12, page 368.

everything than can happen to mankind; but he certainly comes across the analogue and perhaps some things that are unprecedented' (486) - its prominent position suggesting that it is to be understood as a comment on the structure of the text.

The reader and interpreter are being offered a 'field of possibilities' on which to exercise their own creative and critical faculties. This sense of the work as a 'field of possibilities' is underscored in the first version of the novel by the comparison made by Hersilie of Wilhelm's movements through the world of the text with the many possible variations of movement open to the pieces on a chessboard:

> But could you not play your eternal Rouge et noir [red and black] with great skill and artifice in our neighbourhood? One knows how to jump across the whole chessboard with the knight, without landing on the same square again. You should become a master of this trick, then your friends might not have to do without you for so long (1821.85).

Here are stressed both the multiple, variable possibilities of interpretation and the skill demanded of the interpreter.

Hermann Broch has laid emphasis on the role of the 'Totalitätskunstwerk' [art work of totality] as a 'mirror of the age', indicating how such works, among which he counts Joyce's *Ulysses* and Goethe's *Wanderjahre*, are the products of critical, transitional phases of human history, constructed 'from the myriads and more than myriads of anonymous but concrete individual powers which keep the whole thing going', and reflecting within themselves as much as possible of the 'incomprehensible, infinite, infinitely facetted "everyday life of the age"'[19]. The kaleidoscopic world of the *Wanderjahre* highlights many of the central issues of the early nineteenth century: the problems and opportunities of early industrialisation, technological and scientific progress; over-population, emigration and land-reform; educational reform and the pursuit of a system of values which can keep pace with this developing complexity; the growth of both religious tolerance and of anti-Semitism; the relationship between the sciences

---

[19] Hermann Broch, Volume 9.1, page 64.

and the arts and between the different branches of the arts; the increasing complexity of human relationships and changing gender roles. The aim of the work is precisely this delineation of issues: to highlight the areas where the problems might lie and to give reader and interpreter pause for thought. It is a work which recognises the importance of the descriptive and the limitations of the prescriptive. The phrase 'bleibt im Schweben' [hangs in the balance] (447) insists on the fundamental uncertainty and indefiniteness, not only of every act of interpretation, but also of the essential human condition.

Montan articulates the central aim of the work's multi-perspective structure - to highlight problems rather than provide solutions - when he counters Wilhelm's expectation of finding truth in the midst of the conflicting viewpoints with the assertion, 'In the middle the problem remains, perhaps impenetrable, but perhaps also accessible, if one embarks on the attempt'. Montan also provides a programme for the process of interpretation corresponding to the 'zarte Empirie' [subtle practice], which is the novel's combination of fiction and metafiction. When Wilhelm asks, 'But what is it all about?', his reply - 'Denken und Tun' [thinking and action] - suggests that the process of interpreting, too, involves a combination of theory and practice. Montan's affirmation of the problematical recurs in intensified form in the last aphorism in the 'Betrachtungen im Sinne der Wanderer' where the emphasis is laid equally on the impossibility of definitiveness - the incalculability of life - and on the necessity for continued interpretative efforts: 'Das Problem liegt dazwischen, das Unschaubare, das ewig tätige Leben, in Ruhe gedacht' [the problem lies in between, the indiscernible, the ever active life, contemplated in tranquillity] (309). This perception echoes and then re-echoes the description which Goethe, as he contemplated the possibility of a 'Meisterjahre', gave of the infinite and boundless nature of the interpretative task, both that of the reader and that of the writer: 'Jede Lösung eines Problems ist ein neues Problem' [every solution to a problem raises a new problem][20].

---

[20] Conversation with Kanzler von Müller on 8th June 1821. Gräf, 1.2, page 976.

BIBLIOGRAPHY

Editions of Goethe's work:

Goethe, J.W., *Werke*, herausgegeben im Auftrage der Großherzogin Sophie von Sachsen-Weimar. Abteilung I-IV, 1887-1919 (Weimarer Ausgabe = W.A.).

Goethe, J.W., *Werke*, edited by Erich Trunz, 14 volumes, Hamburg, 1949-67 & revised edition Munich, 1981 (Hamburger Ausgabe = H.A.).

Goethe, J.W., *Werke*, herausgegeben von den nationalen Forschungs- und Gedenkstatten der klassischen deutschen Literatur in Weimar, 12 volumes, Berlin und Weimar, 1981.

Goethe, J.W., *Wilhelm Meisters Wanderjahre oder Die Entsagenden*, edited by Ehrhard Bahr, Stuttgart, 1982.

Goethe, J.W., *Wilhelm Meisters Wanderjahre oder Die Entsagenden*, Urfassung von 1821, Bonn, 1986.

Goethes Italienische Reise, edited by Christoph Michel, Frankfurt am Main, 1976.

Goethes Historische Schriften, edited by Horst Günther, Frankfurt am Main, 1982.

Goethes Märchen, edited by Katharina Mommsen, Frankfurt am Main, 1984.

Wilhelm Meister's Journeyman Years or The Renunciants, edited by Jane K. Brown, translated by Krishna Winston, in *Goethe's Collected Works*, Volume 10, New York, 1989.

Wilhelm Meister's Travels, or, The Renunciants, A Novel, translated by Thomas Carlyle, in German Romance: Specimens of Its Chief Authors, with Biographical and Critical Notices, Volume 4, 1827. Reprinted as Goethe's *Wilhelm Meister's Travels: Translation of the First Edition by Thomas Carlyle*, introduction by James Hardin, Columbia, 1991.

Wilhelm Meister's Years of Travel or The Renunciants, by J.W. von Goethe, translated by H.M. Waidson, (Volumes 4-6), London & New York, 1980.

Collections of Conversations and Letters:

Biedermann, F. von, *Goethe: Gespräche. Eine Sammlung zeitgenössischer Berichte aus seinem Umgang*, edited by W.Herwig, Zürich, Stuttgart, München, 1965-84.

Eckermanns Gespräche mit Goethe, edited by Fritz Bergemann, Frankfurt am Main, 1981.

Gräf, Hans Gerhard, *Goethe über seine Dichtungen*, 3 volumes, Frankfurt am Main, 1902, (rep. Darmstadt), 1968.

Riemer, F.W., *Mitteilungen über Goethe*, edited by A. Pollmer, Leipzig, 1921.

Der Briefwechsel zwischen Schiller und Goethe, edited by Emil Staiger, Frankfurt am Main, 1977.

272

Other Primary Texts:

Aristotle, *Works,* translated and edited under W.D.Ross, Oxford, 1924.
Boethius, *Consolations of Philosophy,* translated by Richard Green, Indianapolis, 1962.
Borges, Jorge Luis, *Labyrinths. Selected Stories and Other Writings,* edited by Donald A.Yates and James E.Irby, Penguin, 1970.
Broch, Hermann, *Kommentierte Werkausgabe,* edited by P.M.Lützeler, Frankfurt am Main, 1975.
Cicero, *Works,* Loeb Classical Library in 28 volumes, London and Cambridge (Mass.), 1942.
Eco, Umberto, *The Name of the Rose,* translated by William Weaver, London, 1998.
Gide, André, *Les Faux Monnayeurs,* Paris, 1925.
Hebbel, Friedrich, *Tagebücher - historisch-kritische Ausgabe,* edited by R.M.Werner, Berlin, 1922.
Hegel, G.W.F., *Ästhetik,* Stuttgart, 1971.
Herder, *Sämtliche Werke,* edited by Theodor Matthias, Leipzig and Wien, 1879.
Homer, *The Iliad,* translated by Martin Hammond, Penguin Classics, 1987.
Homer, *The Odyssey,* translated by E.V.Rieu, Penguin Classics, 1985 (44).
Horace, *Ars Poetica,* Stuttgart, 1984.
Humboldt, Wilhelm von, *Werke,* 5 volumes, Darmstadt, 1960.
Jean Paul (Johann Friedrich Richter), *Werke,* 6 volumes, edited by Norbert Miller, Darmstadt, 1970.
Jean Paul, *Vorschule der Ästhetik,* edited by Wolfgang Henckmann, Hamburg, 1990.
Jean Pauls Persönlichkeit in Berichten der Zeitgenossen, Sämtliche Werke Ergänzungsband, edited by E Berend, Berlin, 1956.
Lessing, Gotthold Ephraim, *Emilia Galotti,* Stuttgart, 1987.
Lessing, Gotthold Ephraim, *Laokoon oder über die Grenzen der Malerei und Poesie,* Stuttgart, 1964.
Longus, *The Pastoral Loves of Daphnis and Chloe,* done into English by George Moore, London 1924.
Longus, *Daphnis und Chloë,* translated into German by Arno Mauersberger, Frankfurt am Main, 1976.
Lucretius, *De rerum natura,* Oxford, 1962.
Mann, Thomas, *Gesammelte Werke,* Frankfurt am Main, 1990.
Ovid, *Metamorphoses,* translated by Mary M.Innes, Penguin Classics, 1971 (7).
Plato, *Works* (Loeb Classical Library) ed. G.P.Goold, Cambridge (Mass.) and London, 1982.
Schlegel, Friedrich, *Lucinde,* Stuttgart, 1965.
Schlegel, Friedrich, *Kritische Ausgabe,* Darmstadt, 1979.

Schlegel, Friedrich, *Kritische und Theoretische Schriften*, Stuttgart, 1978.

Sterne, Laurence, *The Life and Opinions of Tristram Shandy*, edited by Melvin New & Joan New, Penguin Classics, London, 1997.

Sterne, Laurence, *A Sentimental Journey and Other Writings*, edited by Tom Keymer, Everyman, London, 1994.

Sterne, Laurence, *Letters*, edited by L.P. Curtis, Oxford, 1935.

Virgil, *Aeneid*, Oxford, 1971.

Wilde, Oscar, *Complete Works*, London and Glasgow, 1970.

Secondary Literature on Goethe's work:

Abbott, Scott, 'Des Maurers Wandeln/ Es gleicht dem Leben'. The Freemasonic Ritual Route in *Wilhelm Meisters Wanderjahre*', in: *DVjs* June 58, 2 (1984), pages 262-288.

Adler, Jeremy, '"Die Sonne stand noch hoch..." Zu Landschaft und Bildung in *Wilhelm Meisters Wanderjahre*', in: Heinz Ludwig Arnold (editor), *Johann Wolfgang von Goethe*, München, 1982, pages 222-239.

Amrine, Friedrich, 'Romance Narration in *Wilhelm Meisters Wanderjahre*', in: *GQ* (1982), pages 29-38.

Bahr, Ehrhard, *Die Ironie im Spätwerk Goethes*, Berlin, 1972.

Bahr, Ehrhard, 'Revolutionary Realism in Goethe's *Wanderjahre*', in: William J.Lillyman (editor), *Goethe's Narrative Fiction: The Irvine Goethe Symposium*, Berlin and New York, 1983.

Bahr, Ehrhard, '*Wilhelm Meisters Wanderjahre oder die Entsagenden (1821-1829)*; From Bildungsroman to Archival Novel', in: James Harden (editor), *Reflection and Action: Essays on the Bildungsroman*, Columbia, 1991.

Bahr, Ehrhard, *The novel as archive: the genesis, reception, and criticism of Goethe's 'Wilhelm Meisters Wanderjahre'*, Columbia, 1998.

Baldwin, Birgit, '*Wilhelm Meisters Wanderjahre* as an Allegory of Reading', in: *Gyb* 5 (1990), pages 213-232.

Bauer, Georg-Karl, 'Makarie', in: *GRM* 25 (1937), pages 178-197.

Berghahn, Klaus L. and Pinkerneil, Beate, *Am Beispiel 'Wilhelm Meister'. Einführung in die Wissenschaftsgeschichte der Germanistik*, 2 volumes, Königstein, 1980.

Birus, Hendrik, *Vergleichung. Goethes Einführung in die Schreibweise Jean Pauls*, Stuttgart, 1986.

Blackall, Eric, *Goethe and the Novel*, Ithaca and London, 1976.

Blessin, Stefan, *Die Romane Goethes*, Königstein, 1979.

Blessin, Stefan, *Goethes Romane. Aufbruch in die Moderne*, Paderborn, München, Wien, Zürich, 1996.

Braun, Julius W., *Goethe im Urtheile seiner Zeitgenossen*, Hildesheim, 1969 (Reprographischer Nachdruck der Ausgabe Berlin 1883).

274

Brown, Jane K., *Goethe's Cyclical Narratives: 'Unterhaltungen deutscher Ausgewanderten' and 'Wilhelm Meisters Wanderjahre'*, Chapel Hill (N. Carolina), 1975.

Boucke, Ewald, *Goethes Weltanschauung auf historischer Grundlage*, Stuttgart, 1907.

Cohn, Jonas, 'Der Erziehungsplan in Goethes *Wanderjahren*', in: *Die pädagogische Hochschule* 4 (1932), pages 1-25.

Degering, Thomas, Das Elend der Entsagung. 'Wilhelm Meisters Wanderjahre', Bonn, 1982.

David, Claude, 'Goethes *Wanderjahre* als symbolische Dichtung', in: *SuF* 8 (1956), pages 113-128. Rep. in: C.D., *Ordnung des Kunstwerks*, Göttingen, 1983, pages 29-44.

Derré, Françoise, 'Die Beziehung zwischen Felix, Hersilie und Wilhelm in *Wilhelm Meisters Wanderjahren*', in: *GJb* 94 (1977), pages 38-48.

Dowden, Steve, 'Irony and Ethical Autonomy in *Wilhelm Meisters Wanderjahre*', in: *DVjs* 68 (1994), pages 134-54.

Dürr, Volker, 'Geheimnis und Aufklärung: Zur pädagogischen Funktion des Kästchens in *Wilhelm Meisters Wanderjahren*', in: *Monatshefte*, 74.1 (1982), pages 11-19.

Emrich, Wilhelm, 'Das Problem der Symbolinterpretation im Hinblick auf Goethes *Wanderjahre*', in: *DVjs.* 26 (1952), pages 331-352.

Emrich, Wilhelm, *Die Symbolik von 'Faust II'*, Bonn, 1957 (2).

Esau, Helmut, 'Die Landschaft in Goethes *Wilhelm Meisters Wanderjahren*. Zur Deutung eines Strukturprinzips in der Landschaftsgestaltung, in: *CollG* 7 (1973), pages 234-251.

Fambach, Oscar, *Goethe und seine Kritiker*, Düsseldorf, 1953.

Fink, Gonthier-Louis, 'Tagebuch, Redaktor, Autor. Erzählinstanz und Struktur in Goethes *Wilhelm Meisters Wanderjahre*', in: *RechG.* 16 (1986) pages 7-54.

Fischer-Hartmann, Deli, *Goethes Altersroman. Studien über die innere Einheit von 'Wilhelm Meisters Wanderjahren'*, Halle, 1941.

Flitner, Wilhelm, 'Goethes Erziehungsgedanken in *Wilhelm Meisters Wanderjahren*, in: *Goethe* 22 (1960).

Fuchs, Albert, 'Makarie', in: *Goethe-Studien*, Berlin, 1968, pages 97-117.

Gidion, Heidi, *Zur Darstellungsweise von 'Wilhelm Meisters Wanderjahre'*, Göttingen 1969.

Gilg, André, *'Wilhelm Meisters Wanderjahre' und ihre Symbole*, Zürich, 1954.

Gille, Klaus, *'Wilhelm Meister' im Urteil der Zeitgenossen. Ein Beitrag zur Wirkungsgeschichte Goethes*, Assen, 1971.

Gregorovius, Ferdinand, *Goethes 'Wlhelm Meister' in seinen sozialistischen Elementen entwickelt*, Königsberg, 1849, Schwäbisch-Hall, 1855 (2).

Grimminger, Rolf, 'Löcher in der Ordnung der Dinge: *Wilhelm Meisters Lehr- und Wanderjahre*', in: R.G., *Die Ordnung, das Chaos und die Kunst*, Frankfurt am Main, 1986, pages 203-244.

Heitner, Robert, 'Goethe's Ailing Women', in: *MLN* 95 (1980), pages 497-515.

Henkel, Arthur, *Entsagung. Eine Studie zu Goethes Altersroman*, Tübingen, 1954.

Henkel, Arthur, '*Wilhelm Meisters Wanderjahre*: Kritik und Prognose der modernen Gesellschaft', in: *GJb* 97 (1980), pages 82-89.

Irmscher, Hans Dietrich, 'Wilhelm Meister auf der Sternwarte', in: *GJb* 110 (1993), pages 275-96.

Jeßing, Benedikt, *Konstruktion und Eingedenken. Zur Vermittlung von gesellschaftlicher Praxis und literarischer Form in Goethes 'Wilhelm Meisters Wanderjahre' und Uwe Johnsons 'Mutmassungen über Jakob'*, Wiesbaden, 1991.

Jung, Alexander, *Göthe's 'Wanderjahre' und die wichtigsten Fragen des 19 Jahrhunderts*, Mainz, 1854.

Karnick, Manfred, '*Wilhelm Meisters Wanderjahre' oder die Kunst des Mittelbaren*, München 1968.

Keller, Werner, *Goethes dichterische Bildlichkeit*, München, 1972.

Klingenberg, Anneliese, *Goethes Roman 'Wilhelm Meisters Wanderjahre oder die Entsagenden'. Quellen und Komposition*, Berlin & Weimar, 1972.

Koch, Franz, 'Goethes Stellung zu Tod und Unsterblichkeit', in: *JbGG* 45, pages 295-320.

Korff, Hermann, *Geist der Goethezeit*, Leipzig, 1953.

Kraft, Werner, *Goethe. Wiederholte Spiegelungen aus fünf Jahrzehnten*, München, 1986.

Lämmert, Eberhard, 'Goethe als Novelist', in: William J. Lillyman (editor), *Goethe's Narrative Fiction. The Irvine Goethe Symposium*, Berlin and New York, 1983, pages 21- 37.

Langen, August, 'Die Wechselbeziehungen zwischen Wort- und Bildkunst in der Goethezeit', *WW* 3.2. (1952/3), pages 73-86.

Langner, Beatrix, *Schöne Praxis. Struktur und Form von Goethes Roman 'Wilhelm Meisters Wanderjahren'*, (dissertation for the Humboldt University, Berlin), 1983.

Larrett, William, '"Weder Kern noch Schale": The "Novel" Epistemology of Goethe's *Wilhelm Meisters Wanderjahre*', in: *PEGS*, N.S. 56 (1987), pages 38-55.

Lehnert-Rodiek, Gertrud, 'Das "nußbraune Mädchen" in *Wilhelm Meisters Wanderjahre oder die Entsagenden*', in: *GJb* 102 (1985), pages 171-183.

Lewes, George Henry, *Life of Goethe*, 2nd Ed., London 1864.

Loeb, Ernst, 'Makarie und Faust', in: *ZfdPh* 88 (1969), pages 583-597.

Lützeler, P.M., (editor), *Romane und Erzählungen zwischen Romantik und Realismus. Neue Interpretationen*, Stuttgart, 1983.

Lützeler P.M. and McLeod James E. (editors) *Goethes Erzählwerk. Interpretationen*, Stuttgart, 1985.

Maierhofer, Waltraud, '*Wilhelm Meisters Wanderjahre' und der Roman des Nebeneinander*, Bielefeld, 1990.

276

Mandelkow, Karl Robert, *Goethe im Urteil seiner Kritiker. Dokuments zur Wirkungsgeschichte Goethes in Deutschland. 1773-1982*, 4 volumes, München 1975-1984.

Martin, Laura, 'Who's the Fool Now? A Study of Goethe's Novella "Die pilgernde Törin" from His Novel *Wilhelm Meisters Wanderjahre*', in: *GQ* 1993, pages 431-450.

Mautner, Franz H., Feise, Ernst, Viëtor, Karl, '"Ist fortzusetzen": zu Goethes Gedicht auf Schillers Schädel', in: *PMLA* 59 (1944), pages 1156-72.

Monroy, Ernst Friedrich, 'Zur Form der Novelle in *Wilhelm Meisters Wanderjahre*, in: *GRM* 31 (1943), pages 1-19.

Müller, Klaus-Detlev, 'Zum Romanbegriff in Goethes *Wilhelm Meisters Wanderjahre*', in: *DVjs* 53 (1970), pages 275-299.

Müller, P. *Der junge Goethe im zeitgenössischen Urteil*, Berlin, 1969.

Mundt, Theodor, 'Rezenzion von Goethes *Wanderjahre*' in: *Kritische Wälder, Blätter zur Beurteilung der Literatur, Kunst und Wissenschaft unserer Zeit*, Leipzig, 1830.

Muschg, Adolf, *Goethe als Emigrant*, Frankfurt am Main, 1986.

Neuhaus, Volker, 'Die Archivfiktion in *Wilhelm Meisters Wanderjahren*', in: *Euphorion* 62 (1968), pages 13-27.

Neumann, Gerhard, 'Der Wanderer und der Verschollene: Zum Problem der Identität in Goethes *Wilhelm Meister* und in Kafkas *Amerika*-Roman', in: J.P.Stern and J.J.White (Eds.) *Paths and Labyrinths* (Nine Papers read at the Franz Kafka Symposium held at the Institute of Germanic Studies on 20 and 21 October 1983), London, 1985, pages 43-65.

Oellers, Norbert, 'Goethes Novelle "Die pilgernde Thörin" und ihre französische Quelle', in: *GJb* 102 (1985), pages 88-104.

Ohly, Friedrich, 'Goethes Ehrfurchten - ein ordo caritatis', in: *Euphorion* 55 (1961), pages 113-145, 405-448.

Ohly, Friedrich, 'Zum Kästchen in Goethes *Wanderjahren*', in: *ZfdA* 91, (1961-2), pages 255-262.

Osterkamp, Ernst, *Im Buchstabenbilde. Studien zu Verfahren Goethescher Bildebeschreibung*, Stuttgart, 1991.

Peschken, Bernd, 'Das "Blatt" in den *Wanderjahren*', in: *Goethe* 27 (1965), pages 205-30.

Peschken, Bernd, *Entsagung in 'Wilhelm Meisters Wanderjahre'*, Bonn, 1968.

Reiss, Hans, *Goethes Romane,* Bern & München, 1963.

Reiss, Hans, '*Wilhelm Meisters Wanderjahre*. Der Weg von der ersten zur zweiten Fassung', in: *DVjs* 39 (1965), pages 34-57.

Riemann, Robert, *Goethes Romantechnik,* Leipzig, 1902.

Ritzenhoff, Ursula, (editor), *Erläuterungen und Dokumente. Johann Wolfgang Goethe. Die Wahlverwandtschaften*, Stuttgart, 1982.

Robertson, J.G., *The Life and Work of Goethe*, London 1932.

Röder, Gerda, *Glück und glückliches Ende im deutschen Bildungsroman. Eine Studie zu Goethes 'Wilhelm Meister'*, München, 1968.

Rothmann, Kurt, (editor), *Erläuterungen und Dokuments. Johann Wolfgang Goethe, Die Leiden des jungen Werther*, Stuttgart, 1987.

Sarter, Eberhard, *Zur Technik von 'Wilhelm Meisters Wanderjahre'*, Berlin, 1914.

Sax, Benjamin C., *Images of Identity. Goethe and the Problem of Self-conception in the Nineteenth Century*, New York, 1987.

Schiff, Julius, 'Mignon, Ottilie, Makarie im Lichte der Goetheschen Naturphilosophie', in:*JbGG* 9 (1922), pages 133-147.

Schings, Hans-Jürgen, 'Wilhelm Meisters schöne Amazone', in: *JbDSG* 29 (1985), pages 141-206.

Schlaffer, Hannelore, *'Wilhelm Meister': Das Ende der Kunst und die Wiederkehr des Mythos*, Stuttgart, 1980.

Schlaffer, Hannelore, 'Gedichtete Theorie - Die "Noten und Abhandlungen" zum "West-östlichen Divan"', in: *GJb.* 101 (1984), pages 218-233.

Schlaffer, Heinz, 'Exoterik und Esoterik in Goethes Romanen', in: *GJb.* 95 (1978), pages 212-226.

Schlechta, Karl, *Goethes 'Wilhelm Meister'*, Frankfurt am Main, 1953.

Schmidt, Julian, *'Wilhelm Meister* in Verhältnis zu unserer Zeit', in: *Die Grenzboten*, 14Jg, 1 Semester, 11 Band, Leipzig, 1830.

Schrimpf, Hans Joachim, *Das Weltbild des späten Goethe. Überlieferung und Bewahrung in Goethes Alterswerk*, Stuttgart, 1956.

Seidlin, Oskar, '"Melusine" in der Spiegelung der *Wanderjahre*', in: Fs.V.Lange, pages 146-162. Rep. as: 'Coda. Ironische Kontrafaktur: Goethes "Neue Melusine"', in: *Vom erwachenden Bewußtsein und vom Sündenfall*, Stuttgart, 1979.

Sorensen, Bengt, 'Über die Familie in Goethes *Werther* und *Wilhelm Meister*, in: *OL* 42 (1987), pages 118-140.

Spranger, Eduard, 'Die sittliche Astrologie der Makarie in *Wilhelm Meisters Wanderjahren*', in: *Die Erziehung* 14 (1939), pages 409-17.

Staiger, Emil, *Goethe*, Zürich, 1959.

Steer, Alfred G., *Goethe's Science in the Structure of the 'Wanderjahre'*, Athens (Georgia), 1979.

Strelka, Joseph, 'Goethes *Wilhelm Meister* und der Roman des 20.Jahrhunderts', in: *GQ* 41 (1968), pages 338-355. Rep. in: J.S., *Auf der Suche nach dem verlorenen Selbst*, München, 1977, pages 9-27, 151.

Strelka, Joseph, *Esoterik bei Goethe*, Tübingen, 1980.

Strich, Fritz, *Goethe und die Weltliteratur*, Bern, 1957 (2).

Trunz, Erich, (editor), *Studien zu Goethes Alterswerken*, Frankfurt am Main, 1971.

Vaget, Hans Rudolph, *Dilettantismus und Meisterschaft. Zum Problem der Dilettantismus bei Goethe*, München, 1971.

Vaget, Hans Rudolph, 'Goethe the Novelist. On the Coherence of His Fiction', in: William J. Lillyman (.editor), *Goethe's Narrative Fiction. The Irvine Goethe Symposium*, Berlin and New York, 1983, pages 1-20.

278

Viëtor, Karl, 'Goethes Gedicht auf Schillers Schädel, in: *PMLA* 49 (1944), pages 142-183 and 1156-1172.

Voßkamp, Wilhelm, 'Utopie und Utopiekritik in Goethes Romanen *Wilhelm Meisters Lehrjahre* und *Wilhelm Meisters Wanderjahre*, in: *Utopieforschung*, (editor) Wilhelm Voßkamp, Volume 3, Stuttgart 1982. (Tb.-Ausg. Frankfurt am Main, 1985), pages 227-249.

Weber, Monica, *Goethe's Conception of the Reader and its Implications for 'Wilhelm Meisters Wanderjahre*, (dissertation for University of Waterloo, Canada), 1986.

Wiese, Benno von, 'Johann Wolfgang Goethe, "Der Mann von funfzig Jahren"', in: B.v.W., *Die deutsche Novelle von Goethe bis Kafka*, Volume 2, Düsseldorf, 1962, pages 26-52.

Wundt, Max, *Goethes Wilhelm Meister und die Entwicklung des modernen Lebensideals*, Berlin, 1913, 1932 (2).

Other Secondary Literature:

Beaujean, Marion, *Der Leser als Teil des literarischen Lebens*, Bonn, 1971.

Berend, Eduard, 'Jean Pauls handschriftlicher Nachlaß. Seine Eigenart und seine Geschichte', in: *JbJPG* 3 (1968), pages 13-22.

Boehm, Gottfried (editor), *Was ist ein Bild*, München, 1994.

Boehm, Gottfried and Pfotenhauer, Helmut (editors) *Beschreibungskunst - Kunstbeschreibung: Ekphrasis von der Antike bis zur Gegenwart*, München, 1995.

Buch, Hans Christoph, *Ut Pictura Poesis. Die Beschreibungsliteratur und ihre Kritiker von Lessing bis Lukács*, München, 1972.

Eco, Umberto, *Postscript to 'The Name of the Rose'*, translated by W. Weaver, San Diego, 1984.

Fried, Michael, *Absorption and Theatricality: Painting and Beholder in the Age of Diderot*, Berkeley, 1980.

Gervinus, Georg Gottfried, *Neuere Geschichte der poetischen National-Literatur der Deutschen*, Leipzig, 1842.

Hettner, Hermann, *Geschichte der deutschen Literatur im achtzehnten Jahrhundert*, Berlin, 1961, (Braunschweig 1872).

Hettner, Hermann, *Literaturgeschichte der Goethezeit*, München, 1970, (dritte Auflage, Braunschweig, 1879).

Hunter, R.L., *A Study of Daphnis and Chloe*, Cambridge, 1983.

Irish University Review, a journal of Irish Studies: John Banville Special, Volume 11, No.1, 1981.

Kindlers Literatur Lexikon, 7 volumes, edited by G.Woerner, Zürich, 1965-72.

Michelson, Peter, *Laurence Sterne und der deutsche Roman des 18 Jahrhunderts*, Göttingen, 1972.

Müller-Vollmer, Kurt, *Poesie und Einbildungskraft. Zur Dichtungstheorie Wilhelm von Humboldts*, Stuttgart, 1967.

New, Melvin, (Ed.), *The life and opinions of Traistram Shandy, gentleman,* New Casebooks Series, London 1992.

Profitlich, Ulrich, *Der Seelige Leser. Untersuchungen zur Dichtungstheorie Jean Pauls*, Bonn, 1968.

Rasch, Wolfdietrich, *Die Erzählweise Jean Pauls*, München, 1961.

Schadewaldt, Wolfgang, 'Der Schild des Achilleus' rep. in: *Homer, Die Dichtung und ihre Deutung*, Joachim Latacz (editor), Darmstadt, 1991, pages 173-199.

Scherer, Wilhelm, *Geschichte der deutschen Literatur*, Berlin, 1883.

Schmidt, Julian, *Geschichte der deutschen Literatur im neunzehnten Jahrhundert*, Leipzig, 1856.

Selbmann, Rolf, *Der deutsche Bildungsroman*, Stuttgart; Weimar, 1994.

Sengle, Friedrich, *Biedermeierzeit. Deutsche Literatur im Spannungsfeld zwischen Restauration und Revolution 1815-1848*, 2 volumes, Stuttgart, 1972.

Soud, Stephen, '"Weavers, Gardeners and Gladiators": Labyrinths in *Tristram Shandy*' in: *Eighteenth Century Studies* 28/4, pages 397-411.

Swales, Martin, *The German Bildungsroman from Wieland to Hesse*, Princeton, 1978.

Thalmann, Marianne, *Romantik und Manierismus*, Stuttgart, 1963.

Theoretical Works:

Alter, Robert, *Partial Magic: The Novel as a Self-Conscious Genre*, London & Berkeley, 1975.

Barthes, Roland, *Le plaisir du texte*, Paris, 1973.

Barthes, Roland, *S/Z*, Paris, 1970.

Barthes, Roland, *Image-Music-Text*, essays selected and translated by Stephen Heath, London, 1977.

Beer, Gillian, *The Romance*, London, 1970.

Blankenburg, Friedrich von, *Versuch über den Roman*, Faksimiledruck der Originalausgabe von 1774. Mit einem Nachwort von Eberhard Lämmert, Stuttgart, 1965.

Dällenbach, Lucien, *Le Récit spéculaire. Essai sur la mise en abyme*, Paris, 1977.

Dieterle, Bernhard, *Erzählte Bilder. Zum narrativen Umgang mit Gemälden*, Marburg, 1988.

Doob, Penelope Reed, *The Idea of the Labyrinth from Classical Antiquity through the Middle Ages*, Ithaca and London, 1990.

Eagleton, Terry, *Literary Theory. An Introduction*, Oxford, 1983.

Eco, Umberto, *The Role of the Reader*, Bloomington, 1979.

Eco, Umberto, *Semiotics and the Philosophy of Language*, London, 1984.

Frye, Northrop, *Creation and Recreation*, Toronto; Buffalo; London, 1980.

Gadamer, Hans Georg, *Wahrheit und Methode,* Tübingen, 1965.

280

Holquist, Michael, *Dialogism: Bakhtin and his world*, London & New York, 1990.

Hutcheon, Linda, *Narcissistic Narrative, The Metafictional Paradox*, London & New York, 1980.

Iser, Wolfgang, *Der Akt des Lesens. Theorie Ästhetischer Wirkung*, München, 1976.

Jauß, H.R., *Literaturgeschichte als Provokation*, Frankfurt am Main, 1979 (6).

Jauß, H.R., *Ästhetische Erfahrung und literarische Hermeneutik*, Frankfurt am Main, 1984.

Jauß, Hans Robert, *Nachahmung und Illusion*, München, 1991.

Josipovici, Gabriel, *The World and the Book: A Study of Modern Fiction*, London, 1977.

Karl Kerenyi, *Humanistische Seelenforschung Werke 1*, Wiesbaden, 1966.

Kittler, Friedrich, *Aufschreibesysteme 1800. 1900*, München, 1995.

Krieger, Murray, *Ekphrasis: The Illusion of the Natural Sign*, Baltimore and London, 1992.

Miller, J. Hillis, *Ariadne's Thread. Story Lines*, New Haven and London, 1992.

Pfotenhauer, Helmut, *Um 1800: Konfiguration der Literatur, Kunstliteratur und Ästhetik*, Tübingen, 1991.

Ricardou, Jean, *Nouveau Roman: hier, aujourd'hui 2*, Paris, 1972.

Said, Edward, *The World, the Text and the Critic*, London, 1981.

Schmeling, Manfred, *Der labyrinthische Diskurs*, Frankfurt am Main, 1987.

Stanzel, Franz, *Theorie des Erzählens*, Göttingen, 1979.

Vogt, Jochen, *Aspekte erzählender Prosa. Eine Einführung in Erzähltechnik und Romantheorie*, Opladen, 1990.

Waugh, Patricia, *Metafiction. The Theory and Practice of Self-Conscious Fiction*, London & New York, 1984.

Willems, Gottfried, *Anschaulichkeit. Zur Theorie und Geschichte der Wort-Bild-Beziehungen und des literarischen Darstellungsstil*, Tübingen, 1989.

INDEX

Abeken, Rudolf   117
Amazons   158, 170, 212, 234
analogy   8-9, 109, 110, 117, 119, 120 140, 155, 173, 208, 212, 229, 242, 245, 246, 252, 265, 267
anatomy   155-6, 197, 247
aphorisms   1, 2, 21-23, 34, 36, 42, 55-6, 61, 62, 69, 71, 72, 74, 75-9, 85, 87-8, 115, 116, 124, 128, 130, 131, 141, 148-50, 154, 169, 175, 176, 178-9, 180, 190, 193, 197, 199, 200, 209, 220-2, 241, 244, 256-7, 260, 265, 267, 269
Apollo 77, 155, 167
archive, archive fiction   36, 62, 76, 78, 125, 132, 135, 136, 144, 159, 175, 176, 178, 180, 191, 193, 199, 209, 220-1, 241, 246, 257,260, 267
Aristotle   30, 32, 120, 198, 235, 263
Augustine   235

Bakhtin, Mikhail   7, 36
Banville, John   10
Barth, John   11
Barthes Roland   4, 75-76
Beckett, Samuel   62
Bible 35-36, 194-196, 202, 208, 222
'Bildungsroman'   102-3
Blanckenburg, Friedrich von 96, 103
Boethius   234-5, 237
Boisserée, Sulpiz   40, 75, 84, 102
Borges, J.L.   237, 263
Brentano, Bettina   115
Brion, Friederike   87, 181-3, 209
Broch, Hermann   52, 57-58, 62, 69, 241-2, 268
Byron 166, 193, 198, 199

Calderon   199
Carlyle, Thomas   20, 192-3, 198
Carter, Angela   11
Cervantes, Miguel   9, 10, 25, 46, 48, 124, 219
Chaucer, Geoffrey   237
Cicero 200-201
Cotta   114, 239

Daedalus   229, 236, 252-3
Dante 237
dialogue, dialogism   7, 18, 22, 36, 41, 48, 82, 83, 86, 90, 92, 97, 107, 110, 116, 126, 151, 180, 256, 258
Diderot, Denis 118, 262
dramatic novel   46, 104, 115, 117, 138

Eckermann, J.P.   11, 12, 19, 38, 56, 63, 71, 72, 79, 89, 113, 114, 121, 131, 166, 191, 193, 198, 213, 259, 265
Eco, Umberto 82, 262-5
editor 51, 90, 91, 92, 124, 132-5, 145, 255
ekphrasis   8, 13, 170, 200, 205-8, 220, 238
Eliot, T.S.   7
encyclopaedia 45-7, 49-50, 262, 224, 231, 262
Enlightenment 95, 99, 262
epic novel   46-7, 55, 104
Euripides   34, 38, 198
Eyck, Jan van 8

fragment   1, 33-37, 43-45, 50-1, 54, 65, 84, 127, 137-8, 178, 191, 196, 199-200, 221, 231, 241 249-50, 261
frame-story   9, 10, 56, 58-9, 62, 133, 136, 183, 188

freemasons   90, 211, 238, 247
Freud, Sigmund   121

Gadamer, H.G.,   78, 154
'Geistesgeschichte'   59
Gide, André   8, 11, 57, 240
Goethe, J.W. von, works:

Claudine   226
Dichtung und Wahrheit   69, 76, 80, 85, 86, 92, 177-8, 181, 182, 195, 224, 231, 236
Essays:
'Einwirkung der neueren Philosophie'   235-6
'Geneigte Teilnahme an den *Wanderjahren*'   129, 248
'German Romance'   198
'Helena in Edinburgh, Paris und Moskau'   193
'Kunst und Handwerk'   84
'Lorenz Sterne'   20-1
'Rembrandt der Denker'   204
'Ruisdael als Dichter' 145-7, 204-5
'Der Sammler und die Seinigen' 83, 84, 85, 87, 155
'Shakespeare und keine Ende' 172
'Über den Granit'   266
'Über Laokoon'   71, 205, 212-3
'Über das Lehrgedicht'   227-8
'Vorwort zum deutschen Gil Blas' 239-40, 250, 254
'Wolkengestalt nach Howard' 266
'Wiederholte Speigelungen'   209
Farbenlehre   77, 86, 87, 88, 112, 173-4, 180, 195
Faust 39, 42, 67, 87, 166, 172, 173, 198, 222, 225, 232-3, 241, 245, 252, 254, 261, 265
*Götz von Berlichingen*81
Italienische Reise   73, 77, 85, 89, 203-4, 230-1

Kampagne in Frankreich   18, 19
Maximen und Reflexionen   42-3, 69, 71, 73, 77, 80, 82, 85, 87-8, 148, 189, 199-200, 201-2, 226
Die natürliche Tochter   225-6, 233-4
Individual Poems:
'An den Mond'   233
'Antepirrhema'   225, 245
'An Werther'   233
'Ein Chinese in Rom'   38
'Eins und Alles'   266
'Epilog zu Schillers Glocke'   173
'Epirrhema'   245
'Gedichte sind gemalte Fensterscheiben'   202-3
'Im ernsten Beinhaus' 141, 259-260
'Im Gegenwärtigen Vergangenes' 146
'Metamorphose der Pflanzen'245
'Metamorphose der Tiere'   245
'Parabase'   245, 265
'Um Mitternacht'   79
'Urworte, Orphisch'   233
'Vermächtnis' 141, 176
'Weltseele'   243
Propyläen   82, 232, 261-2
Das römische Carneval   250-1
Tages- und Jahreshefte   18, 72, 114, 227
Über Kunst und Altertum   20, 79, 191, 192-3, 224, 233, 261-2
Die Wahlverwandtschaften   32, 40, 52, 91-2, 110-122, 163, 165, 256
Werther   19, 52, 69, 80-1, 85, 89-90, 92-7, 101, 113, 233
West-östlicher Divan 39-43, 67, 74, 81, 153, 195, 198
Wilhelm Meisters Lehrjahre 46, 52, 55, 56, 74, 80, 90-1, 97-110, 136-7, 142, 146, 152, 163, 164, 165, 177, 206-7, 224-5, 236

Wilhelm Meisters Wanderjahre (1821 version) 135, 141-44, 191, 219, 268
Xenien 38, 81, 241

Goldsmith, Oliver 21, 108
Griffith Richard 22
Gutzkow, Karl 64

Hamlet 106, 108-109, 236
Hammer-Purgstall, J. von, 39
Hebbel, Friedrich 44
Hegel, G.W.F., 52, 54, 57, 103, 160
Herder, J.G. 27, 36, 38, 48, 77, 84
hermeneutical circle 83, 208
Hesse, Hermann 11
Hippocrates 131, 199
Homer 10, 13, 17, 50, 55, 71, 86, 89, 93, 166, 172, 178, 194, 198, 199, 205-7, 237
Horace 4, 15, 160, 199, 202
Hotho, G.H. 51-54, 61, 66, 160
Hugo, Victor 12
Humboldt, W. von, 42, 82-3, 97-109,166-7, 171-2, 175, 208, 224, 241

Iken, K.J.L. 83, 84, 208
infinity 71-2, 122, 199, 213, 239, 243, 261-2, 264-9
intertextuality 6, 23, 43, 45, 78, 263

Jacobi, F.H. 101-2
Jean Paul 11, 14, 37-50, 104,125, 261
Jerome 235
Jerusalem 93, 96
Joyce, James 7, 57, 62, 237, 239, 240, 264, 268
juxtaposition 64, 197

Kant, Immanuel 121, 170, 189, 235-6

Kayßler, A.B. 129, 248
Keats, John 9
Kerenyi, Karl 243, 261
Kestner, Christian 90, 93-94, 96
Klettenberg, Susanne von 178, 230
Knebel, K.L. von 87, 97, 101
Koran 149, 199
Körner, C.G., 97-109, 106, 108

labyrinth 1, 23, 24, 29-33, 60, 63, 119, 127, 153-4, 176-8, 185-7, 195, 207, 212, 221-224, 230-54, 256-8, 262-3, 265, 267
Laocoon 71, 85, 201, 205-7, 212-13
Lavater 96
Lessing, G.E. 48, 93-95, 96, 199, 200-201, 205-7
Lewes, G. H., 33, 51
Longus 10, 11-18, 42, 229
Lucretius 229
Luther, Martin 27, 36, 223

Mallarmé, S. 264
Mann, Thomas 2, 11, 57, 58, 103, 208
metafiction 2-11,67, 68, 263, 269
Meyer, Heinrich 110, 125, 131, 227-8
Mirabeau 78
mirrors 8, 92, 95, 96, 105, 121, 162, 176-8, 180, 209-10, 256-7, 268
mise en abyme 8, 13, 65, 119, 153, 159, 209, 265
misinterpretation 80-1, 102, 118, 149, 151, 181-90, 212, 257
modernism 10, 58, 64, 67, 68, 222, 240
Morgenstern, Karl 102
Müller, Kanzler von 70, 72, 80, 104, 131, 165, 197, 253, 260, 269
Mundt, Theodor 51-53, 161

284

Musäus   184
Musil, Robert 62

Narcissus   121-2
narrator   5, 14, 25-27, 37, 43,
   47-9, 67, 91, 107, 115, 116, 123-9,
   132-44, 156-7, 184-6, 222, 253-4,
   255-6
Nazarenes   216
Niethammer, 194
nouveau roman   8, 11, 240

openness   1, 5, 239, 254, 264-9
originality   6, 22, 23, 78-79, 179,
   195
Ossian 93
Ovid   89, 121, 199, 223, 225, 228,
   237, 252

Paestum   73
Palladio   204
parody 6, 7, 66, 141, 161, 181, 189,
   190, 216, 220, 255-6
picture galleries   45, 59, 65, 89,
   105, 110, 175, 197, 200, 206-8,
   212-15, 221, 247, 267
Pindar 84
Plato   55, 116, 128, 167, 171, 173-
   4,179, 194, 222, 234
Plotinus   131, 199
Plutarch   201
polyphony   7, 36, 49, 76, 90, 91,
   95, 123, 195
post-modernism   10, 240

Quintilian   223

Raphael   89, 94, 170, 216
Rembrandt   204
readers' expectations 78, 135, 139,
   181
'renunciation' 59, 61, 66, 143, 183-
   4, 244

'repeated reflections' 59, 63, 65, 95,
   109, 121, 158, 197, 208-10, 212,
   260, 267
Ricardou, Jean   4
Riemer, F.W. 38, 75, 82, 111,
   112,166, 205, 207, 259
Robbe-Grillet, Alain 11, 237, 240
Rochlitz, J.F. 33, 74, 83, 84, 105,
   112, 152, 239
Roos, Heinrich   204
Rousseau   95
Ruisdael, Jakob   145-7, 204-5

Said, Edward 6, 17, 35
Sartorius, Georg   101
Schelling   88, 110
Schiller, Friedrich   37-39, 42, 70,
   97-110, 174, 178, 182-3, 186, 193,
   236, 259
Schlegel, Friedrich 33-34,   66,
   105-107, 109, 110, 166, 171
Schleiermacher, Friedrich   83
Schuchardt   86, 191
Scott, Walter 229
self-consciousness   3,   10,   25-
   27,66, 67
self-reflexivity 8, 62, 95, 115, 122,
   238
sentimentality 18-20, 80
Shakespeare, William 172-3,   193,
   194, 199, 236
Shelley, Mary 9
Simonides   200-1
Socrates   126, 234
solar system   41, 43, 105, 167, 172-
   4, 176, 177-8, 180, 243, 245-6,
   252
Soret, Frédéric 78-9
Spinoza, Baruch   76, 260
Stein, Charlotte von   182
Sterne, Laurence   4, 10, 18-37,
   43, 46, 48, 79, 118, 131,135, 154,
   199, 247

285

208, 246

Tischbein, Wilhelm   203-4,   216,
217

Varnhagen von Ense, K.A.   53-4
Velázquez   8
Virgil 152, 229, 237, 242-3, 249
visual arts   13, 28-9, 37, 68, 69,
73, 85, 88-9, 152, 200-22, 226,
232
Voigt, C.G.   112
Voß, Heinrich 81, 194

weaving   31-2, 36, 41, 61, 125,
157, 197, 212, 218, 221-230, 244,
247, 249
Werner, Zacharias   113
Wieland, C.M.11, 56, 101, 173-4
Wilde, Oscar 204
Winckelmann 232, 266-7
Wittgenstein 9
Wolf, Christa 11
'world literature'   191-200

Zelter, K.F.   21, 43, 73, 74, 75, 81,
84, 86, 111, 114, 131, 241, 193,
241, 259, 261, 265

STUDIES IN GERMAN LANGUAGE AND LITERATURE

1. Ulrich Goebel and Oskar Reichmann (eds.) in collaboration with Peter I. Barta, **Historical Lexicography of the German Language, Volume 1**

2. Christoph Meckel, ***Zünd* and Other Stories**, Carol Bedwell (trans.)

3. Christoph Meckel, ***Snow Creatures* and Other Stories,** Carol Bedwell (trans.)

4. Hasan Dewran, *A Thousand Winds May Make A Storm/Tausend Winde-Ein Sturm, Poems and Aphorisms/Gedichte und Aphorismen*, Hans W. Panthel (trans.)

5. William C. McDonald, **The Tristan Story in German Literature of the Late Middle Ages and Early Renaissance: Tradition and Innovation**

6. Ulrich Goebel and Oskar Reichmann (eds.) in collaboration with Peter I. Barta, **Historical Lexicography of the German Language, Volume 2**

7. Ian F. Roe, **An Introduction to the Major Works of Franz Grillparzer, 1791-1872, Austrian Dramatist and Poet**

8. Margaret Littler, **Alfred Andersch (1914-1980) and the Literary, Philosophical, and Cultural Life of the Federal Republic of Germany**

9. *The Nibelungenlied*, Robert Lichtenstein (trans.)

10. Eva Wagner, **An Analysis of Franz Grillparzer's Drama: Fate, Guilt, and Tragedy**

11. Erich W. Schaufler, **Elias Canettis Autobiographie in Der Deutschen Presse**

12. Patrick T. Murray, **The Development of German Aesthetic Theory from Kant to Schiller: A Philosophical Commentary on Schiller's** *Aesthetic Education of Man* **(1795)**

13. Edelgard E. DuBruck, **Aspects of Fifteenth-Century Society in the German Carnival Comedies: Speculum Hominis**

14. Ulrich Goebel and David Lee (eds.), **The Ring of Words in Medieval Literature** (paperback)

15. Albrecht Classen, **The German Volksbuch: A Critical History of a Late-Medieval Genre**

16. Martin Swales, **Studies of German Prose Fiction in the Age of European Realism**

17. **The Alsfeld Passion Play,** Larry E. West (trans.)

18. **Ludwig Achim von Arnim's Novellas of 1812 - Isabella of Egypt, Melück Maria Blainville, The Three Loving Sisters and the Lucky Dyer, Angelika the Genoese and Cosmus the Tightrope-Walker**, Bruce Duncan (trans.)

19. Karl A. Bernhardt and Graeme Davis, **The Word Order of Old High German**

20. Barbara Burns, **The Short Stories of Detlev von Liliencron: Passion, Penury, Patriotism**

21. J.W. Thomas (trans.), **Fables, Sermonettes, and Parables by The Stricker, 13th Century German Poet, in English Translation**

22. **Theodor Storm–Narrative Strategies and Patriarchy; Theodor Storm–Erzählstrategien und Patriarchat,** herausgegeben von David A. Jackson und Mark G. Ward

23. Gordon J.A. Burgess, **A Computer-Assisted Analysis of Goethe's** *Die Wahlverwandtschaften*: **The Enigma of Elective Affinities**

24. Rainer Maria Rilke, **The Duino Elegies**, translated by John Waterfield

25. Paul Bishop, **The World of Stoical Discourse in Goethe's Novel** *Die Wahlverwandtschaften*

26. Heike Bartel and Brian Keith-Smith (eds.), **'Nachdenklicher Leichtsinn'– Essays on Goethe and Goethe Reception**

27. Roger Kingerlee, **Psychological Models of Masculinity in Döblin, Musil, and Jahnn: Männliches, Allzumännliches**

28. Otto Weininger (1880-1903), **A Translation of Weininger's** *Über die letzten Dinge* **(1904/1907) /** *On Last Things*, translated from the original German, and with an introduction by Steven Burns

29. G. Peter McMullin, **Childhood and Children in Thomas Mann's Fiction**

30. Gillian Pye, **Approaches to Comedy in German Drama**

31. Hajo Drees, **A Comprehensive Interpretation of the Life and Work of Christa Wolf, 20th-Century German Writer**

32. Regina Angela Wenzel, **Changing Notions of Money and Language in German Literature from 1509-1956**

33. Joan Wright, **The Novel Poetics of Goethe's** *Wilhelm Meisters Wanderjahre*: **Eine zarte Empirie**